VALUE-BASED METRICS FOR IMPROVING RESULTS

An Enterprise Project Management Toolkit

VALUE-BASED METRICS FOR IMPROVING RESULTS

An Enterprise Project Management Toolkit

Mel Schnapper, Ph.D.
Steven Rollins, PMP

Copyright ©2006 by J. Ross Publishing, Inc.

ISBN 1-932159-25-8

Printed and bound in the U.S.A. Printed on acid-free paper
10 9 8 7 6 5 4 3 2 1

Library of Congress Cataloging-in-Publication Data

Schnapper, Melvin.
  Value-based metrics for improving results : an enterprise project management toolkit / by Mel Schnapper, Steven Rollins.
    p. cm.
  Includes index.
  ISBN 1-932159-25-8 (hardcover : alk. paper)
  1. Project management—Quality control. 2. Performance standards. 3. Work measurement. I. Rollins, Steven C., 1950-. II. Title.
  HD69.P75S365 2006
  658.4′04—dc22   2006001079

    This publication contains information obtained from authentic and highly regarded sources. Reprinted material is used with permission, and sources are indicated. Reasonable effort has been made to publish reliable data and information, but the author and the publisher cannot assume responsibility for the validity of all materials or for the consequences of their use.
    All rights reserved. Neither this publication nor any part thereof may be reproduced, stored in a retrieval system or transmitted in any form or by any means, electronic, mechanical, photocopying, recording or otherwise, without the prior written permission of the publisher.
    The copyright owner's consent does not extend to copying for general distribution for promotion, for creating new works, or for resale. Specific permission must be obtained from J. Ross Publishing for such purposes.
    Direct all inquiries to J. Ross Publishing, Inc., 5765 North Andrews Way, Fort Lauderdale, Florida 33309.

Phone: (954) 727-9333
Fax: (561) 892-0700
Web: www.jrosspub.com

TABLE OF CONTENTS

Preface vii
Acknowledgments xi
About the Authors xv
Web Added Value™ xix

Part 1: Defining the Methodology
Chapter 1: Introduction 3
Chapter 2: The Value of a Metrics Methodology on Business 13
Chapter 3: What Is Value? 29
Chapter 4: How to Create and Exceed Value 63
Chapter 5: Alignment of All Metrics 73
Chapter 6: Skills-Building Exercises 81

Part II: 3Ms Measurement Program for the Organization
Chapter 7: Metrics and Program/Project Management 89
Chapter 8: Role/Authority/Decision Making 99
Chapter 9: Metrics and Corporate Culture 105
Chapter 10: Initiatives That Support the 3Ms 111
Chapter 11: Other Applications of the 3Ms Methodology 123
Chapter 12: Applying Theory of Constraints Metrics the TOC Way 131
Chapter 13: The Value Proposition of an Organizational Project-Based
              Metrics Program 145

Part III: 3Ms Measurement Tools for the Organization
Chapter 14: The 3Ms Metric Profile 157
Chapter 15: Project Management Context 169
Chapter 16: Management Oversight 175
Chapter 17: Project Integration Management 185

v

Chapter 18: Project Scope Management 211
Chapter 19: Project Time Management 233
Chapter 20: Project Cost Management 259
Chapter 21: Project Quality Management 275
Chapter 22: Project Human Resource Management 293
Chapter 23: Project Communications Management 305
Chapter 24: Project Risk Management 317
Chapter 25: Project Procurement Management 331
Chapter 26: Project Fraud Management 351
Chapter 27: Project Management Office Management 365

Part IV: Realizing the Value Proposition of an Implemented Measurement Program for Your Organization
Chapter 28: Metrics Maturity Model 381
Chapter 29: Road Map Schedule for Implementing a 3Ms
 Metrics Program 395
Chapter 30: Business Case for Implementing a 3Ms
 Measurement Program 405
Chapter 31: Summary 419

Index 423

PREFACE

A great many years have passed since the Egyptians built the Pyramids, but the use of measures in our work remains the same. We know we need measures. The key question is which measures.

Most of the time, measures are easy to create and apply. We know that measures or metrics are necessary to help us gain the knowledge we seek in completing any task.

Should we not expect that, through the years, best practice metrics would have been documented in some shape or fashion for the benefit of mankind in a collective set of metrics that, when applied, would assure the user of finite or infinite knowledge? Should we not expect that these metrics would be continuously improved upon time and time again to the point that the same collection of metrics would have evolved to a deity-like state? Where can we find this published collection of metrics today that promises the universe to us? Surely it exists. Did not humankind land a man on the moon?

We have searched the world over and have not found one instance of a published collection of metrics that, when applied to the completion of work tasks, ensures understanding of the resulting information so that the outcome cannot be misunderstood.

Inside the covers of this book sits a treasure trove of metrics. We have framed this collection of metrics in relationship to the rigor and discipline of universal project management standards as defined by the Project Management Institute, the largest association of project management professionals in the world today.

Furthermore, we realize that metrics can be created for almost any need. Our focus in this work is to identify metrics that have long been applied in successful management of the delivery of projects. Given that this is a new endeavor, a methodology is now introduced that can be applied over and over to any project, business unit, or business. The 3Ms methodology has enabled us to offer you more than 200 metrics that focus on the primary benefits of successful project management application, answering questions like "Are we there yet?" and *"Are we on budget or better?"* Nothing else really matters when considering what is satisfactory compared to what was expected.

Key to our approach is the requirement to align the delivery expectations of the workforce in a linear behavioral fashion. This behavior traverses the organization, from the executive team down to the project team member. The prime axiom of this behavior is that workers at all levels place how the business expects them to perform their jobs first and ahead of their own personal expectations of how they believe they should perform their jobs. This means that instead of leaving at four o'clock each workday, working until five o'clock or later when you can make a difference toward success must become the norm and not the rule.

For all of the interest in metrics of both general performance management approaches and project management specifically, there has never been a methodology that fully and rigorously aligns the relationship between monies, values, results, standards, and rewards as the essence of the methodology. For all of the books, presentations, and articles on project management metrics that are available, we can confidently conclude that whoever masters the 3Ms approach will quickly find that all of the additional approaches will become quite marginal to a total enterprise metrics approach.

The 3Ms not only offers a rigorous and mathematically precise way to measure project management performance at the organization, team, and individual levels, but also includes, in its essence, and in the very definition of metrics, the social, linguistic, and teamwork dynamics that are largely ignored by most all of the other project management metrics approaches.

As an example, consider the Project Management Institute Project Management Body of Knowledge (PMBOK®). When the 3Ms is applied to the PMBOK® standard for businesses and organizations, the result is significantly clearer opportunities for delivery achievement, thus yielding significantly improved collaborative decision making because the quantitative data have been made more discernible.

None of this is to say that any other approach is inadequate. In fact, we contend the opposite. If you adopt or adapt the 3Ms approach, initially you will want to keep much of your legacy metrics approach and add the 3Ms to complement the existing cafeteria of metrics you may already be using. As you continue to implement 3Ms, you will reduce the number of metrics you are using while focusing on fewer and more value-added and value-defined metrics that help create the total enterprise alignment for greater clarity of purpose, accountability, roles, and vision of your project management efforts at any level for any function.

This book is designed to be a reference and teaching aid. We will tell many stories throughout this book that will assist in our observations, but in the end it is your choice as to whether you will buy into this approach. We believe that the overriding tenet of value behind this book is that the achievement of value from the application of project management and its related metrics is the essence of transforming any organization to provide greater value. We also believe that the business governance/Project Management Office is the facilitator of successful work delivery that directs and provides this value in all businesses.

Passion can get a person in trouble!

ACKNOWLEDGMENTS

STEVE ROLLINS

The creation of this book represents a personal fulfillment to document the delivery metrics that I have utilized in many different shapes and fashions over my career. I often wondered why I was reinventing the wheel each time I worked in or led a project team. The answer soon became obvious and thus the motivation to create this work.

Writing this book was the easy part, as the writing was accomplished in record time due to the vast knowledge stores that I and Dr. Schnapper each possess. The hardest portion of this work was controlling the emotion that came out as I recalled past work experiences. Each of these past work events proved further that without people working together for a common cause with common beliefs, achievement would be difficult. There were as many good references as there were bad. Someone once said that to know success, one must know failure in order to recognize success.

I have become very active within the Project Management Institute (PMI) through many of its component chapters. It was as a member of the Metrics Specific Interest Group (MetSIG) that I had the good fortune to meet Dr. Mel Schnapper. Mel founded the MetSIG and was the presiding SIG Chair at the time of our meeting back in 2000 as I stood around for a while stewing over my innate need to become more involved with an area of sincere personal interest. The MetSIG was essentially just beginning to find itself at this time, as most new organizations do, but something struck me about Mel and his focus on metrics. It was from encounters with him and his 3Ms methodology that I finally was able to connect my project delivery thinking with his approach, and that led to our working together on this book. I appreciated his work so much that I initially became an officer of the MetSIG Board of Directors. Today, as the SIG Chair for the Metrics SIG (www.metsig.org), I can see the true value proposition of the MetSIG, and I do feel it will become a leading factor in helping us all achieve the promise of project management value that leads business toward achievement of business growth. I am thankful for meeting Mel and gaining the perspective of his 3Ms methodology, as well as everything else he has helped me with.

There are many good books on measurements and metrics available today. There is only one commonly accepted standard in project management, as evidenced by the large membership of the PMI. PMI has developed the Project Management Body of Knowledge (PMBOK®), which includes nine areas of knowledge. It is to this standard that the message in this book is aligned. I thank PMI for placing a stake in the ground for best project management value and for the potential of continuous improvement as mankind continues its evolutionary march. We will "raise the bar" with this literary contribution!

The impact of human behavior in the project management space must be harnessed by project management professionals everywhere if businesses that apply project management rigor and discipline are ever to achieve the benefit from the promise of project management — *business prosperity*. Much of my understanding of human behavior in project management I learned firsthand from Dr. Edwards Deming through his Total Quality Management paradigm and later Dr. Eli Goldratt through his teachings of the Theory of Constraints paradigm. I am ever so grateful to these men for their contributions so that others like me can leverage their concepts with new ideas toward new and improved techniques.

I also wish to thank Gerry Kendall, who contributed Chapter 12 on Theory of Constraints. Gerry's insight into influencing human behavior with value-based metrics through the Theory of Constraints is consistent with the message of this book. Gerry and I wrote *Advanced Project Portfolio Management and the PMO: Multiplying ROI at Warp Speed*, which has become the best-seller in the business governance/PMO space. That book and now this book on metrics form a powerful one-two punch in how to get value from a PMO that will lead to business transformation. I encourage you to also pick up a copy of my book *Essential Project Investment Governance and Reporting: Preventing Project Fraud and Ensuring Sarbanes-Oxley Compliance* if you have an interest in safeguarding business and project investments.

Finally, I encourage you to consider the value of measurement systems in helping organizations transform themselves as the business climate changes around them — sometimes every day. If companies are to be competitive, they must understand that invisible value exists all around, awaiting discovery. Measurement systems do lead to "raised visibility," eventually resulting in improved cross-collaboration. Thus, let it be understood that if you cannot measure, you cannot control. If you cannot control, you cannot manage. Thus, if you cannot measure, you cannot manage. This leads us to the ever-present question: What is your value proposition and how do you know, and is the value you seek sufficient or are you unknowingly leaving money on the table?

My hope and prayer is that this book will help you find new methods to become more successful in your delivery work. I am interested in your stories. Please send your thoughts, comments, and stories to me at Steve@PMOUSA.com. I encourage you to help improve business standards by sharing your thoughts about the content shared with you in this book.

MEL SCHNAPPER

A few words about some unique aspects of the 3Ms approach: As you read further about this methodology, you will see statements that metrics are "social," "linguistic," and "not valid until at least two people agree as to what the metrics are." These statements are not typical of the "normal" metrics-oriented individual, who usually comes from a statistical, engineering, or otherwise technical/business background.

Apart from the metrics of passing tests in school, my first formal encounter was when I was a Peace Corps volunteer in Nigeria and became fluent in the Yoruba language. By fluent I mean that I had a Foreign Service Institute (FSI) rating of 2+ on a scale ranging from 0 (knows nothing about the language) to 5 (native language proficiency). I bring this up because my first encounter with the rigor of metrics was in the qualitative domain of linguistic fluency as measured by the FSI testers.

When 10 testers are trained by the FSI and they test 10 people for their language fluency, they will never differ by more than a (+) or (5) with intervals of 9, +, 1, 1+, 2, 2+... on a scale of 0 to 5. The precise metrics below the level of the ratings are accent, grammatical structure, use of idioms and colloquialisms, proper level of formal or informal word selection, etc. All are very specific to the conversation held with the tester.

My second experience in determining metrics was when I became a trainer of Peace Corps volunteers and had to develop a "training by objectives" curriculum to identify, in measurable terms, what defined "intercultural sensitivity," "cross-cultural flexibility," "tolerance for ambiguity," etc. All of these are critical skills for working effectively in another culture. My thanks to the work of Al Wight, Center for Research in Education, in Estes Park, Colorado, where I spent two weeks in 1968 learning the rigor of measuring training objectives and learning how to accurately observe and describe human behavior. This also was developed in my work with nonverbal intercultural behavior, which involved how to describe and not interpret it or judge it, just measure it.

My other experience which led to the development of the 3Ms methodology with its linguistic, social, and behavioral elements was getting my master's degree in applied linguistics and Ph.D. in organizational behavior. I also consult to and have been employed by major corporations like Quaker Oats, G.D. Searle, and the Chicago Board Options Exchange. At the Oracle Corporation, I was the quality manager of the Global Project Management Service Line. It was through Oracle that

I became involved with PMI and the more technical way to create metrics; in fact, that was 100% of my job, aspects of which you will find detailed in the book.

As I learned at Oracle and elsewhere in the information technology space, metrics was given only enough attention and time to satisfy urgent requests to justify why a project should continue, to explain why a project was not doing well, or to defend a budget that was supposed to be trimmed. Otherwise, metrics was far from a part of the corporate culture.

My work at Oracle allowed me to apply this generic approach to the very technical aspects of project management. It was there that I had to learn the information technology language and the PMI PMBOK® terms and synthesize all of this into what became the 3Ms methodology. Later, I would create an online version for virtual project management in an e-commerce start-up, where my traditional organization development approach of face-to-face meetings was impractical because of the chaotic nature of the start-up and because the project teams were geographically dispersed.

Prior to entering the formal PMI world, my work had been in facilitating teamwork and general performance improvement, so I came to the PMI world with a highly evolved process of measuring all kinds of performance and simply applied it to the world of project management.

Thus, I am humbly honored to present for your utilization my contribution to the world of project management metrics, which I hope helps you transform your work results to the best that they can be!

ABOUT THE AUTHORS

Mel Schnapper, Ph.D., is the founder and past chair of the Metrics Specific Interest Group (SIG) of the Project Management Institute (PMI). As Director of Organization Development for Halo Branded Solutions, he implemented the "3Ms of Performance: Measure, Manage, and Magnify," a methodology that supports baselining, managing, and aligning metrics for monitoring and rewarding progress to support the kind of success that is defined in measurable terms before the task and/or project begins.

He also developed an online application and tutorial that enabled staff to input their own metrics for measuring, managing, and rewarding performance. He typically reports to the chief technology officer, chief information officer, or those with adequate authority to support any kind of metrics implementation. He was formerly Quality Manager of the Global Project Management Service Line at Oracle Corporation and Senior Consultant at Oracle's Change Management Practice. Additionally, his organization development background enables him to bring "high performance to high tech through metrics." His approach to metrics comes from his training in organization behavior (metrics are social products) and linguistics (metrics must have a common meaning among those who work together). He also prides himself on being able to measure anything!

Dr. Schnapper's current consulting activity is in the areas of performance management systems, career development, succession planning, leadership skills, teamwork skills, and, of course, measuring the effectiveness of all of these interventions. His current international consulting activity is in Afghanistan and Nigeria, where he is bringing his metrics approach to democratization and government reform projects.

His clients are domestic and international companies and organizations that want to examine and improve their various systems to baseline, support, manage, improve, align, and reward *any* kind of performance at *any* level for *any* function.

He has a Ph.D. in organization behavior and is widely published in the fields of organization development, training, and international development. He can be reached at mel@schnapper.com.

Steven C. Rollins, MBA, PMP, PMOP, is President, CEO, and founder of the ALLPMO Network (www.PMOUSA.com), which offers 18 PMO niche-specific websites free to the public.

He is a well-known global subject matter expert in enterprise project management implementations and improvements whose background includes extensive experience in industries such as financial services, government, healthcare, human resources, information technology, insurance, and telecommunications. He has been a featured keynote speaker at many project management events, speaking on "Growing the Business: The Value Proposition of Project Managers" to Project Management Institute (PMI) chapters and businesses across the United States, Canada, Europe, and Asia.

Recent clients include 2XCL Training, Royal Sun-Alliance, IBM, iDLSystems, Duquesne University, Satyam Corporation, American Century Financial Services, Fortis Benefits Insurance Company, Guilford Tech Community College, Honeywell, HR Block, International Institute for Learning, Jasmine Networks, Kaiser Permanente, Principal Financial Group, Sprint, State of Kansas, Systemcorp, Westell Technologies, Lowes Corporation, Blue Cross Blue Shield of Michigan, McNeilus Companies, and U.S. Marine Corp.

Additionally, Mr. Rollins is the PMI Metrics Specific Interest Group Chair and the Executive Chair of the Mid-America PMO Regional Group that operates as a chapter of the PMI PMO SIG with a membership of more than 700 people serving seven states in the Midwest.

He is co-author of the best-selling book *Advanced Project Portfolio Management and the PMO: Multiplying ROI at Warp Speed* (J. Ross Publishing, 2003) and *Essential Project Investment Governance and Reporting: Preventing Project Fraud and Ensuring Sarbanes-Oxley Compliance* (J. Ross Publishing, 2005).

In collaboration with iDLSystems, he has developed state-of-the-art e-learning content in the discipline of business governance, including offerings in Sarbanes-

Oxley, metrics, and project management, that is today being used at universities, colleges, and businesses worldwide.

Mr. Rollins has also authored white papers on "How to Get Value from a PMO," "How to Market Your PMO," "Growing the Business: The Value Proposition of Project Managers," and "The Value Proposition of an Organizational Metrics Program." He can be reached at Steve@PMOUSA.com.

*Free value-added materials available from
the Download Resource Center at www.jrosspub.com*

At J. Ross Publishing we are committed to providing today's professional with practical, hands-on tools that enhance the learning experience and give readers an opportunity to apply what they have learned. That is why we offer free ancillary materials available for download on this book and all participating Web Added Value™ publications. These online resources may include interactive versions of material that appears in the book or supplemental templates, worksheets, models, plans, case studies, proposals, spreadsheets and assessment tools, among other things. Whenever you see the WAV™ symbol in any of our publications, it means bonus materials accompany the book and are available from the Web Added Value Download Resource Center at www.jrosspub.com.

Downloads available for *Value-Based Metrics for Improving Results: An Enterprise Project Management Toolkit* consist of a 3Ms metrics maturity model, PMO case study, project management metrics business case, and 3Ms metric profile examples.

PART I: DEFINING THE METHODOLOGY

1

INTRODUCTION

If you are working in a typical project management environment, think about how you would answer the following and similar questions about metrics:

- Are you confused about all the metrics that you have considered for your project?
- Do you find that different metrics have different emphases and make it hard or impossible to compare apples to bananas?
- Does every function in your company insist on its own metrics methodologies for measuring performance?
- Do you find it impossible to compare the value metrics are supposed to show?
- Do the metrics people not even define "value" in the same way?
- Are your metrics not compatible with organizational culture, leadership style and managerial procedures?
- Do you find it difficult to impossible to measure the qualitative dimensions of performance and try to "wing" or obscure them?
- Is there lack of a hierarchy of metrics so individuals, teams, projects, and functions have a "clear line of sight" to the driving corporate objectives?
- For some of your functions, is change so dramatic and frequent that metrics have a short life span?

Your answers to the above questions most likely are yes. This book will help you change all of your answers to no, which in this case is, paradoxically, the positive answer.

By following the 3Ms process as described in the following chapters, your answers for all of the questions above can change to positive. Not only that, but by having explicit and rigorous project management metrics that have been created by the 3Ms process, your project is guaranteed a level of visibility and attention from senior management that is rarely achieved otherwise. As a result, the people involved will have a greater sense of fulfillment.

This is because the 3Ms is a process of hierarchical alignment that "marries" the metrics of your project to the metrics of your division/department and all the way up the corporate hierarchy to the corporate objective that defines the functionality of your project. This is true whether your project is in sales, engineering, R&D, human resources, finance, or whatever. One of the many criteria of a 3Ms project metric is that the value and the deliverables be defined and sourced to a corporate objective. Therefore, your corporate management team, your C-level executives, *must* be aware of your existence and potential contribution. In fact, one of the metrics instruments in this book helps executives realize that either their corporate metrics are a valuable management tool that supports alignment throughout the organization or the current metrics do not and the metrics development process creates metrics as an end in themselves and are not a powerful tool for executives to use to manage the enterprise.

Whether you are a CEO, Program/Project Management Office director, project team member, trainer, or internal or external organization development consultant, at some point you need to be accountable for achieving measurable results that satisfy you and your employer or client. The authors have developed a process called the *3Ms of Performance: Measure, Manage, and Magnify,* which is a structured sequence of exercises and questions that lead you and others (as many others as are involved in the interdependent task or project) to an agreement about what is to be achieved *in any function, for any individual, for any team, at any level* and then establish standards for this performance. This enables all parties to manage all resources to achieve the results they get paid to produce and then magnify the results so that they measurably exceed the client/customer/employer expectations.

The original 3Ms process began its genesis as a modified and, according to George Odiorne, the "godfather" of management by objectives (MBO), "improved" version of MBO. The essence of MBO is this: Before beginning any project or task, before committing any resources of people, time, or money, *first* define in measurable terms (objectives) what the successful task or project will look like. This is the first step of the 3Ms — Measure.

As simple as this concept sounds, and as frequently as people use this process to manage important events in their lives, it is too often neglected in the project management profession. When the organizational dynamics are putting overwhelming pressure on project teams to do something now and show results even when those results statements are very ambiguous, this first step of the 3Ms and of the traditional MBO planning process often goes out the window.

This is one reason why so many projects are over budget and late. Project team members spend too much time defining expected results long after the project has begun. Although project outcomes need some degree of redefinition during the life of the project, most of this could be dramatically reduced if the project team defined its successful metrics criteria in the way that will be described in this text.

Before going into the value and benefits of a metrics methodology and, more specifically, the 3Ms methodology, let's begin with a brief summary statement of the *3Ms of Performance: Measure, Manage, and Magnify.*

MEASURE

First determine the key value areas of the project itself. What value does the project have, or what benefits will it create for the customer/client? How many critical or "key" value dimensions does it support?

Then determine in qualitative and quantitative terms or units what a successful completion of the project will be like when all of these value categories or key value areas are successful. This is first done for the project team and then, for alignment, up and down the corporate metrics hierarchy for any level of the organization. This is critical to create a "line of sight" between the project metrics and those (going upward) of the:

1. Executive sponsor of the project
2. Project and/or Program Management Office
3. Ultimately the corporate objectives and/or goals

The basic standard of performance is Satisfactory. From this standard, an additional two standards are defined as Very Good and Excellent. How and why these additional standards are used will be explained later.

Everything is measurable and scalable. The only issues are to what degree the effort has value and to what degree you want:

- Accuracy
- Frequency
- Quantity
- Quality

As will be explained later, what many people in the project management world interpret as "not measurable" are the qualitative metrics which are ignored or weakly translated into quantitative metrics. Later chapters will demonstrate that qualitative metrics can be as rigorous and precise as quantitative metrics when the proper words are used and when these words have buy-in from all stakeholders.

Remember that everything is measurable and everything is scalable, another important feature of the 3Ms approach. Some of these dimensions are:

1. **Accuracy** — For money, the range is from 1 million to 0.01
2. **Frequency** — From annual, quarterly, weekly, daily, hourly...to every second

3. **Quantity** — From <0 to infinity to >0 to infinity
4. **Quality** — From perfect to "regardless of any quality variables"

The following quote is from the book *Reinventing Government*,* which at first you might think is far afield from the world of project management. However, it is the most accurate description of the dynamics of what occurs when companies and project teams begin any kind of metrics program and why there is initial frustration with any metrics approach.

The reader who is seriously considering a commitment to the 3Ms or any other rigorous metrics approach should read and reread the following quote. This will help him or her anticipate the dynamics of questions that have never been asked before and the initial frustration of not having answered them. The following comments also describe the three phases of the 3Ms approach — Measure, Manage, and Magnify. The 3Ms phases are inserted in parentheses.

Comments on the Utility of Measuring Results

This pattern — adoption of crude performance measures (Measure), followed by protest and pressure to improve the measures (Manage), followed by the development of more sophisticated measures (Magnify) — is common where performance is measured. It explains why so many public [and private] organizations have discovered that even a poor start is better than no start, and even crude measures are better than no measures. All organizations make mistakes at first. But, over time, they are usually forced to correct them.

The simple act of defining measures is extremely enlightening to many organizations. Typically, public agencies [and corporations] are not entirely clear about their objectives, or are in fact, aiming at the wrong objectives. When they have to define the outcomes they want and the appropriate benchmarks to measure those outcomes, this confusion is forced into the open.

Measure

People begin to ask the right questions, to redefine the problem they are trying to solve, and to diagnose that problem anew. When the measurement process starts, people immediately begin to think about the goals of the organization.

Not only will there not have been a history of good or relevant metrics, it is likely that standards of performance have never been clearly defined beyond a binary pass/fail or its equivalent. The first stage of 3Ms requires predefining four

---

* David Osborne and Ted Gaeble, *Reinventing Government,* Addison-Wesley Publishing Company, 1993.

standards of performance. Defining these four standards forces project teams to more fully identify the metrics that distinguish between each standard. It also encourages the project team to at least define standards that exceed minimum expectations.

As an example of 3Ms forcing people to focus on the correct metrics, Dr. Schnapper served as a consultant to the Ministry of Health, Government of Namibia in the 3Ms area and was teaching physicians, managers, and administrative staff how to measure their performance. He mentioned that he was going to have surgery on his right shoulder and that, by his standards, if he were playing tennis again within six weeks, that would be Satisfactory; if within four weeks, that would be Very Good; and if within two weeks, that would be Excellent.

One of the physicians who performed such surgeries then said: "What if you are playing tennis within two weeks and need surgery again within a year? Would your metrics still define a standard of Excellent?" That question made Dr. Schnapper realize that his metrics were totally wrong. It wasn't a matter of how quickly he was back on the tennis court; it was a matter of needing no additional surgery or heavy-duty physical therapy. It was *those* metrics that were the most valuable. And so, within the workshop, he and the doctor who asked the question developed the following metrics: After waiting for at least eight weeks to play tennis again, if he didn't need anything more than occasional (every three months or so) physical therapy over the next ten years of active tennis playing, that would be Satisfactory; if he only needed some annual physical therapy, that would be Very Good; and if he needed no physical therapy over the next ten years, that would be Excellent.

The dynamics of this exchange is what happens in the project management world as well. People will initially focus on what they initially believe is the most value-add metric and realize later (hopefully not too much later) that their initial metrics were way off.

MANAGE

Once you have identified all of the metrics that define success or the 3Ms standard of Satisfactory, the next step is *Manage*.

The beauty of the 3Ms program is that you will be led through the step-by-step process of developing metrics just by filling out the 3Ms template and creating a project profile.

In fact, the issues described in the preceding quote ("Comments on the Utility of Measuring Results") arise even in the first few hours of a 3Ms introduction because the 3Ms questions have never been asked before, not even by other metrics approaches.

These organizations will be asking questions that have not been asked before and will not always readily find the answers. Through the cycle of Measure and Manage, project teams will hypothesize initial key value area weightings and performance objectives with weightings, metrics, and standards. Not having lived in the consciousness of metrics, teams discover from the beginning and throughout the cycles of the Measure and Manage phases how erroneous their first "measures" were.

This first-time cycle of implementing the 3Ms can only be considered a hypothesis for several reasons:

1. Most project organizations do not have good metrics-based baselines to use as history or as an indicator of what is achievable.
2. As the paragraphs below explain, initial metrics may seem very attractive and intuitively obvious. Often, the most important metrics do not emerge as important until the more immediate metrics are discovered not to be a measure of value.
3. Organizations will go for the readily measured metrics of profitability, cost, waste, sales, etc., which are good macro- or corporate-level metrics. However, these metrics are aggregations of many, if not dozens of, lower level metrics that are hidden until the higher level metrics are used for at least one cycle of the Measure/Manage states of 3Ms.

Manage means to identify all variables that will help or hinder the success that has been defined by the Measure step. Ensure that all systems (personnel, technical, operations, information, reward, performance review, etc.) and programs (diversity, organization development, training, etc.) are appropriate to support all results (performance objectives) at a minimum standard of Satisfactory.

This stage of the 3Ms will not be highly elaborated on here as *any* model of managing task accomplishment is compatible with the 3Ms. The point we want to make here is that regardless of what managerial approach the project team or organization uses, the implementation of the 3Ms process will highlight, in precise terms:

1. What the deliverables are
2. Who (the project manager, team members individually and collectively) does what (as defined by performance objectives) by when and how well (as defined by the four standards — Excellent, Very Good, Satisfactory, and Unsatisfactory)
3. Accountabilities and appropriate authority

As will be discussed later, the 3Ms is style free and can work whether the managerial style is autocratic or democratic. We have seen, however, that when the managerial culture and leadership style support candor and sharing of mistakes without fear of punishment, 3Ms works best.

By using metrics to manage, the results are easier to achieve at higher standards. Certainly the learning curve is steeper as well. Every managerial effort and investment can be linked to a performance improvement result. The cost and results of that cost, or return on investment, can be determined with *no* ambiguity. Ratios of investment to outcome can be tracked on a precise 1:1 or 1:10 or 1 basis, however many multiples there are from the initial cost. This can be measured at the project level by using the performance scorecard that will be explained later. One can even track the payoff or value for any individual performance objective for any individual team member. That is just one of many dimensions of the 3Ms scalability feature.

When the 3Ms is maintained as an online application, management can access any objective at *any* level for *any* function at *any* time. Management can then create program-level, project-level, or individual-level "dashboards" for a quick and real-time assessment of progress, or lack thereof, toward predefined measures and standards of success. This will facilitate being able to "turn on a dime," make immediate managerial changes, and not wait for some quarterly or even weekly report when efforts may have already proved costly. This is in almost total contrast to the typical ability of project management organizations to make changes in their project organization, staffing, and other resource allocations.

MAGNIFY

As the Measure and Manage steps are nearing completion — and this cycle may take at least a year of introduction and modification (improve all management systems and programs to support standards of at least Very Good and Excellent and/ or change the standards so that the measures previously described as Satisfactory are now Unsatisfactory, Very Good is Satisfactory, Excellent is now Very Good) — a new standard of Excellent is created.

Many organizations that began programs dependent on measurement with considerable enthusiasm and then allowed their focus to languish when results were not as expected blamed the approach rather than their own skills and diligence. This is especially true in the objectives-setting process. Studies of several 3Ms-like programs led to the conclusion that an improved format for setting objectives would produce better results. However, metrics alone will not improve results. Metrics just might provide the rigorous measurement skills to more fully realize that performance has been languishing and not improving. As will be elaborated in the discussion of systems, when metrics achieve a clarity not previously sextant, the clarity of metrics using this approach will highlight everything else in the larger corporate system that is lacking in ways that could support a metrics corporate culture.

According to an old cliché, "what gets measured gets managed" and by implication improved. Those of us who get on the scale frequently know that the metrics of weight management is but the beginning. These metrics can give us a baseline (current weight) and help us determine weight management objectives (a successful body weight). We also know that without diligent management of eating and exercise, the metrics will contribute nothing. To magnify one's weight loss with additional health benefits takes quantum leaps of effort beyond the managed weight loss.

The same dynamics and additional effort are at least as true in the project management realm, where, in most organizations, achieving at least Satisfactory (meeting project budget and deadline) is itself a formidable task. Magnifying this standard to Very Good and Excellent is truly formidable. The metrics dimension of the 3Ms model will not guarantee success, just as getting on the scale in itself does not lead to weight loss. The Manage and Magnify phases will be successful only when the leadership and corporate culture support excellence, or in 3Ms terms — are Excellent and/or at least Very Good.

It's a chicken or egg thing. If there is already a managerial commitment to total quality management (TQM) or performance excellence, the 3Ms model will totally support it with the kind of metrics, dialogue, transparency, accountability, executive support, and hierarchical alignment that any TQM program requires. If no TQM-oriented program exists, the 3Ms process is in itself a TQM program at the standards of Very Good and Excellent. If a company is committed to 3Ms, it will need no other TQM approach to support continuous improvement and similar efforts.

SUMMARY

This chapter introduced the basic framework of the 3Ms methodology and defined the three most critical terms: Measure, Manage, and Magnify. Measure is the first step of defining all outputs in measurable terms. Manage is to identify all variables that will help or hinder the successful accomplishment of the results that were defined in the Measure phase. Magnify is to create at least 110% value for the cost of accomplishing results at a standard of Satisfactory. The essence of 3Ms is built on the concepts of MBO in that objectives drive all other managerial decisions and investments. However, 3Ms has expanded this framework to make objectives more precise with weightings and standards, sourced to value, to equate value to money and to emphasize the social and linguistic nature of improved clarity, productivity, and efficiency. Standards define the level of value that was received, where value is defined as getting what you expected for the price you paid. In other words, whether in corporate life or personal life, we place a value on everything we buy, and our pleasure or displeasure is a function of whether or not the product or service met, did not meet, or exceeded our expectations.

The 3Ms methodology gives project managers a very precise way to create and/or measure value about their entire project and the individual contribution of project team members. This is all calculated by standards and weightings per project objective. 3Ms also enables project managers to drill down to metrics that ultimately sum up to the standard categories of "on time and within budget."

When projects go through the three phases of Measure, Manage, and Magnify, they use the metrics to first (Measure) define in measurable terms what outcome will define success, then (Manage) identify all variables (systems, procedures, resources, etc.) that will help or hinder achieving the success that has already been defined in the Measure phase, and finally (Magnify) create work methods that deliver more than 100% of value for no more than 100% of the original project budget.

QUESTIONS

1-1. The 3Ms methodology is compatible with:
   a. Management by objectives
   b. Total quality management
   c. Organization development
   d. All of the above
1-2. In the Measure phase of 3Ms, the project manager and team members:
   a. Identify the metrics that define the standards of Satisfactory, Very Good, and Excellent
   b. Identify the metrics that define the standards of Satisfactory
   c. Identify the metrics that define the standards of Very Good
   d. Identify the metrics that define the standards of Excellent
1-3. 3Ms is linguistic because certain linguistic rules must be learned by the project team members. True or false?
1-4. 3Ms teaches a particular set of social rules to make the project more enjoyable. True or false?
1-5. The basic human unit of the 3Ms-oriented project team is:
   a. An individual
   b. At least two persons
   c. The entire team
   d. Gender equality
1-6. The three dimensions of scalability of the 3Ms are:
   a. Timeliness
   b. Quantity
   c. Quality
   d. Team membership
1-7. The definition of value within the 3Ms context is getting more than you expected for the price you paid. True or false?
1-8. Alignment of metrics is hierarchical and not horizontal. True or false?
1-9. The theme of "the utility of measuring" is that measuring forces project teams to ask questions they otherwise would not. True or false?
1-10. The 3Ms methodology is compatible with any other performance improvement process. True or false?
1-11. The 3Ms process allows you to compare the equivalent value of radically different metrics. True or false?
1-12. The 3Ms process can be successful even without top management support and involvement. True or false?

1-13. When the 3Ms is maintained as an online application, management can access any objective at *any* level for *any* function at *any* time. True or false?

1-14. The advantage of the 3Ms approach is that it can be isolated from corporate culture. True or false?

1-15. The 3Ms can only work when the corporate culture is democratic and open. True or false?

THE VALUE OF A METRICS METHODOLOGY ON BUSINESS

Let there be no doubt about it: 3Ms is neither a quick fix nor a Band-Aid. It is a profound alteration in the way everyone in the organization will think about their work and what they deliver for the remuneration they accept.

This is a new "social contract" in that those who engage in the 3Ms culture are accepting accountability, transparency, and productivity measures that hold everyone to produce at a standard of at least Satisfactory, where that standard is so clearly defined that there is no room for ambiguity. Therefore, it behooves those with task interdependency, as is true for any project team, or any work relationship, for that matter, to go through the Measure phase with the realization that this phase will hold them accountable in a way hitherto unknown to anyone on the project team.

Our argument, as will be articulated in the rest of the book, is that the start-up investment in time, money, and effort to create metrics will repay itself in multiples. This even occurs at the initial stage when people gain clarity as they never had before about the precise metrics of the respective and mutual results they are paid to achieve.

The cost of starting up a 3Ms metrics methodology are considerable, and the benefits are even more so. This chapter presents summary statements of the 3Ms benefits that can be achieved through a committed implementation of the 3Ms methodology.

Some benefits can be realized almost immediately during the introduction and implementation phases, some within the first year and others after the first year and the ensuing years of the reiterations/recycling of the Measure, Manage, and Magnify phases of the process. Ultimately, the greatest value is realized when the 3Ms reaches the stage of being *the* corporate culture — the way people think about project accomplishment, measurement, judgment, rewards, and even tasks.

One thing we can promise is that *any* time invested in this process will be returned back to the productive aspects of work accomplishment *at least* at a ratio of 2:1 and up to 10:1 very quickly. As the same skills are repeated and improved, the ratio *in time alone* can be even 30:1 or 40:1. This is only for the savings of time and does not include the other benefits of improved project teamwork, role and authority clarity, reduced ambiguity of expectations, reduced conflict, and the many other benefits amplified in the summary list below and detailed within the book.

The following is a partial list of benefits that accrue from the implementation of the 3Ms approach as has been experienced by previous and current users.

AT THE HIGHER CORPORATE LEVELS

1. At the highest levels of the corporation, a process for aligning strategic, annual, functional, and departmental objectives

In creating and clarifying the corporate objectives, the executive team has to articulate objectives that are more than the usual financials (sales, profit, cost, etc.). To truly support the 3Ms rigor of project management, corporate objectives have to embrace *all* of the aspects of project management including human resources management and development metrics, corporate culture metrics, process improvement metrics, and quality improvement metrics. Without these metrics at the corporate level, project management metrics will have no highest level objectives for alignment for creating project management metrics for the monitoring, evaluation, and rewards for the project management community.

As those who are the most experienced know, the more common project management dilemma is to create, even perfect, project management objectives and scopes of work in an ambiguous corporate context and hope that the alignment is more or less accurate. There is typically no "line of sight" between project management and the corporate objectives. Depending on the size and complexity of the total corporate structure, the project might be 5 to 10 levels removed from the corporate objectives.

This book will discuss examples of how specific key value areas (KVAs) and performance objectives (POs) were used to create alignment within and between technology teams, business development teams, and cross-functional teams and between strategic and operational objectives. It offers a common procedure and language that accelerate all of the alignment efforts across every function at every level.

The 3Ms secures the place of strategic planning as a working, living process that drives decision making, even on a daily basis. This is in contrast to so many strategic planning processes that have ambiguous and immeasurable vision/mission/purpose and goals statements. These lengthy and detailed documents gather dust on the shelf, because without metrics they lack the power and specificity to serve as a powerful management tool.

2. An internal monitoring system to initiate when these objectives need to be fine-tuned to make them more responsive to changing external market conditions and internal organizational changes

There are many strategic planning, performance review, appraisal, and other management processes that are supposed to take place at least annually and often do not. The 3Ms methodology should be an almost daily discussion regarding how project teams and team members are constantly driven to create greater value for the company by referencing their KVAs and POs to all decision-making and project-planning activity. 3Ms uses the corporate objectives as the larger context and the project objectives as the more focused context.

The 3Ms scorecard format supports the more frequent monitoring, appraisal, and reorganizing of resources (people, money, time, etc.) to stay on target for the standard that was already predefined in the Measure phase of the 3Ms.

3. A methodology to align functional objectives across the top of the organization

3Ms is a process of getting executives to commit to teamwork, interdependencies, and allocation of resources to save their downward hierarchies the time, effort, and even anguish when highest level objectives are ambiguous and highest level conflicts have not been resolved.

When the CEO, COO, and C-level executives or vice presidents of any organization get together to create the strategic objectives of the strategic planning process, inevitably there will be conflict between various corporate functions. If costs are to be reduced across the enterprise and the vice president of sales/marketing wants to expand into a new market at greater cost or R&D wants to pursue a new line of product development at greater cost, this will create conflict at the corporate levels of objectives. Although inevitable, the resolution of these conflicts is typically avoided, creating conflict all the way down the corporate hierarchy and contaminating the project management environment as well. Worse yet, only the corporate executive team has the authority to resolve the conflict.

For this reason and many others, a key project management team-building exercise, the role/authority/decision grid, is included in Chapter 8. It is one of the most useful exercises for resolving the surface kind of conflict. The conflict was not created by the 3Ms process. It was there anyway; the 3Ms just clarifies it with metrics and describes the conflict in a way that can, if the leadership will is there, lead to resolution.

By using the 3Ms approach, these conflicts can be resolved at their inception and at the highest level, saving the project management environment endless time and angst trying to resolve these same conflicting demands. Usually these efforts are futile because the project level was never the source of the conflict, and at this level, project managers typically do not have the proper authority for resolution.

A key part of the 3Ms start-up dynamics clarifies conflicts that were hidden because of ambiguous metrics, typically in the form of goals, instead of objectives (this distinction will be made later). Goals are different from objectives. A goal is directional, like "improve delivery date"; an objective would be "reduce delivery date by three days or by an average of three days by September 1, 2007."

The now-heightened role clarity and accountability for results in sharper metrics terms surface these conflicts for resolution.

4. Metrics are exclusively about future outcomes
Though articulated by many, and seldom really followed, metrics are a description of the future state of the project. Project scope of work (SOW) documents are supposed to articulate in precise terms what the project deliverables are. Yet, a lot of time and effort is wasted when well into the life cycle of the project, the project manager and customer are often arguing about whether or not the project is on time and/or delivering what was promised. These inevitable arguments result from ambiguous SOWs that seemed clear at the inception of the project, but prove to be ambiguous when deliverables are not meeting client expectations.

By using the 3Ms Measure methodology, these misalignments between project deliverables and customer expectations can be totally eliminated when the 3Ms kind of dialogue occurs with adequate frequency. It is also inevitable that any original project SOW will be modified as soon as the ink dries on the contract. This is not preventable. What is preventable is the widening chasm over time that occurs because frequent alignment dialogues do not occur.

AT THE OPERATIONAL LEVEL

1. Near absolute clarity regarding project manager–team member deliverables, expectations of supervisory support, and the nature of interdependencies
Because of the project team focus of the 3Ms and its primary focus on the team (and not the individual), the metrics are developed as a team product. This is done in a team setting with transparency and consensus building regarding who (team member) does what (POs) by when (delivery date) and how well (standards) as determined by what measures (the metrics of the 3Ms process). This book will discuss the precise questions and in what sequence and format they are to be answered by the collective team.

All of the expectations of supervisory support are made explicit by the 3Ms template, which provides the structure for conducting a dialogue to create a 3Ms profile, which there are many examples of in this book.

2. Ability to measurably define what constitutes value and priorities
When the KVAs are defined as weighted proportions of 100% of the value of the project when project delivery meets customer expectations, the team will have total clarity regarding the project value as it aligns with the project SOW. This clarity of alignment will be between project team members and between the project team

and the executive(s) accountable for the project, whether this executive authority resides in a Project or Program Management Office (PMO) or at the vice-president of operations level. This total alignment of the KVA level ensures that there is agreement about "values and priorities" from the beginning.

It is inevitable that this clarity will erode over time due to customer changes in the SOW, scope creep, changes in personnel, and the dozens of other things that can happen, especially with multiyear, multilocation, big and complex projects. When a project is heavily information technology oriented, the rapid change in the applications will create additional erosion of the original clarity that was achieved. For this reason and many others we will articulate, the Measure phase of the 3Ms should be repeated at least quarterly at the team level. This quarterly review might last only minutes, but it should be assumed that the initial KVAs and POs need to be changed to some degree in response to changing realties. We will explain how to do this as well.

3. A linguistics for resolving conflict

As will be explained later, the 3Ms methodology is linguistic and social. This is in contrast to the many other metrics methodologies, derived from the engineering, financial, and information technology worlds. The 3Ms was derived from the world of the Peace Corps, organization development, communications, and even Gestalt therapy. All of these contributions and perspectives give the 3Ms approach a unique focus on the interpersonal and even emotional dimensions of project management metrics. Project management conflict is so often, at its source, the ambiguity of project management terms that are not rigorously defined by the population that will use these words repeatedly — the project team. While doing health checks for project status, terms frequently used by these formats are "customer satisfaction," "quickly resolved," and "effective teamwork," among others. Seldom are any of these terms defined in response to one basic question: As defined by what metrics?

4. A reward system that makes sense and is based on predefined standards of results

As defined by the 3Ms scorecard, 3Ms metrics are defined by the value of the delivery of what the customer expected for the cost of the deliverable. This constitutes value. The scorecard makes each proportionately weighted PO explicit regarding the four possible standards of performance and the value created by each standard. All of the value of each PO is summed up to create the total value of project team and team member performance. This total value is then aligned with predefined ranges of rewards. Although the reward ranges illustrated in this book are based on project team performance only, a company may wish to add additional rewards based on team member performance, overall company performance, PMO performance, cost-of-living adjustments, or any other factor. The 3Ms is infinitely scalable in this regard as well.

5. Increased teamwork resulting from well-defined objectives that are interdependent both within and between departments and functions

The 3Ms provides a process for creating rigorous alignment at *any* level of the company, for *any* function and to *any* degree of granularity or specificity. All of these metrics cascade downward from the corporate objectives or bubble up to the corporate objectives. The universal 3Ms procedures will guarantee that, for any point in time, a picture of total clarity regarding objectives will be created.

At the project team level, the process may be inductive or deductive. Preferably, it is deductive in that the more generalized objectives from the hierarchical level above the project are already clearly defined. The project team then develops its team-level objectives, and then each individual develops his or her objectives to support team objectives. All objectives at the team and individual levels share the same 3Ms template format, described later.

When this process occurs inductively, there might be greater ambiguity regarding the project SOW to allow individual team members to first define their objectives and then summarize their collective objectives as team- or project-level objectives. This process of hierarchical alignment can occur inductively, bottom up, or from the specific to the general. This typically means that there will be greater ambiguity at the top in that corporate objectives have been "dictated" from the lowest performance unit of the organization — the individual. This might be appropriate under some limited circumstances, but the 3Ms preference is top down, from the general to the specific objective.

Ideally, when the corporate culture supports upward as well as downward communication and feedback, there will be a simultaneous inductive/deductive process going on. Through the dimension of time, corporate objectives are being redefined as a result of real-time feedback from the bottom, and project team objectives are being redefined because of the internal and external changes that are tracked by the corporate objectives. This picture needs to be reiterated repeatedly.

6. Focused and appropriate investments of time, effort, and money into improvements of results

Once the KVAs and POs are agreed to, the next step is that there be an action plan per PO. POs define the *what* to be delivered, by *when* and *how well*; an action plan describes the *how*. Regardless of how detailed the action plan is and the format being used, it has to identify the tasks, the time of each task, and the resources (people, money, physical resources like equipment, expertise, etc.) of each task. This book provides two templates for an action plan, both of which are very skeletal, but they do provide the essential questions or categories for building a more elaborate action plan per PO.

In using the 3Ms to monitor progress, the resources allocated to each action plan will be rearranged to accommodate which areas of accomplishment need more, or sometimes less, attention and investment. The 3Ms is also compatible with MS Project® or *any* other project management software that helps projects allocate level of effort and determine what kind of skills are needed at what phase of the project. Also, the POs and metrics may change per project phase, and this will be reflected in the performance scorecard, which can be aligned with project phases instead of calendar time frames. Within the scorecard, objectives and their weightings and standards can change, as can the dependent action plans.

7. Greater accountability for training efforts whether on the job or in the classroom

The 3Ms template also articulates both short- and long-term training needs of the project team and the individual members. Briefly here, and in greater detail later on, Section V.A of the 3Ms template identifies short-term training objectives and is focused on those skills and knowledge that can make an immediate impact on the POs identified for the immediate project. Section V.B identifies long-term training objectives and focuses on skills development that supports the individual's or project team's next project and the same or different skill sets that ought to be developed in anticipation of that next project even when those skills cannot be used on the immediate project.

This is what development is in contrast to training. Development is for long-term improved performance; training is typically for short-term improved performance. Training has to be built into the total planning process. It is seldom the case that all members of the project team are fully competent for the task at hand, especially if the project involves a new technology or another challenge never faced before.

When training is tied to specific POs of the 3Ms template, then the performance improvement can be tracked to either identify objectives where the same standards of Satisfactory, Very Good, or Excellent are achieved in ways that are "better, faster, or cheaper" or there is a consistent upgrade of overall standards of accomplishment.

8. Resolution of the potential conflict between individual and team effort and rewards

So often, there is the spurious argument regarding the conflict between individual and team effort and rewards. Unfortunately, the argument is not so spurious when certain kinds of reward systems set up the conflict. Within the 3Ms process, the transparency of the project-team-level objectives, which represent the cumulative output of team members, eliminates these dynamics. This potential conflict can be further managed by how management established the weightedness between team and individual accomplishment.

One extreme would be the development of *only* project team KVAs and POs, so that *no* individual accomplishment is ever developed. This is the essence of the self-directed work team, which requires a very mature team corporate culture, cross-training, and teams that can work very autonomously.

The essence of the 3Ms objectives-setting exercise is that all the objectives at the individual level are sourced to the objectives at the project team level. Most individual objectives will be mutual to two or more team members; only a few will be exclusive to an individual. Therefore, with this dynamic and mathematical precision of setting up project team objectives, there is little legalistic or formal basis for internal competition. Appropriate leadership and a corporate culture should take care of the rest.

9. A corporate culture where everyone speaks the same language about performance issues
The initial development of 3Ms KVAs and POs requires attention to the use of terms such as "measured by," "manifested by," "we will know when these factors occur or appear," etc. As the project wends its way toward completion, other terms and concepts inevitably will "contaminate" what at first was a pure and totally clear dictionary. Hence, the linguistics must also be attended to on a continuous basis.

10. Objective language and measures for discussing teamwork, leadership, commitment, and quality
Although anyone reading this statement "knows" what it means, there are many definitions of what constitutes "teamwork, leadership, commitment, and quality." Our definitions of these terms are seldom universal and often contextual. Therefore, these terms must also have a metric shared by everyone. This metrics of words and even corporate culture is addressed in Chapter 9.

11. A shift in thinking from activity, input, and throughput to results: start with the "what" and then develop the "how"
So often, project teams immediately focus on the work plan. This is even encouraged by dominant project management applications like MS Project®. It is often assumed that clarity exists regarding the "what" or outcome of the project as should have been articulated by the SOW. And this may be "mostly" true. What is also true is that under the pressure of showing results and dramatic activity, what is ambiguous is left for later discussion for clarification. The 3Ms process is just that: In the first M, Measure, what is meant by success is defined in measurable terms. In the second M, Manage, all those variables that will help or hinder success are identified and plans to manage them are created. These two phases of the 3Ms often are reversed, with project teams jumping into planning without first arriving at total clarity on what is supposed to be achieved.

12. Empowered individual and team efforts because management's support for accountabilities and results is also clear
Many a project team is left floundering without adequate executive leadership, corporate mandates, staffing, and other resources. This is often due to the disconnect or lack of alignment between the project objectives and the corporate objectives that

should supply the source and accountability for project success. By using the 3Ms methodology for corporate hierarchical alignment, the project team can create a "clear line of sight," targeting the highest level objectives and office/executive that have ultimate accountability to support the project.

13. Realization of team member potential to achieve standards that are greater than "satisfactory"

It has been our experience that the project SOW states only the minimum performance criteria for the deliverable. There is seldom any articulation of what might exceed the scope in terms of "better, faster, or cheaper." Occasionally, there is an implicit or even explicit reward for faster accomplishment, but not better or cheaper. With the 3Ms approach, all outcomes are not only weighted to define their relative "importance," but there is a predefined set of standards per outcome. The standard of "Satisfactory" typically defines the initial SOW, the contract and/or customer expectations.

The standards of Very Good and Excellent define, in metric terms, what will exceed the agreement, but with no accountability for achieving these higher standards. What happens is that the articulation of these two additional standards creates the motivation and creativity to exceed Satisfactory. Typically, there is not even a vision or concept and therefore no motivation to achieve what would be better than "meets expectations."

14. A system that can be applied to any managerial model already in place or anticipated

Other programs that can be strengthened by 3Ms are self-directed work teams, balanced scorecard, open book management, diversity, etc. The 3Ms methodology can certainly function as a stand-alone and exclusive way to manage any project. Additionally, it can complement *any* other managerial model of project management and add greater clarity and rigor.

15. Create management practices which include a corporate culture and reward system that support the constant improvement of current results

Because the initial phase of Measure defines the standards of Satisfactory, Very Good, and Excellent, project teams are always describing standards that exceed project scope and customer expectations. They also can see from the performance scorecard that exceeding Satisfactory has greater rewards. When the entire team is working toward Very Good and Excellent, people will tap creative insights into achieving higher standards with less time and less effort. Although this is contrary to what we call the "factory mentality," project teams can first conceptualize through the Measure stage, with its demands of POs, weightings, and four distinguishing standards, that the achievement of Very Good and Excellent is a function of thinking creatively and *not* a function of working harder or longer hours.

16. Improved fraud prevention and detection
Metrics raise visibility to opportunity and threat. The greater the degree of visibility, the lower the opportunity for fraud to be committed. The context of this is related to normal work culture that makes workers defensive and protective of their jobs and reputation from reprisal. Thus, reducing the opportunity for fraud to be committed is a key benefit.

17. Improved cognitivity for everyone in determining value in their work
Metrics define "minimum goodness" at the moment of completed action when comparing the result to the expectation.

AT THE INDIVIDUAL LEVEL

1. Reward system
Create a rational reward system so that project team members can self-manage their efforts and know at the beginning of any performance period (quarterly, annually) what kind of results deserves what kind(s) of rewards.

2. Other rewards
In addition to monetary rewards of increased base pay, bonuses, stock options, etc., other rewards per standard (Satisfactory, Very Good, Excellent) of performance can be negotiated when the 3Ms profile is being developed.

3. Greater detail
Create greater detail at the individual and team levels to support the operational metrics templates and ultimately the strategic objectives. This hierarchy for alignment and a clear line of sight is shown in Figure 5-1.

TARGET POPULATION

The management team of any organization can be most effective when there is clarity, stability, and security. The 3Ms format provides the outline for the dialogue between project manager and team members. This book, the public workshops sponsored by the Project Management Institute and its chapters, and the consulting services we offer provide guidelines to coordinate the initial process for setting KVAs and POs, for quarterly performance reviews, and for annual performance/reward reviews.

This book gives the greatest level of detail regarding the 3Ms process. We have also encountered a few non-3Ms environments and relationships where there was so much implicit understanding regarding task accomplishment expectations and an at least Satisfactory standard of performance that many of these detailed dialogues and procedures might be abbreviated without compromising the essential value of the 3Ms integrity. Some variables affecting the dialogue are the longevity of the relationship, knowledge of the job, stability of the environment, and clarity of the several levels of objectives above and objectives of the levels below.

Assumptions about the typical 3Ms participant population are as follows. The reasons for making these assumptions explicit is that the 3Ms methodology requires a certain degree of interpersonal skills and abilities to engage in sometimes tense dialogues, so at least one of the parties should have the qualities listed below. These represent the ideal. To the degree that a project environment lacks these general qualities, the 3Ms will be more difficult to implement, requiring more time, effort, and perhaps training to teach 3Ms populations the skills and qualities they may initially lack.

The management level is composed of people who:

- Understand and use the concepts of KVAs and standards of performance
- Can conduct a mature dialogue with their supervisors and subordinates regarding mutual expectations
- Identify and negotiate differences of opinions, approaches, and areas of joint and mutually exclusive responsibility and authority
- Initiate changes (upward or downward) in their objectives (weights and standards) when performance conditions change
- Look for added value within their POs for improving their performance; improvement may be measured by cost, productivity, quality, efficiency, new organizational concepts and approaches, teamwork, training, etc.
- Conduct face-to-face dialogue as the essence of management, as opposed to filling out forms or the ever-popular escalation of issues
- Want to perform well, be of service, and advance themselves
- Add your own!

TRAINING

No matter how good the forms, manual, and any other supportive material, there can be no substitute for *training* to:

- Initiate the start-up of this process
- Sustain the process as it matures
- Modify the process to respond to changing environments, structures, and workforce

SKILL MASTERY

Within the repeated application of the 3Ms cycle, you will learn new ways to define what results you are paid to produce. Adopting and adapting these changes will mean using new skills to gain almost complete clarity about the project manager/team member job and how these roles reward for performance.

These skills will not come immediately and, like any skill, will require effort, practice, and continued use until they are a part of the project management repertoire. The benefits of mastering these skills are greater clarity, team member commitment, motivation, and a committed relationship for negotiating expectations and changes as they inevitably occur within the project team and the environment.

The 3Ms approach is a variation of *and compatible with* balanced scorecard, performance management, management by objectives, total quality management, and any approach that motivates team members to strive for continuous improvement in their productivity, quality, efficiency, costs, or whatever variable determines added value of their contributions to their job.

The approach is a logical exercise between project manager, management, and team members that supports a dialogue which produces mutually agreeable output measures. At a level of Satisfactory, team members earns their paychecks and at levels of Very Good and Excellent exceed in value what they are paid. By supporting and delivering outputs at the Very Good and Excellent standards, staff and management will realize that any money for salaries, benefits, and bonuses is being spent well (i.e., that additional value has been produced).

Other indicators of a successful 3Ms of Performance include:

- Increased individual and team productivity
- Clarity of performance standards
- Objectively reached decisions about rewards for performance
- Adequate authority delegated to the level of responsibility
- Improved teamwork of the project management team, resulting in:
    - Reduced conflict at the executive level
    - An accelerated implementation of programs and initiatives
- A disciplined approach to implement a host of other human resources management and development activity:
    - Career planning
    - Recruiting
    - Team building
    - Succession planning
- An organization where extra performance is rewarded and poor performers are either:
    - Trained
    - Transferred to a position where they will be at least Satisfactory
    - Terminated
- Transparent management processes within each function and at each level
- A more effective utilization of available resources (human, material, financial)

BENEFITS OF REGULAR REVIEWS OR HEALTH CHECKS

Inherent in the 3Ms is all of the best of any performance management and review process, with additional advantages for the specific project management context.

Reviews should be done at least quarterly or more frequently, depending on the dynamics of the project and its vulnerability to inevitable changes of scope, membership, customer demands, executive priorities, etc. Reviews or health checks can support any changes in standards and weightings to keep the potential rating of performance in line with changing realities. With the commitment to quarterly reviews, the annual review should not hold any surprises or great drama regarding judgment of performance, rewards, recognition, career potential, etc.

The 3Ms also advocates frequent reviews of objectives, priorities, and standards. In this approach, *quarterly reviews are as critical as or even more critical than the initial and mutual setting of objectives.* In this process, the objectives equate to the value of the job and the contributions of performance. Remember that to manage effectively is to get the greatest value from team member efforts.

The quarterly review process is truly a way of managing ongoing performance — the primary job of any project manager. It is both amusing and upsetting when project managers say they do not have time to review objectives. Isn't that the primary job of the project manager?

3Ms is, in part, a particular language that ensures clarity between people in any performance relationship. Although theoretically supplied by job descriptions, most team members and their project managers cannot specify the relative importance of their KVAs; others simply rank all KVAs as equal or near equal in importance.

SUMMARY

This chapter highlights the many, but not exhaustive, benefits of the 3Ms process, for both the short term and especially the long term, when 3Ms becomes the social and linguistic culture of how projects are managed. All of the negative dimensions of project management are improved, and some can be eliminated if not prevented from ever occurring. The rigorous nature of the three phases "forces" project teams to start with total clarity regarding their statement of work and to develop metrics that reflect any inevitable changes that will occur. Because the 3Ms is about a continuous dialogue and is the "way people talk about their work," which they do all the time anyway, the alteration of metrics to define changes in work and changes in the project to reflect altered metrics is a continuous process, with many benefits to all levels of the corporate hierarchy as described in this chapter.

QUESTIONS

2-1. Which of the following are 3Ms benefits at the corporate level:
   a. Top leadership of the corporation is forced to align objectives
   b. Specific measurable corporate objectives are developed by consensus
   c. Any strategic planning has strategic objectives
   d. Leadership uses the 3Ms methodology for frequent realignment

2-2. The three factors built into the 3Ms methodology are accountability, transparency, and security. True or false?
2-3. The 3Ms methodology can only yield benefits if it becomes the corporate culture. True or false?
2-4. Which of the following benefits will 3Ms produce almost immediately:
   a. Improved project teamwork
   b. Role and authority clarity
   c. Reduced ambiguity of expectations
   d. Reduced conflict
   e. All of the above
2-5. The difference between goals and objectives is that goals define results and measurable terms and objectives are more general. True or false?
2-6. The difference between inductive and deductive thinking is that inductive reasoning is from the general to the specific and deductive reasoning is from the specific to the general. True or false?
2-7. Training is aligned with performance objectives by asking the team what skills it might newly acquire or dramatically improve to perform at a higher standard or at the same standard more easily. True or false?
2-8. Many if not most scopes of work sometimes contribute to conflict because what are called objectives or criteria of success are often ambiguous. True or false?
2-9. Which of the following are benefits of 3Ms at the operational level:
   a. Near absolute clarity regarding project manager–team member deliverables, expectations of supervisory support, and the nature of interdependencies
   b. Increased teamwork resulting from well-defined objectives that are interdependent both within and between departments and functions
   c. Ability to measurably define what constitutes "value and priorities"
   d. A reward system that makes sense and is based on predefined standards of results
   e. All of the above
2-10. The 3Ms creates alignment at the corporate level of objectives because corporate objectives are strategically force ranked, with standards of performance by the entire executive team, who must reach agreement on *all* of the corporate objectives. True or false?
2-11. For 3Ms to be most effective, corporate objectives have to embrace *all* of the aspects of project management, including human resources management and development metrics, corporate culture metrics, process improvement metrics, and quality improvement metrics. True or false?
2-12. The 3Ms creates better teamwork in that the Measure phase requires that the entire team develop its performance objectives, with weightings and standards, together for total transparency. True or false?

2-13. The 3Ms scorecard is a powerful management tool in that at the individual and team levels you can spot who is not contributing to the group's success. True or false?
2-14. The target audience for the 3Ms methodology can be anyone employed in any position for any length of time. True or false?
2-15. The most critical review of performance objectives is:
   a. Annual
   b. Quarterly
   c. Monthly
   d. Weekly

This book has free materials available for download from the Web Added Value™ Resource Center at www.jrosspub.com.

3

WHAT IS VALUE?

One of the unique features of the 3Ms approach is that the term value is defined very precisely and adds rigor to the corporate rhetoric of "added value," "value for the customer," and "the value proposition," which imply that someone is going to get more than what they paid for. The 3Ms definition of value is simple and profound: *Value is when you get what you pay for when the deliverable meets your expectations as described in measurable terms.* This standard of value is called Satisfactory.

When you buy a car and are promised 70,000 miles of maintenance-free driving and that actually occurs, you have received the value of that promise. When you order a pizza and the promise is that for $10.99 you will get a hot pizza delivered within 30 minutes and that happens, you have received value. When a software project team has a budget of a million dollars to deliver a project management application with 10 features with specific performance indicators and a delivery date of a year from inception and that happens, that too is value or a standard of Satisfactory (Table 3-1).

The central theme of this entire book is *not* metrics. It is how to create the metrics that define the increased value of a project managed by the 3Ms process. Figure 3-1 shows the three phases of the 3Ms process. The chapters on the 3Ms template and the action plan formats will show how to complete each phase. This chapter will take you through the steps of creating a 3Ms profile from a 3Ms template.

The project-level 3Ms template presented below will be replicated over and over within the 3Ms methodology description and the tool kit portion of the book. Eventually, the reader will realize that regardless of the specific context or level of function, the logic and processes are always the same. All of this will support the 3Ms mantra: a universal methodology for infinite metrics.

Table 3-1. A Hierarchy of the Standard of Satisfactory Showing the Hierarchical Alignment of the Corporate, Program, Project, and Project Team Member Objectives

Organizational Level	Standard of Satisfactory	Value (All Areas Were Predefined at the Standard of Satisfactory)
Corporate	Profits, sales, personnel costs	Increased profits, stock market credibility
Program Management Office	Timeliness, cost, deliverables	Efficiency, effectiveness
Project team	Meeting project objectives of time and cost	Customer satisfaction
Individual	Complete performance objectives	Project team members are creating value at the level of their costs/salaries

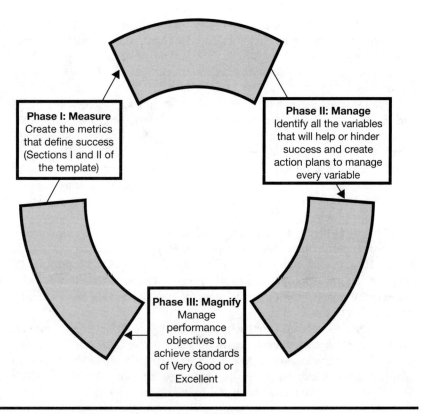

Figure 3-1. 3Ms Measure, Manage, Magnify Cycle

The next chapters will walk you through the sections of the 3Ms template and identify the questions to answer and how to answer those questions to produce a 3Ms profile.

The following is a sample 3Ms template. It is not intended for your complete understanding, but rather as your initial exposure.

Project-Level 3Ms Template

Project Name: Product Widget
Project Manager: Steve Rollins
Version Date: 9/6/06

I. Key Value Areas Weighting (%)
   A. Timeliness = 30%
   B. Budget = 30%
   C. Risk management = 20%
   D. Quality = 20%
II. Project Performance Objectives — Measurable with weightings (%) and distinguishing standards of performance (see Table 3-2).
   A. Timeliness = 30%: 4 = 10% early; 3 = 5% early; 2 = by due date; 1 = later than due date.
   B. Budget = 30%: 4 = 10% below budget; 3 = 5% below budget; 2 = within budget; 1 = exceeds the budget.
   C. Risk management = 20%: 4 = accepted change requests 10% more requirements; 3 = additional features; 2 = met customer requirements; 1 = did not meet customer requirements.
   D. Quality = 20%: 4 = plus 5% fewer tasks; 3 = improved quality above industry standards; 2 = all performance meets industry standards; 1 = change in the schedule.
III. Performance Scorecard (see Table 3-3) — 4 = Excellent; 3 = Very Good; 2 = Satisfactory; 1 = Unsatisfactory.
IV. Performance Factors
   A. Team Members — Project schedule is critical path. Project team manages the critical path of the project schedule for its work.
   B. Project Manager — Critical path, intra- and interproject, relative to the corporate objectives, between projects and between corporate goals.

Table 3-2. Standards and Their Numerical Equivalent

Excellent	4
Very Good	3
Satisfactory	2
Unsatisfactory	1

Table 3-3. Performance Scorecard

Key Value Areas	Weighting	Performance Objectives	Weighting (W)	Performance (P)	Value (V) W × P = V
Timeliness	30	Timeliness	0.30	2	0.60
Budget	30	Budget	0.30	3	0.90
Risk management	20	Risk management	0.20	2	0.40
Quality	20	Quality	0.20	3	0.60
	100%		100%		TOTAL VALUE = 2.50

V. Training Objectives
   A. Short Term for Team — Improve estimating abilities, skill of how to recognize delivery opportunity and threat within own work and that of peers, and how to calculate critical path management.
   B. Long Term for Team — Learn to optimize the delivery opportunity for short term and how to navigate their project vis-à-vis other projects.

ESTABLISHING KEY VALUE AREAS (SECTION I OF THE TEMPLATE)

The first step of deducing performance standards is to develop a forced weighting of all key value areas (KVAs) so the sum is 100%. These KVAs do not describe results per se; they describe the major areas of potential value to the company. Remember to focus on KVAs first and then specific objectives.

Again, What Is Value?

Value is what the employee, team, and organization deliver when the results achieved were predefined to be a standard of Satisfactory (2). This value earns the paycheck. Some companies label this standard as competent, meets expectations, good, etc. The actual words are irrelevant as all of these terms imply the same concept — performance at this standard earns the paycheck, project cost, or consulting fee.

Returning to the 3Ms template for Project Widget, which is really a very generic project, the KVAs and their weightings are:

Timeliness   = 30%
Budget   = 30%
Risk management   = 20%
Quality   = 20%

The project team reached consensus that these four were the project areas of value.

As an example, assume that the replication of this process occurs within a group setting (the project team) where individuals are, for the first time, developing their individual 3Ms profile. If the individual who initiates the 3Ms wants to start at the project team level, it does not matter technically. It is just that the project level may be farther removed from the emotional involvement of the team members, especially if the team is cross-functional and there is not yet a common project team understanding. In this case, it is better to reproduce the template at the individual level and then at the project level afterward. If you want to create the project-level template first based on the scope of work and other formal and legalistic documents, that is fine. In that case, the second step would be to deduce the team members' templates. By doing both at the same time, the dynamics are more likely to create the alignment of team and individual metrics and minimize, if not eliminate, the mostly artificial conflict between individual and team objectives and rewards.

The following are hypothetical examples of the KVAs for professions everyone can relate to. They illustrate the proportionate value of the KVAs as a percentage of each dollar of the salaries of these roles. Later these KVAs will represent the proportionate cost of the project or consulting fee or the percentage per $1, $10,000 or $1 million of the project. Regardless of the absolute amount, the weightings per KVA define the importance or priority of each value or KVA.

Examples of KVAs

Teacher	Teaching	= 60%
	Parent conferencing	= 20%
	Administration	= 20%
Car salesperson	Sales	= 80%
	Customer relations (after sales)	= 20%
Restaurant manager	Kitchen	= 60%
	Service	= 20%
	Customer relations	= 20%
Regional sales manager	Sales	= 40%
	Recruiting	= 20%
	Training	= 20%
	Customer relations	= 20%

These KVAs represent areas of value and *not* the specific deliverables or the metrics of those deliverables. Those are defined at the next level: performance objectives.

To derive the KVAs of a project team, team members answer certain questions, all of which have a number of different variations. The following questions for the project manager and team, if this is a collective effort, are the ones we advocate. These questions are basically all the same, but different people understand one format better than the other, even though the answers are all the same (i.e., the KVAs above).

- Looking at your current project (Project Widget), how do you think it ought to be to create greater value than it does? What are the KVAs of this

project? Look at the corporate objectives of your company, department, division, etc.
- Per $100 of the project budget, what are the most important areas of value to the customer and/or your project team?
- Of the areas you have identified, what is their proportionate value?
- What weighting would you give to each so that altogether they equal 100% of the project's value?

Look at the examples above and follow the rules below. The answers to these questions at the level of the familiar roles above (teacher, car salesperson, restaurant manager, regional sales manager) are answered above. At the level of a Project Widget, the answers are:

    Timeliness   = 30%
    Budget   = 30%
    Risk management   = 20%
    Quality   = 20%

To ensure harmony and the same format and language across multiple projects, with many team members, multiple units of an enterprise, and multiple levels of management, we have developed several useful rules that all project teams should follow.

This KVA level is the first experience of the social and linguistic dynamics of the 3Ms process. Team members will find themselves in "violent agreement" as they use different terms for the same thing, until they agree on the one best or temporary term. Team members will sometimes use the same term with different meanings, which will surface in Section II of the 3Ms template when these terms are further defined as specific measurable outcomes (performance objectives) and in a metrics format.

When developing KVAs, the few rules below are very powerful and ensure uniformity, even in very complex environments, where specific projects are radically different, with different KVAs and subsequent differences in performance objectives, metrics, and weightings. The rules simply work. Use them.

Rules for KVAs

- Limit your answers to no more than five categories.
- The fewer, the better for immediate focus.
- Give each category a two- or three-word label based on your functions.
- Each KVA has its own category, meaning no "and" should be used (e.g., not sales and marketing = 40%, but sales = 20%, marketing = 20%).
- Each KVA must be at least 20% of the total value of the job. These proportions will ensure your focus on the most critical aspects of the job. If there were any more than five KVAs or any percentage less than 20, then "key" value areas would no longer be "key" or significant.

- KVAs greater than 20% increase in only 10% increments (not 25%, but either 20% or 30%) because KVAs at this level do not need a 5% degree of specificity.

During the initial stages of the 3Ms, KVAs may change as teams agree to common labels and weightings per KVA. Additionally, the initiation of the 3Ms may see a manifestation of other change dynamics going on, so the KVAs also must respond to changing internal and external environments.

ESTABLISHING PERFORMANCE OBJECTIVES (SECTION II)

As a quick review, an objective is a measurable statement of results with a time limit and other suitable qualitative and quantitative criteria. The criteria of these performance objectives (POs) are equal to those of the traditional management by objectives criteria: **s**pecific, **m**easurable, **a**chievable, **r**elevant, and **t**ime framed or SMART. Additionally, 3Ms objectives have weightings and four standards of performance. There must be at least one objective per KVA as value is only created when the manifestation is a deliverable for which someone has paid.

Although each KVA in Project Widget has only one objective, more than one objective could be identified per KVA had there been two different products, markets, time frames, or widgets, each with a different production deadline or separate budget.

The POs are also developed through a series of questions which can be either very direct or a more formal sequence of questions to create more ideas and metrics before zeroing in on the one initial choice.

This section both describes and shows how to begin to use the 3Ms as a rigorous tool to establish POs with weightings, metrics, and standards of performance, as well as their relative value to different KVAs and objectives. Although there are many other issues regarding this approach (degree of participation, compatibility with corporate culture, payoffs, etc.), the focus here is on the explicitness of specifying objectives and their weightings. This helps to define priorities and standards of distinguishing performance.

With KVAs established, the next step is to develop POs.

Questions for Producing Performance Objectives

Assuming an annual performance period and project cycle for reviews of Project Widget performance, if one of the KVAs that was just created produced results that are *at least* Satisfactory, how would you know it? By what measures would you know that you have produced results that are at least Satisfactory?

The following are the types of questions that will produce POs:

- What are all possible variables or measures? (This question could lead into a formal brainstorming session where project team members produce at least 10 metrics, knowing that some are not going to be used.) For the KVA of

quality, these metrics might be life of product, compatibility with existing machinery, replacement cost, maintenance, ingenuity of design, etc.
- Which are nonnegotiable? (Nonnegotiable means imposed from the outside, such as budget limitations, deadlines, minimum performance standards, human resources available, etc.)
- Which POs do you want to make nonnegotiable? (Self-imposed POs would be tighter deadline, with less money, fewer people, a higher standard, etc. or for quality would be conformance to industry standards, safety margins, etc.)
- Which measure from all of the above will you use to establish the standard of Satisfactory?
- Other questions that help are: What performance reflects Excellent versus Unsatisfactory performance? What distinguishes between Excellent versus Unsatisfactory? What is the general description of a job well done? Satisfactory might be conformance to industry standards at a cost per unit not to exceed some dollar value and compatible with a dollar value >90%.

Some examples of different standards of quality are given in Table 3-4. In the first example, quality is a function of life span of the unit. In the second example, quality is a function. This illustrates how ambiguous the word "quality" is. Both examples are valid, and there are many more metrics that would validly define the different quality standards.
- Which measure(s) will you add to Satisfactory to create Very Good? Very Good is usually "better, faster, and cheaper" than Satisfactory. *This standard earns more than the paycheck and creates value that exceeds what the individual or team is getting paid to deliver.* In financial terms, this is usually >105% of cost, meaning that for the cost of a standard performance, the customer received "very good" performance.
- Which measure(s) will you add/use to create Excellent? Excellent is a quantum leap larger than the interval between Satisfactory and Very Good, a conceptual breakthrough, even discontinuous from Very Good. Creating even more additional value, or a standard of Excellent (4), exceeds Very Good by being

Table 3-4. Different Definitions (Metrics) of Quality

Quality	4 = +20% of normal life span, shelf life 3 = +15% 2 = +10% 1 = <10%
Quality	4 = exceeds safety standards by >20% or recognized in the industry as setting a new world standard 3 = exceeds safety standards by >10% 2 = meets safety standards 1 = does not meet safety standards

exceptionally creative or better, faster, and cheaper to a dramatic degree. This value earns even more than the monetary value of the standard of Very Good. In financial terms, this would be >110%, meaning that for the cost of creating the standard of Satisfactory, the customer received the value created by the standard of Excellent.

By not prejudging distinguishing standards of performance, project manager and team member may have different judgments of the same performance standard (i.e., what is Satisfactory, Very Good, or Excellent). Agreeing to explicit prejudgment of distinguishing standards eliminates frequent ambiguity.

Many practitioners of similar approaches tend to set priorities of "high," "medium," and "low." For all the lists of priorities, so many are set at "high." This is the same as setting all of them at "low." There is nothing to distinguish between priorities. This failure may have the effect of setting three or four priorities, each of which is 60% of the job — 240% of the job is a logical impossibility! Forced weightings in a total universe of 100% is a more explicit way of expressing priorities.

Thus, the following POs and standards for the sales project team (with KVAs of sales = 40%, staffing = 30%, budget = 30%) might be:

>550 units for a performance standard of Excellent
>400 units for a standard of Very Good
>300 units for a standard of Satisfactory
<300 units for a rating of Unsatisfactory

Another example of Excellent might be to keep the sales units at >400 with no additional increase of units for that year, but creating a website for the dealership with an e-commerce function that might, in the second year of its existence, create sales that greatly exceed the 550 units of the original Excellent. This is an example of the creative aspects of Excellent. It is not just more — it is a qualitative leap of creating the potential for "more."

The alignment of terms such as "Excellent" with measurable outcomes eliminates ambiguity, anxiety, and confusion for the project team being managed. For year-end reviews, we translate the judgment to a numerical value (Excellent = 4, Very Good = 3, Satisfactory = 2, and Unsatisfactory = 1) and multiply the standard of performance (e.g., 4 = Excellent) by the weighting of the objective (40% or 0.4), yielding 1.6 as the overall value of that objective or contribution. This will be further explained in Section III of the 3Ms template, which is the performance scorecard. In the online application, the scorecard can be accessed 24/7 for input or to monitor progress for any KVA/PO of any project team.

Rules for Performance Objectives

Just like the rules for KVAs, to ensure conformity across multiple projects, the rules for POs support uniformity across projects and KVAs within projects:

- No weightings less than 10%.
- No "ands," as in internal and external customers = 20% weighting; it has to be internal customers = 10% and external customers = 10% weighting.
- No more than 10 POs for the entire profile (Section II).
- At least one PO per KVA. If there are no results, there is no value being created.
- Objectives do not use adjectives or adverbs. These grammatical terms only introduce ambiguity. What do "quickly," "efficient," "effective," "good customer relations," etc. mean? These words only have meaning when further defined by the metrics of greater precision, so that "quickly" means "within 24 hours," "by close of business" etc. Therefore, there is no need for adjectives and adverbs and they are not allowed within the 3Ms methodology.

Format for Creating Performance Objectives

For a human resources management project to reduce overtime, write the objectives using the following format: Adjective/ Results/By when (date)/Optional/Cost not to exceed:

Results: Reduced overtime in Department 23 from 150 hours to 50 hours per month

By when (date): August 1 = 4; September 1 = 3; October 1 = 2; later than October 1 = 1

Optional:

Cost not to exceed: $50,000

Exercise

Produce objectives that vary the standard of cost and overtime while making timeliness nonnegotiable. The variables you build into your original statement define what is nonnegotiable, what should not be compromised, and therefore what is the most important part of the objective.

The following three statements illustrate different POs. In statement 1, the most important variables are cost and timeliness and therefore do not contribute to the definition of distinguishing standards. In statement 2, they are timeliness and amount of overtime reduced. In statement 3, they are amount of overtime reduced and cost. Although all are important in the objective, the variable that distinguishes between standards of performance is still important, *but* the least important.

Statement 1: Outcome is the metric for distinguishing standards.
By August 1 (timeliness) at a cost ≤$50,000 (cost) reduce overtime from 150 hours to (metrics for distinguishing standards) <40 = Excellent (4); <45 = Very Good (3); <50 = Satisfactory (2); >51 = Unsatisfactory (1).

Statement 2: Cost is the metric for distinguishing standards.
By August 1 (timeliness) reduce overtime (results) from 150 hours to 50 hours at a cost of <$40,000 = 4; <$45,000 = 3; <$50,000 = 2; >$50,000 = 1.

Statement 3: Timeliness is the metric for distinguishing standards.
Reduce overtime from 150 hours to 50 hours at a cost ≤$50,000 by August 1 = 4; by September 1 = 3; by October 1 = 2; later than October 1 = 1.

QUALITATIVE METRICS: THE WHY, WHAT, AND HOW

> *It's either quantifiable or it's not measurable.*
> *It's either quantifiable or it's subjective.*
> *We have to quantify it in order to measure it.*

Most, if not all, who read the statements above will:

1. Agree with them
2. Equate the word "measure" with the word "quantify," and consequently
3. Avoid and/or neglect the explicit qualitative dimensions of measuring your project management progress

Even staff with a quality-management-related role are not likely to have rigorous metrics of quality that are qualitative in nature. In this section, we will establish the foundation of qualitative metrics, illustrate how we use them, and then show how to use them in the project management world, as illustrated by the qualitative metrics of a director of a Project Management Office.

There is an almost total lack of qualitative metrics in the project management world. The *3Ms of Performance: Measure, Manage, and Magnify* is a methodology in which qualitative metrics are as rigorous and as precise as quantitative metrics. In fact, much of the 3Ms methodology reflects how most people think about most of their lives, but at a level that is implicit and seldom articulated. The exceptions are in conflict resolution or crisis situations, when people individually or as parties in a dispute, are forced to spell out, in detailed fashion, the metrics of the resolution for mutual understanding, agreement, and commitment. Therefore, after presenting some examples from the project management world, examples from other areas will be considered to see the kind of rigor and precision provided by qualitative metrics.

Qualitative Metrics for a Project Management Office

In the 3Ms profile for a director of a Project Management Office (PMO), the metrics in the performance arena are an appropriate mix of quantitative and qualitative metrics. The 3Ms profile is the performance metrics or objectives by which this position would be measured.

This mix is derived from the 3Ms process and template, where the first step is to define at any level (individual, team, project, function, or even the dashboard or corporate objectives level) what the value of one's contribution is. The word "value," as previously defined, is the delivery of products and/or services that meet the expectations of the purchaser. Value is the metrics/quality of the deliverable and is judged as being at least equal to and/or fair for the price/fee/salary being paid.

Another dimension of developing qualitative variables is to develop distinguishing standards to tease out the qualitative metrics of any performance outcome. These standards and their definitions are as follows:

- **Satisfactory** — Meeting customer expectations, competent, delivering value, or whatever words are used in your environment
- **Very Good** — Some degree of "better, faster, cheaper" with an added value of at least 5% as defined by the customer
- **Excellent** — Some multiples of Very Good or a creative/conceptual breakthrough beyond Very Good, with an added financial value of at least 10%
- **Unsatisfactory** — Anything less than or missing from what is defined by Satisfactory

Instead of the rigorous four standards above, standards are supposedly defined by the use of the many tools of project management. These tools are typically focused on risk management and health checks, typically with use of green, amber, and red levels of "health," which are themselves aggregated ambiguous labels of other and more lower level ambiguities.

The question (to a project team) is framed thusly: In order to obtain at least a performance level of Satisfactory, what are the metrics that would determine this? Satisfactory is defined as delivering all of the project features as defined by the scope of work. Whether the money was "satisfactorily" earned is judged based on metrics defined by the company (project on schedule, under budget, results desirable). The answers are typically:

- **Timeliness** — Is it on time?
- **Financial** — Is it within budget?
- **Customer satisfaction** — Does it meet the customer's expectation?
- **Efficient** — Did it maximize customer resources?
- **Effective** — How well does it work?
- **Problem resolution** — Was there minimum conflict and time needed to resolve issues at the level where they exist, or did issues need to be "escalated" or moved upward within the reporting hierarchy of authority?

Examples of Business Governance/PMO Qualitative Standards

The same logic is used for the qualitative standards of a project management health check:

- **Satisfactory (2)** — Project management health checks are delivered on a monthly basis and are complete.

- **Very Good (3)** — Health checks are delivered bimonthly, for greater timeliness to correct errors of performance.
- **Excellent (4)** — Create an online application that enables all project management data to be input at *any* time and to be calculated in a health checks database or by real-time monitoring, which eliminates the separate task of doing health checks. The concept of health checks becomes like breathing, gravity, etc.

The following 3Ms profile for a director of the PMO uses the concepts presented above:

I. Key Value Areas Weightings (%)
   A. Build PMO = 40%
   B. Direct PMO = 40%
   C. Staff development = 20%
II. Performance Objectives (with weightings, metrics, standards)
   A. Build PMO = 40%
      1. 20% = issue initial program management process/templates: 4 = by June 30; 3 = by July 15; 2 = by August 30; 1 = not issued in third quarter.
      2. 20% = staff PMO: 4 = >90%; 3 = >50% of identified PMO; 2 = roles and responsibilities of PMO resources documented; 1 = unspecified.
   B. Direct PMO = 40%
      1. 20% = PMO project life cycle: 4 = no project moves forward without following PMO processes; 3 = all required documents are completed on targeted projects; 2 = complete pilot project by October 1, 2006; 1 = later than October 1, 2006.
      2. 20% = create master schedule: 4 = all project interdependencies identified; 3 = all projects on schedule included; 2 = key targeted projects included; 1 = unspecified.
   C. Staff development = 20%
      1. 10% = PMO compliance to 3Ms process: 4 = performance rewards based on 3Ms process; 3 = PMO team 3Ms externally aligned; 2 = PMO team members all have 3Ms profiles; 1 = unspecified.
      2. 10% = PMO staff learning: 4 = 100% of learning goals completed; 3 = PMO team members complete 50% of learning objectives; 2 = all PMO team members have learning objectives; 1 = unspecified.

The following project involving security provides more examples of qualitative metrics with standards of performance for the areas of virus protection, hiring security staff, clearance of employees, and physical entry:

Virus protection	1 = opened with damage; 2 = opened and disabled; 3 = not opened; 4 = never gets in.

Hiring security staff   1 = no security-related certification; 2 = Certified Information Systems Security Professional (CISSP); 3 = CISSP with experience; 4 = has held a role with corporate security accountability.

Another hiring PO for a project organization is:

- **Excellent (4)** — Hire three project managers by January 1, 2007 who average 15 years of project management experience where at least one person has managed projects that are comparable to ours and requires no training.
- **Very Good (3)** — All three project managers have an average of 10 years of managing projects closely related in substance and require half the normal training time.
- **Satisfactory (2)** — All three project managers have PMP®, an average of five years in project management, and require a normal training investment.
- **Unsatisfactory (1)** — Failure to achieve any one of the factors of Satisfactory.

Clearance of employees   4 = top secret; 3 = secret; 2 = confidential; 1 = no clearance.

Physical entry   4 = deterred from entry; 3 = failed attempted entry; 2 = entry with no loss; 1 = entry with loss and/or damage.

To further support the rigor of qualitative metrics, here are a few examples from areas other than project management.

Example 1 — The Foreign Service Institute of the U.S. State Department measures linguistic fluency for nine distinguishable standards of linguist fluency ranging from 0 = "knowing nothing" to 5 = "native speaker competency and accent." Among certified testers, the interjudge correlation of ratings is 0.9, as proof that amongst judges who judge grammar, syntax, and even the nonverbal accoutrements of the linguistic behavior, all the variables are known and accounted for.

Example 2 — Olympic performances that are balletic (ice skating, ring tossing, etc.) demonstrate that 10 judges from 10 different countries will rate this kind of performance 90% of the time with a deviation or interval of 1 point and about >80% of the time with a deviation of only 0.5. And yet, the performance itself is about form, rhythm, poise, and level of difficulty (with its own metrics!).

Example 3 — For a fast-food restaurant, the metrics of the value for the $2.99 a customer pays are:

- Provide an accurate order within five minutes
- The food is hot
- At least one napkin and plastic knife, fork, and spoon
- Food in a bag or on a cardboard tray
- The food is conveniently arranged so that you can grab each item, even while you drive and are on the cell phone at the same time!

What Is Value?

All the above are a mix of qualitative and quantitative metrics. The quantitative metrics are price = $2.99, timeliness = within five minutes, and utensils = at least one of each. The qualitative metrics are hot food, cardboard tray, and convenience of access to the food while driving.

Other examples of qualitative metrics come from wine tasting, ballroom competition, and reviews of restaurants, movies, theater, art, literature, and music. In these fields where the metrics are qualitative, agreement among experts in the respective fields, or in statistical terminology interjudge correlation (the degree of agreement between different judges), is near 1.

The way people describe their life and their relationships, with spouse, lovers, children, parents, and colleagues, is also a mix of qualitative and quantitative metrics. A child is doing "well" in school, where the term "well" is a cumulative qualitative based on judgment of grades, friendships, completion of homework, participation in extracurricular activities, etc. Thus the term "well" is an aggregated metric that summarizes a myriad of qualitative and quantitative metrics. In fact, examples 1 to 3 of qualitative metrics above are what people usually access to describe their work and social life.

CHANGES IN WEIGHTINGS OF KVAS AND POS

When a project begins, the weightings of the KVAs may very well reflect the proportionate value. Later, during the next phases of the project, especially if the schedule is slipping and depending on the longevity of the project, the proportionate value of timeliness will increase (Table 3-5). More resources will be brought to bear to justify the greater weighted value of that KVA, and the POs supporting the KVAs may change not only their weightings but the nature of the metrics, the standards, and the action plans. This is but one example of how 3Ms is a total management methodology.

Tailor Objectives to the Changing Environment

To be more explicit about changes in expectations because of other changes, objectives and standards should be changed. In terms of the sales manager example

Table 3-5. 3Ms for Changing Weightedness

Initial POs		When Schedule Is Slipping		When Cost Is Excessive	
Timeliness	30	Timeliness	40	Timeliness	20
Budget	30	Budget	20	Budget	40
Risk avoidance	20	Risk avoidance	20	Risk avoidance	20
Quality	20	Quality	20	Quality	20
	100%		100%		100%

Table 3-6. Altered Standards for New Situation

Original Standards	New Standards Responding to Situations
>550 units = Excellent (4)	>400 units = Excellent (4)
>400 units = Very Good (3)	>300 units = Very Good (3)
>300 units = Satisfactory (2)	>200 units = Satisfactory (2)
<200 units = Unsatisfactory (1)	<100 units = Unsatisfactory (1)

used earlier in the chapter, the objectives should change to meet changing conditions. Before, only the project KVAs in sales were altered from 40% to 60%.

Certain performance levels may be easier or more difficult to achieve later. If the company is willing to sacrifice some sales, the weightings could remain the same and the standards could be realigned with the new realities, so that the sales standards would change from the original, as shown in Table 3-6.

Although the focus of this book is at the project team level, we cannot ignore the fact that teams are composed of individuals, and sometimes individuals are in conflict because their own POs are competing for resources of time, money, and other people. When project teams are evolved with 3Ms, this is unlikely to happen. When two project teams evolve, they many not have aligned to their next common source of their own KVAs and POs or may have interpreted them differently.

HOW TO SET JOINT OBJECTIVES

Very often, when individuals have clear objectives, they may be so independent of others that they neglect the supportive behavior on which others depend. This is likely to happen when individuals see their support of others as detracting from their own performance. When others are dependent employees with independent objectives (objectives that do not rely on input or support from others), just rework the independent objectives so they become a joint objective *with* the other party (individual, department, team, etc.).

For example, salesperson A is supposed to sell 100 items as an objective at a standard of Very Good and relies on a customer service follow-up function whose objective, at a standard of Satisfactory, is a complaint rate of less than five per month. If the customer service function is not meeting that objective, then set the objective for both as a sales objective of 100 items and a condition of no more than five complaints a month, as shown in Table 3-7. To give the salesperson greater support due to a dependency on satisfied customers and enable the salesperson to achieve standards of Very Good and Excellent, the customer service standards would be raised as shown in Table 3-8.

The next case involves a sales team and a customer service team. The sales team interpreted that its KVAs were 80/20 for sales/customer service and the customer service team that its KVAs were customer service/sales 80/20. This

What Is Value? 45

Table 3-7. Salesperson Performance Standards

Salesperson — Sales Objectives	Customer Service — Customer Complaints
Excellent = >150	Excellent = <2 per month
Very Good = >100	Very Good = <4 per month
Satisfactory = >75	Satisfactory = <5 per month
Unsatisfactory = <75	Unsatisfactory = >5 per month

Table 3-8. Improved Salesperson Performance Standards

Salesperson — Sales Objectives	Customer Service — Customer Complaints
Excellent = >150	Excellent = <2 per month
Very Good = >100	Very Good = <3 per month
Satisfactory = >75	Satisfactory = <4 per month
Unsatisfactory = <75	Unsatisfactory = >4 per month

Table 3-9. How to Set Up Joint Objectives

Product Development Team	Research and Development
Sales = 80%	Sales = 20%
R&D = 20%	R&D = 80%
Sales Team	**Customer Service Team**
Sales = 50%	Customer service = 50%
Customer service = 50%	Sales = 50%

weighting so heavily toward one function and so little toward the other resulted in behaviors that reflected these weightings. The resolution through the KVA level of the 3Ms approach was to have both teams share the very same KVAs with a weighting of 50/50 and review both teams as *one* team. The metaphor is that before each team was in a separate canoe with a different destination, and now both are in one canoe, as illustrated in Table 3-9.

ANOTHER 3MS FORMAT: KVAS AND CONTRIBUTING VALUE AREAS

The 3Ms methodology lends itself to an almost infinite variety of formats. The basic 3Ms format only needs to create the KVA level at 100% of total value, at increments of not less than 20%, and allocate proportionate value across the subordinate POs at increments of not less than 10%. One company insisted on creating 20% KVAs at a weighting of 100% and then creating contributing value areas (CVAs) that were in increments of no less than 20%. Although this violates a "rule" of the 3Ms, it does not violate the integrity of the process of weightings, standards, and metrics. It would then be within the CVAs to create the POs at weightings of no less than 10% that would show the metrics, weightings, and standards of the POs and the ultimate value results for the performance scorecard of Section III of the template.

As an example, a security consultant wanted to create a 3Ms profile for a security assessment of a bank. The basic KVAs at the normal 3Ms level were:

IT security	= 20%
Physical security	= 20%
Technology	= 20%
People	= 20%
Process	= 20%

Where the normal 3Ms process would then create POs from each KVA, the consultant decided that he wanted to manage in a granular fashion (some might say micromanage), but as will be discussed later, 3Ms is style neutral. As long as you have the weighted KVAs and at least one PO with weightings, metrics, and standards per KVA, you are maintaining the essential integrity of the 3Ms process. Whatever you do beyond that is a function of corporate culture, leadership, history, etc.

The security consultant then took each KVA and gave it a weighting of 100%, and from that 100% created CVAs that were an allocation of that 100%. The results are displayed in Table 3-10. Though not complete, you can see how the template provides the format for the description of each CVA for standards of Excellent, Very Good, Satisfactory, and Unsatisfactory. You can also see that a company that would want to take this to a next level downward could take monitoring compliance at 100% and then allocate the greater specificity of what monitoring compliance means in measurable terms.

For the security consultant and the corporate culture that was evolving, the management team wanted this in a format that could be easily produced in Excel® (Figure 3-2). This is but one example of the many ways in which the 3Ms can be modified by any company without violating or even compromising the rigor of the methodology. In fact, one might argue that this modification lends itself to even greater rigor in that each PO with a larger weighting could even go down to the weightings, standards, and metrics of yet a third level, which is not required by the basic 3Ms methodology. If a company wanted to expand that third level into proportions of another 100% per third-level task, it could go down to yet a fourth level and theoretically to a level where every task and breath could be measured and given standards of performance.

For some, this adds even greater clarity of management results; for others, it is micromanagement or even madness!

Table 3-10. **Another Format of the 3Ms Profile: KVAs with CVAs — No POs**

KVAs	Weighting	CVAs	POs/Metrics
IT security	20%	Encryption = 30% Authentication = 30% Firewalls = 40%	Standards for each CVA
Physical security	20%	Access control = 40% CCTV = 20% ID cards = 20% Guards = 20%	
Technology	20%	Integration in ERP = 30% Current technology = 70%	
People	20%	3Ms info for key job design = 50% Training = 50%	
Process	20%	Monitor compliance = 50% New hires/fires = 50%	
	100%		

ANOTHER TYPOLOGY FOR CREATING PROJECT OBJECTIVES

Another approach which still utilizes the basic weightings and standards is to create a typology of objectives that is a mix of those defined by KVAs and those that are based on innovative and/or problem-solving objectives. By emphasizing the latter, you can encourage team members to go after innovative and problem-solving objectives that create even greater value for the company than those based exclusively on KVAs. The following KVA typology would have weightings and be a proportion of the original 100%, forcing the original KVAs to be reduced in weightings.

Of course, the tension here is between innovation and still getting KVA-based objectives done that are necessary. Can you handle all the creativity?

1. **Innovative objectives** — This involves doing something new on one's own initiative through the application of new technology, new ideas, or new systems. You ask: "What should I concentrate on over the next year to make the greatest improvements in my unit?"
2. **Problem-solving objectives** — These identify existing, recognized problem areas and state a time period for solution. You ask: "If my position functioned at the highest level of effectiveness over the next year, what specific problems should I solve?"
3. **Project objectives** — "What special efforts will be required which are innovative and not a normal part of my job?"

48 Value-Based Metrics for Improving Results

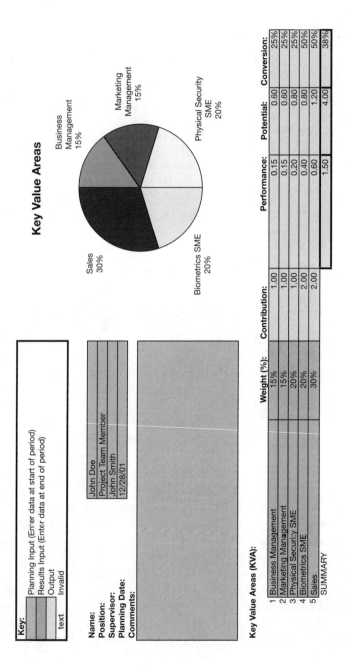

What Is Value? 49

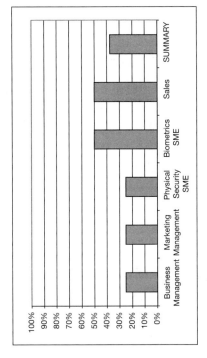

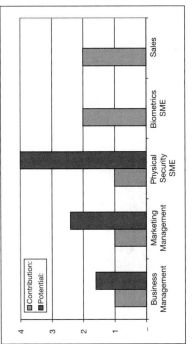

Figure 3-2. 3Ms Profile Template Example

50 Value-Based Metrics for Improving Results

Performance Objectives

KVA - 1: Business Management
Detail: More in line with organizational development and business management than with sales and marketing.

Evaluation Date:

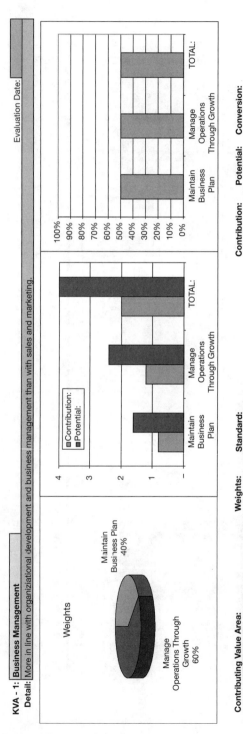

Contributing Value Area:	Weights:	Standard:
1 Maintain Business Plan	40%	2
2 Manage Operations Through Growth	60%	2
TOTAL:		

Maintain Business Plan	
4 - Excellent	Below plus - Secure 100% of funding as needed on the strength of the business plan
3 - Very Good	Below plus - Business plan to functionally serve as an ongoing strategic roadmap. Estimates within +/- 25% of actuals, in FY1
2 - Satisfactory	Document planned current and planned business activities as needed.
1 - Unsatisfactory	

What Is Value? 51

Manage Operations Through Growth
4 - Excellent Below plus - Manage development of web-based/integrated business systems.
3 - Very Good Below plus - Create tools and replicable processes for business planning and service order to cash cycle
2 - Satisfactory Manage cash flows, new hires, subcontractors, vendors, service providers, etc.
1 - Unsatisfatory

#REF!
4 - Excellent
3 - Very Good
2 - Satisfactory
1 - Unsatisfatory

#REF!
4 - Excellent
3 - Very Good
2 - Satisfactory
1 - Unsatisfatory

#REF!
4 - Excellent
3 - Very Good
2 - Satisfactory
1 - Unsatisfatory

Figure 3-2. 3Ms Profile Template Example (continued)

52 Value-Based Metrics for Improving Results

KVA - 2: Marketing Management

Detail: Evaluation Date:

Weights

- Market Responsiveness / Customer Sat. 20%
- Marketing Research & Analysis 20%
- Maintain Strategic Marketing Plan 20%
- Manage Promotional Activities 20%
- Manage Public (and Investor?) Relations 20%

Contribution: ■
Potential: ■

Categories (x-axis): Marketing Research & Analysis, Manage Promotional Activities, Market Responsiveness/Customer Sat.

Y-axis: 0% – 100%

TOTAL: Maintain Business Plan

Contributing Value Area:	Weights:	Standard:	Contribution:	Potential:	Conversion:
1 Marketing Research & Analysis	20%	2	0.40	0.80	50%
2 Maintain Strategic Marketing Plan	20%	2	0.40	0.80	50%
3 Manage Promotional Activities	20%	2	0.40	0.80	50%
4 Manage Public (and Investor?) Relations	20%	2	0.40	0.80	50%
5 Market Responsiveness / Customer Sat.	20%	2	0.40	0.80	50%
TOTAL:			2.00	4.00	50%

What Is Value?   53

Marketing Research & Analysis
- 4 - Excellent
- 3 - Very Good
- 2 - Satisfactory
- 1 - Unsatisfatory

Conduct primary MR&A as needed.
Construct analysis of secondary MR&A to synthesize comprehensive picture of market enabling strategic decision making
Collect secondary MR&A to synthesize picture of targeted segments

Maintain Strategic Marketing Plan
- 4 - Excellent
- 3 - Very Good
- 2 - Satisfactory
- 1 - Unsatisfatory

Develop a Strategic Marketing Plan to create / exploit some sustainable competitive advantage. (e.g., IP)
Develop a Strategic Marketing Plan to create / exploit some competitive advantage. (e.g., TTM)
Develop a Strategic Marketing Plan to leverage corporate strengths.

Manage Promotional Activities
- 4 - Excellent
- 3 - Very Good
- 2 - Satisfactory
- 1 - Unsatisfatory

Host Security Awarenes Seminars (as revenue stream?)
Exhibit at 1 / Speak at 2 Trade Shows / Conferences / Seminars
Manage creation of collateral materials, including web site content and brochures/*.PDF, advertising.

Manage Public (and Investor?) Relations
- 4 - Excellent
- 3 - Very Good
- 2 - Satisfactory
- 1 - Unsatisfatory

Make COMPANY newsworthy
Ensure that press presents COMPANY in neutral to favorable light in 100% stories
Develop process for issuing press releases and partner/practitioner publications.

Market Responsiveness / Customer Sat.
- 4 - Excellent
- 3 - Very Good
- 2 - Satisfactory
- 1 - Unsatisfatory

>15% business ($) is repeat in client organizations / client referrals
Ensure that every engagement results in 2.5 or better on 3Ms scale of customer satisfaction metrics
Develop service offerings that respond to market needs, delivering as promised 100%.

Figure 3-2. 3Ms Profile Template Example (continued)

54 Value-Based Metrics for Improving Results

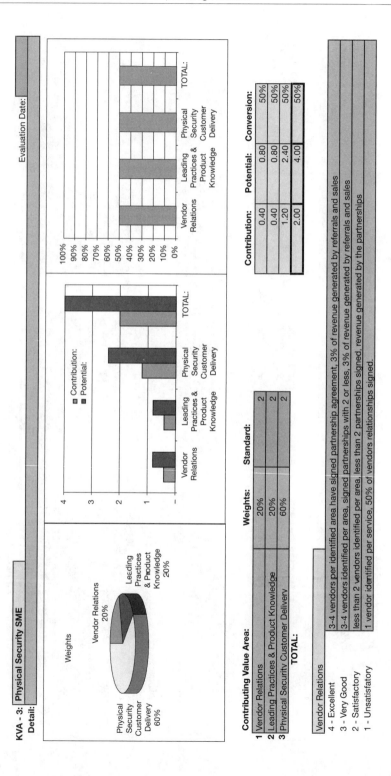

What Is Value? 55

Leading Practices & Product Knowledge
Develop partnership with manufacturer/service providers to provide market requirements for product/service development.
Recommend and implement appropriate products/solutions
Recommend appropriate products/solutions

4 - Excellent
3 - Very Good
2 - Satisfactory
1 - Unsatisfactory

Physical Security Customer Delivery
Publish / Sell Physical Security Consulting Engagement Process / Methodology
Develop Physical Security Consulting Engagement Process / Methodology - Train COMPANY
Conduct Physical Security Consulting Engagements

4 - Excellent
3 - Very Good
2 - Satisfactory
1 - Unsatisfactory

#REF!
4 - Excellent
3 - Very Good
2 - Satisfactory
1 - Unsatisfactory

#REF!
4 - Excellent
3 - Very Good
2 - Satisfactory
1 - Unsatisfactory

Figure 3-2. 3Ms Profile Template Example (continued)

56 Value-Based Metrics for Improving Results

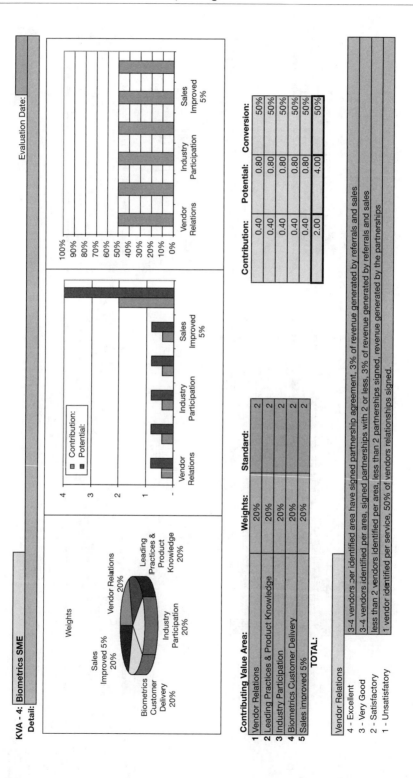

What Is Value? 57

Leading Practices & Product Knowledge
Develop partnership with manufacturer/service providers to provide market requirements for product/service development.
Recommend and implement appropriate products/solutions
Recommend appropriate products/solutions

4 - Excellent
3 - Very Good
2 - Satisfactory
1 - Unsatisfactory

Industry Participation
Contribute to / Lead standards / industry organizations
Join standards / industry organizations
Stay abreast of developments in industry (e.g., standards, legislation, methods)

4 - Excellent
3 - Very Good
2 - Satisfactory
1 - Unsatisfactory

Biometrics Customer Delivery
Publish / Sell Bioemtrics Consulting Engagement Process / Methodology
Develop Biometrics Consulting Engagement Process / Methodology - Train COMPANY
Conduct Biometrics Consulting Engagements

4 - Excellent
3 - Very Good
2 - Satisfactory
1 - Unsatisfactory

Sales improved 5%

4 - Excellent
3 - Very Good
2 - Satisfactory
1 - Unsatisfactory

Figure 3-2. 3Ms Profile Template Example (continued)

58 Value-Based Metrics for Improving Results

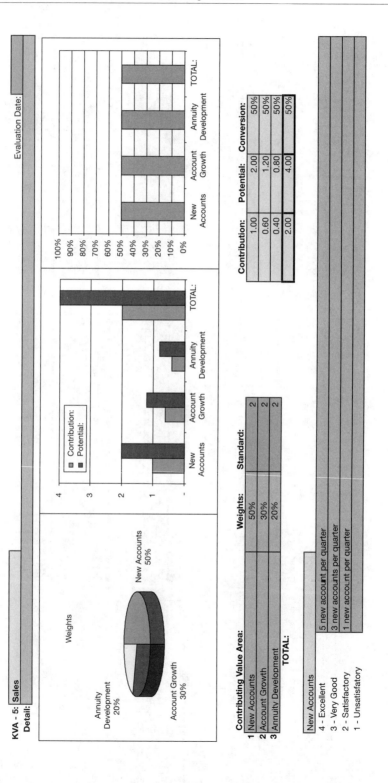

What Is Value? 59

Account Growth	
4 - Excellent	Extend 50% of existing account base.
3 - Very Good	Extend 25% of existing account base.
2 - Satisfactory	Extend 15% of existing account base
1 - Unsatisfactory	

Annuity Development	
4 - Excellent	Create annuity relationship in 15% account base
3 - Very Good	Create annuity relationship in 10% account base
2 - Satisfactory	Create annuity relationship in 5% account base
1 - Unsatisfactory	

#REF!	
4 - Excellent	
3 - Very Good	
2 - Satisfactory	
1 - Unsatisfactory	

#REF!	
4 - Excellent	
3 - Very Good	
2 - Satisfactory	
1 - Unsatisfactory	

Training Objectives
Short-Term — Technical training in IT security and system integration and implementation. CISSP certification.
Long-Term — Ongoing technical and business training and development.

Performance Factors
Employee
Supervisor

Promotability

Figure 3-2. 3Ms Profile Template Example (continued)

4. **Team objectives** — These are objectives that need to be accomplished with another member of management on an equal or subordinate level. Team objectives could be a subset of regular routine objectives or subsumed by KVAs-based objectives. On the other hand, if these team-building objectives are to establish a new relationship or dramatically improve existing ones, then the team building might be a subset of innovative or problem-solving objectives. The nature of the task will determine this.
5. **Regular/routine objectives** — These have to do with the basic KVAs and answer the question: "What results are expected of me on a regular, daily basis?"

Of course, the tension here is between innovation and still getting KVA-based objectives done that are necessary. Can you handle all the creativity?

We could also argue that this "different" typology is really included within the action plans to create Excellent and Very Good within the normal 3Ms format. This is but one of many ways to modify the 3Ms approach.

SUMMARY

This chapter demonstrated the rigor and precision of working the project team down the hierarchy of value creation. Ideally, the team's KVAs are aligned to the KVAs and POs of the PMO or to corporate objectives. Unfortunately, this is seldom the case, as most project teams are left "hanging," with no precise corporate objective for alignment. Fortunately, successful project teams make good guesses as to what the corporate objectives should have been.

The rigor of 3Ms is that first value is defined as KVAs in weighted terms. Then POs are created that describe value in measurable terms that include metrics, weightings, and standards. The Measure phase of 3Ms creates total clarity for the project team. We advocate that this clarity be done in a collaborative manner, either starting with the KVAs and objectives at the team level and working down (deductively) or beginning with individual team members and working upward to the team level (inductively). Ultimately, for the Manage and Magnify stages, it should not matter. In fact, as internal and external conditions change over time, the dynamics of the dialogue will be both inductive and deductive at the same time.

In addition to presenting a standard template that has KVAs and POs with a performance scorecard, several other formats that adhere to the principles of the 3Ms were also provided. In fact, if a year later the 3Ms looks the same as it was originally introduced, you are probably not using it.

We also showed that qualitative metrics are as rigorous as quantitative metrics. Additionally, you can adhere to the basic KVA and PO format and change weightings and standards to accommodate changes in the project management environment.

QUESTIONS

3-1. Value is getting what you expected for the price you paid. True or false?
3-2. A KVA has a minimum weighting of 10%. True or false?
3-3. A KVA measures the results to be achieved. True or false?
3-4. Which of the following are three rules of KVAs:
   a. No weighting less than 20%
   b. No intervals of 5%
   c. All KVAs together must sum up to 100%
   d. KVAs can combine two functions
3-5. POs must have a weighting of at least 10%. True or false?
3-6. If a KVA has a weighting of 70%, it can have up to eight performance objectives. True or false?
3-7. The three phases of the 3Ms process are Measure, Manage, and Multiply. True or false?
3-8. Qualitative metrics are impossible to measure. True or false?
3-9. The 3Ms can be a useful conflict resolution tool with the use of KVAs and POs. True or false?
3-10. Which of the following factors can erode even the perfect clarity that was achieved during the Measure phase of 3Ms:
   a. Changes in priorities
   b. Changes in resources
   c. Changes in personnel
   d. Changes in customer expectations
3-11. The integrity of the 3Ms methodology can be preserved even while changing the look and format of the KVAs and POs. True or false?
3-12. The value of anything can be measured very precisely with metrics. True or false?
3-13. Each standard of performance represents a specific financial return on investment of time, energy, and money. True or false?
3-14. Various typologies can be used to enhance a project team's investment in creativity and value creation. True or false?
3-15. When companies try to use contributing value areas, they distort the weightings of the KVAs. True or false?

This book has free materials available for download from the
Web Added Value™ Resource Center at www.jrosspub.com.

4

HOW TO CREATE AND EXCEED VALUE

The second and third phases of the 3Ms are Manage and Magnify. As was described in Chapter 1, as part of the Manage phase, the project team identifies all variables that will help or hinder progress toward the predefined measures of success that were created in the Measure phase. This is where the team looks at its internal and external environment and decides how its action plans will accomplish the performance objectives at a standard of at least Satisfactory.

At this point, every individual team member and the team as a whole will have key value areas (KVAs) and performance objectives (POs), so there is no ambiguity regarding what the various standards of Satisfactory, Very Good, and Excellent represent.

The "game" of the 3Ms methodology is to create value beyond Satisfactory, especially since creating the standards of every PO gives team members a clear statement of what the standards are. This is unlike the typical ambiguity of how good is good, very good, or excellent as these terms are typically used in corporate America.

By identifying all the variables that will help or hinder success, team members can create action plans to improve all of these variables. Many of the variables will be technical to the project itself, such as having the latest software, best qualified people, and financial and physical resources to get the job done. Of equal importance, the team will have a hierarchy of corporate objectives to which the project itself can align.

Additionally, there are the generic management variables such as promotional opportunity, rewards for above satisfactory performance, corporate culture, leadership style, etc. Much of why project teams fail to be successful is in the human element, especially having leadership and followership skills in times of stress and overwhelming deadlines to meet.

Project teams, by definition, are temporary systems created to achieve specific objectives. Thus, project team environments should have or train people to quickly create teamwork with role clarity and conflict resolution skills, along with the skills of the 3Ms metrics repertoire. These skills with clear and flexible action plans will win the day.

ACTION PLANS PER PERFORMANCE OBJECTIVE

Action plans PO are not a formal part of the 3Ms template, as almost all companies already have their own action plan format. Many use MS Project® and other formats, all of which are compatible with the 3Ms.

Once the project manager and team member agree on the POs (weightings, measures, and standards), they must develop an action plan for all of the POs. The complexity of the action plan will depend on the clarity of procedures, resources, and team member knowledge, skills, and experience, as well as challenges of the environment. Below are two action plan formats. Use any format you find useful.

- Who will do what by when?
- How often will progress be monitored?
- What resources will be needed (people, time, money)?
- Whose approval is necessary?
- Who should be kept informed?
- How frequently?
- What are potential dangers to success?
- What should project manager and team member pay attention to?
- What are alternatives if this course of action should fail, be untimely, be too costly, or otherwise run into difficulties?
- What are additional critical success factors, if any?

You can use the format shown in Table 4-1. Add as many columns or factors as you want to include in an action plan.

Another consideration for action plans is the longevity of KVAs/POs/tasks. Depending on the management style, the team might want to describe only KVAs, or KVAs and POs, or KVAs, POs, and tasks together. We fully support using the

Table 4-1. Project Team Assignments

Who	Does What	By When	Approved By
Project manager			
Project team member 1			
Project team member 2			
Project team member 3			
Project team member 4			
Project team member 5			

Table 4-2. Aspects of Team Accomplishment

3Ms Level	Longevity	Why
KVAs	Annual, unless there is a major shift in why the project was created	It is the reason the project was created, and most of its value (as determined by the weightings) should have a year or more of contribution.
POs	At least quarterly	These are the results by which KVA values are manifested, produced, and documented by metrics, weightings, and standards.
Tasks	As long as the task takes and could be weekly, daily, hourly	There are hundreds of tasks a day, and most (60 to 70%) are directly supportive of the POs. A great many others are not directly supportive of the project POs, but are part of team or collegial effort, as when a colleague asks for an opinion or asks to attend a project meeting. This is all part of teamwork and is not restrained by having individual and/or team KVAs and POs. The only conflict is when project managers or team members are doing so much to support others' POs that they neglect their own.

MS Project® work breakdown structure. Its hierarchy of tasks and additional levels of subtasks support the rigor or the 3Ms as an equally rigorous way to manage people and tasks with near zero ambiguity.

Depending on the dynamics of the environment, KVAs, POs, and tasks will have different degrees of longevity, but in general, Table 4-2 illustrates the durability relationship between these three aspects of team accomplishment.

PERFORMANCE SCORECARD (SECTION III)

The process of developing the performance scorecard or total value of the project team contribution is summarized in this section.

How to Arrive at Overall Value of Performance

The procedure is to multiply the weighting (proportionate value) of each PO by the standard that has been achieved (and previously defined) to arrive at the value of each PO. The overall value contribution of the project team is calculated by summing up all of the values. This same performance scorecard is also used to derive the total value of individual team member contributions.

As shown in Table 4-3, which aligns value with rewards, the project team with a total value creation of 3.1 should get between 10 and 13% in salary rewards. Rewards could also be additional vacation, recognition, promotion, attendance at conferences, or anything else mentioned in the book *1001 Way to Reward Employ-*

Table 4-3. Performance Scorecard for Project Widget

KVAs	%	Objectives with Standards	Weightings of Objectives	Standards (Achieved or in Progress)	Year-End Performance × Weighting = Value
Timeliness	30	4 = 10% early 3 = 5% early 2 = due date 1 = later than due date	30%	3	0.9
Budget	30	4 = 10% below budget 3 = 5% below budget 2 = within budget 1 = exceeds the budget	30%	4	1.2
Risk avoidance	20	4 = accepted change requests 10% more requirements 3 = additional features 2 = met customer requirements 1 = did not meet customer requirements	20%	3	0.6
Quality	20	4 = plus 5% fewer tasks 3 = improved quality above industry standards 2 = all performance meets industry standards 1 = change in the schedule	20%	2	0.4
Total	**100**		**100%**		**3.1**

ees by Robert Nelson. Another level of rewards is bonuses based on project performance, corporate performance, etc. We will not go into all the possible levels of reward systems for a project management environment.

Another level within the project team reward alignment could be a comparable reward system for individual performance within the team (Table 4-4). This alignment process can be a very powerful tool to shape corporate cultural along the continuum of individual versus team culture. A reward system could be based exclusively on team value and nothing for individuals.

Notice that as the intervals between monetary reward levels become larger, the greater the rewards are, so as to incentivize better performance. Too often, the incentives for Excellent performance are just incremental and of the same interval as between any other two or three standards, which is really a disincentive. The

Table 4-4. Aligning Total Value to the Reward System

3.6–4.0	14–25% pay increase
3.1–3.5	10–13% pay increase
2.5–3.0	7–9% pay increase
2.0–2.4	5–6% pay increase

internal monologue among employees is: Why work so much harder for so little difference between doing average and really excelling?

PERFORMANCE FACTORS (SECTION IV)

Although implicit in many metrics formats, 3Ms makes the human resources development activity at least equal to the technical in value. For most other metrics methodologies, technical competency is 100% of what is developed. 3Ms brings the same rigor to the human resources development area as to the KVAs and POs themselves.

For such factors as leadership, teamwork, creativity, and other style factors, project manager and project team members might agree that these account for 10% of the overall performance. In cases where leadership was excellent, the performance scorecard of 3.4 could be increased by 10% or 0.34, yielding a total performance value of 3.74.

It is critical that these nonresults objective performance factors be clear to both the project manager and the team, so they are out of the realm of the subjective. Leadership could be explicitly defined as initiating appropriate changes in schedule, confronting issues that are impeding progress, or whatever other behaviors project manager and team member agree define leadership. These performance factors will help you fill in the performance scorecard (Section III) and identify under performance factors (Section IV) those behaviors on the part of team member (A) and project manager (B) that each should attend to for improved accomplishment of the POs (Section II).

The list below suggests categories of behavioral skills for the 3Ms profile and for performance-related discussions. These discussions should be specific. For example, instead of "show initiative," state "will initiate discussions about problem areas of work when they are still minor," or instead of "observation," state "will give immediate feedback about events and conditions that will have a positive or negative impact on the performance objectives."

The following series of questions to further identify performance factors are asked by the team member to the project manager and asked by the project manager to the team member:

- What is it I do well that I ought to continue?
- What is it I do poorly that I ought to improve?

- What is it I do that I ought to stop doing?
- What is it that I do not do that I ought to start doing?

With all the hoopla about 360-degree processes for giving feedback to individuals and the complicated psychometric tools, both in hard copy and online, these four questions posed to the following populations are as or more powerful than any 360-degree process:

- Self
- Colleagues
- Project manager/team leader
- Direct reports (most valuable feedback)
- Clients, vendors, consultants, etc.

The project manager might say to the team member: "Now that we've developed your POs with weightings and standards, let's review them and scan the environment to identify what performance factors should get attention and which ones will help you accomplish your objectives. Let's look at all potential factors to see which one or two are most critical to your performance."

The project manager and team member could ask each other: "Now that we've identified and discussed your performance factors, what are some of mine to maintain support of your accomplishment?" The discussion might involve how the project manager should keep team members apprised of changes, delegate his or her authority to have direct access to people, etc.

TRAINING OBJECTIVES (SECTION V)

Once project manager and team member have established the POs with weightings and standards, they are ready to identify developmental or training objectives. Training objectives are skills building for immediate or long-term improvement. Categories include personal skills:

- Interpersonal communication
- Confrontation skills
- Effective meetings
- Public presentations

technical skills:

- Business knowledge
- Computer literacy (MS Project®, Visio®, etc.)

and managerial skills:

- Delegating
- Training

- Reorganizing
- Supporting
- Team building
- Career planning
- Budgeting
- Writing skills
- Financial planning

Short-Term Training Objectives

Short-term training objectives are skills or knowledge that will make an immediate contribution to all or some of the annual project POs. Any team member may find that he or she is spending a lot of time on the administrative chores of keeping manual records of reports, surveys, etc. If using a computer with an appropriate software package would increase the accuracy, timeliness, and speed of producing reports, then a training objective would be "learn to use an appropriate software package to manage project record keeping aspects of my job by year end."

This training objective does not require a weighting and is usually outside of the performance evaluation process. The training objective could have a formal weighting with standards of performance. This is done when performance is marginal or unsatisfactory and the team member requires the incentive of being evaluated on the skills development as well as results. This is especially useful when the overall performance is unsatisfactory or true of one critical PO.

The project manager might ask the team member: "As we scan the project POs, what are the skills you should improve or acquire to help you perform your objectives faster, cheaper, easier, better, etc.?"

Such skills might be exclusive to one or more of the POs. For example, if one objective requires a lot of reading, then a speed-reading course would certainly be of benefit. If revising procedures is an objective, then gaining greater knowledge of those procedures from a historical, comparative, or conceptual perspective would be useful. Additionally, these training objectives should not only focus on activity, but define a performance measure as well (e.g., not just take a speed-reading course, but achieve a rate of reading that is three times the current rate with no loss of comprehension).

Long-Term Training Objectives

Long-term training objectives are the same as short-term objectives, but may or may not impact immediate project objectives. Long-term objectives are skills building and oriented toward some long-term career objective, such as a promotional opportunity or particular project, task, or role for which the team member is not now prepared. A team member who wants to manage a project would find out what he or she needs to develop to be qualified for that position. The long-term developmental objective might be a commitment to get a certificate in project management or as a Project Management Professional (PMP®) or to learn particular management skills and concepts as extra course work or through additional work assignments.

The agreement here between employee and boss is that there is no negative impact on current objectives unless the boss sees some long-term benefit. The better the fit and the criticality between current POs and long-term developmental objectives, the greater support for the time, money, and effort in this area.

Use of long-term training objectives invites a career-planning discussion between team member and project manager and a career-planning system for the company. This will not be elaborated on here, as very few companies have a project management career track, but the following questions would be appropriate:

- "As you think about your career movement over the next three to five years, what position or area of responsibility would you like to have?"
- "What skill or skills does it require?"
- "To what extent do you have or not have it/them?"
- "What can you do to acquire it/them?"
- "What schedule/action plan do you have to develop/acquire it/them?"
- "What actions do you need me/the company/management to take to assist you in attaining your goals?"

PROMOTABILITY (SECTION VI)

This section has to be filled in by a specific company's policies regarding what makes a team member promotable. The general concept is that when a team member's performance is consistently at a standard of at least Very Good, increasing the reward system without getting into career mobility is not likely to continue to motivate. The theme for exploration is this: Performance reviews and rewards without career planning are data without a vision; career planning without performance data is a vision without a reality check.

Now that we have covered all of the sections of the 3Ms template, Table 4-5 summarizes the key questions per section of the template.

SUMMARY

This chapter focused on the Manage phase of the 3Ms, Sections III, IV, V, and VI. Section III is the performance scorecard, which summarizes the KVAs and weightings, the POs and weightings and standards, and how value is defined per PO for the total project team. Once the scorecard is calculated, which in the online version of 3Ms is done automatically, then the total team value is aligned with various reward systems. All of these are predefined, so team members know exactly what they will get for which standard of performance. There are various models of reward systems which are weighted toward either individual performance or team performance. Either way, 3Ms will support the explicit metrics for rewarding people for effort.

Table 4-5. Summary of Questions per Section of the 3Ms Template

3Ms Profile Data Entry Field	Questions
I. KVAs	a. What are your major contributions to the project team/department/function? b. What is the proportionate value of these contributions?
II. PO	By what metrics are the standards of your contributions being judged? How do you determine the standards of your POs? What is the proportionate value of each PO?
III. Scorecard	a. How do you know, in advance, what kind of reward your performance will bring? b. How do you get agreement about this with your project manager?

IV. Performance factors
  A. Team member
  B. Project manager
	a. What should you pay attention to in order to successfully complete your objectives?
	b. What should your project manager pay attention to in order to support your success?

V. Training objectives
  A. Short term
  B. Long term
	a. What skill(s) should you/the team acquire or improve to be more successful?
	b. What skill(s) should you/the team acquire or improve to get ahead (promoted, bigger assignment, more responsibility)?

VI. Promotability (This is for the individual team member and could be used for a project team that is likely to remain intact, which is a rarity. Teams seldom end up with any more than 50% of the staff they started with. This depends, of course, on the longevity and competition for human resources within the project community.)	What do you see as your next career move in terms of increased accountabilities, new task, or new position within the project management career path?

Section IV is where project teams identify the crucial factors of awareness as they work. These factors are typically "political" and attend to leadership, values, corporate culture, and those factors that will increase effectiveness.

Section V describes the short- and long-term training objectives, much of which can occur on the job. The focus here is to develop skills for their immediate impact on POs and long term for career mobility or increased accountability.

Section VI very briefly introduces the concept of promotability in a more formal career mobility sense and is left up to the company environment in terms of how much attention this should get. Ideally, a company with a heavy investment in project management will develop a special career path for project management and support people on this path with sponsorship of PMP® certification and other Project Management Institute activity.

QUESTIONS

4-1. The first step of the Manage phase is to recruit the best people for the project. True or false?

4-2. The Manage and Magnify steps must occur sequentially. True or false?

4-3. Some performance objectives will not need action plans. True or false?

4-4. The MS Project® work breakdown structure is not compatible with the 3Ms. True or false?

4-5. The 3Ms reward system aligns different standards of performance with equal intervals of the reward hierarchy. True or false?

4-6. The performance scorecard is used by management to ensure that project teams are performing at their maximum level. True or false?

4-7. A typical question for getting feedback on performance factors is: "How am I doing?" True or false?

4-8. The longevity of key value areas and performance objectives is equal. True or false?

4-9. Which of the following populations should be used for getting feedback:
a. Self
b. Colleagues
c. Project manager/team member
d. Direct reports
e. Clients, vendors, consultants, etc.
f. All the above

4-10. The three areas of short- and long-term training objectives are personal, technical, and managerial. True or false?

4-11. Performance factors are about how well people do technically. True or false?

4-12. By what metrics the standards of your contributions are being judged is most relevant to the performance scorecard. True or false?

4-13. In the 3Ms, there is typically a conflict between individual and team performance. True or false?

4-14. Promotional opportunities are not necessary as long as project teams are getting sufficient rewards. True or false?

4-15. 3Ms is unique in that all of its metrics are a measure of value. True or false?

This book has free materials available for download from the Web Added Value™ Resource Center at www.jrosspub.com.

5

ALIGNMENT OF ALL METRICS

ALIGNING THE ORGANIZATION TO OPTIMIZE PROJECT DELIVERY SPEED AND FULFILLMENT

Hierarchical Alignment

Most organizational metrics identify metrics at only the level of the project deliverables themselves, and those monitoring functions only track metrics at that level. This has useful purposes for the "dashboard" level, but when those metrics are at a standard of Unsatisfactory, typically there are no metrics that, when drilled down to a lower level, can allow access to data to find the source or cause of why these dashboard-level performance standards are not being met. In other words, the scope of these metrics is internalized to the collection of observable data. If that collection of data does not contain data from other like groups of data, then no relationship can be measured between any like data group that is not directly or indirectly correlated.

Behavioral Alignment

Most businesses set forth fiscal year business plans that they wish to achieve. When the fiscal year strategic plans are finally approved, work begins to meet these needs, with an expected delivery within that fiscal year for work that has been funded. These plans produce role-level result expectations throughout the organization that, unless linked to other role levels, horizontally and vertically, will most often fail to meet executive-level expectations for success. You can test this by performing a simple test on yourself. When you come to work each day, how do you determine what work will be performed first? Do you make your decisions based on your personal needs ahead of what the business expects of you, or do you place the business needs ahead of your own in everything you do while you are at work?

Hopefully, what you should be doing is obvious, but we all know what usually occurs.

The 3Ms method is designed to link together the hierarchical and behavioral aspects of the organization being measured so the data collected can be measured in a way that influences the speed of work at the entity level. Without this integration, optimization of business resources applied to project delivery cannot be incrementally improved because no one will truly know what aspect of the fiscal year work plan is most important to the business. No one will ever have all the facts; even the CEO will not be sure. People's instincts will have to guide them. Most CEOs we know want to be sure when making project investment decisions that will impact the bottom line.

GETTING STARTED

Step 1 — Collect all baseline data pertinent to the strategic fiscal year work plan that is to be measured. This 12-month cycle will become the focus interval for measuring achievement. Typical data collected are:

- Number of funded projects
- Corporate goals and their meanings
- Lists of resource pools
- Amount of project delivery work to be funded
- Primary corporate goal supported by each corporate objective
- Who is accountable for the achievement for each corporate goal at the executive level
- A force ranking of corporate objectives within the overall project portfolio for the fiscal year measured (usually performed by corporate governance)

Step 2 — Calculate all costs for each corporate goal from assigned corporate objectives (planned costs) and summarize. This information will specify how money will be invested for a specific corporate goal.

Step 3 — Determine the overall planned start and end dates for work in each corporate goal. This information will specify when a certain corporate goal is expected to be achieved in the fiscal year. This also means planned start and end dates have been estimated for all corporate objective work assigned within a corporate goal.

Step 4 — Force rank the corporate goals by determining which corporate goal is the most strategic and/or tactically important to the business. This information should specify which corporate goal has preference over other corporate goals if a change in the business climate occurs that requires a direct change to the order or number of planned corporate goals to be achieved for the fiscal year. Usually, the corporate goal with the largest investment is rated the most important. The force ranking may depend on available time, resources, government regulation, or any combination of those parameters.

Step 5 — Determine the baseline organizational 3Ms profile and answers to the related metrics:

1. Total overall planned project investment for the fiscal year in dollars
2. Total overall planned corporate goal investment for the fiscal year in dollars
3. Total overall planned fulfillment date (month/date/year)
4. Most important planned corporate objective
5. Most important planned corporate goal
6. Top 10 planned corporate objectives (projects) in strategic order
7. Planned strategic order of corporate goals
8. Planned force-ranked corporate objectives for the fiscal year
9. Develop the organizational planned 3Ms profile for the fiscal year
10. Develop the corporate goal planned 3Ms profile for the fiscal year
11. Develop the corporate objectives planned 3Ms profile for the fiscal year

The organization's 3Ms baseline model for the fiscal year is considered constructed when this information has been developed. This information is utilized to measure achievement when compared to what was actually performed. Ongoing review of these metrics on a monthly basis is considered favorable when a positive result is calculated from the current fiscal-year-to-date actuals. Estimated level of effort to complete the "getting started" phase should require three to five workdays from one person. The socialization of this information requires further time to gain consensus. Gaining agreement on these metrics and their results is vitally important to aligning the organization hierarchically and behaviorally.

Other pertinent and supportive data include the following elements:

- Corporate mission (why the company exists, raison d'être)
- Corporate vision
- Corporate goals
- Corporate objectives
- Individual objectives (typical level of team members' 3Ms profiles)
- Regional, departmental, product line, or business unit objectives (may want to have mission, vision, and goals)
- Functional objectives (could repeat mission, vision, and goals for every level)
- Intraproject team-based objectives (the collective 3Ms profile of team members or that of the project manager)

As you will see in the many processes and alignment templates, the process of creating metrics at *any* level *always* includes the metrics of *every* other level (see Figure 5-1). Thus, at *any* time, the highest level metrics (corporate/enterprise/project) are inextricably synced with those at the lowest level (individual performance). By using the templates and online application, an enterprise can identify any lack of performance at *any* level that will impact any other level in real time. Of course, this real-time check is the ideal and necessitates that every level is being monitored

76 Value-Based Metrics for Improving Results

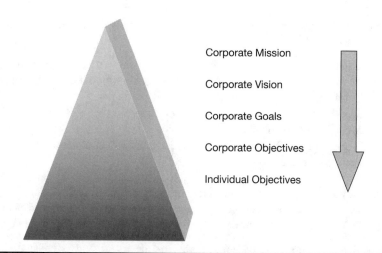

Figure 5-1. Generic Hierarchy of Corporate Goal Achievement Expectations

and realigned all the time, which is impossible. The closer this is approximated, the more accurate, timely, and effective corrections can be made at any level of corporate performance.

The national sales project team depicted in Figure 5-2 illustrates the horizontal alignment between different project teams that aggregate up to the regional project team level of results and how the regional project teams aggregate up to the national project level.

The organizational chart of a delivery project team illustrates several important 3Ms principles. The principles are given first, followed by why each is crucial for the total methodology and profound mind-set shift that occurs with 3Ms.

- **Principle 1**: 3Ms will support precise hierarchical and horizontal alignment for both qualitative and quantitative metrics.
- **Principle 2**: Equivalent standards can equate between radically different results.
- **Principle 3**: Standards set for project teams and individuals are, in part, dependent on their skills and history for comparable projects.

Principle 1: 3Ms will support precise hierarchical and horizontal alignment for both qualitative and quantitative metrics — The hierarchy in Figure 5-2 shows the aggregation (top down) of the 1,000 unit sales at the national level being allocated across the three regions and then per regional team to individuals. Although this may appear simplistic, by using product units and an easily quantifiable metric of number of units, the process is the same for qualitative objectives.

These numbers for the regional project teams are determined during the setting of regional key value areas (KVAs) and project team performance objectives (POs),

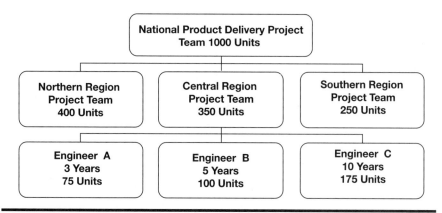

Figure 5-2. Hierarchy of Sales Project Multiteam Objectives

which take their "marching orders" to align upward to the product delivery project level at the national or corporate level.

Principle 2: Equivalent standards can equate between radically different results — Assume that the product deliverable is a software application that automatically regulates heating in a manufacturing environment by section of the facility. It could reasonably be expected that equivalent project teams with equivalent experience and expertise and with equivalent effort produce nonequivalent results because the company's three regional environments are not equivalent. The function of heating is less critical for the southern region of the country, more critical for the central region, and even more critical for the northern region. Then equivalent efforts would yield greater results in the northern region for a standard of Satisfactory or 400 units, lesser results in the central region or 350 units, and dramatically less results in the southern region or 250 units. In other words, the standard of Satisfactory creates equal value to the company, even when the results are not equal.

Principle 3: Standards set for project teams and individuals are, in part, dependent on their skills and history for comparable projects — This principle applies down to the level of individual POs of the regional product development team members, each of whom brings a unique length of experience to the team where all conditions are the same for all team members.

This is simply using the everyday logic of not expecting the same results from junior team members as from senior team members. In the 3Ms approach, this is made very explicit during the transparent negotiation of setting the KVAs and POs of the project and then the KVAs and individual POs of the team members to support and align upward with the project-level KVAs and POs.

Suppose the company employs three engineers with different levels of experience. Engineer A, with 3 years of experience and a PO of 75 units, creates value

Table 5-1. Value Comparison Among Engineering Roles

	Engineer A	Engineer B	Engineer C
Total compensation	$100,000	$150,000	$200,000
PO units	75	100	175
At 50% weighting	50,000	75,000	100,000

equal to engineer B, with 5 years of experience and a PO of 100 units, who creates value equivalent to engineer C, with 10 years of experience and a PO of 175 units. The reason the value is equal is that the engineers are creating the expected results for the money they are getting paid. When all three deliver their POs at a standard of at least Satisfactory, each one has created value for that PO. If all three had equal remuneration packages, then the value they create would *not* be equal.

Table 5-1 summarizes this logic. The value for all three engineers is equal in that the expected result is less in absolute terms for the standard of Satisfactory, but the compensation for this same standard of accomplishment is also unequal. Remember what value is: getting the results you expect for the money you pay.

The variables that are impacted by Principles 1, 2, and 3 can be infinite, as are the circumstances of project environments, staffing, funding, leadership, etc.

Suppose the KVAs of this project team are 100% sales, complete and aligned with the generic corporate hierarchy of objectives in Figure 5-1, although it skips two levels of alignment, functional and intraproject team-based objectives. If the KVAs were 60% sales, 20% customer relations, and 20% new product development, then the two 20% KVA would have to be aligned with the functional objectives of the R&D function and the customer service function.

Figure 5-3 is a real example from a 3Ms-oriented company that established KVAs at the corporate level and one PO per KVA. From this document, the management team took the PO level as its own KVAs and created 3Ms profiles with its staff.

SUMMARY

This chapter described how the entire methodology of 3Ms metrics is based on a systems approach, so that any change in any metric impacts at least those metrics above and below that level. If metrics were also aligned interfunctionally, then to maintain that alignment, metrics of other functions would also have to be re-aligned. The hierarchical nature of metrics promotes the teamwork dimensions of dialogue between levels of the organization so that any output at any level is the appropriate input at the next level. The process can be managed with mathematical precision, although the human dimensions of this process must also be an intrinsic part of it.

Alignment of All Metrics   79

MISSION STATEMENT

*Preeminent Provider of Products and Services
to Empower the Pharmaceutical Functions of the Health Care Industry*

Vision (for team members and customers)
- The highest levels of service and quality
- Commitment to personal and professional development
- Personal integrity and adherence to highest ethical standards
- Open and honest communication

Goals
1. Increase sales
2. Increase profits
3. Develop new streams of income
4. Be the best quality human resource company for the pharmaceutical industry
5. Support team members, customers, and staff — personally, professionally, and financially

Objectives
1. Gross sales of $3.6 million by end of year
2. Profits of 10% per annum (up from 5% last year)
3. Claims project manager, full-time placement, outsourcing, CD-ROM, and Internet
4. As determined by customer and pharmacist surveys
5. Pay 50% of staff expenses for personal and professional growth programs up to $1,000 per team member per year

---

Figure 5-3. Corporate Hierarchy of a Personnel Agency

QUESTIONS

5-1. The 3Ms gives you access to metrics well below the project objectives. True or false?

5-2. The hierarchical alignment of metrics in 3Ms is no different from that of other metrics approaches. True or false?

5-3. Equal standards must always produce equal results. True or false?

5-4. 3Ms allows radically different functions to have equivalent value. True or false?

5-5. Every key value area must have at least one performance objective. True or false?

5-6. Corporate goals are the level at which measurable results are identified. True or false?

5-7. If one engineer produces 100 units at a standard of Satisfactory and is paid $100,000 and another engineer produces 50 units at a standard of Satisfactory and is paid $50,000, both have created equal value. True or false?

5-8. Equivalent standards can equate between radically different results. True or false?

5-9. Goals indicate directionality of accomplishment, and objectives define outcomes in measurable terms. True or false?

5-10. Any corporate objective must have at least two performance objectives. True or false?

5-11. The following is a correct allocation of weightings to support a goal: sales = 25%, customer relations = 25%, new product development = 50%. True or false?

5-12. The performance objectives with weightings and standards set at the beginning of the year are good for the entire year. True or false?

5-13. In the project-dominated environment, project objectives and corporate objectives can be the same. True or false?

5-14. The only kinds of alignment are hierarchical and horizontal. True or false?

5-15. Standards set for project teams and individuals must be equal regardless of skills and history on comparable projects. True or false?

This book has free materials available for download from the
Web Added Value™ Resource Center at www.jrosspub.com.

6

SKILLS-BUILDING EXERCISES

This chapter consists of metrics skills-building exercises that are best done with the entire project team. After these exercises are completed, the project team should duplicate the exercises using its own real metrics and performance objectives.

EXERCISE

Create equivalent individual performance objectives for your project administrative assistant.

1. **Result Area — Filing Effectiveness**
   Objective — Updated master file for project reports every 21 days = 4; <28 days = 3; <35 days = 2; >35 days = 1.
2. **Result Area — PowerPoint® Effectiveness**
   Objective — Completed PowerPoint® presentations showing project progress with maximum 10% rejection rate from the Project Management Office due to errors. Rejection rate of <5% = 4; <7% = 3; <10% = 2; >10% = 1.
3. **Result Area — Purchasing Effectiveness**
   Objective — Project management training supplies such as case studies, special articles, climate surveys, etc. in stock with no instances of out-of-stock supplies during fiscal year 2006 = 4; ≤3 = 3; ≤6 = 2; ≥7 = 1.
4. **Result Area — Training Inquiries**
   Objective — All project training inquiries concerning nonexecutive training programs such as letter-writing courses, public speaking, etc. responded to within 24 hours = 4; 48 hours = 3; 72 hours = 2; >72 hours = 1.
5. **Result Area — PMP® Credentials**
   Objective — Monitor all PMP® certificate programs to ensure that >90% of all project team members are taking a PMP®-related course each quarter = 4; >80% = 3; >50% = 2; <50% = 1.

PAIR EXERCISE: SETTING PROJECT KEY VALUE AREAS AND PERFORMANCE OBJECTIVES

This exercise is typically conducted during a 3Ms introductory training session with all of the project managers and project team members. After reading this book, you should be able to find a colleague to participate. It is best if that colleague is your project manager or a member of your project team.

In this exercise, person A acts as the interviewer of person B, who sets one objective for his or her job to be achieved by a specific date. The reason for having an interviewer is simply to make things go smoother and faster. It will be easier for person B to come up with his or her project key value areas and performance objectives this way.

It is up to the interviewer to be very insistent that:

1. The statement arrived at is not a statement of an "activity" (e.g., call on 20 more dealers)
2. The statement meets the following criteria:
   - It is completely specific and concrete, not general
   - It is attainable
   - It is desirable
   - It describes a result that is measurable (observable and describable)

After person B has produced his or her statement, roles can be reversed and person B can become the interviewer for person A, who proceeds to formulate one of his or her objectives. This exercise continues until all objectives for the team member's key value areas are complete and approved by the entire team and project manager.

STEPS IN SETTING PROJECT OBJECTIVES

1. Break down the project into no more than five major key value areas.
2. To identify the measurable output of the performance objective per key result area, ask: "What performance reflects good versus bad performance?" or "What distinguishes a good job from a bad job?" or "What is the general description of a job well done?"
3. Write the objective using the following format: Results/By when (date)/Optional/Cost not to exceed. For example:
   - **Results** — Reduced overtime in Department 23 from 150 hours to 50 hours per month.
   - **By when (date)** — August 1 = 4; September 1 = 3; October 1 = 2; later than October 1 = 1.
   - **Optional** —
   - **Cost not to exceed** — $50,000.
4. Be sure the objective specifies what (with metrics) and when.

Exercise

Produce project objectives that vary the standard of cost and overtime while making timeliness nonnegotiable. The variables you build into your original statement define what is not negotiable, what should not be compromised, and therefore what is the *most* important metric of the objective.

The following are three sample performance objectives:

1. By August 1 at a cost ≤$50,000 reduce overtime from 150 hours to ≤40 = 4; ≤45 = 3; ≤50 = 2; ≥51 = 1.
2. By August 1 reduce overtime from 150 hours to 50 hours at a cost ≤$10,500 = 4; ≤$11,500 = 3; ≤$50,000 = 2; ≥$50,000 = 1.
3. Reduce overtime from 150 hours to 50 hours at a cost ≤$50,000 by June 1 = 4; by July 1 = 3; by August 1 = 2; by September 1 = 1.

In statement 1, the most important variables are cost and timeliness. In statement 2, they are timeliness and amount of overtime reduced. In statement 3, they are amount of overtime reduced and cost. Although all are important in the objective, the variable that distinguishes between standards of performance is the least important.

SELF-TEST ON OBJECTIVES: GOALS VERSUS OBJECTIVES

The 3Ms system cannot be practiced until vague or general goals are converted into specific objectives. The manager who thinks he or she is practicing 3Ms by wanting to increase sales, reduce costs, and increase profits is deceiving himself or herself. Such general objectives have to be put into exact metrics for amount, time, place, and other pertinent dimensions. And they must be expressed in terms that require some form of measurement.

Exercise

Indicate which of the following statements are goals by writing yes, no, or almost in each blank. For the statements that are not objectives, add measurable variables that will make them specific, measurable, agreed to, realistic, and timed (SMART) objectives.

1. A return on investment of 7% in Division A by December 31, 2006   _____
2. Increased production   _____
3. Better communication between company and foremen   _____
4. Six PMP® hired by October 2006   _____
5. Improved quality   _____
6. Construction of a one-story, 20,000-square-foot air-conditioned office building next to the main plant by July 1, 2007 at a cost of $75,000   _____

7. Employment of two international project managers fluent in French and English by December 1, 2006 _____
8. A 20-minute color film at a cost of $50,000 depicting in a humorous and interesting way how the company started its metrics program _____
9. 30% of shareholders know the names of three of the company's products by December 2006 _____
10. By 2007, 20% of all management positions to be held by women _____

Exercise

Improve the following objectives:

1. **Result Area — Administration**
   Objective — Complete MS Project® update assignments within time completion date set by project manager.

2. **Result Area — Personal Development**
   Objective — Complete all project organization charts using Visio® v. 10 within 30 days of each change.

3. **Result Area — Special Project**
   Objective — Locate a project management certificate course for three members of the project team by March 2007.

SUMMARY

This chapter presented a number of exercises that can improve the metrics skills of project team members. It is best if these are done as a project team activity, so that real issues will emerge during the activity.

QUESTIONS

6-1. The acronym SMART stands for special, measurable, achievable, relevant, and time framed. True or false?
6-2. Is "increased production" a goal or an objective?
6-3. In the following performance objective, the most important metrics are cost and reduced overtime: By August 1 at a cost ≤$50,000 reduce overtime from 150 hours to ≤40 = 4; ≤45 = 3; ≤50 = 2; ≥51 = 1. True or false?
6-4. In the following performance objective, the most important metrics are timeliness and overtime: By August 1 reduce overtime from 150 hours to 50 hours at a cost ≤$10,500 = 4; ≤$11,500 = 3; ≤$50,000 = 2; ≥$50,000 = 1. True or false?

Skills-Building Exercises

6-5. In the following performance objective, the most important metrics are overtime and cost: Reduce overtime from 150 hours to 50 hours at a cost ≤$50,000 by June 1 = 4; by July 1 = 3; by August 1 = 2; by September 1 = 1. True or false?

6-6. What is missing from the following performance objective? Complete MS Project® update assignments within time completion date set by project manager.
   a. Weighting
   b. Standards
   c. Metrics
   d. Nothing is missing

6-7. What is the worst feature of the following objective? A 20-minute color film at a cost of $50,000 depicting in a humorous and interesting way how the company started its metrics program.
   a. Ambiguity
   b. Weightings
   c. Film is too expensive
   d. Twenty minutes is too long

6-8. The following is a valid performance objective: 30% of shareholders know the names of three of the company's products by December 2006. True or false?

6-9. A performance objective should also include "how" it will get done. True or false?

6-10. A performance objective should also include "why" it is being done. True or false?

6-11. All performance objectives can be sourced to a goal. True or false?

6-12. Some goals may not have performance objectives. True or false?

6-13. Six PMP® hired by October 2006 is a valid performance objective. True or false?

6-14. Improved quality is a valid performance objective. True or false?

6-15. Construction of a one-story, 20,000-square-foot air-conditioned office building next to the main plant by July 1, 2007 at a cost of $75,000 is a valid performance objective. True or false?

This book has free materials available for download from the Web Added Value™ Resource Center at www.jrosspub.com.

PART II:
3MS MEASUREMENT PROGRAM FOR THE ORGANIZATION

7

METRICS AND PROGRAM/PROJECT MANAGEMENT

GLOBAL PROJECT MANAGEMENT SERVICE LINE

The 3Ms was implemented at a large software corporation when Dr. Schnapper was quality manager of the Global Project Management Service Line (GPMSL). This service line was created to baseline 18 categories of project management metrics. The company was losing the consulting business that should have been the follow-up to the sales of its software. Too many customers were buying the software and engaging other consulting firms to install and implement the applications.

The corporation did not have a clear picture of what areas of its project management delivery were creating this bad reputation in the marketplace. To remedy the situation, it created the GPMSL and decided to use the 3Ms as a way to get a clear metrics-based picture of current performance and create project management metrics.

Project managers were faced with:

- Incompatible systems for measuring project performance
- No corporate hierarchies of objectives
- A corporate culture that did not support metrics
- A reward system not aligned with performance metrics

Some of the more imaginative project managers could visualize having:

- Total clarity about what they were getting paid to produce
- Improved metrics-based contracts with supervisor, co-workers, subordinates, clients, and others relevant to their success
- Everyone accountable for and committed to their contribution for mutual success
- Results that supported going beyond their own conventional thinking

The 3Ms, as you have already read, is also a linguistics process to achieve clarity of terms like value, priorities, teamwork, leadership, commitment, quality, etc. 3Ms was initiated to:

- Use weightings, measures, and standards to describe results project managers were paid to achieve
- Show how metrics defined the value chain
- Create alignment among corporate, project, and individual performance objectives
- Clarify the reward systems at any level for any function

Although there are many approaches to developing project management metrics for the issues listed above, the 3Ms process represented a universal logic that can be applied to any environment, for any function, at any level. Whether the people involved in the GPMSL were project managers in a major corporation or project team members, the 3Ms of Performance could help them develop clarity about the results they were paid to produce. This approach has the concepts, skills, and procedures to produce clarity about the value of any individual, team, department, or project function at any level and the return on investment for any cost, effort, or investment in personnel, equipment, or new procedures.

The steps of the 3Ms are to:

1. **Measure** — Describe in qualitative and/or quantitative terms what your success criteria are
2. **Manage** — Identify, anticipate, and exploit all of the managerial variables that will help or hinder your efforts
3. **Magnify** — Develop a new way of thinking about how to produce better results for less cost and effort

3MS BACKGROUND

The project management service line at this corporation was suffering from a number of conditions that were reducing the effectiveness, income-producing potential, sales efforts, and development of more experienced project managers. In addition to the immediate effects of these conditions, no immediate solution was being implemented that would alleviate these conditions and lead to a stronger, more credible project management presence in the market amongst current and potential customers.

Customers saw it as optional whether or not to use this firm's project management staff. By improving project management capacity, the firm had the potential to make its project management expertise as value added, necessary, and nonnegotiable as other aspects of its applications projects.

The solution was to create GPMSL to improve the overall performance of project management competencies and metrics. Because of Dr. Schnapper's extensive background in the measurement of corporate, team, individual, and project performance, he was hired as quality manager to work with the service line to accomplish the long-term goal, which was to develop universal measures and standards to evaluate how well projects were developed, implemented, and evaluated.

To accomplish this, the GPMSL had to:

1. Describe the elements of measurement in qualitative and quantitative terms
2. Identify the key metrics and support systems of project management:
   a. Baseline metrics
   b. Current competency levels
   c. Number of projects
   d. Managers/level/role
   e. Delivery experience for size and complexity
   f. Success rating (red to green, based on health check instrument)
   g. Continuity for duration (not part time/short duration)
   h. Recruiting/attrition/retention
   i. Number of peer reviews
   j. Ratio of projects to project end reports
   k. Health check statistics
   l. Customer satisfaction results
   m. Proposed project management/delivered project management
   n. Project management level of training
   o. Number of projects where proprietary software was used versus number of projects (custom development method, project development method) that used commercial software
3. For each of the metrics, distinguish between the performance standards of Satisfactory, Very Good, and Excellent
4. Identify the baselines of the above metrics
5. Assign weightings to every component of a project
6. Use weightings to calculate the value of:
   a. Results
   b. Improvement
7. Identify processes that will create consensus for all of the above
8. Identify areas for immediate project performance improvement
9. Identify best practices (internal and external) for project management performance
10. Identify a core team with clarity about roles, authority, and objectives that could identify the interdependent integrity of these metrics

The long-term objectives of the GPMSL were to create:

1. Universal measures/metrics for determining project success
2. Universal repertoire of project management competencies
3. Global common template for project management metrics with conditions for local modifications

4. Baseline for metric categories above
5. Process of continuous improvement for all of #4
6. Dramatic improvement of those project-related systems that impact #5 (career and individual performance management systems, reward systems, organizational structure, etc.)

THE PROCESS

The 3Ms developed rigorous metrics by having project team members respond to the following questions and answer them based on mutual agreement and alignment:

- What are your major contributions to the project?
- What is the proportionate value of these contributions?
- By what metrics are the standards of your contributions going to be judged?
- How will we determine the standards of your individual and collective performance objectives?
- What is the proportionate value of each performance objective?
- How will you know, in advance, what kind of reward your performance will bring?
- How do you get agreement about this within the corporate hierarchy?

Both individual and consensus agreement are then recorded in a format called a 3Ms profile, shown in Figure 7-1 and elsewhere in this book. Figure 7-1 is a 3Ms profile for a director of the Project Management Office (PMO).

The benefits of this approach are many. At the corporate level:

1. At the highest levels of the corporation, a process for aligning strategic, annual, functional, and departmental objectives in an effective project management context
2. An internal monitoring system to initiate when these objectives need to be fine-tuned to make them more responsive to changing external market conditions and internal organizational changes
3. A methodology to align all project management functional objectives across the top of the organization
4. A process of getting executives to commit to teamwork, interdependencies, and allocation of project management resources.

At the operational level:

1. Near absolute clarity regarding supervisor-employee deliverables, expectations of supervisory support, nature of interdependencies, etc.
2. Ability to measurably define what constitutes "value and priorities"
3. Linguistics for resolving conflict
4. A reward system that makes sense and is based on predefined standards of results

I. **Key Result Areas Weighting (%)**
   A. Build PMO = 40
   B. Direct PMO = 40
   C. Staff Development = 20
II. **Performance Objectives**
   A. Build PMO = 40%
      1. 20% = issue initial program management: 4 = by June 30; 3 = by July 15; 2 = by August 30; 1 = not issued in third quarter.
      2. 20% = staff PMO: 4 = >90%; 3 = >50% of identified PMO; 2 = roles and responsibilities of PMO resources documented; 1 = unspecified.
   B. Direct PMO = 40%
      1. 20% = PMO project life cycle: 4 = no project moves forward without following PMO processes; 3 = all required documents are completed on targeted projects; 2 = complete pilot project by October 1, 2000; 1 = later than October 1, 2000.
      2. 20% = create master schedule: 4 = all project interdependencies identified; 3 = all projects on schedule included; 2 = key targeted projects included; 1 = unspecified.
   C. Staff Development = 20%
      1. 10% = PMO compliance to 3Ms process: 4 = performance rewards based on 3Ms process; 3 = PMO team 3Ms externally aligned; 2 = PMO team members all have 3M profiles; 1 = unspecified.
      2. 10% = PMO staff learning: 4 = 100% of learning goals completed; 3 = PMO team members complete 50% of learning objectives; 2 = all PMO team members have learning objectives; 1 = unspecified.
III. **Performance Factors**
   A. Employee — Keep current on Starbelly.com project status, and strongly enforce project management processes.
   B. Supervisor — Ensure that the PMO is actually given the authority and resources required to accomplish its charter.

Figure 7-1. 3Ms Profile for Project Manager

5. Increased teamwork resulting from well-defined objectives that are interdependent both within and between departments and functions
6. Focused and appropriate investments of time, effort, and money into improvements of results
7. Greater accountability for training efforts whether on the job or in the classroom
8. Resolution of the potential conflict between individual and team effort and rewards
9. A corporate culture where everyone speaks the same language about performance issues

10. Objective language and measures for discussing teamwork, leadership, commitment, and quality
11. A shift in thinking from activity, input, and throughput to results that starts with the "what" and then develops the "how"
12. Empowered individual and project team efforts because management's support for accountabilities and results is also clear
13. Realization of employee potential to achieve standards that are greater than "satisfactory"
14. A system that can be applied to any managerial model already in place or anticipated (self-directed work teams, balanced scorecard, open book management, diversity, etc.)

The list of metrics for baselining continuous improvement efforts in Figure 7-2), though not exhaustive, is very comprehensive. Once completed, it would have provided the total framework for any further granular metrics.

THE DEMISE OF THE GPMSL

About four months into the project, as those people involved in the various subcomponents of the corporate consulting practice were beginning to realize how critical this metrics effort was, the GPMSL was terminated by the vice president of operations. Although the head of the GPMSL team had not established a direct relationship with the vice president or ever had the opportunity to even make a presentation to gain support, he was assured by those at levels below the vice president that his efforts were being monitored and welcomed. However, these assurances were never really tested for their veracity. Examples that should have been warnings about lack of support were numerous.

For example, the team discovered that there were up to $50 million of annual customer credits. A customer credit at this company meant that the customer was unhappy about something, and instead of getting a refund, credit for that same amount was extended for additional services and/or products. However, there was no breakdown of that $50 million. The source could have been an accounting error or total customer dissatisfaction with some or all of a project delivery schedule. When the billing department was contacted, the answer was that reasons for the credits were identified at the beginning, and there was no way to determine the sources of the money.

The total cost of the GPMSL was about $500,000 a year to the company, including all salaries and benefits. The team figured that on this metric alone, if it could save 10% of the dissatisfaction that resulted in the $50 million, or $5 million, then the team would have returned its investment 10 times. And this was only one of 18 metric categories. Still, these figures had no impact on the decision not to terminate the team.

Metrics and Program/Project Management   95

I. Capacity
  A. Number of project managers by level and role
  B. Current competency level of these project managers
  C. Delivery experience by size and complexity (of these same project managers and/or the consulting service line as a whole)
  D. Project manager level of training demand versus delivered (corporate education, etc.) and how relevant
  E. Recruiting (success in getting qualified candidates and actually hiring them)
  F. Attrition (why people leave)
  G. Retention (how long people stay)

II. Projects
  A. Success ratings (red to green) of projects (tied to a specific project manager or overall) or determined by other variables (size, complexity, division, application, etc.)
  B. Continuity for duration (of each project manager) by practice
  C. Health check statistics (performance measures checklist, etc.)
  D. Customer satisfaction results as determined by surveys
  E. Ratio of proposed corporate project managers to delivered project managers per project (of what size, nature, etc.)
  F. Ratio and number of projects where corporate methods were used versus number of projects
  G. Contribution of GPMSL to sales, traceability, loyalty, partnering, etc.

III. Personnel/Human Resources
  A. Number of peer reviews/performance appraisals

IV. Methods/Procedures
  A. Ratio of projects to project end reports (what was done, how used, intellectual capital, reusability, etc.)
  B. Ratio of projects to customer satisfaction reports

Figures 7-2. List of Metrics for the GPMSL

In many other ways, the team was able to identify other metrics which if improved by 5% would have returned the team's expenses to the company by multiples of the team's cost.

SUMMARY

This chapter described the attempt to implement the 3Ms approach at a major software corporation. It explained why the project to improve metrics was implemented and how these improved metrics were intended to improve the market position of the corporation's consulting service line. The consulting service line was seen as having the greatest potential for corporate growth of income. After three months of dramatic progress, the team was suddenly discontinued. There had been no warning about its demise, and everyone with whom it was working agreed that the effort was very worthwhile.

The GPMSL is an example of how lack of proper corporate positioning, lack of a discipline like organizational change management, and lack of alignment with high-level corporate objectives all contributed to its ultimate demise. How to position the metrics function is also described. It's too bad that this team existed before this book was published. We are not saying that all of the caveats and admonitions in the book would have saved the GPMSL or even extended its life, but there is always that possibility.

QUESTIONS

7-1. The GPMSL was established to create the following number of metric categories:
   a. 12
   b. 14
   c. 16
   d. 18
   e. None of the above

7-2. The GPMSL was created because the company was rapidly increasing its share of consulting contracts to install its own software applications. True or false?

7-3. Project managers were faced with:
   a. Incompatible systems for measuring project performance
   b. No corporate hierarchies of objectives
   c. A corporate culture that did not support metrics
   d. A reward system not aligned with performance metrics
   e. All of the above

7-4. Some of the more imaginative project managers could visualize having:
   a. Total clarity about what they were getting paid to produce
   b. Contracts with supervisor, co-workers, subordinates, clients, and others relevant to their success
   c. Everyone accountable for and committed to their contribution for mutual success
   d. Results that support going beyond their own conventional thinking
   e. a, c, and d

7-5. In this case study, 3Ms was able to:
   a. Use weightings, measures, and standards to describe results project managers are paid to achieve
   b. Show how metrics can define the value chain
   c. Create alignment among corporate, project, and individual performance objectives

d. Clarify the reward systems at any level for any function
e. All the above

7-6. 3Ms process represents a universal logic that can be applied to:
a. High-tech environments
b. Construction companies
c. Companies with highly developed metrics
d. Companies with a history of success
e. Any environment, for any function, at any level

7-7. The 3Ms approach has the concepts, skills, and procedures to produce clarity about the value of any individual, team, department, or project function at any level and the return on investment for any cost, effort, or investment in personnel, equipment, or new procedures. True or false?

7-8. By improving project management capacity, the firm described in this chapter had the potential to make its project management expertise as value added, necessary, and nonnegotiable as other aspects of its applications projects. True or false?

7-9. The goal of the quality management function was to develop universal measures and standards to evaluate how well projects are developed, implemented, and evaluated. True or false?

7-10. The following list describes all of key metrics and support systems of project management. True or false?
a. Baseline metrics
b. Current competency levels
c. Number of projects
d. Managers/level/role
e. Delivery experience for size and complexity

7-11. The long-term objectives of the GPMSL were to:
a. Create universal measures/metrics for determining project success
b. Create a universal repertoire of project management competencies
c. Create a global common template for project management metrics with conditions for local modifications
d. Establish a baseline for metrics categories
e. Save the company money

7-12. Increased teamwork resulting from well-defined objectives that are interdependent both within and between departments and functions is always a result of the 3Ms process. True or false?

7-13. Empowered individual and project team efforts because management's support for accountabilities and results is clear is not necessarily a result of applying 3Ms. True or false?

7-14. Capacity, projects, personnel, and methods/procedures are four of the five major categories of assessing project management metrics. True or false?

8

ROLE/AUTHORITY/ DECISION MAKING

Role clarity is the understanding team members have of their mutual and mutually exclusive territory or areas of accountability. Another refinement of this is their respective levels of authority in terms of any area of accountability that they share as a team. This will enable team meetings to conclude with concrete statements of action in the linguistic format of "who does what by when" instead of the all-too-common conclusions of "greater commitment," "improved communication," and "more cooperation." Although such statements make people feel good at the conclusion of a meeting, they lead to little or no action and only greater cynicism about these meetings and rhetoric for the future.

A further refinement of the general role clarity defined above is the role/authority/decision grid. Although this chapter explains the process clearly, you should experience the process as a participant with a role and decision for which you share accountability.

To develop role/authority/decision clarity, participants fill in Table 8-1, where the first column is a list of decision-making areas, and the remaining columns are the individual roles that participate in those decisions. The table should include a column for the team leader and each team member. The number of columns is extended until all relevant team members and/or stakeholders that have an investment in a particular decision are included by a respective column and ideally have participated in the exercise.

Someone who is not present to participate in the exercise will not have the benefit of hearing others explain why they agreed to their respective levels of authority. The participation is really critical, as often the level of authority one wants for oneself or ascribes to another will change radically by hearing the arguments against one's initial position.

Table 8-1. Role-Level Authority

Decision Area	Role A	Role B	Role C
Buy new project management software	A D C I	A D C I	etc.

A = approve, D = decide, C = consult, I = inform.

The other thing that typically happens is the levels of authority can be pushed down when everyone is present. This often means that those with the initial approve authority will ascribe it downward and accept decide, consult, or even inform for themselves. This can change the dynamics of the total project going forward.

This is not a grid for ascribing levels of authority to an entire project or effort; it is for each critical decision that has produced conflict or is likely to. Ascribing levels of authority for the entire effort is too macro and will lead to conflict later. During the length of any project, no one person will have the same level of authority regarding *all* decisions for the duration of the project. Again, this is a role/authority/decision grid, not a role/authority/project authority grid. It is used to determine what role has what level of authority over what decision.

The exercise consists of explaining the idea of role, authority, and decisions. Authority is defined as the level of power a person has over an action, decision, or specific series of actions/decisions to be taken by himself or herself or someone he or she reports to, works with, or supervises. Each level has a specific definition:

- **A = approve** — This is the authority to take action.
- **D = decide** — This is the authority to come to a conclusion regarding what should be done, but must await someone with approval authority before taking action.
- **C = consult** — This is the obligation to receive input from others or to be available to give input, but allows that advice, whether given or received, to be ignored in the final decision.
- **I = inform** — This is the obligation to inform others of a decision that has been made, is being made, or is being contemplated. Whether this has to occur before, during, or after can also be defined within the exercise.

During the exercise, the team picks a decision area that has created conflict or confusion in the past and responds to the question: With regard to this decision, what degree of authority should each of you have? Individuals then fill out the respective cells for themselves and each other by indicating A, D, C, or I along the row even with the decision being considered.

When everyone has completed the row for themselves and each other, the facilitator puts all the responses on a collective table (Table 8-2), so everyone can

Table 8-2. DAM Project Role Authority Matrix

Name	Authorize	Decision	Consult	Inform
DAM steering committee				
President	X			
Chief technology officer		X		
Member A*		X		
Member B*		X		
Member C*			X	
Member D*			X	
Consultant			X	
Member E*			X	
Member F				X
Member G				X
Member H				X
DAM project team				
Member				X
Member				X
Member				X
Member				X
Member				X
DAM others				
Member				X
Member				X
Member				X
Member				X
Member				X

* Denotes member of the steering committee and the project team.

see their own opinions and those of others. The negotiation process consists of everyone participating until there is resolution regarding who has what level of authority for what decision (under normal circumstances). "Under normal circumstances" is assumed, as levels of authority can be quite different per person when someone leaves the team, is on temporary leave, or just didn't make a particular decision-making meeting. There should also be an understanding of how the levels of authority might shift when members are absent and the decision must be made.

The ideal conclusion is that everyone is in agreement on who should have the ultimate approval authority, who should decide, who should be consulted about it (which may include people outside of the team), and who should be informed about it and when.

This chapter cannot describe all of the dynamics of this process. The dynamics will necessarily go into some depth or at least touch upon many other elements identified as critical for effective teamwork. The process will be easier and faster when the team already shares a communication model that includes how to listen, resolve conflict, and reach general decisions. There are many comprehensive communication models available, and this should be part of the commitment to the whole team-building process.

SUMMARY

When the 3Ms program is begun, one of the many issues that surfaces almost immediately is who has what degree of authority to approve what. Without 3Ms, authority is ambiguous, and it is ambiguous authority over ambiguous decisions that leads to ambiguous results. And people learn to live with it. With the stark clarity of the 3Ms metrics in place, authority has to be defined in a much more rigorous manner. It is defined by four levels: approve, decide, consult, and inform. Although there are other versions of this hierarchy of authority, some seven levels deep, these four levels are really all that is needed for the 3Ms approach.

This role/authority/decision grid is a simple but profound exercise that *must* be done by all of those who have some degree of authority vis-à-vis a specific decision. Each decision, even within the same category of decision making, may have different degrees of authority from those who participate. This chapter showed the ultimate resolution of what has been a very contentious area of decision making.

QUESTIONS

8-1. The 3Ms approach is all one needs to make project teams more effective. True or false?

8-2. The nature of authority is pretty clear to most project team members. True or false?

8-3. Approve, decide, recommend, and inform are the four levels of authority in this model. True or false?

8-4. The hierarchy of authority necessarily follows the same hierarchy of reporting relationships. True or false?

8-5. When teams commit to greater clarity and greater communication, these commitments are usually carried out. True or false?

8-6. The role/authority/decision exercise can be used for specific decisions and for decision making in general. True or false?

8-7. Decide is the level of authority for taking action. True or false?

8-8. Inform is the level of authority for letting others know that action has, is being, or will be taken. True or false?

8-9. The consult level obligates others to listen to that person, but not necessarily follow his or her advice. True or false?

8-10. Although it would be helpful to have supportive communication models to facilitate the role/authority/decision process, this process in itself is also a communication model regarding authority. True or false?

8-11. One theme that haunts most project efforts is the ambiguity of authority. True or false?

8-12. Once authority is defined at the beginning of the project's life cycle, it does not need to be defined again. True or false?

8-13. Negotiation is the key to a successful role/authority/decision session. True or false?

8-14. The more transparent the role/authority/decision process is, the better. True or false?

8-15. A project scope of work is totally adequate for defining which role has what level of authority. True or false?

9

METRICS AND CORPORATE CULTURE

The ultimate goal of the 3Ms methodology and rigorous metrics is to have a level of 3Ms mastery so that all of what is done in the project management space relies on the incremental cognitive skills to realize results of measurement and collaboration among the workforce. As for the business itself, the goal is an accelerated delivery opportunity with high confidence and reduced threat of noncompliance, no matter how complex the project criteria.

When 3Ms has achieved the level of being *the* corporate culture, the way projects are conceived and for all phases, metrics are a key ingredient of the initial project scope and all of the conversations, documents, health checks, and project reviews in the format of key value areas and performance objectives as previously defined in the 3Ms template.

This will be achieved by some after only several iterations of the 3Ms cycle, which will include the three phases of Measure, Manage, and Magnify. For others, it will take more exposure, training, and actual coaching. As will be detailed later by way of steps to take, templates, and the online application, the first time the Measure phase takes place, it is created as a hypothesis. This is at a time when it is unlikely that the organization has:

- Rigorous measures for valid baselines
- Conducted team-based meetings where individual 3Ms profiles are created collectively and transparently
- Documents or objectives at each level of the corporate hierarchy
- A process for executives to examine metrics as a corporate management tool for managing the future

At best, the metrics will have been used as a scorecard or some other form of historical document. The Measure phase is all about the future: Given what we now know about current baseline performance and future internal strengths and weaknesses in the areas of resources, competencies, capacities, demands, etc. and future external opportunities and threats in terms of the market, competition, income projections, recruiting efforts, etc., by what relevant and reasonable metrics (quantitative and qualitative) can we define Satisfactory? This process will also include the key value areas and performance objectives with metrics, weightings, and standards.

Ideally, the strengths, weaknesses, threats, and opportunities (SWOT) analysis will already have been developed by a strategic planning process where this kind of data is generated. Many strategic planning processes produce plans and goals (directionality) and lack the distinction of strategic objectives (statements of measurable achievement with due dates).

When this is completed by the total organization (ideally) or at least those functions committed to the 3Ms process, the next Manage phase begins. As stated before, in this phase all those variables that will help or hinder the accomplishment of the now predefined standards of success are identified and then an action plan is aligned to each variable so those that management anticipates will hinder success are eliminated or reduced in influence and those that will support success are strengthened.

For the first year, we suggest that the Measure and Manage phases be done quarterly, as the organization is still learning about the methodology, terms, and communication processes that are part of these phases. The more ambitious organization might even want to include the Magnify phase in its third or fourth quarterly cycle.

For those who imagine this process to be time consuming and burdensome, you are half right. It is time consuming, but it takes no more time than resolving the arguments, correcting the mistakes, and reallocating resources that result from ambiguous performance measures, as is almost universal. The problem with this other kind of wasted time is that it is so ever-present, like gravity, that it has become "normal" and invisible.

When a company has gone through three to four cycles of the 3Ms phases, the language of the 3Ms template and 3Ms scorecard will become the way people talk to each other about changes in priorities (weightings), accomplishments becoming more or less difficult to achieve (standards), and changing what it is that people should focus upon to determine success (metrics). Remember that these discussions are occurring *all the time anyway*, but in ways that sustain ambiguity, argumentation, and debate. With the 3Ms methodology as the way people talk, *there is no ambiguity* in conversation. Any changes that will necessarily occur will occur with the rigor of 3Ms linguistics and precise use of the few terms of the phases.

Here is an example of a normal exchange:

> *Steve*: Hey, Mel, I've got something that's a real priority.
> *Mel*: Sure, what is it?

Steve: The recruiting effort we discussed has to be done with greater urgency. We need that project manager right away.

Mel: But I don't have enough resources to increase the recruiting effort and attend to my other accountabilities.

Steve: I'm sure you can work it out.

Here is a 3Ms exchange:

Steve: Remember that recruiting key value area that now has a weighting of 20%?

Mel: Yes, and the supporting performance objective was to have a PMP®-certified project manager on board within the quarter.

Steve: Right, well now we need the project manager within six weeks. So I want you to increase the recruiting key value area to 40%, reallocate the weightings of the other 80%, and change the performance objective standard of Satisfactory to 6 weeks from now, instead of 12 weeks from now. Also, lower the results of one or two of the other performance objectives, which will recognize that you've had to reallocate resources of staff and time and that the previous standards did not take into account this new urgency. So, work on this for now, and let's review your 3Ms profile in a few days.

Mel: I'm sure glad we invested in learning about 3Ms and how to reallocate weightings and standards to accommodate new realities. Before 3Ms, I would have been in a panic and really resented this new priority and been confused regarding your expectations of me for my other tasks that will necessarily suffer.

Steve: Yeah, you're right. The 3Ms was a *very* worthwhile investment.

Even though the discussion above is fairly stilted, it was written that way to show in very explicit terms how a 3Ms culture would sound. You will have to imagine, from your own experience, how effective the first conversation would be compared to the 3Ms conversation.

Even in the social arena, people learn to use the 3Ms linguistics by just playing with it. For instance, if someone has completed a task according to expectations, a colleague or their boss will compliment them by saying: "That was really satisfactory," which in normal language sounds like an insult, but in the 3Ms culture it will be understood by everyone that the task or objective was accomplished at the standard that was expected — no more and no less, and that in other linguistic domains the adjective would be "good," "competent," or "meets expectations." Terms like "very good" and "excellent" are used sparingly and only for those outcomes that truly have created value of 105 or 110% as previously defined.

In some corporate cultures, doing all that you are supposed to do is considered "excellent"; in 3Ms culture, doing all you are supposed to do is Satisfactory. It is only when you exceed expectations that the recognition is Very Good or Excellent.

We have introduced the 3Ms culture where people were rewarded for "excellent" performance when in fact their deliverables were "satisfactory." This is what we call an "inflationary reward system," and it takes a while for people to realize that there are real distinctions between various standards of performance, especially if they have been working with a binary pass/fail system, where pass equals "excellent" and people seldom are judged as less than that.

The good news about these inflated systems is that the rewards are excessive for the results being delivered and people seldom get less than excessive rewards. The bad news is that people do not really have an incentive to exceed minimum performance. There are no distinguishing standards above "pass," and results seldom exceed what 3Ms defines as Satisfactory.

When there is a 3Ms culture, alignment occurs almost automatically, not only because the standard 3Ms profiles are reviewed as often as is necessary, but also because all of the disputes and wasted time and effort in the typical project management environment are nearly absent. By using the 3Ms methodology, the role/authority/decision grid, and other organization development methods and techniques, conflict will not disappear, but it will be quickly surfaced, defined, and resolved.

As described in Chapter 8 on the role/authority/decision grid, as soon as performance metrics are explicit, and it is recognized who does what with what standard, people realize how ambiguous their own efforts and those of others are, and in order to get things done, they demand greater explicit accountability.

SUMMARY

This chapter described some of the dynamics that occur when 3Ms language and behaviors are fully part of the corporate culture. People talk to each other differently regarding tasks and objectives, especially when they may be changing on a frequent basis. People think differently about their work, their accountability, and their reward systems, and conflict is easily and quickly identified and resolved.

QUESTIONS

9-1. A typical comment one would hear in the 3Ms culture is: "This is really important." True or false?
9-2. The 3Ms methodology, when part of the corporate culture, will accelerate the resolution of conflict. True or false?
9-3. When the 3Ms corporate culture is flourishing, there is no additional need for greater clarity of authority. True or false?
9-4. Which of the following is more likely to be heard within a 3Ms culture:
 a. "Thanks for staying late last night. That was really excellent."
 b. "Your sales have increased by 105%, and that is really very good."
 c. "You missed the deadline for the report, but it is still satisfactory."

9-5. Inflationary reward systems are the result of ambiguous standards of performance. True or false?

9-6. Managing the 3Ms profiles at the team and individual levels in a transparent manner will undermine the effectiveness of 3Ms. True or false?

9-7. The concepts of 3Ms standards are implicit in many project-related discussions. True or false?

9-8. One cycle of the 3Ms process usually is sufficient for people to master the methodology. True or false?

9-9. It does not really matter if strategic planning occurs prior to or parallel to the introduction of 3Ms. True or false?

9-10. Most project management organizations have executives who use metrics as a corporate management tool for managing the future. True or false?

9-11. The 3Ms Manage phase will indicate to what degree the Measure phase has set reasonable standards. True or false?

9-12. The 3Ms process will guarantee that documents or objectives at each level of the corporate hierarchy exist. True or false?

9-13. Most project management organizations have rigorous measures for valid baselines. True or false?

9-14. In many non-3Ms corporate cultures, doing all you are supposed to do is considered "excellent." True or false?

9-15. When the 3Ms becomes *the* corporate culture, there is *no* conflict. True or false?

This book has free materials available for download from the
Web Added Value™ Resource Center at www.jrosspub.com.

10

INITIATIVES THAT SUPPORT THE 3MS

This chapter examines two major organizational initiatives that will profoundly support the 3Ms program, as both deal with how people *feel* regarding change, their role, and their relationships with others. The first of these methodologies is organization development, or OD as it is known to its practitioners and those who support it. The second methodology is organizational change management, or OCM. It is important to use the complete name so as not be confuse it with change management as used in the project management and information technology worlds for changes to scopes of work and even as used by programmers to describe the management of changes to a program.

The basic focus of the OD effort is to teach people new skills, concepts, and awareness that will support the 3Ms culture and methodology. The basic focus of OCM is to prepare people for the profound changes that the 3Ms will bring about. Both deal with the people dimension of change.

ORGANIZATION DEVELOPMENT

OD is usually initiated with a workshop or retreat following a needs analysis. These needs analyses can be done using interviews, focus groups, or questionnaires, both in hard copy and as part of an online application. Two sessions that are typical of the team-building exercises normally conducted by OD consultants are on the themes of teamwork skills and corporate culture. OD, unlike more conventional consulting approaches, makes, among others, the following assumptions:

1. The client system has a great deal of knowledge, wisdom, and experience regarding its own organizational problems, how to solve them, and how to improve overall effectiveness.

2. The OD consultant is there to facilitate, teach problem-solving skills, and introduce concepts that enable the client organization to mature and incorporate those same skills on its own. Over time, the client can incorporate these new skills *without the need for continued consulting,* at least for whatever the client has begun to internalize as part of its own repertoire.
3. If the consultant is used after that, it is for additional skills, one-on-one coaching, and/or working with subteams of the larger organization.
4. OD can also involve the development of human resource management systems regarding performance, rewards, career, succession, recruiting, etc. All of these are developed with the full participation and ownership of those who will be accountable for implementing these systems.

The following describes a typical OD introductory workshop to support the 3Ms program. On day 1, participants are seated around tables in groups of six. Groups are then given the assignment of representing the theme of teamwork at their company. They do this by drawing a picture using various colored markers and are not allowed to use numbers or words to highlight the creative nature of this exercise. This kind of exercise also notifies participants that this will be a different kind of session, not like the typical classroom lecture and discussion. It also sends the message that everyone participates. After the groups finish their pictures, a spokesperson from each group then describes to the total group what that picture represents. When all groups have presented, the total group summarizes the major themes that were apparent.

A brief introduction to the idea of teamwork skills is given. Rather than lecturing or having people read about these skills, they identify, list, and prioritize only those skills that they believe are relevant to their project's improved teamwork. The staff already has presented the context of these more specific skills through their pictures and teamwork themes. Therefore, these skills are not theoretical or generic to organizations in general, though many are. These skills are specific to the project and most relevant to participants and their immediate needs for improved performance.

The participants seated at each table list specific skills they think would be most helpful to project staff to demonstrate improved task accomplishment. When all of these skills have been presented, the consultant then facilitates highlighting those skills where there is consensus. With the limited time of these presentations, groups are asked to incorporate these skills into their future teamwork activity.

In a full-blown or complete OD consulting relationship, the next steps would be some combination of the following:

1. Training sessions on what behaviors manifest these skills would include real tasks faced by teams and the staff as a whole. After the skills training sessions are over, these skills should begin to be incorporated into the actual task.
2. Participants read brief articles related to these skills, since a conceptual understanding of why certain skills are valuable can be helpful. Also, different people learn differently.

3. Brief lectures are given regarding these specific skills. Participants demonstrate these skills by role playing them in various situations that have already occurred between or within project teams. Other situations that need improved teamwork skills might be expressed by project staff during these team-building sessions or be the result of some previous diagnostic process.
4. As the team-building sessions continue, with a focus on actual work being accomplished, teams will show their growing mastery of some of the skills as newer skills are introduced.

On day 2, the second session focuses on corporate culture. A brief presentation is given on the general use of the word culture, and then corporate culture is defined. Corporate culture is, among many other things, the way people behave in a particular organization. Another theme of the presentation is that corporate culture is a culture that can be created and managed by everyone's daily behavior, although it is most dependent on the behaviors of the highly visible leadership. The subtheme of corporate culture is how 3Ms is itself a profound shift from the current corporate culture to one of near absolute clarity of measurable results, accountability, and a transparent reward system.

Again, in groups of about six staff per table, participants are asked to identify behaviors within the project that are desirable and frequent, desirable and infrequent, undesirable and frequent, and undesirable and infrequent. Each table presents its list to the entire group, and again a consensus is established regarding these behaviors. That is where the session ends.

In a more comprehensive OD process, the next steps would be to:

1. Decide what behaviors within all four categories are most critical to change (either eliminate, reduce, or increase)
2. Create actions at the individual and groups level that accomplish what was identified in #1 above
3. Revisit this exercise every three months or so to determine how well the corporate culture is changing to support staff effectiveness
4. Add or delete behaviors in all four categories with each review of corporate culture
5. Identify and align all of the above with specific performance objectives of both the project teams and individuals

The specific design of the introductory OD workshop follows.

Corporate Culture Team-Building Workshop

The purpose of the corporate culture team-building workshop is to be able to use corporate culture as a team-building tool. As a result of this workshop, participants will be able to:

1. Describe corporate culture as defined by observable behaviors
2. Identify behaviors that are desirable and frequent, desirable and infrequent, undesirable and frequent, and undesirable and infrequent

3. Develop action plans at the individual and team levels to sustain desirable and frequent behaviors, increase desirable and infrequent behaviors, reduce undesirable and frequent behaviors, and decide what to do about undesirable and infrequent behaviors
4. Align all the above to specific performance objectives

The typical schedule for the workshop is as follows:

8:00 a.m.	Introduction to corporate culture
8:30 a.m.	Each group of five develops a list of the four categories of behavior as it has observed them in its environment and lists them on a flip chart
9:00 a.m.	Report out
9:30 a.m.	Create a combined list of the four categories and pick the top four for each category
10:00 a.m.	Break
10:15 a.m.	Develop individual and team action plans to accomplish #3 above
11:15 a.m.	Describe how the new corporate culture will improve teamwork, effectiveness, and satisfaction

ORGANIZATIONAL CHANGE MANAGEMENT

With the many OCM approaches around, our approach is heavily reliant on the 3Ms methodology in that we help the client define success in measurable (qualitative and quantitative) terms, or as Covey would say, "start with the results."

We engage the client with an organizational assessment process using surveys, focus groups, interviews, etc. to scope out what areas will need special attention to achieve the success that has already been defined. The rest of the effort is to manage all variables (systems, processes, procedures, corporate culture, leadership, etc.) to achieve that success. Metrics are used to monitor progress and to align all efforts to support the results.

Our mission is to enable solutions to improve the project and business performance of new applications by integrating human and organizational factors with the new technology, in alignment with the business strategy. All of this is project based.

Introduction

The fairly new discipline of OCM recognizes that corporate America is changing significantly as customer expectations and competitive pressures grow. These pressures often result in reorganizations, different technology, decreased development cycles, and changing missions. This has a tremendous impact on the staff and management of an organization.

Employees undergoing such pressures will experience many fears and frustrations. These employees realize that their responsibilities and work processes will change, necessitating new "people" management systems. The managers of the organization have to cope with the miscommunication and rumors that abound in such situations, as well as manage, develop, and train employees whose jobs have changed drastically.

Specifically, if the 3Ms is introduced after or preceding some kind of profound organizational change, such as massive layoffs, restructuring, mergers, or new leadership, OCM is used to allay the fear and expectations that this rigorous performance measurement process is another way to get rid of people.

A "storming" phase is natural during this state of transition to the 3Ms discipline. In fact, most employees expect a period of transition that serves to reinforce the magnitude and significance of the change. If the "storming" phase is expected, planned for, and controlled through effective "people" management systems, it can positively influence the long-term success of the frame-breaking change.

We help clients control employee dynamics during the "storming" phase through proven methodologies based on extensive experience in technology implementation. We focus our expertise to help clients create "people" systems that not only manage transition but position the organization to successfully manage the inevitable changes that are part of doing business, but with the additional rigor of 3Ms metrics.

Technology, Process, and People

We subscribe to the philosophy that there is a triad that an organization must have in place to successfully operate and change: *people, process, and technology*. We achieve success by developing OCM strategies that help industry and government become more efficient and competitive. We understand that when an organization implements technology, the work processes must also change to align with the technology. In a similar fashion, when the technology and process are aligned, the organization must align employees with their new corporate, functional, team, and individual performance objectives.

All too often, organizations address process and technology independently and fail to recognize the importance of the people aspect. OCM assists in implementing integrated "people" management systems. Technology and processes are but two pieces of the puzzle. By providing services that support the technical objectives, we significantly improve the value of the technology through system-based "people" solutions. These solutions significantly increase the probability of successful change implementations and generate cost-effective and timely results.

The Integrated People Solution

Our philosophy is that all aspects of employee management must be integrated to achieve success. For example, certain areas should be addressed as part of the project: organizational effectiveness, training, leadership development, employee skills, reward systems, and communication. To successfully change, an organization must address all of these categories in a holistic manner, as no single category will completely address the people issues.

The 3Ms Components of OCM

We offer four services to meet the "people" needs during a project life cycle:

- Organizational assessments
- Leadership development
- Organizational communication
- Human performance and development

Through these services, we perform organizational readiness and communications assessments, develop performance management metrics and compensation systems, and address corporate culture issues in organizations undergoing significant change. Our metrics approach is, as you might guess, 3Ms.

The methodologies for each of the services follow an open system approach to organizations and are integrated with the technology implementation. Furthermore, each of the services has metrics built into the methodology to assure clients of quality deliverables and measurable results.

The following sections provide a brief description of our services. Also included are the benefits organizations can expect to receive through our practical application and delivery of these services.

Organizational Assessment

We strongly believe that an organizational assessment is the intelligent front end to all technology implementations. The result of this assessment allows the benchmarking of current effectiveness and prescribes the necessary organizational improvements to achieve effective transitions of any sort.

Initially, we work with the client's designated change leaders, senior managers, and, of course, project managers to identify the factors relevant to the technology implementation, including culture, change readiness, reward systems, reporting relationships, leadership, values, skill sets, and goals. These factors, specific for any client, ensure that the assessment is relevant to the specific "business case" which prompted the change in the first place.

Through the analysis of the assessment results, we develop an organizational change strategy that outlines specific training plans, performance and reward systems, internal communication programs, and strategic planning and leadership effectiveness programs. This allows us to concentrate only on those areas where a deficiency exists, while reinforcing identified strengths.

This assessment provides:

- Reduced costs by focusing resources on those areas that are identified as weakest relative to achieving project goals
- A baseline for each participant, team, and functional area from which the individual's and team's development can be measured throughout the change process

- A baseline from which organizational development can be measured throughout the change process life cycle

Leadership Development

In many companies embarking on significant technological change, the change leaders are not fully prepared to guide employees through the change process. This may be the result of the leaders not having the technological expertise required or having a mind-set that does not truly accept an open system organization. These problems can mitigate the success of the implementation, but can be overcome through practical guidance and shared experience of our change management consultants.

We offer in-depth planning services to help change leaders understand the new vision, renew their commitment, and shape their future. We work with leadership to identify and delineate both individual and departmental goals and objectives, tie them to the mainstream vision, and set measurement systems to track progress, using a combination of workshops, seminars, and facilitated sessions.

The benefits clients experience through change leadership development are:

- Executives and change leaders who have the appropriate level of technical knowledge to make implementation decisions and set personal and organizational goals
- Increased leadership buy-in to the change through a shared understanding of the company goals and the implementation plan
- Increased synergy throughout the organization as leaders establish their respective departmental objectives aligned with the new technology objectives
- A 3Ms repertoire of skills to measure change at *any* level, for *any* function

Organizational Communication

Effective communication is vital to the success of a technology implementation. In fact, our experience with communication planning shows that "good communication cannot guarantee success, but poor communication guarantees failure."

To fully understand the new technology vision and the organization's role in it, employees must first buy-in to the need for change. In some organizations, there already exists a collective agreement that change is needed. However, in those organizations where employees do not perceive the need for change, the probability of success is drastically reduced.

There are two principal deliverables to organizational communication:

- Technology implementation communication model which outlines the communication strategy and presents the feedback processes for the life of the program
- Communication plan which presents an organization-specific audience matrix outlining the various audiences, the obstacles to communication, the key

messages to be communicated, and the appropriate media in which the messages should be communicated

Through the communication model and communication plan, feedback programs are created to achieve a unified vision and facilitate open communication among all levels of the organization. These programs reduce resistance to change, uniformly communicate benefits and objectives of the implementation, and create a shared understanding of the need to move forward. In addition, the structure provided by a good project communication plan and model will have lasting benefits beyond the scope of the technology implementation.

Human Performance and Development

To receive the maximum benefit of the new technology, the technology implementation will, in all likelihood, necessitate changes in job responsibilities and functions. We help define new job descriptions, skill profiles, and competencies for each job. In addition, we assist clients in developing the tools to interview and appraise those who fill the new roles. Included with these tools is an interviewing protocol for selecting appropriate people to fill new roles and designing new compensation and incentive programs that reflect realigned responsibilities.

In today's business environment, it is critical that performance management be linked to new objectives. This fact gets to the heart of the integration of all OCM approaches. By incorporating training, communication, and leadership initiatives, employee performance and development is enhanced and directly related to overall business and technology goals.

The benefits of a well-designed human performance and development system are:

- Increased employee understanding of roles and performance expectations
- A structured process through which goals can be aligned with specific work-related tasks for future performance reviews
- Efficient performance-enhancing training resulting from training objectives based on objective and 3Ms metrics
- Increased employee satisfaction as people are rewarded for work that directly relates to overall personal and business objectives

Action Plan

Listed below are the anticipated actions, divided into four major steps and many substeps, that are performed to ensure an effective OCM program and successful implementation. The major four steps are identified by the cumulative time involved per step and the absolute amount of time per action. Depending on many as yet unknown variables, some actions may be skipped and other actions may be added or subdivided.

The overall completion of these steps is a 90-day process, which can be scheduled over any number of calendar days depending on how aggressively the project organization wants to complete the process. This is dependent on a client's commitment of resources, time, priorities, availability, etc. Some actions are sequential and some can be concurrent, and the process can be graphed on a project management flowchart.

Step 1: 25 Days

Identify participating populations and initial scan of organizational readiness for the change management effort.

Actions
1. Identify criteria, describe the mandate, and recruit for membership of the following groups: executive sponsors, executive advisory committee, user advisory committee, executive project manager (an individual or group), audit/internal control, steering committee, and users/subject matter experts.
2. Train/advise each group about its role(s), skill sets, etc.
3. Conduct an organizational assessment that benchmarks the organization's current effectiveness in terms of change readiness, culture, leadership, rewards, metrics, and teamwork. Based on the assessment results, a detailed change management program is custom developed to the company's specific needs. The major activities include:
   a. Gather and review assessment-related data.
   b. Identify employees to participate in an organizational assessment.
   c. Using previously developed organizational assessments, customize an assessment.
   d. Announce organizational assessment to the organization (performed in conjunction with Step 3).
   e. Administer organizational assessment, process data, and analyze results.
   f. Confirm analysis and results with organizational assessment participants and relevant groups in Action 1.
   g. Prepare organizational assessment report, including overall change strategy to drive remaining steps.
   h. Prepare key staff to implement change strategy via facilitated session(s).
   i. Transfer knowledge around organizational assessment to appropriate staff.

Results — The assessment shows the organization's readiness, capacity, and resources to facilitate the change and the change management infrastructure to initiate and sustain the change effort.

Step 2: 20 Days

This step is designed to allow leadership to develop a new vision for the technology and organization, renew its commitment for the project's success, tie individual and departmental objectives together, reinforce teamwork, and set 3Ms measurement systems to track progress. It ensures effective sponsorship and achievement of business objectives regarding the technology initiative.

Actions
1. Gather and review leadership-related data.
2. Confirm leaders, at all levels, needed to sponsor the project.
3. Using previously developed leadership assessments, customize an assessment.
4. Announce leadership assessment to organization (performed in conjunction with Step 3).
5. Administer leadership assessment, process data, and analyze results.
6. Confirm analysis and results with leadership assessment participants.
7. Prepare leadership assessment report highlighting change roles for appropriate change leaders.
8. Transfer knowledge around leadership assessment to appropriate staff.

Results — Clarity of roles, functions, interdependencies, and critical paths for accomplishing the leadership, managerial, and followership accountabilities of the change effort. Also provides real-time profiles of leadership capacities or lack thereof.

Step 3: 25 Days

Develop and implement communication and feedback programs to achieve a unified vision and facilitate open communication among all levels of the organization. This step reinforces stakeholder involvement, commitment, and buy-in to reduce employee resistance to organizational and technological changes.

Actions
1. Gather and review communication (formal and informal)–related data.
2. Identify employees, at all levels and locations, needing communication regarding project, achieved via audience analysis.
3. Develop initial key messages regarding project based on audience analysis.
4. Determine timing of key messages based on audience analysis.
5. Prepare communication strategy, including alternative communication methods, based on audience analysis.
6. Transfer knowledge around communication to appropriate staff.

Results — A communications strategy, networks, and protocols that keep *all* stakeholders fully informed about the progress of the change effort.

Step 4: 20 Days

Analyze the gap between existing and future employee skill sets and job responsibilities based on the new technology and organizational changes. This step is designed to identify skill set differences for use in developing new or current job profiles.

Actions
1. Gather and review current job-related data.
2. Confirm employees whose job functions/skills are impacted by the technology.
3. Determine existing skill sets of employees/job roles based on current technology.
4. Identify skill sets needed by employees/job roles to successfully operate the new technology.
5. Prepare a skills gap analysis that highlights the differences and similarities between current and needed skills.
6. Confirm analysis and results with participants.
7. Include this information in the training needs assessment to understand training needs regarding impacted employees/job roles.
8. Transfer knowledge around skills gap analysis to appropriate staff.

Results — A training strategy, tactics, and curricula that develop the skill set for the future state of the organization. Also identifies those staff who may lack the capacity to develop the new skill set and will be outplaced or reassigned to exploit what they can contribute to other company efforts.

SUMMARY

This chapter introduced two distinct methodologies that are very supportive of initiating and sustaining the 3Ms methodology. By the nature of the 3Ms, many of the OD and OCM dynamics and skills will be introduced anyway, but having OD and OCM as "separate" initiatives will accelerate the acquisition of 3Ms skills and concepts.

OD focuses on interpersonal skills of communication, conflict resolution, teamwork, managing corporate culture, and facilitating change in relationships, teams, or the entire organization. OCM focuses on the management of communication about the anticipated change and ensures understanding and support of the change process. This is done by conducting meetings for focus groups, feedback, and informing the leadership and followership what their responsibilities are regarding the change. A subset of OCM is training in new skills sets that might be necessary for improved performance after the changes are completed.

QUESTIONS

10-1. The 3Ms process can sustain itself without any other supportive methodologies. True or false?

10-2. Typical themes of the OD approach are collusion and creating a power base. True or false?

10-3. OD is focused on the project team as the fundamental work unit. True or false?

10-4. An OD facilitator is always necessary to make the OD process successful. True or false?

10-5. An assumption of OD is that company systems can learn and change. True or false?

10-6. Although OD might introduce some theory of organizational effectiveness, the focus is on the "here and now." True or false?

10-7. The OD approach uses experiential exercises for skills practice, more so than lectures or reading. True or false?

10-8. A common exercise used in OD is identifying behaviors that are desirable and frequent, desirable and infrequent, undesirable and frequent, and undesirable and infrequent, so everyone will change immediately. True or false?

10-9. The organizational assessment process is the fourth step of the OCM initiative. True or false?

10-10. The three components of the OCM process are people, process, and technology. True or false?

10-11. Four services provided by the 3Ms OCM are organizational assessments, leadership development, organizational communication, and human performance and development. True or false?

10-12. The organizational assessment is used to "prove" that the business case for the change is valid. True or false?

10-13. The only benefits of the organizational assessment are establishing a baseline for each participant, team, and functional area from which individual and team development can be measured throughout the change process and establishing a baseline from which organizational development can be measured throughout the change process life cycle. True or false?

10-14. The only benefits of a well-designed human performance and development system are increased employee understanding of roles and performance expectations and a structured process through which company goals can be aligned with specific work-related tasks for future performance reviews. True or false?

10-15. The total amount of time required to fully implement an OCM program is 90 days. True or false?

This book has free materials available for download from the Web Added Value™ Resource Center at www.jrosspub.com.

11

OTHER APPLICATIONS OF THE 3MS METHODOLOGY

Although we believe that the application of the 3Ms methodology is almost infinite, we will present just three examples of how to fully exploit the basic thinking process of 3Ms. After a while, you will just think this way about so many of your professional and even personal performance areas. The three applications are executive leadership, conflict resolution, and project management team building. They are different enough from each other so you can see the common 3Ms approach in all of them.

EXECUTIVE LEADERSHIP

There are dozens if not hundreds of leadership models and concepts and hundreds of courses that teach leadership skills (leader effectiveness training, situational leadership, managerial grid, etc.). All of the concepts and skills-training programs purport to show how to effect desirable outcomes for project management. This may be the only universal factor across all of the models and training programs. And yet outcomes are sometimes so vague that leaders are not sure what they are leading toward.

Typically, executives are leading toward bigger, better, faster, and cheaper. Without objectives, there is no way to get specific feedback about objectives and no way to reallocate human, physical, and financial resources to greater advantage.

Our typical clients are presidents of companies or vice presidents of major divisions (R&D, marketing, operations, international, etc.) of Fortune 500 companies. Our work with them is usually in the areas of team building, leadership issues, strategic business planning, defining operational objectives, and developing a rational reward system.

Their frequent complaint to us is that however technically qualified their next level of executives/managers and no matter how many years with the company, the client alone has a total company or division-wide perspective on any specific issue that might arise. For example, if the vice president of sales wants to go after a new market, he or she may not give proper attention to its impact on the total corporate strategy or the strategic and operational objectives of the R&D, marketing, and personnel functions. If the vice president of international wants to alter a pricing strategy for one segment of exported products, he or she may not consider the impact on production and legal/regulatory implications. It is most often the president who will remind them there are other players on the team.

Another area where presidents are frustrated is often they are the only ones preoccupied with creating a vision of the company's future. This future usually relates to new R&D efforts for completely new products, challenges and dangers of the international marketplace, and new ways to reorganize and produce to increase productivity, respond to new regulatory guidelines, or cut costs.

In all of these areas, these CEOs ask us: "Why don't others think about these things?" Our discussions usually go like this:

Question: "Let's take the vice president of sales who hasn't proposed new product lines to you in two years. What was his salary increase and bonus last year?"

President: "The most I could give him. It was very generous. That's what I don't understand. He and the others are earning well beyond their value in the marketplace, and yet they don't contribute as leaders — with foresight and vision."

Question: "That's it. You reward them for what they give you. You have not defined your reward system to reflect what you want."

President: "But I have told them repeatedly how unhappy I am with their contribution as leaders and visionaries."

Question: First of all, did you tell them you expected a futuristic or global or CEO-type input when you hired them?"

President: "No. At their level, they should assume that as part of their job.

Question: "...and obviously they haven't."

President: "Yes, but..."

Question: "...and in all the years you have paid them considerably well for being your managers, good subordinates, and for not taking the initiative in regard to company-level strategies and futures?"

President: "Yeah, I guess you're right. So what do I do?"

Our answer, with variations on this theme, has been to develop key value areas (KVAs) and performance objectives with metrics, weightings, and standards that incorporate leadership, vision, and strategic thinking. This behavior becomes a formal accountability, not just a hope. Depending on the situation, these account-

Table 11-1. Changing KVA Weightings to Change Behavior

Old KVAs		New KVAs	
Sales	50%	Sales	40%
Training	30%	Training	20%
Recruiting	20%	Recruiting	20%
		New product development	20%

abilities can affect base salary, bonuses, or both, the last of which sends the strongest message. The next strongest depends upon whether the proportion and absolute dollars of salary or bonus represent the next largest amount of dollars.

Here is the approach. If the vice president of sales has not been responsive in the area of contributing to new product development when he or she and his or her staff necessarily know what the market might want, alter the basic KVAs, assuming they were formalized in the first place. Use the 3Ms approach to alter the weightings of the objectives (Table 11-1). The new profile of weightings of the vice president's objectives now has the individual looking at new product development as 20% of his or her KVAs (key result areas).

There is an even more specific level of handling this issue based on the 3Ms approach to setting standards per objective (Table 11-2). Thus, the president could establish distinguishing standards for this objective, for example a 20% weighting of the new objective with specific standards to evaluate measurable outcomes. In this way, the vice president will know, without ambiguity, what level of performance is expected in the area of new product proposals. The impact on the vice president's reward system becomes a matter of mathematics — not subjectivity and not an interpersonal debate with the president.

Ideally, the vice president of sales will accept the reconfiguration of his or her KVAs and performance standards for the new objectives and agree that both are fair, required of the role, necessary for the company's continued growth, etc. On the other hand, there may be no agreement about these new priorities. After all, this change may be difficult after years of being rewarded without contributing in this area.

If there is an impasse, there might be other tough choices to make. Does the president want to find another vice president of sales that will deliver this 20%

Table 11-2. Performance Objectives to Support New KVA

At least three product proposals accepted by the lab and marketing as having high potential	Excellent
At least two	Very Good
At least one	Satisfactory
No new product proposals	Unsatisfactory

contribution? Does the president hire someone else to deliver these results, create a new position of vice president of strategic planning, or hire a consultant? Would any of these moves be accepted by the vice president of sales, or would the individual leave, taking all he or she knows about products, technology, and marketing?

These decisions are not easy and must be considered along with a whole host of other variables. Each instance has a different resolution. One thing all of our client presidents do have is a conceptual framework for realizing how they can get new behaviors where the reward system has not demanded these behaviors and contributions in the past.

CONFLICT RESOLUTION

When there is any kind of conflict between individuals or functions within a company, the first thing we do is determine if the source of the conflict lies in objectives at that level or above. The objectives might be absent, ambiguous, nonaligned, mutually exclusive, antagonistic, weighted in a noncomplementary fashion, etc.

This enables us to approach the conflict with a focus on agreed upon results as the largest context. Typically, the resolution works out quite easily when the first step is the determination of what outcomes have the greatest value to the company. The dynamics then become company focused, not person focused.

Whenever you commit to an objective, your boss must make a commitment to you in terms of time, money, and effort, both his or her and/or other staff. You can expect, as most people have experienced, that often these commitments seem to disappear during the year. Most employees hold their tongue or get defensive when they cannot accomplish all they promised, even when others withdrew their committed support.

We always take this 3Ms approach first, even though we teach a lot of interpersonal conflict resolution skills that rely on active listening, confrontation, and joint problem solving. We still consider the objectives-focused approach to be the more simple and efficient.

With this 3Ms approach, the measures of outcomes are so precise that the concomitant support is built into the achievement of the outcomes. To achieve these outcomes, you are obligated to confront your boss and/or others whose withdrawal of support is affecting you. The more explicit you make this at the beginning, the easier it will be midyear. Do not wait until year end to explain why you did not do what you were supposed to. Actually, your quarterly reviews should realign your support with your objectives. This whole paragraph could have been titled "How to Manage Your Boss."

This objectives-based conflict occurs when someone reneges on their commitment to you and/or you did not realize while setting your objectives that you were dependent on someone else doing something for you or with you. If that individual does not feel obligated to help you because, apart from being a good person, he or she does not have any formal objectives-based reason to, go back and confront your boss about the situation to be resolved in several ways:

1. Your boss will support your confronting the other person to get his or her support.
2. If your boss refuses, he or she will support your confronting the other person's boss.
3. Your boss will confronts the other individual and/or that individual's boss.
4. All three or four of you sit down and negotiate who is to change what and by when, which may include changing your objective's weighting (so it is less of a priority), the standard (so you are not expected to perform as well), or the deadline (you are given longer to complete it).

When Manager and Subordinate Disagree

First of all, with weighting and standards, there is little left to subjective judgment. There can be disagreement about the KVAs, weightings, and objectives. However, the boss is paying the salary and has the legitimate authority to determine the relative value he or she is paying for.

A valid difference of opinion occurs when there is no resolution about the standards of performance for a particular objective. The employee may suffer because the standards are truly set too high. In this case, there are at least several options:

1. Establish a first-quarter objective as a valid (from the boss's perspective) indicator of progress toward the annual objective.
2. Use one quarter to monitor effort and results so both have data to reevaluate the annualized objective standards.
3. Both parties must be open to having their beliefs proven wrong. Perhaps the boss had different assumptions about the conditions, sources of help, etc. Perhaps the employee did not anticipate how easy certain aspects would be or how much support he or she would get from the boss and others.

It would be impossible to cover every possible kind of conflict that might exist even within the 3Ms context, but we have described one of the most common and how to resolve it.

PROJECT MANAGEMENT TEAM BUILDING

A 3Ms Fantasy: Total Agreement About Everything!

Imagine there's no countries
It isn't hard to do
Nothing to kill or die for
No religion too
Imagine all the people
Living life in peace

As fantastic as John Lennon's lyrics are, it is thought by many to be just as fantastic to have a work group in total agreement about each other's priorities and the performance standards of these priorities. To have this with full participation of the manager, and beyond that to have complete agreement about what performance standard will have what performance appraisal judgment is the best that can be expected.

Yet this was achieved, with perfection up and down five levels of a software engineering environment. At every level, consensus was developed about all individual KVAs, objectives, the weightings (priorities) per objective, the standards of everyone's performance objective, and how total performance would be judged and ultimately rewarded. Everyone knew exactly who had to support who and to what extent. The understanding and potential for teamwork at this point were near perfect; the challenge was to maintain this level throughout the performance period.

Impossible, you say. Performance appraisals are at best, you say, a necessary evil for altering, usually in a positive direction, someone's paycheck. Yet we accomplished this over a period of a year working with the director and top 40 managers of a division of about 100 engineers and technicians.

Without getting too technical, here is how we did it:

1. Made an overall presentation about 3Ms as a way of defining the results they were getting paid to produce
2. Showed how all of their work was measurable (qualitatively and quantitatively)
3. Showed how each objective could get a weighting proportionate to the value of each person's total job
4. Showed how each objective could have distinguishing standards of performance and how each standard equated with a shared judgment about how well the results were achieved

Why was this seemingly impossible project accomplished with near mathematical and group perfection?

1. **Collaboration** — Tied in with the director's openness to this approach was his modeling of a total collaborative effort. This approach affected four levels of managers. The director met with his direct reports and modeled a total collaborative effort in setting objectives. His guidelines were goals, or statements of general direction, and even these were negotiated.
2. **History** — The performance appraisal system we encountered was focused on personality traits rather than results oriented. We call this the psychiatric approach. It had been introduced during a period of layoffs, and people thought it would be used to support termination decisions. There had been little training to support its implementation, and even that soon ended.

    The downside of this history was that people were very skeptical and even cynical. The upside is once they saw that the new system could rationalize salary decisions, it appealed to their sense of an orderly world.
3. **Longevity** — Engineers in this division had worked with each other for decades and had a pretty good idea of what each other's jobs were, although they did not know this in the precise terms that this 3Ms approach de-

manded. They were all bright and eager to learn more about the potential for greater mutual cooperation and support.
4. **Secure environment** — The initial introduction of the current approach was long past, and except for its lasting bitterness, there was no suspicion that the new approach would in any way endanger job security.
5. **Technology of measurement** — In our approach, anyone's performance objectives with absolute precision cannot take more than one page. Additional information that may be critical in some relationships, such as purpose of objectives, needed resources, reasons, constraints, and action plans, is optional and can be documented if someone wants to.
6. **Supportive director** — The director was willing to support this new approach. The rest of the organization was still committed to an approach that had people documenting monthly staff luncheons (as many as 10 pages for some). The director decided that he would not abandon the old approach, but would use our approach for internal consumption initially and the traditional approach for the external world, at least until his division felt comfortable with our approach.

SUMMARY

The 3Ms approach is more than another way to measure, manage, improve, and reward performance; it is a way of thinking about how to define the value you bring to your job (or any relationship) and how to measure the value you create. With the 3Ms approach, you have a particular logic that can be applied to almost any area of your life. In many ways, most people have learned some of the 3Ms approach, but never in the same disciplined and rigorous manner.

This chapter described how the 3Ms thought process and technology have been applied to executive leadership, conflict resolution, and project management team building. In each case, the same processes and steps were used: Define the value of the role, deliverable, etc. Create KVAs that give weightings to the value. Create performance objectives that describe the results in measurable terms with metrics, weightings, and standards. When people have mastered this mode of thinking, all kinds of usually frustrating situations are quickly defined and resolved.

QUESTIONS

11-1. The 3Ms is a logical, technical process for defining value and outcomes and is useful for an almost infinite number of applications. True or false?

11-2. As shown in the executive leadership case, the 3Ms can be used to create a reward system that makes subordinates pay attention to executive needs. True or false?

11-3. Many reward systems are out of sync with what the executive really wants. True or false?

11-4. The 3Ms allows disputants to lessen the emotionalism of disagreement by focusing on measurable outcomes that both can agree are desirable. True or false?

11-5. By creating performance objectives with metrics, weightings, and standards, ambiguity about expected deliverables or performance can be reduced to zero. True or false?

11-6. The 3Ms approach can fully resolve all conflicts that any executive might have. True or false?

11-7. Even with the 3Ms there may be a difference of opinion regarding how to establish the measures defined by the standards. True or false?

11-8. In using the 3Ms for conflict resolution, the four variables that can bring disputants closer together are modify the metrics, weightings, standards, and time frames of the performance objectives. True or false?

11-9. Ambiguous objectives are always the root cause of project management conflict. True or false?

11-10. The 3Ms process is able to exploit traditional ways of managing people and processes. True or false?

11-11. Annual performance objectives are always the most practical for managing progress toward predefined success. True or false?

11-12. In a project management environment, alignment cannot occur beyond four levels of the organization. True or false?

11-13. The components of success for the project management case study in this chapter were longevity, history, technology of measurement, supportive director, collaboration, and secure environment. True or false?

11-14. Though the 3Ms is useful for work-related tasks, it has limited use for the social environment. True or false?

11-15. The three case studies in this chapter show how the 3Ms approach can be used for everything that is performance related. True or false?

This book has free materials available for download from the Web Added Value™ Resource Center at www.jrosspub.com.

12

APPLYING THEORY OF CONSTRAINTS METRICS THE TOC WAY

By Gerald I. Kendall, PMP

"Tell me how you measure me, and I'll tell you how I will behave. If my measurements are not clear, no one can predict how I will behave, not even me." This adage, from Dr. Eli Goldratt,* gives the direction for a metrics solution, according to a methodology called the Theory of Constraints, or TOC for short. TOC assumes that there are very few factors governing the throughput of any organization and that the best results come from finding the simplicity in the midst of all the complexity we face.

What is the problem with most metrics today? There are really two problems:

- Encouraging people to do the wrong things
- Not driving people to focus on doing the few right things

If you find yourself in a hole, the first thing to do is stop digging. The TOC approach recognizes that human beings are probably *not* going to be driven correctly by 8 or 12 measurements, such as advocated in a balanced scorecard system. In such a complex system, measurements are almost always in conflict with each other. Whenever you put efficiency or cost reduction measurements on the same scorecard as throughput or getting work done, the person being measured will frequently find himself or herself in a conflict. This person has the perfect excuse for missing a number of measurements in any time period. At the same time, the

---

* Goldratt is the author of the multimillion-copy best-selling book *The Goal* and several others, including *Critical Chain, Necessary But Not Sufficient, It's Not Luck, The Haystack Syndrome,* and *The Theory of Constraints.*

boss has the perfect reason to crucify someone, because in any time period it is likely that one or more measurements will be missed. As Jim Collins points out in his bestseller *Good to Great,** the difference between good and great companies is that the great companies get rid of their bad measurements, the ones that demotivate or confuse people.

The TOC approach is a holistic approach. It advocates simplicity over complexity. One primary measurement and one secondary measurement are usually enough to drive the correct human behavior in any given situation. This chapter introduces the TOC metrics for senior management, for support organizations in a supply chain, and for project management.

CHARACTERISTICS OF GOOD METRICS

A good measurement should drive a person in any function to do what is good for the organization as a whole. While this may sound obvious, some further background and examples show why, in many organizations, people in functional areas are actively encouraged to do things that are *not* good for the organization as a whole.

The problem really begins with how organizations deal with today's complex world. One way to deal with complexity is to divide the organization into "manageable pieces," which are usually functional areas. The senior management then gives specific metrics to each functional area. Most functional areas are cost centers (e.g., production, engineering, finance, administration, IT). Therefore, when measuring these areas, it is natural to see a strong emphasis on cost or its equivalent, efficiency.

One real-life example comes from the armed forces of a country that I will, kindly, leave nameless. The sergeant responsible for equipment maintenance for his unit, which was active in the field, noticed that one of the missiles was not functioning. Further diagnosis found a part that was bad. The sergeant called the parts manager, who said that he had the part in stock but couldn't ship it to the sergeant. "Why not?" asked the bewildered sergeant. "Because this is my last part, and if I ship it to you, it will show up on a report as an out-of-stock situation, which gives me a bad rating." So the sergeant had to leave his unit partially defenseless for two weeks, until the parts manager was able to fully stock up.

To illustrate that this is not an isolated case but in fact very common throughout industry, consider the following story, which is also true. A procurement manager who was primarily measured on cost of materials was very proud that he had saved his company $1.3 million per year by changing vendors. At the same time, the plant manager proved that the new materials, which were causing dozens of problems

---

* Jim Collins, *Good to Great,* HarperCollins, New York, 2001. Collins calls "great" companies those that outperformed their peers by an average of at least 7 times over a 15-year period.

daily on the shop floor, were costing the company over $25 million per year in lost sales.

The problem with these metrics is that they only consider the impact of any decision on one part of the organization and not on the organization as a whole. Therefore, one of the most important characteristics of any good measurement system is that it reflects the impact on the entire system, not on one isolated piece.

This brings home the second problem with many measurement systems today — the distortion of cost accounting and cost allocations. Two examples will illustrate the distortions.

Cost Accounting Distortion Example 1: Judgment of the System as a Whole

One of the distortions of cost accounting is how it measures the performance of the system as a whole. As just one example, ask yourself why companies in so many industries, such as communications, automotive, and computers, continue producing at a high rate long after the end consumers stop buying. One reason is that cost accounting measures the production silo on efficiencies, encouraging these companies toward high utilization of their resources. The higher the machine and labor utilization, the greater the efficiency reported. Cost accounting also lists the resulting excess inventories as "assets" on the company's financial report. Cost accounting then reports these burdensome inventories as artificial higher company profits, by reducing the cost of goods sold.*

Also, when one company in the supply chain, such as an automotive manufacturer, is able to pass its inventory off to the dealers (the next link in the supply chain), in the short term the cost frame of reference makes its results look good, by recording these transfers as sales. However, unless the end consumer has bought, no one in the supply chain has sold. Inventory in the supply chain may be well beyond the level needed to satisfy end consumer demand. The fact that the inventory was recorded as "sales" in the manufacturer's profit-and-loss statement is totally distorted. It is the manufacturer that must now provide incentives to consumers, reducing its own profits and the dealers' profits and cutting into sales of the next model year. In reality, the entire supply chain is actually worse off than before — the opposite of the way the current frame of reference, cost accounting, reports it!

Today, whether a company uses traditional cost accounting or its popular replacement, activity-based costing, the distortions of allocated costs still apply. These distortions represent another failed attempt to deal with complexity by breaking down a system into smaller parts and trying to optimize within each part.

---

* By a distortion of cost accounting, when a company has more inventory at the end of a reporting period than it had at the beginning, the cost of goods sold (which includes the difference between starting and ending inventory) appears to decrease artificially.

The distortions are so subjective that there is a popular joke in the accounting profession. When you ask an accountant how much something costs, the answer is "How much would you like it to cost?" This chapter does not put blame on the accounting profession for distortions. Accountants look continually for better ways to help managers make more effective decisions. Rather, I am simply pointing out the distortions embedded within current systems.

Cost Accounting Distortion Example 2: Judgment on Make/Buy Alternatives

Cost accounting, as a way to manage complexity, can lead a company to wrongly believe that outsourcing will be "more cost effective." This has happened in both outsourcing some manufacturing and also outsourcing of services such as IT. With cost allocations, a company looks at the "cost" per manufactured part, for example, as the actual cost of raw materials plus the allocated cost of labor and other overhead. The more you allocate, the better the outsourcing alternative looks. Often, cost allocations are made very subjectively, without really understanding the impact on the organization as a whole.

For example, when a manager decides to transfer the manufacturing of a part to an outside supplier, many of the allocated costs do not, in reality, go away. If 10% of a worker's time is allocated to producing a part, and that part is subcontracted, does the worker lose 10% of his or her wages? Not at all. Does 10% of the depreciation on the machine used to produce the part disappear? No way! What about the heat, electricity, and other operating expenses? While there may be some decrease, it usually is nowhere near what has been allocated to individual parts.

At the same time that some of the allocated costs are not realized as savings, the subcontractor is charging much more than the raw material cost to supply the part. Much of the "savings" is pure fiction! In effect, in many cases, the subcontracted part costs more and, at the same time, reduces flexibility and profit.

However, the effects can go much further than this immediate negative impact on profit. Consider what happened to some U.S. companies that decided to outsource their manufacturing to the Far East. The lead time for products and services went up, so inventories in the supply chain increased dramatically. At some companies, the lead time increase meant that they were less responsive to consumer demand. The resulting shortages of some popular products meant that they eventually lost customer sales and at the same time got stuck with huge inventories of less popular products. Leverage was diminished.

Similarly, cost accounting can distort judgment on investment in new equipment, judgment of profit centers, and judgment on product line profitability.* A

---

* A detailed discussion of these distortions appears in the self-learning tool *TOC Insights into Finance and Measurements* by Eli and Rami Goldratt (available at www.tocinternational.com).

- THROUGHPUT – T
- INVESTMENT – I
- OPERATING EXPENSE – OE

Figure 12-1. Throughput Flow

company will be quickly distracted from the company goals if it continually makes bad decisions driven by poor management accounting support.

METRICS FOR THE SYSTEM AS A WHOLE

In the new frame of reference, there are only three global parameters needed to measure the impact of any management decision at any level (Figure 12-1). *Throughput* (T) is the rate at which the organization generates goal units. In for-profit organizations, goal units are expressed in dollars. Throughput is calculated by taking the revenue received from customers in a given time period and subtracting amounts paid in raw materials and direct expenses to outside suppliers for each product or service sold. Every dollar of throughput generated is money that is left in the company's bank account after paying raw material vendors. Since throughput is a "rate," it can be expressed per hour, per week, etc. Note that throughput is not recognized until money has been received from the customer.

In order to generate throughput, a company makes *investment* (I), both in terms of capital (buildings, equipment, computer systems, etc.) and in terms of inventory (raw materials, work in process, finished goods).

The money that the organization spends every month to turn investment into throughput is called *operating expense* (OE). This money includes salaries, depreciation expense, costs of supplies, heat, electricity, rent, etc.

From these three global parameters, two derivatives are:

- Net profit = Throughput – Operating expense (NP = T – OE)
- Return on investment = Net profit divided by Investment [ROI = (T – OE)/I]

Driving Change in Behavior by T, I, and OE

Using the new frame of reference, any manager, in judging what actions to take, will use the impact on throughput, investment, and operating expense as his or her guide. If a manager is recommending a decision and has no idea what the impact will be on the company in terms of throughput, investment, and operating expense, then how dare he or she make such a recommendation!

There are now many documented examples that illustrate the simplicity, guidance, and power that this new frame provides.* In the example discussed above, a procurement manager made a decision to replace materials suppliers with cheaper vendors, using cost savings as his frame of reference. The savings were U.S. $1.3 million. In the new framework, this manager would be required to calculate the net impact of his decision on throughput, investment, and operating expense for the entire company, not just the operating expense savings for procurement.

How could a procurement manager possibly estimate, in advance, what the impact of a change in materials would be on production? Since this decision impacts both operating expense and throughput, the procurement and operations managers would need to conduct tests with the new materials to assess the impact before the final decision is made. The real-life calculations for this example were as follows:

- Impact on throughput
    - Cost of raw materials decreased by $1.3 million
    - Lost revenues due to material problems were $82,800 per day, based on production tests
    - Revenues decreased by $29.8 million per year
- Impact on operating expense
    - Waste increased by $4,000 per day, based on production tests
    - Operating expense increased by $1.44 million per year
    - Carrying cost on $200,000 reduction in inventory saving, at 10%
    - Operating expense reduced by $20,000 per year
- Impact on investment
    - Switching vendors requires new testing equipment
    - Investment increased by $35,000 total
    - Raw materials inventory can be reduced by $200,000

If the decision is executed as described, the following summarizes the expected results (note that Δ means "change in"):

$$\Delta T = \$1.3 \text{ million} - \$29.8 \text{ million} = -\$28.5 \text{ million}$$

$$\Delta OE = \$1.44 \text{ million} - \$0.02 \text{ million} = \$1.42 \text{ million}$$

$$\Delta I = \$35,000 - \$200,000 = -\$165,000$$

---

* For example, see Statements on Management Accounting #4HH, Institute of Management Accountants, Montvale, NJ, 1999; Thomas Corbett, *Throughput Accounting*, North River Press, Great Barrington, MA, 1998; Victoria J. Mabin and Steven J. Balderstone, *The World of the Theory of Constraints*, St. Lucie Press, Boca Raton, FL, 2000.

In the example, even though investment in inventory was reduced by $165,000, the devastating impact on throughput and operating expense means that this would obviously be a bad decision if implemented as is. However, the procurement manager had a great idea to begin with — to procure materials through different vendors, reducing lead time and reducing cost. The idea has some horrible negative consequences if executed without cooperation from operations.

When operating in silos, it is guaranteed that decisions will be executed without considering the negative consequences on the company as a whole. With holistic metrics, understanding the impact on throughput, investment, and operating expense globally across the company, the procurement manager will work to find suppliers that he can bring up to current standards. He will see part of his mission as minimizing the impact of any transition on production. He will *not* be measured on local improvements in isolation. As a result, he will not be satisfied until global improvement is achieved.

METRICS FOR A SUPPLY CHAIN

Two key measurements are needed to cause each member of the supply chain and each supporting department to operate in perfect alignment with each other:

1. **Throughput $ days (late)** — A supply chain must recognize that shortages of product increase the risk of losing both the current sale and future business. For some products, the end consumer will tolerate some shortages, but not for too long. To take this into account, this measurement multiplies the late throughput, valued at the point of end consumer sale, by the number of days that the throughput is late. If one line item on an order is missed, throughput $ days is calculated based on the value of the total order, recognizing the client's irritation that one item was missed. The objective is 0.
2. **Inventory $ days** — People usually describe inventory either in terms of its dollar value or in terms of how many days of consumption it represents. This measurement considers both attributes by multiplying the value of the inventory within the supply chain (at raw material cost) by the number of days that the material is held within the supply chain at any level. The objective is to reduce, without negatively impacting throughput $ days (late).

Throughput $ Days (Late)

In many supply chains, the end product has a high price tag (hundreds or thousands of dollars), while many components of that product have minimal cost (dollars or even pennies). The entire supply chain benefits if the supplier of a $1 component reacts urgently when it is blocking a $25,000 sale.

To help each organization within a supply chain determine what is urgent to downstream links, a daily or weekly report is needed showing throughput $ days (late) from their customers — the next link down in the supply chain. The throughput $ days are expressed using the pricing of the end consumer. Such a report tells each organization the magnitude of a problem order to the entire supply chain and how to prioritize its actions.

For example, assume that company A manufactures a $1 shear pin that is used in building a transmission by company B. Company B ships its transmission to company C, a major automotive manufacturer. If company A is one day late with an order of 100 shear pins, it might ordinarily look at this order as unimportant, since it only represents $100 to the company. However, each shear pin is holding up a $25,000 sale at the end consumer level, representing $20,000 throughput to the entire supply chain. Company A receives a report showing $2 million throughput $ days for the shear pins (100 × $20,000). Now company A understands the importance of this order and how to prioritize its efforts.

If the same order is late for a second day, the report would show $4 million throughput $ days (100 × $20,000 × 2). The amount will continue to increase until this order is satisfied.

Another example deals with quality problems. If company A in the above example ships the shear pins on time, but a quality problem shows up at the automotive manufacturer on the day the shipment is due, the transmissions are returned to company B. Company B now has $2 million throughput $ days assigned to it — the order is now late. It is a hot potato for company B. It examines the transmissions and determines that the problem is with the shear pins. The throughput $ days are now assigned to company A and will stay with company A until the problem is resolved.

If the problem requires another two days to resolve, and company A ships the corrected shear pins to company B, the order, which is now three days late, has an assigned throughput $ days of $6 million (3 days × $2 million). It is an even hotter potato for company B.

Similarly, if the problem resides with a materials or packaging supplier to company A, the procurement department in company A has the hot potato until the problem is resolved. By combining both dollars and days in this measurement, the supply chain is more likely to retain customers by avoiding long stock-outs and long repair periods for quality problems. In order for throughput $ days to be effective, the members of the supply chain must agree to use this measurement to drive priorities throughout the supply chain.

Inventory $ Days

Too much inventory in a supply chain hurts in several different ways:

- It increases the cost of obsolescence. When replacement products are released, the more inventory there is in the supply chain, the greater the cost of obsolescence.

- It delays the introduction of a new product into the market. Distributors and retailers will be reluctant to stock the new product until they get rid of their supply of old product.
- It spoils sales for the new product. As soon as a retailer, for example, knows that one of its products will soon be obsolete, it puts the product on sale. Everyone who buys the sale product will not buy the new product.
- When retail shelves are stocked with too much inventory of individual items, sales opportunities are missed. Due to the constraint of the amount of shelf space available, retailers cannot have the variety of product on display, which means that they miss some consumer sales.
- The more inventory, the greater the carrying costs and the greater the other operating expenses (shipping, cost of rework, etc.).

The inventory $ days measurement is secondary to throughput $ days. Therefore, it is very important that reductions in supply chain inventory do not cause problems in missing orders. Some inventory is necessary in the supply chain as protection against Murphy — fluctuations and problems in transportation, manufacturing, and end customer demand.

By making this a supply chain measurement, rather than an individual entity measurement, the behavior within the supply chain drives a holistic result. For example, the correct distribution of inventory within most supply chains is to hold the most inventory where the forecast is most accurate and the fluctuations are smallest. This implies that more inventory should be held at or close to the manufacturer, with smaller inventories at the distributor and smallest inventory at the source closest to the end customer.

Today, many organizations within a supply chain try to reduce their inventory investment by pushing the inventory on to the next link in the supply chain. They can then claim this as a "sale" on their books. However, this behavior hurts the performance of the supply chain in terms of both total inventory carried within the supply chain and stock-outs.

Therefore, as with the throughput $ days measurement, agreement is needed across all supply chain organizations to look at the overall inventory rather than an individual organization's inventory.

PROJECT MANAGEMENT METRICS

I am a personal witness to the fact that the same problems that existed in projects over 30 years ago still exist today. The only difference is that today the problems of finishing projects late, over budget, and not within scope are far more common and significant. From the analysis done by Goldratt in project management,[*] the metric that drives behavior contrary to the goal is to measure people to finish their tasks according to an estimated time.

---

[*] See Eliyahu M. Goldratt, *Critical Chain,* North River Press, Great Barrington, MA, 1997.

Goldratt claims that as soon as a person gives an estimate for a project task, it becomes a commitment. Since resources on projects are rated according to how reliable they are, it is natural for a resource to take the uncertainty of project work into account by inflating its estimate. In fact, there are many pressures to inflate estimates, including:

- Murphy exists in projects.
- Project work, by definition, includes many tasks that were not done in exactly the same way before.
- Management is likely to cut back on task time estimates to gain a more aggressive schedule.
- Dependencies exist that can delay the start of your work, thereby delaying the finish (i.e., you are dependent on having other resources finish their work on time, and the more dependencies exist within a project, the greater the chance of slippage).
- You cannot always be certain of which resources will be assigned to a project. Often, the "best" resources are already tied up on other projects. This means that many projects suffer from being forced to use less experienced resources.

There are three considerations for success in project management:

- Choosing the right project mix
- Ensuring the correct scope in each project
- Driving projects through to completion as quickly as possible

The first two items above are the subject of strategy, which is discussed extensively in two other books by this author.* For metrics, I will concentrate on the last issue — speeding up project delivery.

With most project task estimates having extra time embedded in inflated estimates, how can we possibly explain why so many projects finish later than planned? An examination of human behavior on projects shows that this safety embedded in task estimates is often misused.

In juggling work on different projects and operational responsibilities, the project team member must decide what to work on right now. People, knowing that they have safety in their estimate, often delay starting work on a given project task until much later than they had originally planned. Instead, they choose more urgent tasks. Goldratt terms this behavior Student Syndrome. This refers to the behavior of students who have three weeks notice of an exam, but wait until the night before

---

* See Gerald I. Kendall, *Viable Vision: Transforming Total Sales into Net Profits,* J. Ross Publishing, Ft. Lauderdale, FL, 2005 and Gerald I. Kendall and Steven C. Rollins, *Advanced Project Portfolio Management and the PMO: Multiplying ROI at Warp Speed,* J. Ross Publishing, Ft. Lauderdale, FL, 2003.

the exam to start studying. When a team member starts a task much later than originally planned, and Murphy does occur, the task finishes later than its estimate. The effect of Student Syndrome is made worse by the dependencies between tasks on a project. While a team member delays the completion of his or her task, all following tasks, dependent on this task, are waiting. If some of the following tasks are also subject to Student Syndrome, the delay in getting a project completed will be substantial.

Another common behavior further delays vital project work. Project managers are under tremendous pressure from executives to show progress *now*, so they push team members very hard to cut task time estimates. As a result, when a team member puts up a tough fight and wins a concession on a task estimate, the team member and project manager both consider that estimate a due date.

Team members know that if, by some miracle, they finish a task in less time and turn it in earlier than the due date, next time they will be expected to finish tasks in record time. Therefore, in cases where team members do finish the specified work early, they prefer to work up to the due date, adding unneeded bells and whistles and doing extra checking. This behavior is called Parkinson's Law, where work expands to fill the time available. The devastating waste to the company occurs with the combination of Student Syndrome and Parkinson's Law. These behaviors drive up individual task time durations, resulting in longer projects. While these negative effects are serious, there is another sinister factor driving project durations through the roof in the multiproject environment.

THE MULTIPROJECT ENVIRONMENT

Most organizations today operate in a multiproject environment — an environment where different projects share one or more common resources. In fact, in real life, managers are not so polite in their description. They usually call it "fighting" over resources rather than "sharing."

Once again, local optima reign supreme. Functional heads initiate projects, irrespective of the capacity of the organization to do the work. They are doing this for an excellent reason: if they do not meet their goals by the next review period, they may no longer be employed or they may miss a significant measurement. Executives assume that the sooner a project is initiated, the sooner it will be completed.

Each senior executive, who is accountable for results, sees project initiation as his or her right. By comparison, this is like giving each functional executive an unlimited numbers of blank checks with the instruction to make whatever capital investments he or she feels are necessary.

The only difference with projects is that we are dealing with limited human capital, in addition to dollars. Every organization has many more opportunities to improve, using projects, than it has the resources with which to execute those projects. When too many projects are activated simultaneously, the result is bad multitasking — a huge waste of resource time.

Bad multitasking occurs when team members split their time between multiple tasks such that the combined duration of all projects is dramatically increased. There are two potential negative effects when a resource takes on multiple tasks at once and juggles, doing parts of each task every few days. One negative effect of bad multitasking is that the level of effort for each task increases. Due to effort to regain concentration each time the same task is restarted, a task with three weeks of effort can easily turn into four weeks or more.

The other negative effect is the extended duration of each task. When the effect of multitasking is combined with additional start-up time, a task that could have been finished in 10 days of dedicated time is spread over 4 weeks or more. In new product development, this means that a company loses or defers many weeks of sales and may miss a competitive window. For projects that bring internal benefits, it means those benefits were delayed or missed for several or many weeks.

Correct Metrics for Projects

It is not important if an individual task finishes on time. What is most important is that the project finishes on time, at the earliest possible time to drive benefits to the organization. Therefore, to discourage Student Syndrome and Parkinson's Law behavior, implement the following changes:

- Cut all task estimates in half. Thus, when a team member sees a very aggressive time estimate, he or she is unlikely to delay starting the task and is unlikely to try to add bells and whistles to the task when finished.
- Do not measure people on finishing their tasks on time, formally or informally. Make it clear to all team members that you no longer care if a task finishes on time or not. It is the project deadline that is most important.
- Implement the "relay runner" work ethic. When a resource is assigned a task, the task is completed as quickly as possible and the baton is passed on to the next resource as early as possible.

To take care of the bad multitasking problem, the new metric is to stagger projects according to the capacity of one resource, the organization's strategic resource in the multiproject environment. This resource is the resource that is most heavily loaded, or the resource that is most badly multitasked. Another way of identifying the strategic resource is to look for the resource that delays the entire collection of the organization's progress the most.

When projects are staggered according to this one resource, project success rates increase dramatically and flow much more quickly through the organization. Numerous real-life case studies now show project durations being cut by half or more through the methodology, including the new metrics.

SUMMARY

Every organization has two choices for metrics — complexity or simplicity. The frame of reference described in this chapter, based on a methodology called TOC, has been implemented in many companies across the supply chain. This approach looks for the simplicity inherent in every complex system. It has been applied to marketing, production, engineering, project management, distribution, and company strategy. In a study conducted by Mabin and Balderstone[*] of dozens of reported cases, the following mean improvements were noted:

- Lead time: 70%
- Due date performance: 44%
- Inventory reduction: 49%
- Revenue improvement: 83%
- Profitability improvement: 116%

Over 20 books have been published about TOC and many self-study materials are available. You are welcome to investigate further at www.tocinternational.com or by e-mail to Gerryikendall@cs.com.

QUESTIONS

12-1. The TOC approach encourages a balanced scorecard system. True or false?

12-2. Whenever you include efficiency or cost reduction measurements on the same scorecard as throughput or getting work done, the person being measured will frequently:
   a. Perform better
   b. Remain unclear
   c. Find himself or herself in conflict
   d. Blame others

12-3. The difference between good and great companies is that in great companies:
   a. Project work is aligned with corporate objectives
   b. Executives have more oversight
   c. Project teams are happier in their work
   d. Bad measurements, the ones that demotivate or confuse people, are eliminated

12-4. A good measurement should drive a person in any function to do what is good for the organization as a whole. True or false?

---

[*] *International Journal of Operations and Production Management,* Spring 2003.

12-5. One of the distortions of cost accounting is how it:
   a. Measures the performance of the system as a whole
   b. Improves team speed-to-market performance
   c. Optimizes work throughput
   d. Supports business growth
12-6. Cost accounting, as a way to manage complexity, can lead a company to:
   a. Fast business growth
   b. Wrongly believe that outsourcing will be more cost effective
   c. Properly measure worker value
   d. Better recognize work fulfillment
12-7. Return on investment is derived from the net profit divided by the investment. True or false?
12-8. There are three considerations for success in project management. Which of the following is not one of them:
   a. Choosing the right project mix
   b. Ensuring the correct scope of each project
   c. Keeping the project scorecard current
   d. Driving projects through to completion as quickly as possible
12-9. When work estimates are given, it is often found that work expands to meet these estimates. This is known as Parkinson's Law. True or false?
12-10. When safety exists in work estimates, people often delay starting work on a given task until much later than planned. This is knows as Student Syndrome. True or false?
12-11. Bad multitasking often occurs when team members split their time between multiple tasks such that:
   a. Overworked team member quits
   b. Work needed now is not started until it is late
   c. Combined duration of all work is dramatically increased
   d. Project fails
12-12. It is not important if an individual task finishes on time. What is most important is that the project finishes on time, at the earliest possible time to drive benefits to the organization. True or false?
12-13. A strategic resource is that resource that is most multitasked in a multiproject environment. True or false?
12-14. Team members know that if, by some miracle, they finish a task in less time and turn the task in earlier than the due date, next time they will be expected to finish tasks in record time. True or false?
12-15. Today, when a company uses traditional cost accounting or its popular replacement, activity-based costing, the distortions of allocated costs still apply. True or false?

13

THE VALUE PROPOSITION OF AN ORGANIZATIONAL PROJECT-BASED METRICS PROGRAM

Have you heard the old adage "Figures don't lie, but liars sure can figure"? How about "If you can't measure, you can't control, and thus you cannot manage"? This statement says you must be able to measure the subject in order to better manage it. Well, we don't know about your business, but with all the job outsourcing happening, one has to wonder just what in the heck is being measured to cause management to outsource jobs. You probably know the answer. If you said the "bottom line," you are very correct. But just how the organization measured this to get the answer remains the question.

In most businesses, project delivery success or failure often means the difference between that business remaining competitive and no longer operating. Standish Group, in its "Chaos" report, indicated that five of six information technology projects fail every year! Thus, making project investments is a risky proposition for most every business. What are businesses doing about this? Where is the safety net to catch failing project investments and put them back on track? We are smarter than this, aren't we?

What would you do if suddenly your organization was asked to deliver value that was three times its annual operating budget over the fiscal year or else all of the jobs in the organization would be eliminated? This is exactly what is occurring today as businesses are moving jobs to cheaper labor markets in order to gain this organizational value. Is this necessary? Just how are these businesses determining the value they need to recognize the opportunities and threats they need to consider managing toward? In this chapter, focus is toward the riskiest part of business, project delivery. If 10% of failed project investments were saved in a business, would that be sufficient to save jobs? To save the company? To save you? What about 20%?

METRICS PROGRAM MODELS

What are the best approaches to a project-based metrics program? What types of metrics program models are there? Essentially, there are four types, and they can be combined as follows:

1. Project based versus resource based
2. Throughput optimization versus cost optimization
3. Project-based cost optimization
4. Project-based throughput optimization
5. Resource-based cost optimization
6. Resource-based throughput optimization

For the purpose of this chapter, a project-based throughput optimization model is the recommended model. This emphasis is based on speed-to-market project delivery brought about by incrementally improving tactical project progress visibility to the workforce that enables more complex cross-collaboration (improved behavior) within the workforce to recognize the identified opportunities and threats to complete project work.

Since you have already been immersed in the 3Ms methodology, we can use this methodology to analyze the paragraph above. The first step is to define the key value areas (KVAs) of this model. We could say that they are speed to market, visibility to workforce, cross-collaboration, recognition of threats, and recognition of opportunities. The weightings of these KVAs will depend on the particular context of this project, but let's say for now that these five KVAs are co-equal in value or 20% each.

The next 3Ms step is to ask for each KVA: If by year end the results of speed to market were performed at a standard of at least Satisfactory, what would that be? Let's say the answer is "due date of project delivery." In value terms, which is what our metrics approach is all about, that 20% weight KVA delivered its value relative to the cost of 20 cents per dollar of cost. This is Satisfactory.

If the KVA were to create value in excess of Satisfactory or a value of 21 cents at a cost of 20 cents, then the delivery time might be 5% quicker than expected. Depending on resources, all might agree that a 3% quicker delivery time created 5% greater value. That will be determined by the customer. That standard of at least 5% greater value is called Very Good. The highest standard in 3Ms is Excellent, where the value created is 10% above cost.

Thus we have:

                Excellent = >10% ahead of due date
                Very Good = >5% ahead of due date

Satisfactory = due date
Unsatisfactory = later than due date

The same sequence of questions will be asked of the other four remaining KVAs, and the three standards will be created. Note that there are always actually four standards. The fourth is Unsatisfactory, but this is easily measured because Unsatisfactory is when any factor that defines Satisfactory is missing.

In a project-based metrics program, all work measured is considered to be project work. This can include any or all of those initiatives that are necessary, including those that "keep the lights on." Utilizing a project-based model enables the estimate for cost and time for each project to be baselined so as to define "minimal goodness" when defining Satisfactory performance in comparing progress for a project. Thus the actual progress against cost and time becomes the variable to control for evaluating performance toward delivery. This constitutes the Measure phase of the 3Ms.

When project information collected in this manner is shared among related other projects, inter/intraproject predecessor and successor relationships in any combination can also be measured and shared. This is the scalability of the 3Ms. This helps influence (improve behavior of) other project teams to reset their sense of urgency to complete their project work. Relative to the throughput optimization versus cost optimization models, only throughput optimization brings about practical value in a project-based environment. *This is given since the impact to business expectations aligns the behavior of the workforce to that of what the business expects in achievement in the corporate objectives as long as the workforce has that visibility and values that information.* The visibility and alignment are essential to the 3Ms process as KVAs and project objectives are aligned from the top down and from the bottom up, as part of the continuous alignment process. This process enables the executive group to manage projects as it sees to what degree objectives are aligned and performing to a standard of at least Satisfactory. Not providing this awareness to the workforce often results in personal selection of what work to perform each day instead of what the business expected. Is this good? When every individual has access to his or her own performance scorecard and that of the project team, this provides even daily monitoring of results against expectations. With the use of the 3Ms online application, this can even be done 24/7, although that would be extreme.

The cost optimization model focuses on spending money on projects and resources that are allocated without much regard for the resulting influence this information has on inter/intraproject and resource behavior sense of urgency. Thus resources not on the critical path of a project receive as much attention as those that are. The same is true for projects assigned primarily to a corporate objective. Focus on which project is most important to a particular corporate objective is the key, and often this is missed in this approach. With 3Ms, the Measure phase guarantees that all project objectives are aligned with corporate objectives. It would be impossible during a Measure phase for a project to not be aligned with corporate objectives. If a new project should be created after a Measure phase, that project would be captured in the next quarterly review of the Measure phase, which is continually being updated during the Manage phase.

A resource-based metrics program places primary value on cost-optimizing resource performance and is typically measured for utilization first and effectiveness second. Businesses that are likely to utilize this model are those that provide staffing services. Resource management in these businesses is critical to their survival.

Businesses that can clearly choose between a project-based model and a resource-based model to manage development costs and throughputs must understand the significance of their choice and the resulting impact on the workforce's ability to react in a timely manner to new cyclical metric analysis given the mutual exclusivity of these two metric models. If the 3Ms model is used, it can embrace what other metrics models deem as mutually exclusive.

This cyclical "new" data will present cause and effect opportunities to drive work completion and the behavior of those who perform that work. Give this workforce sufficient time to adapt to the new information, and the results will be dramatic. Give the same workforce insufficient time to adapt, and the results may cause more rework than the original work if panic sets in; the rush to do something may impact the desired solution in the rush to perform.

Resource-based metrics programs are much more dynamic in change from year to year than project-based metrics programs. What may be key resources this year may be the lowest rated resources relative to need the following year. This radical shift in resource value is much more difficult for the business leadership to manage than the project-based option. Thus, this understanding is a major justification for businesses to become project based versus resource based in their metrics program. In application of the 3Ms approach, there is no such conflict between the two.

BENEFIT REALIZATION OF A METRICS PROGRAM

In any organization, a well-defined metrics program may yield many of the following viable benefits.

1. Strategic and tactical alignment of business expectations with those of the workforce — Each day when you come to work, how do you prioritize your work? How do you establish the sense of urgency for the workday? Are you organizing your workday based on what you need personally or what the business expects you to do?

2. Raised visibility of work delivery acceleration opportunities and/or work delivery threats for the planned and current work in the fiscal year — In other words, creating value that exceeds the standard of Satisfactory. If management, work teams, and/or team members had visibility to the opportunity that by working one more hour in a certain work week they could accelerate work completion that would result in advancing work delivery by 30 calendar days and this would impact a significant number of people and other interrelated work initiatives, would they do it? Of course they would. The question is how they would know this.

3. Incrementally improved cognitive skills so the workforce can recognize delivery acceleration opportunities and/or delivery threats to the strategic fiscal year work plan in their daily work — Changing the work attitude of how people recognize work value while performing their work is the objective. It is no longer sufficient to just perform work. Robots can do that. We must use more of our cognitive skills that have remained so underutilized in our jobs, to begin adding more value to the output we produce without raising the cost to do so. Failure to adopt this work attitude will impede the ability of a business to make competitive gains in added intrinsic value to work products and the like. A metrics program will help facilitate recognition of work delivery opportunities and threats, particularly if all work is linked and related to specific corporate objectives and made visible to the workforce for the related cause and effect results. This is exactly the mentality of the workforce when the 3Ms is part of the corporate culture.

4. Improved risk management of corporate objectives — How important is it to know that in the second quarter of the fiscal year a particular corporate objective and all related project investments can be canceled and those monies not "sunk" can be reallocated to other project investments, instead of waiting until all the monies are sunk and lost later in the year when it becomes apparent that the corporate objective effort was wasted? Certainly a metrics program can "shine a flashlight" on this information for the workforce. But the metrics program is only the messenger. Management governance must be in place to close the information loop of awareness between executives and team members.

5. Return on investment on project investments — A 10 to 40% improvement is brought about by raised visibility of tactical progress from all project investments. By adjusting the project portfolio from month to month to take advantage of business climate changes, funded work can be added, modified, or even canceled. If a business can save 20% of a funded $100 million fiscal year strategic work plan, what do you suppose the business could do with that unexpected $20 million? A metrics program is a critical tool for sustaining and growing the competitive business advantage from year to year. In the application of 3Ms, this unexpected $20 million could define a new KVA.

6. Return on investment on resource investments — A 5 to 20% improvement is realized in utilization and effectiveness for all resources in the fiscal year. Understanding what resources are working on and in what order relative to the fast-paced world of business can quickly become a quagmire for a business if the members of the workforce individually determine what work they will do each day. Consider this point in relationship to the rolling 12 months ahead. Managing all resources to be in alignment with what the business expects is worth 5% by itself. This 5% can be worth millions in saved productivity, not to mention opportunities to collect revenue sooner from these efforts. This can be documented in the performance scorecard of the project team.

7. Return on investment on specific corporate objectives — A 10 to 40% improvement in cost and achievement versus failure is possible. Managing a corporate objectives portfolio will assist in understanding what work initiatives are most critical to the benefit of everyone even in a dynamic environment. Viable visibility is a key objective for any metrics program because of the good it can bring to a business, yielding a multitude of positive effects for the work expected to be completed.

8. Return on investment on project fraud management — This is undeterminable if your organization does not have a policy. But be assured that a project fraud management program can significantly influence all aspects of project delivery, and project fraud must be measured to assess its impact against all of the above. The safer it becomes for the workforce to work at speed, the better the bottom line will appear over time if the cause and effects from the metrics are made visible to the workforce to act upon.

9. Moves a business from a cost optimization model to a model that is more focused on throughput — Filling the project delivery pipeline with more is much more fulfilling to business aspirations than optimizing cost allocations for work that is not strategically important or on the critical path. Utilizing the 3Ms Measure phase, a business will know in precise terms what measures define success and how each better standard with its focus on *output* will better focus any throughput or input efforts.

MANAGING AN ORGANIZATIONAL METRICS PROGRAM

Every fiscal year, a business plans its budget for the next fiscal year. The end result is often the fiscal year strategic work plan. Typically, this plan identifies what the corporate objectives will be, what project investments are required to achieve those corporate objectives, and what resource skills are necessary in that support. This information becomes the baseline for the fiscal year for any metrics program. Strategic planning normally prepares and facilitates the development and approval of the fiscal year strategic work plan. Strategic planning also reports on progress against the fiscal year strategic plan in a regular fashion to its primary customers, the C-level executives, corporate governance, and key stakeholders.

The Project Management Office (PMO) has been growing in prominence in businesses everywhere. The PMO has been proven to deliver 10 to 40% return on investment on the fiscal year strategic work plan* for businesses that establish the PMO function to support project delivery efficiencies. Given the tactical nature of

---

* Gerald I. Kendall and Steven C. Rollins, *Advanced Project Portfolio Management and the PMO: Multiplying ROI at Warp Speed,* J. Ross Publishing, Ft. Lauderdale, FL, 2003.

the PMO versus the strategic nature of strategic planning, and given that the PMO cyclically reports overall tactical project progress against project expectations, the metrics function should reside within the PMO and assist with interpreting organization progress value and risk.

DETERMINING AND JUSTIFYING THE NEED FOR AN ORGANIZATIONAL METRICS PROGRAM

Take a good look around the company you work for and consider the following 10 questions.

1. Do you know your job value today? Can you state the value proposition for your job in a measurable manner? If you cannot describe your job value, then of what value is your job? Guess who is also asking this question? Your boss. An excellent rule of thumb to determine your job value is to calculate your total compensation per year and multiply by (a minimum of) three to define the *total expected value* from your job at minimum expectations. By creating KVAs from your job total expected value, you will have a value profile of your job and the performance objectives with measures, weightings, and standards that emanate from each KVA to "prove" to your boss what value you have created.

If you are not delivering the total expected value of your job, your job is at risk. On the average, outsourcing your job can deliver up to 30 times the bottom-line dollar value. How important is it to you to keep your job? Again, creating KVAs and performance objectives at standards of Very Good and Excellent will "prove" that your value exceeds your job total expected value.

2. Can you list your company's top 10 strategic project initiatives in strategic order? Not being aware of what the business wants to achieve for the fiscal year in its key project investments only hurts your chance to contribute more personal value and hurts the business that pays you. If you do not know, how can you possibly do anything to help the business add value or prevent the business from failing? It does not cost you anything to become cognizant. Ignoring the apparent value for the benefit of the business and yourself can cost you everything.

3. Can you clearly state the value proposition of your business unit in measurable terms for the current fiscal year? Your business unit must deliver at least three times its annual operating budget for the fiscal year. Is that happening? How do you know? You would know if you delivered at standards of Very Good and Excellent performance levels, which were set to measure three and four times cost.

4. Outside of your boss and friends, who do you go to for help in your work when failing? The PMO can help facilitate work completion issues if you approach them in a timely manner.

5. Are you aware of what the corporate objectives delivery plans are for the fiscal year and how your work relates to them? Ignore this opportunity at your own peril. With 3Ms, you participate in the Measure phase and the alignment process, which guarantee that you know how your project aligns with corporate objectives.

6. **Can you identify who at the executive level is accountable for each corporate objective strategically and tactically?** Answering "the CEO" is not acceptable. If your business is not measuring objective achievement risk and no one is accountable for a specific corporate objective, a great deal of money, value, and opportunity is being missed. If you doubt this, revisit the stated value proposition of the business for the fiscal year and ask yourself how not managing this risk helps the business grow. Again, the 3Ms alignment process will ensure that you know which C-level officer is accountable for your project.

7. **Is the work you personally perform clearly linked to a primary corporate objective?** Understanding this linkage helps to define your value to the business. It is the same as knowing where you keep your personal money. You know where your money is, don't you?

8. **Is there a project fraud management policy in your business that focuses on prevention and detection?** Companies with an appropriate project fraud prevention and detection policy can save 6% or more of their fiscal year budget. An important side benefit is that the trust those in the workforce have in each other begins to improve over time. This leads to positive risk taking by the workforce in project delivery acceleration opportunities.

9. **Do the project teams in your organization perform their work without fear of losing their jobs if the work they perform is delivered too early?** Most project teams rely on the project executive and sponsor to help clear hurdles in the delivery path. But what project fraud controls are there on the project executive and project sponsor that will prevent and/or detect project fraud on their behalf? If your organization does not have a project fraud policy in place, how do you know that project fraud does not exist in the workplace?

10. **Do you have visibility to the project schedule critical path for the work you perform?** Using critical path scheduling for a project team is an excellent method to raise team member visibility as to roles and effect on what is important to project success. Any team member who ignores this increases the risk that the project will be less than successful, since team member reaction to project unplanned events will be much more reactive instead of much more proactive.

CASE STUDY

Let's assume that your company has:
- $100 million in project investments planned for the fiscal year
- 500 resources planned for at 70% utilization that will cost the business $50 million in compensation for the fiscal year

Value Proposition of an Organizational Project-Based Metrics Program 153

- $200 million in business assets to be considered in project selection
- Five corporate objectives for the fiscal year, each funded at $20 million, with 20 projects each

An organizational metrics program that measures for speed to market in project delivery and links that work to the fulfillment of corporate objectives yielded a 10% delivery improvement in time and cost. This was the result of the raised visibility to accelerate work because it was identified.

This result yielded the following effects:

- $10 million savings in project investments delivered in less than 11 calendar months, allowing the business to start more work than was planned with $10 million it did not expect to have
- $5 million more than was expected in resource productivity utilization improvement
- $20 million more than was expected in leverage improvements to the most valued corporate assets that gave the most value to the business
- Earlier than expected achievement of the five corporate objectives, thereby enabling corporate resources and assets to work on those initiatives that were not planned and also enabling business benefit to be realized sooner than expected due to raised visibility to achieved corporate objectives

Total benefit gained by the business from the metrics program was $35 million for the fiscal year, plus on time and on budget or better work delivery because delivery acceleration opportunities were visible to more people, who could take positive action.

The total cost of the metrics program for the organization was very nominal, certainly much less than was gained. Reporting to metrics was a basic tenet required of everyone in the organization. Failure to do so is similar to failing to pay your electric bill — sooner or later, the lights will go out.

SUMMARY

The overridding message of this chapter and one that you should take away is that businesses are based on how people react to the business output, customers, and workers alike. Implementing an organization metrics program that ignores the peer-peer influences from unforeseen opportunities and threats, which could have been made visible by a viable metrics program, is unfulfilling to the business itself and to your job value in particular. You must seek to always raise the value of your skill in your job every day to produce the expected results that are achieved or expect that others that compete with you or your business will. The choice is clearly yours.

QUESTIONS

13-1. In a project-based metrics program, all work measured is considered to be project work. True or false?

13-2. The cost optimization model focuses on spending money on projects and resources that are allocated, without much regard for the resulting influence this has on inter/intraproject and resource sense of urgency. True or false?

13-3. A resource-based metrics program places primary value on cost-optimizing resource performance and typically measures utilization first and effectiveness second. True or false?

13-4. Resource-based metrics programs are much more dynamic in change from year to year than project-based metrics programs. True or false?

13-5. In any organization, a well-defined metrics program can yield the viable benefit of strategic and tactical alignment of business expectations with those of the workforce. True or false?

13-6. Not being aware of what the business wants to achieve for the fiscal year in its key project investments only hurts your chance to contribute more personal value and hurts the business that pays you. True or false?

PART III:
3MS MEASUREMENT TOOLS FOR THE ORGANIZATION

14

THE 3MS METRIC PROFILE

In the following chapters, a great deal of detail is provided that maps to the third edition of the Project Management Institute's *A Guide to the Project Management Body of Knowledge* (PMBOK®). For each area of knowledge, each specific output from each specific defined process is profiled in a 3Ms-oriented template to provide you with a baseline perspective of essential measurements. In most all cases, each 3Ms metric profile is based on performance standards against time and cost. These performance standards are Excellent, Very Good, Satisfactory, and Unsatisfactory.

In mapping the PMBOK® area of knowledge outputs in this manner, we have created more than 200 metrics that can be implemented and monitored in predictive and detective analysis techniques to help the project manager control project risk to delivery. Because the focus of the third edition of the PMBOK® is based on the single project culture, we have organized our approach in a similar manner. This correlation enables holistic and uniform measures that provide common language and process, which will greatly assist any organization using these templates to bring into alignment all project teams internally and all project teams within business objectives. The cognitive ability for people to comprehend what is essential or "satisfactory" versus what is too much ("Excellent" or "Very Good") is critical to delivering projects on time and on budget — all the time! The worst thing that should ever happen to a project is being on time and on budget.

Use these measures and you will be on your way. Create you own 3Ms project profiles based on the prescribed methodology in the preceding chapters, and you will never fail in knowing the quantification of any project output relative to progress expectations. "To know that you know" is far better than "to know that you do not know"!

DEFINING THE 3MS METRIC PROFILE

The 3Ms metric profile (Figure 14-1) is an Excel® worksheet with predefined macros to roll up calculations derived from assessed performance measures as

3Ms Metric Profile for: Date: Completed by:

		Weight (%):	Contribution:		Performance:	Potential:	Conversion:
1	Business Management	15%	-		-	0.60	0%
2	Marketing Management	15%	-		-	0.60	0%
3	Physical Security SME	20%	-		-	0.80	0%
4	Biometrics SME	20%	-		-	0.80	0%
5	Sales	30%	-		-	1.20	0%
	SUMMARY		-		-	4.00	0%

Performance Objectives

KVA - 1: Business Management   Evaluation Date:

Detail: More in line with organizational development and business management than with sales and marketing.

Contributing Value Area:	Weights:	Standard:	Contribution:	Potential:	Conversion:
1 Maintain Business Plan	40%	Std. Must = 1, 2, 3, or 4	-	1.60	0%
2 Manage Operations Through Growth	60%	Std. Must = 1, 2, 3, or 4	-	2.40	0%
3	0%	Std. Must = 1, 2, 3, or 4	-	0.00	#DIV/0!
4	0%	Std. Must = 1, 2, 3, or 4	-	0.00	#DIV/0!
5	0%	Std. Must = 1, 2, 3, or 4	-	0.00	#DIV/0!
TOTAL:				4.00	0%

Maintain Business Plan

- 4 - Excellent — Below plus - Secure 100% of funding as needed on the strength of the business plan
- 3 - Very Good — Below plus - Business plan to functionally serve as an ongoing strategic roadmap. Estimates within +/- 25% of actuals, in FY1
- 2 - Satisfactory — Document planned current and planned business activities as needed.
- 1 - Unsatisfactory
- 0

Manage Operations Through Growth

- 4 - Excellent — Below plus - Manage development of web-based/integrated business systems.
- 3 - Very Good — Below plus - Create tools and replicable processes for business planning and service order to cash cycle
- 2 - Satisfactory — Manage cash flows, new hires, subcontractors, vendors, service providers, etc.
- 1 - Unsatisfactory
- 0

- 4 - Excellent — 0
- 3 - Very Good — 0
- 2 - Satisfactory — 0
- 1 - Unsatisfactory — 0
- 0

- 4 - Excellent — 0
- 3 - Very Good — 0
- 2 - Satisfactory — 0
- 1 - Unsatisfactory — 0
- 0

- 4 - Excellent — 0
- 3 - Very Good — 0
- 2 - Satisfactory — 0
- 1 - Unsatisfactory — 0

The 3Ms Metric Profile   159

KVA - 2:	Marketing Management						Evaluation Date:	
Detail:	0							
	Contributing Value Area:	Weights:	Standard:			Contribution:	Potential:	Conversion:
1	Marketing Research & Analysis	20%		Std. Must = 1, 2, 3, or 4		-	0.80	0%
2	Maintain Strategic Marketing Plan	20%		Std. Must = 1, 2, 3, or 4		-	0.80	0%
3	Manage Promotional Activities	20%		Std. Must = 1, 2, 3, or 4		-	0.80	0%
4	Manage Public (and Investor?) Relations	20%		Std. Must = 1, 2, 3, or 4		-	0.80	0%
5	Market Responsiveness / Customer Sat.	20%		Std. Must = 1, 2, 3, or 4		-		0%
	TOTAL:					-	4.00	0%

Marketing Research & Analysis
4 - Excellent — Conduct primary MR&A as needed.
3 - Very Good — Construct analysis of secondary MR&A to synthesize comprehensive picture of market enabling strategic decision making
2 - Satisfactory — Collect secondary MR&A to synthesize picture of targeted segments
1 - Unsatisfactory — 0

Maintain Strategic Marketing Plan
4 - Excellent — Develop a Strategic Marketing Plan to create / exploit some sustainable competitive advantage. (e.g., IP)
3 - Very Good — Develop a Strategic Marketing Plan to create / exploit some competitive advantage. (e.g., TTM)
2 - Satisfactory — Develop a Strategic Marketing Plan to leverage corporate strengths.
1 - Unsatisfactory — 0

Manage Promotional Activities
4 - Excellent — Host Security Awarenes Seminars (as revenue stream?)
3 - Very Good — Exhibit at 1 / Speak at 2 Trade Shows / Conferences / Seminars
2 - Satisfactory — Manage creation of collateral materials, including web site content and brochures/*.PDF, advertising.
1 - Unsatisfactory — 0

Manage Public (and Investor?) Relations
4 - Excellent — Make COMPANY newsworthy
3 - Very Good — Ensure that press presents COMPANY in neutral to favorable light in 100% stories
2 - Satisfactory — Develop process for issuing press releases and partner/practitioner publications.
1 - Unsatisfactory — 0

Market Responsiveness / Customer Sat.
4 - Excellent — >15% business ($) is repeat in client organizations / client referrals
3 - Very Good — Ensure that every engagement results in 2.5 or better on 3Ms scale of customer satisfaction metrics
2 - Satisfactory — Develop service offerings that respond to market needs, delivering as promised 100%.
1 - Unsatisfactory — 0

Figure 14-1. 3Ms Profile Print Format

KVA - 3: Physical Security SME

Detail: 0

Evaluation Date:

#	Contributing Value Area:	Weights:	Standard:		Contribution:	Potential:	Conversion:
1	Vendor Relations	20%	Std. Must = 1, 2, 3, or 4		-	0.80	0%
2	Leading Practices & Product Knowledge	20%	Std. Must = 1, 2, 3, or 4		-	0.80	0%
3	Physical Security Customer Delivery	60%	Std. Must = 1, 2, 3, or 4		-	2.40	0%
4	0	0%	Std. Must = 1, 2, 3, or 4		-	0.00	#DIV/0!
5	0	0%	Std. Must = 1, 2, 3, or 4		-	0.00	#DIV/0!
	TOTAL:				-	4.00	0%

Vendor Relations
- 4 - Excellent: 3-4 vendors per identified area have signed partnership agreement, 3% of revenue generated by referrals and sales
- 3 - Very Good: 3-4 vendors identified per area, signed partnerships with 2 or less, 3% of revenue generated by referrals and sales
- 2 - Satisfactory: less than 2 vendors identified per area, less than 2 partnerships signed, revenue generated by the partnerships
- 1 - Unsatisfactory: 1 vendor identified per service, 50% of vendor relationships signed.

Leading Practices & Product Knowledge
- 4 - Excellent: Develop partnership with manufacturer/service providers to provide market requirements for product/service development.
- 3 - Very Good: Recommend and implement appropriate products/solutions
- 2 - Satisfactory: Recommend appropriate products/solutions
- 1 - Unsatisfactory: 0

Physical Security Customer Delivery
- 4 - Excellent: Publish / Sell Physical Security Consulting Engagement Process / Methodology
- 3 - Very Good: Develop Physical Security Consulting Engagement Process / Methodology - Train COMPANY
- 2 - Satisfactory: Conduct Physical Security Consulting Engagements
- 1 - Unsatisfactory: 0

0
- 4 - Excellent: 0
- 3 - Very Good: 0
- 2 - Satisfactory: 0
- 1 - Unsatisfactory: 0

0
- 4 - Excellent: 0
- 3 - Very Good: 0
- 2 - Satisfactory: 0
- 1 - Unsatisfactory: 0

The 3Ms Metric Profile   161

KVA - 4:	Biometrics SME						Evaluation Date:	
Detail:	0							
	Contributing Value Area:	**Weights:**	**Standard:**			**Contribution:**	**Potential:**	**Conversion:**
1	Vendor Relations	20%		Std. Must = 1, 2, 3, or 4		-	0.80	0%
2	Leading Practices & Product Knowledge	30%		Std. Must = 1, 2, 3, or 4		-	1.20	0%
3	Industry Participation	20%		Std. Must = 1, 2, 3, or 4		-	0.80	0%
4	Biometrics Customer Delivery	30%		Std. Must = 1, 2, 3, or 4		-	1.20	0%
5	0	0%					0.00	#DIV/0!
	TOTAL:					-	4.00	0%

Vendor Relations	
4 - Excellent	3-4 vendors per identified area have signed partnership agreement, 3% of revenue generated by referrals and sales
3 - Very Good	3-4 vendors identified per area, signed partnerships with 2 or less, 3% of revenue generated by referrals and sales
2 - Satisfactory	less than 2 vendors identified per area, less than 2 partnerships signed, revenue generated by the partnerships
1 - Unsatisfactory	1 vendor identified per service, 50% of vendor relationships signed.
Leading Practices & Product Knowledge	
4 - Excellent	Develop partnership with manufacturer/service providers to provide market requirements for product/service development.
3 - Very Good	Recommend and implement appropriate products/solutions
2 - Satisfactory	Recommend appropriate products/solutions
1 - Unsatisfactory	0
Industry Participation	
4 - Excellent	Contribute to / Lead standards / industry organizations
3 - Very Good	Join standards / industry organizations
2 - Satisfactory	Stay abreast of developments in industry (e.g., standards, legislation, methods)
1 - Unsatisfactory	0
Biometrics Customer Delivery	
4 - Excellent	Publish / Sell Biometrics Consulting Engagement Process / Methodology
3 - Very Good	Develop Biometrics Consulting Engagement Process / Methodology - Train COMPANY
2 - Satisfactory	Conduct Biometrics Consulting Engagements
1 - Unsatisfactory	0
0	
4 - Excellent	0
3 - Very Good	0
2 - Satisfactory	0
1 - Unsatisfactory	0

Figure 14-1. 3Ms Profile Print Format (continued)

162 Value-Based Metrics for Improving Results

KVA - 5:	Sales					Evaluation Date:	
Detail: 0							
	Contributing Value Area:	Weights:	Standard:		Contribution:	Potential:	Conversion:
1	New Accounts	50%		Std. Must = 1, 2, 3, or 4	-	2.00	0%
2	Account Growth	30%		Std. Must = 1, 2, 3, or 4	-	1.20	0%
3	Annuity Development	20%		Std. Must = 1, 2, 3, or 4	-	0.80	0%
4	0	0%		Std. Must = 1, 2, 3, or 4	-	0.00	#DIV/0!
5	0	0%		Std. Must = 1, 2, 3, or 4	-	0.00	#DIV/0!
	TOTAL:					4.00	0%

New Accounts
4 - Excellent   5 new account per quarter
3 - Very Good   3 new accounts per quarter
2 - Satisfactory   1 new account per quarter
1 - Unsatisfactory   0

Account Growth
4 - Excellent   Extend 50% of existing account base.
3 - Very Good   Extend 25% of existing account base.
2 - Satisfactory   Extend 15% of existing account base
1 - Unsatisfactory   0

Annuity Development
4 - Excellent   Create annuity relationship in 15% account base
3 - Very Good   Create annuity relationship in 10% account base
2 - Satisfactory   Create annuity relationship in 5% account base
1 - Unsatisfactory   0

4 - Excellent   0
3 - Very Good   0
2 - Satisfactory   0
1 - Unsatisfactory   0

4 - Excellent   0
3 - Very Good   0
2 - Satisfactory   0
1 - Unsatisfactory   0

Training Objectives
Short-Term   Technical training in IT security and system integration and implementation. CISSP certification.
Long-Term   Ongoing technical and business training and develoment.

Performance Factors
Employee   0
Supervisor   0

Promotability

Figure 14-1. 3Ms Profile Print Format (continued)

predetermined from the performance standard baseline. Each key value area (KVA) scorecard is baselined at 4.0 because there are four performance standards. Percentages are applied as a function of 4.0. Thus, "maintain business plan" as a contributing value area with an assigned standard of 2 would be 40% of 4.0 or 1.60. Stating this differently, the contribution of satisfactory performance would equate to a contribution of 1.60 for this specific KVA and contributing value area.

To complete this template for each 3Ms metric profile utilized, complete the following steps:

Step 1   Identify the KVAs and list them (two to five items)
Step 2   Assign weighting (5% minimum)
Step 3   Populate performance objectives for each KVA in Step 1 (state contributing value areas and associated weighting)
Step 4   Populate performance standards for each contributing value area by defining what is Excellent, Very Good, Satisfactory, and Unsatisfactory. Repeat this step for each contributing value area of the KVA.
Step 5   Repeat Steps 3 and 4 until all KVAs have been decomposed into specific performance standard definitions for each specific contributing value area
Step 6   Populate training objectives
Step 7   Populate performance factors
Step 8   Populate promotability factors

Steps 1 and 2 (Figure 14-2) will automatically populate the chart based on the data entered for contribution. All weights for KVAs must total 100%. Performance is automatically calculated when contribution is entered as a conversion (difference between potential and actual).

Enter standard (result) and contribution data (Figures 14-3 and 14-4). Potential data are calculated at Excellent performance.

Save and store the profile template. You have completed the construction of the performance objectives (Figure 14-5).

SUMMARY

Project delivery has long been a mystery to businesses everywhere. We see this as a result of a large percentage of failed projects in businesses everywhere. These project investment failures have made project investing a very risky proposition in an environment of tight money. This combination has made business executives gun-shy toward investing in worthy projects. This unnatural restraint is the result of failure and diminishing trust in those who work and deliver projects for the business. When an executive neck is chopped as a result of project failure, people tend to take it very personally, when often the problem emanated from poor business alignment within the project itself.

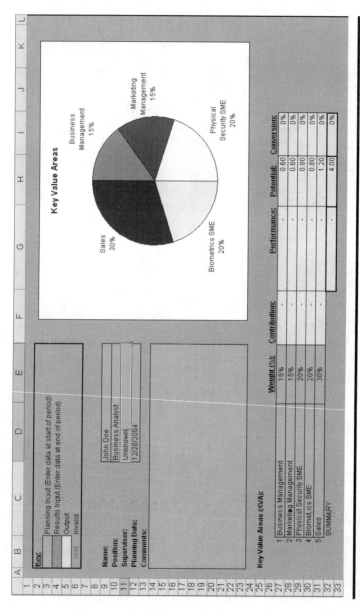

Figure 14-2. Steps 1 and 2

The 3Ms Metric Profile   165

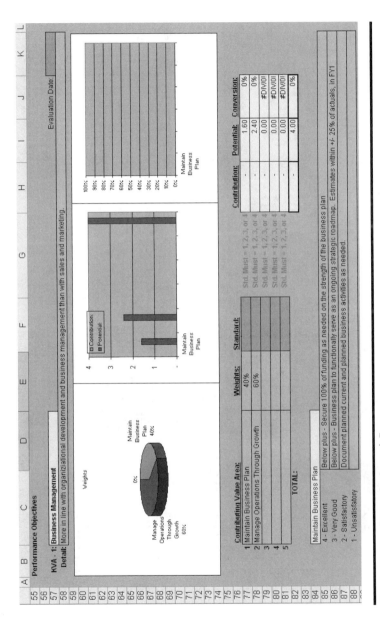

Figure 14-3. Steps 3, 4, and 5

166 Value-Based Metrics for Improving Results

	Contributing Value Area:	Weights:	Standard:		Contribution:	Potential:	Conversion:
1	Marketing Research & Analysis	20%	Std. Must = 1, 2, 3, or 4		-	0.80	0%
2	Maintain Strategic Marketing Plan	20%	Std. Must = 1, 2, 3, or 4		-	0.80	0%
3	Manage Promotional Activities	20%	Std. Must = 1, 2, 3, or 4		-	0.80	0%
4	Manage Public (and Investor?) Relations	20%	Std. Must = 1, 2, 3, or 4		-	0.80	0%
5	Market Responsiveness / Customer Sat.	20%	Std. Must = 1, 2, 3, or 4		-	0.80	0%
	TOTAL:					4.00	

Marketing Research & Analysis
4 - Excellent — Conduct primary MR&A as needed.
3 - Very Good — Construct analysis of secondary MR&A to synthesize comprehensive picture of market enabling strategic decision making
2 - Satisfactory — Collect secondary MR&A to synthesize picture of targeted segments
1 - Unsatisfactory

Maintain Strategic Marketing Plan
4 - Excellent — Develop a Strategic Marketing Plan to create / exploit some sustainable competitive advantage (e.g., IP)
3 - Very Good — Develop a Strategic Marketing Plan to create / exploit some competitive advantage (e.g., TTM)
2 - Satisfactory — Develop a Strategic Marketing Plan to leverage corporate strengths.
1 - Unsatisfactory

Manage Promotional Activities
4 - Excellent — Host Security Awareness Seminars (as revenue stream?)
3 - Very Good — Exhibit at 1 / Speak at 2 Trade Shows / Conferences / Seminars
2 - Satisfactory — Manage creation of collateral materials, including web site content and brochures (*PDF, advertising
1 - Unsatisfactory

Manage Public (and Investor) Relations
4 - Excellent — Make COMPANY newsworthy
3 - Very Good — Ensure that press presents COMPANY in neutral to favorable light in 100% stories
2 - Satisfactory — Develop process for issuing press releases and partner/practitioner publications.
1 - Unsatisfactory

Market Responsiveness / Customer Sat.
4 - Excellent — > 15% business ($) is repeat in client organizations / client referrals
3 - Very Good — Ensure that every engagement results in 2.5 or better on 3MS scale of customer satisfaction metrics

Figure 14-4. Another Example of Steps 3, 4, and 5

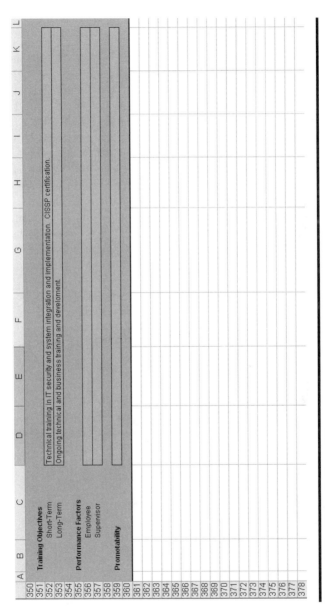

Figure 14-5. Steps 6, 7, and 8

A well-structured metrics program managed by the organization's business governance entity or Project Management Office can begin the process to reverse the trend of project failures through sound alignment of corporate objectives with available resources. This raises strategic and tactical visibility to delivery acceleration opportunities versus delivery threats.

We submit that our experiences and the related information in this book are subjective. However, where is there another source that provides you the tools and a standard that you can utilize to add measurable value to your employer through your efforts? Where is there another "stake in the ground" on a metrics application that correlates to the PMBOK®? Where are there other references that combine this value with information on how to deliver projects with a true and measured sense of urgency through metrics? Where are the references that will help you align the business value proposition for the purpose of a greater good? You have one in your hands now. Follow us through the remaining chapters as we uncover value-based metrics to help you and your employer prosper and grow.

The material in this reference is our commitment to further the value proposition of project management for you and your employer. A soft copy of all the templates and metrics from this book is available for purchase at www.jrosspub.com and www.pmousa.com.

This book has free materials available for download from the
Web Added Value™ Resource Center at www.jrosspub.com.

15

PROJECT MANAGEMENT CONTEXT

Can you define the value proposition of project management to the organization? How about the value proposition of the organization? Why should businesses everywhere seek to utilize project management rigor and discipline? What happens if they do not?

Measurement and management have gone hand in hand for years. As the old adage goes, "if you can't measure, you can't control." And "if you can't control, you can't manage." Thus, "if you can't measure, you can't manage very well" stills rings true in many situations today. It is also true that all the measures in the world without management will not get anything done.

This is where the 3Ms is a highly integrated and "seamless" process. Again, by owning the metrics that define the three standards of success — Satisfactory, Very Good, and Excellent — the project team has already agreed to the metrics that define its value. The project team also is aligning with the corporate objectives that define the value of the organization. Thus, the 3Ms answers the first two questions in the first paragraph above.

In the Manage phase, the project team and/or business governance/Project Management Organization (PMO) corporate executives are aligning hierarchically all of the resources and variables that will help (or hinder) the accomplishment of *all* the objectives at *every* level of the business governance/PMO hierarchy. As the organization, from top to bottom *and* bottom to top, moves through the Manage phase, it will necessarily have to reconsider the metrics, weightings, and standards that were initially created. This is mostly because the organization *never* had rigorous metrics to measure *anything*, certainly not with the rigor of metrics, weightings, and standards for objectives at *any* level or weightings for the value proposition (key value areas) at any level.

So, intrinsic to the whole 3Ms process is the concurrent setting of metrics and managing toward predefined success. For the first time, this is a linear, sequential process. First Measure, then Manage. However, after the first time, or start-up phase, these two phases are circular and feeding data back and forth between the steps and up and down the entire organization. After some time, when Magnify, the third phase, is initiated, then the cycle is concurrently between the three phases.

This is the "beef" of the 3Ms. The organization (project team, business governance/PMO executives) is simultaneously measuring, managing, and magnifying and doing this in terms of behavior and, most importantly, when the 3Ms *is* the corporate culture, doing this as a way of thinking about everything related to the attainment of corporate objectives.

In Part III of this book, you will find numerous examples of project management metrics that focus on defining opportunities, threats, and the potential to magnify accomplishments in speed to market for any type of program/project initiative. To further assist your understanding, these metrics are correlated into topical categories as defined by the Project Management Institute's Project Management Body of Knowledge (PMBOK®) nine areas of knowledge. We also identified three additional areas of knowledge that are essential (in our humble opinion): management oversight, project fraud management, and PMO management.

In the following 12 chapters, we provide close insight into how you can enable these techniques in your area of work based on our combined 70-plus years of project delivery experience:

Chapter 16	Management Oversight
Chapter 17	Project Integration Management
Chapter 18	Project Scope Management
Chapter 19	Project Time Management
Chapter 20	Project Cost Management
Chapter 21	Project Quality Management
Chapter 22	Project Human Resource Management
Chapter 23	Project Communications Management
Chapter 24	Project Risk Management
Chapter 25	Project Procurement Management
Chapter 26	Project Fraud Management
Chapter 27	Project Management Office Management

Each of these chapters offers numerous 3Ms-oriented metric key value areas and project and individual performance objectives designed to help you and your business identify opportunity and threat in project delivery.

THE VALUE OF PROJECT MANAGEMENT

Determining what is value versus what is not requires expertise, cognitive skills, and ownership to make this assessment. A key objective of this book is to help you improve your expertise in measurement and your cognitive skills in envisioning project delivery opportunities and threats regarding success. Another key observation is that you cannot do this alone! Much of this support should come from the experts in project management, who are often located in the PMO of most businesses and organizations. Chapter 27 delves into the detail regarding the business governance/PMO role in managing the business metrics program. A great deal of emphasis is placed on business governance/PMO in this book since we envision it to be accountable for the management of the business project management metrics program. There is no substitute! Further insight into how business governance/PMO can add value and support a business can be found in *Advanced Project Portfolio Management and the PMO: Multiplying ROI at Warp Speed*.*

Essentially, the value proposition of project management is to facilitate business growth and prosperity. In the application of project management within any business, change often occurs. These changes take the form of either opportunity or threat to some relative aspect of the business. Many of these changes have a direct impact on transforming the business. When these changes are organized in some aggregated discernible manner, the impact can be astounding to the business. This is known today as "change management." But let's not consider this impact on business as change as much as it is value.

Most people struggle with change, often resisting it. However, when faced with improving their value on the job, they are less likely to resist change if they can see their options. A key and compelling reason for this observation is how people react to change when faced with embracing it. Many people see change as unplanned and thus avoid it. Since so many of us plan everything we do every day, we have choices to make when change is forced onto us. Having the visibility into cause and effect of the decisions we make based on these changes would make those decisions much easier. But that is the problem, isn't it? We don't have the visibility into the cause and the potential effect because we are so busy doing our job. We are isolated by our work because how we work is driven by the need of business to optimize resource costs. This optimization reduces the opportunity to improve project delivery throughput across the organization since people only have time to perform the minimum level of effort in their job, and it's not getting any better.

The globalization of the world economy is forcing businesses to reduce project teams in resource size to bare bones in order to remain competitive. This reduction further reduces the ability of project teams to have the necessary visibility to understand project delivery acceleration opportunities and/or threats (change). This is a key and compelling reason for business governance/PMO to support your metric needs. The business governance/PMO entity has this vision through its tools and techniques, such as portfolio management processes.

As you learn to address new changes in the workplace, we encourage you to speak and think of them as value opportunities and/or threats as opposed to changes. Consider all project delivery information flow as a decision loop. In this case, the information flow is often flawed by lack of understanding or visibility into value-

---

* Gerald I. Kendall and Steven C. Rollins, J. Ross Publishing, Ft. Lauderdale, FL, 2003.

oriented opportunities or threats. In fact, the information flow is like a curved line, where change is created and eventually applied unevenly, to the detriment of the organization. But there is an answer. The solution is unique to each business since each typically has its own business model. If a business could actually control the information loop, then visibility into work completion throughput would become much better. This improvement actually induces "alignment" within the organization based on what the business expected to achieve in the fiscal year versus what is actually occurring. This alignment embraces all the corporate objectives to the lowest level of assigned work. The business governance/PMO entity actually brings control to this information loop and completes the circuit. It becomes the backbone of support for project teams striving for success.

In accounting for the value proposition of you in your job, the project team, the department, or the business unit, use the value audit form (Figure 15-1) to document this value whenever and wherever it becomes acquired. To utilize this process, at the end of the business fiscal year, total the documented value from all of the value audit forms that have been provided by and to you or other entities. As each

---

Date reported (month/date/year) _____

Who is reporting the acquired value? _____

What customer benefited? _____

What business unit benefited from this value? _____

What type of value improved is this? (circle one)

    Increased revenue   **Avoid cost**   **Improve service**

If possible, state the value gained in measurable terms:

_____

_____

_____

Describe how this value was determined:

_____

_____

_____

Approved (month/date/year): _____   Supervisor: _____

Figure 15-1. Value Audit Form

organizational unit (you included) is mapped back to the total value acquired (that was unplanned for at the beginning of the fiscal year), give attention to those areas of the business that achieved three or more times their annual costs during the course of the fiscal year.

Once you have completed the value tabulation, ask yourself if you could have produced more! We always can, can't we? The main question is how we become better at doing so. Most people find that answer in their level of desire to add value and their relative passion for their job. Need we say more?

The value audit form (Figure 15-1) is where you state your relevant key value area and its weighting and the specific project objectives where value was measured by the weighting and the performance standard that was achieved. This process is mathematically precise. As previously defined, the standard of Satisfactory is the minimum or 100% of value for 100% of proportionate cost, typically the standard of Very Good is a value of >5% or a monetary gain that exceeds the cost, and typically Excellent is a standard of at least >10% or creation of a monetary worth that exceeds the cost of that result by at least 10%. As has been suggested, if you want to look for value that is in multiples of cost, then you would set the standards accordingly. Thus, Satisfactory might be a value of two times cost, Very Good might be three times cost, and Excellent might be four times cost. This is the scalability of 3Ms. You are free to set the standards as ambitiously as you like.

SUMMARY

This book is dedicated to establishing a standard for developing metrics for project management and related areas. Application of the material in this chapter was contrived to help you in your journey to continuous process improvement in metrics.

Metrics influence behavior. Since the result of a measured event enables decision making, we can clearly understand why that would be. One of the key questions we must answer is in which direction the result will lead us. Is it from boss to subordinate, peer to peer, or business unit to the enterprise? We must look to what value we are seeking to find the directional answer because if we do not know which way to go, how will we ever get there? We have seen many businesses that have developed their cultures like circular race tracks, with nowhere to go, but with the "just be there first" mentality. That's nice if they are paying you to be first.

Thus, the following chapters are provided as a reference model for your utilization. We have chosen as a standard performance theme on time and on budget for Satisfactory performance or better. Does your organization manage this way or is it all or nothing? The templates contained within this book are also available on CD at www.jrosspub.com.

What about taking credit for the improvements that you have delivered as measured by the 3Ms model? Can you imagine what your boss would say to you if you reported at your annual merit review that you added to the bottom line $75 million in cost avoidance that was not expected? That is what this entire book is all about. We seek to help you find this kind of value, but we cannot do it all for you. You must be a partner — after all, it is your value improvement that is gaining, not ours. We beseech you to implement the value audit form (Figure 15-1) in everything you do at your job. You will learn and improve if you adopt this process into your work "way of life." It's just like going to the bank!

QUESTIONS

15-1. The value proposition of project management is best described as:
  a. Grow business prosperity
  b. Keep costs low
  c. Manage risk
  d. Improve your job value
15-2. If you can't measure, you can't manage. True or false?
15-3. The PMO closes the information loop as a means to help project teams be successful in delivery. True or false?
15-4. Change management is often avoided by project teams. True of false?
15-5. Metrics program management should operate from internal auditing. True or false?
15-6. The value audit form collects the relevant information to document the unexpected value derived from the output of a work result. True or false?
15-7. Economic globalization is forcing project team size (resources) to become smaller and smaller. True or false?
15-8. Applying project management rigor and discipline to achieve project delivery in alignment with corporate objectives can bring about value-based business transformation. True or false?
15-9. Across most business, project investment has become a risky business. True or false?
15-10. The Project Management Institute's PMBOK® areas of knowledge are a critical standard for any metrics-based program. True or false?

This book has free materials available for download from the
Web Added Value™ Resource Center at www.jrosspub.com.

16

MANAGEMENT OVERSIGHT

Generally speaking in the course of business management, the cause and effect of successful project delivery efforts can have a profound effect on a business. Many businesses organize themselves into multiple lines of business that focus on specific products and/or services. In this model, these lines of business often operate with a large degree of autonomy from each other. The exception is cross-functional project investments, which add more complexity and commitment to managing project delivery initiatives. This additional complexity increases the risk to tangent project initiatives within the line of business. Often, intra-line-of-business projects utilize the same human capital in numerous projects, all working toward a different delivery goal. Management of these resources becomes more and more difficult and less and less effective each time another project is added that requires some of the currently allocated resources. Over time, it becomes increasingly clear that a higher authority is needed within the business to prioritize work that determines what is strategically important to the business so the assigned resources can work the work in the correct order. That higher authority is corporate governance.

CORPORATE GOVERNANCE ROLE

The role responsibility of corporate governance is to effectively steer the business to produce in the most optimal manner each fiscal year (throughput). In order to provide the very best senior management direction, the corporate governance team needs a tactical understanding of current progress from the projects identified as strategic to the business. The fiscal year strategic plan represents the baseline expectations of the business for the assigned fiscal year. These already have been defined by the 3Ms process and format of creating and aligning corporate objectives that then drive all of the subordinate goals and objectives, including those of the Project Management Office (PMO).

Tactical progress results from the strategic projects listed in the fiscal year strategic plan are collected and interpreted by the supporting PMO, typically in the form of a monthly report that identifies interproject dependencies and potential delivery opportunities and threats from gap assessments of reported progress of strategic projects as compared to baseline expectations of the fiscal year strategic plan. Again, these already will have been created according to the 3Ms format. The monthly report published by the PMO is distributed to key stakeholders such as corporate governance team members for their careful consideration in determining management action at their next governance meeting.

FORMING THE CORPORATE GOVERNANCE TEAM

Economic change is all around us and is forcing many companies to become better at managing what it is they expect the business to achieve each fiscal year. Those companies that do not change to the business climate will eventually lose their place in the market to their competitors. In consideration of this, does your business have an effective corporate governance team in place? Consider the following questions to help you determine your current comfort level:

Question 1 — Who is responsible for the strategic and tactical achievement of each specific corporate objective stated by the business for the current fiscal year?

Question 2 — Is your business in business? If so, does the supply side of the business drive business, or does the market side drive business?

Question 3 — Are the corporate objectives for the fiscal year readily visible to the workforce? Can employees readily state what they are when asked? Do you have a 3Ms process for ensuring this visibility and alignment of hierarchical objectives or "line of sight" from the bottom to the top?

Questions 4 — Do employees readily know what the top 10 project initiatives are for the fiscal year and how they are progressing?

Question 5 — Is project fraud prevention and detection under control?

In question 1, if you cannot identify these people, then who is managing the achievement of each stated corporate objective? Is anyone? If you are using the 3Ms process, then you have specific ownership of *all* objectives in terms of who does what and how well. Do you know what the planned achievement date is for each corporate objective in the current fiscal year? No? Your job may depend on this knowledge. What if corporate governance does know this information and it is available to you? Should you care? Absolutely! If the business does not have an executive on point for each corporate objective effort, then the risk of not meeting achievement expectations is high. What corporate objective does your project support? Who is the executive in charge of that corporate objective? What if it is determined that the corporate objective your project is supporting is unobtainable, and as a result all related project work is to stop and resource assignments are eliminated? What would that mean to you? Do you care now? By using the 3Ms process, you will have explicit knowledge to answer all of the questions just posed.

Question 2 is more about what side of the business is towing the barge. What side of the business drives decision making? Consider that in most supply-sided organizations, the supply-side leadership typically does not possess the functional skills of its internal business partners, such as the market-side leadership, to make project decisions that are functional in nature. Project selection falls into this category. In a changing business climate, how adept will a supply-side-driven business be in conforming to business climate changes (i.e., 9/11)? CIOs, CFOs, and COOs often are placed in this circumstance. In many instances, saying no to the internal customer (market side) is not an option. If the business remains driven by the supply-side leadership before the market side can act, there will always be extra and unnecessary costs associated. Our approach is for the market side of the business to do its job. Let the supply side do its. Managing this relationship through corporate governance is critical to the success of this relationship and the success of the business.

Question 3 is about the workforce being aware of opportunity and/or threat related to what the business wants to achieve. Paying attention to and increasing your awareness of the desires of the business enable you to be more cognitive of potential cause and effect impact on the business. In other words, if you were going to a car wreck, would you want to know about it before or after?

Question 4 is similar to question 3 but more tactically focused. By staying aware of the progress of the top 10 strategic projects even though you are not involved, could you still assist? Certainly! Consider the following scenario. Suppose that one of the top 10 projects, in order to complete on schedule, requires a resource that is working on your project team. That resource can complete the assignment on your team if you complete yours. You determine that you can complete your work this week by working Saturday morning. This means that the dependent critical resource's work could be completed next week, thus allowing that resource to complete work on the strategically critical project weeks early, resulting in significant positive impact to the business. Would this be of value to you?

In August 2002, President George W. Bush signed into law legislation known as the Sarbanes-Oxley Act. The essence of this law is to prevent corporate fraud from occurring. Does fraud occur within your business? Is there a fraud policy in place within your business? If not, then fraud is probably occurring or has occurred. How about project fraud? Is it occurring today in your business? Question 5 is about the management of project fraud — the prevention and detection of project fraud.

To best manage for fraud is to reduce the opportunity for fraud to be committed. One of the very best mechanisms for reducing opportunity for fraud is to raise the visibility of work. As in baseball, to hit the ball, you must see it. Even if the baseball is coming at you at over 100 miles per hour, it is still your job to swing the bat. Corporate governance is your baseball team. If it can't (or won't) hit a fraudulent 100-mile-an-hour pitch, you won't have to worry long.

Corporate governance can exist at the enterprise, business unit, or program level. The key is to provide effective management oversight (visibility) that induces business alignment with all funded project work. At whatever level of the organization corporate governance exists, membership on this team should include the leaders or their delegates from all participating suborganizations. Those who choose not to participate do so at their own risk. As this group prioritizes project work in an ongoing manner, those organizations not participating are sure to find their requests for project support near the end of the line.

The following 3Ms-oriented metrics support the corporate governance function:

1. Achieve the Fiscal Year Strategic Plan for the Business
2. Improve Workforce
3. Improve Project Throughput
4. Manage Project Fraud Prevention
5. Manage Project Fraud Detection
6. Improve Corporate Asset Value
7. Manage Project Selection
8. Improve Profitability

Scoring for Section III: Performance Scorecard for these metrics is as follows: 4 = Excellent; 3 = Very Good; 2 = Satisfactory; 1 = Unsatisfactory.

ACHIEVE THE FISCAL YEAR STRATEGIC PLAN FOR THE BUSINESS

I. Key Value Areas Weighting (%)
   A. Establish corporate governance board = 20%.
   B. Operate corporate governance board = 30%.
   C. Manage business fiscal year strategic plan = 50%.
II. Performance Objectives
   A. Establish corporate governance board = 20%.
   B. Operate corporate governance board = 30%.
      1. 30%: 4 = all board members are participating and working together outside of governance meetings to navigate initiative opportunities and/or threats, and all strategic projects have been force ranked and are known; 3 = all board members are participating and working together outside of governance meetings; 2 = all board members are participating; 1 = not all board members are participating.
      2. 20%: 4 = all corporate objectives are assigned to specific senior executives, corporate objectives are force ranked, and most critical project investments within

each corporate objective are known; 3 = all corporate objectives are assigned to specific senior executives and corporate objectives are force ranked; 2 = all corporate objectives are assigned to specific senior executives; 1 = not all corporate objectives are assigned to specific senior executives.
3. 50%: 4 = all strategic projects are mapped one-to-one to a specific corporate objective, the most critical project for each corporate objective is known, and projected corporate objective achievement date is known for each corporate objective; 3 = all strategic projects are mapped one-to-one to a specific corporate objective and the most critical project for each corporate objective is known; 2 = all strategic projects are mapped one-to-one to a specific corporate objective; 1 = not all strategic projects are mapped one-to-one to a specific corporate objective.
C. Manage business fiscal year strategic plan = 50%.
1. 20%: 4 = all board members are participating and working together outside of governance meetings to navigate initiative opportunities and/or threats, and all strategic projects have been force ranked and are known; 3 = all board members are participating and working together outside of governance meetings; 2 = all board members are participating; 1 = not all board members are participating.
2. 20%: 4 = all corporate objectives are assigned to specific senior executives, corporate objectives are force ranked, and most critical project investments within each corporate objective are known; 3 = all corporate objectives are assigned to specific senior executives and corporate objectives are force ranked; 2 = all corporate objectives are assigned to specific senior executives; 1 = not all corporate objectives are assigned to specific senior executives.
3. 60%: 4 = all strategic projects are mapped one-to-one to a specific corporate objective, the most critical project for each corporate objective is known, and projected corporate objective achievement date is known for each corporate objective; 3 = all strategic projects are mapped one-to-one to a specific corporate objective and the most critical project for each corporate objective is known; 2 = all strategic projects are mapped one-to-one to a specific corporate objective; 1 = not all strategic projects are mapped one-to-one to a specific corporate objective.

IMPROVE WORKFORCE

Improving the competencies of the project management workforce is measured by how projects are completed on time and on budget. Anything less than 90% is Unsatisfactory performance.

I. Key Value Areas Weighting (%)
A. Improve resource productivity = 25%.
B. Improve resource alignment with corporate objectives = 25%.
C. Projects on time = 25%.
D. Projects completed within budget = 25%.
II. Performance Objectives — Based on all projects linked to specific corporate objectives.
A. 25%: 4 = >8%; 3 = >5%; 2 = >2%; 1 = <2%.

B. 25%: 4 = all resource work is completely linked to specific corporate objectives and resources are working the correct priority order; 3 = 95% of all resources are completely linked to specific corporate objectives and resources are working their work in the correct work order; 2 = 90% of all resources are completely linked to specific corporate objectives and resources are working their work in the correct work order; 1 = less than 90% of all resources are completely linked to specific corporate objectives and resources are working their work in the correct work order.
C. 25%: 4 = >5% ahead of schedule; 3 = <5% ahead of schedule; 2 = on time; 1 = not on time.
D. 25% 4 = >5% ahead of budget; 3 = <5% ahead of budget; 2 = on budget; 1 = not on budget.
III. Performance Scorecard
IV. Performance Factors
V. Training Objectives
   A. Short Term
   B. Long Term

IMPROVE PROJECT THROUGHPUT

I. Key Value Areas Weighting (%)
   A. Improve project throughput = 50%.
   B. Complete more projects than planned in the fiscal year = 50%.
II. Performance Objectives — Based on the total number of projects planned to be funded for the fiscal year.
   A. 50%: 4 = 15% more project throughput; 3 = 10%; 2 = 5%; 1 = <5%.
   B. 50%: 4 = 15% more projects than planned; 3 = 10%; 2 = 5%; 1 = <5%.
III. Performance Scorecard
IV. Performance Factors
V. Training Objectives
   A. Short Term
   B. Long Term

MANAGE PROJECT FRAUD PREVENTION

I. Key Value Areas Weighting (%)
   A. Reduce opportunity for project fraud = 50%.
   B. Audit top 25 projects in portfolio during fiscal year = 50%.
II. Performance Objectives — Based on the total number of projects planned to be funded for the fiscal year.
   A. 50%: 4 = all portfolio projects are utilizing critical path scheduling technique in project teams; 3 = 95%; 2 = 90%; 1 = <90%.
   B. 50%: 4 = all top 25 projects are audited twice each in fiscal year; 3 = 95%; 2 = 80%; 1 = <80%.
III. Performance Scorecard

IV. Performance Factors
V. Training Objectives
   A. Short Term
   B. Long Term

MANAGE PROJECT FRAUD DETECTION

I. Key Value Areas Weighting (%)
   A. Project status reporting = 50%.
   B. Project schedule reporting = 50%.
II. Performance Objectives — Based on the total number of projects planned to be funded for the fiscal year.
   A. 50%: 4 = all portfolio projects are consistently reporting progress to the PMO using PMO procedures scheduling technique in project teams; 3 = 95%; 2 = 90%; 1 = <90%.
   B. 50%: 4 = all portfolio projects are consistently reporting project schedule to the PMO using critical path technique; 3 = 95%; 2 = 90%; 1 = <90%.
III. Performance Scorecard
IV. Performance Factors
V. Training Objectives
   A. Short Term
   B. Long Term

IMPROVE CORPORATE ASSET VALUE

I. Key Value Areas Weighting (%)
   A. Asset status reporting = 50%.
   B. Asset schedule reporting = 50%.
II. Performance Objectives — Based on the total number of projects planned to be funded for the fiscal year and that are mapped to a specific and primarily supported asset.
   A. 50%: 4 = all portfolio assets are consistently reporting progress to the PMO using PMO asset reporting procedures; 3 = 95%; 2 = 90%; 1 = <90%.
   B. 50%: 4 = all portfolio assets are consistently reporting asset schedule (for the fiscal year) to the PMO using critical path technique; 3 = 95%; 2 = 90%; 1 = <90%.
III. Performance Scorecard
IV. Performance Factors
V. Training Objectives
   A. Short Term
   B. Long Term

MANAGE PROJECT SELECTION

I. Key Value Areas Weighting (%)
   A. Manage project prioritization = 50%.
   B. Corporate governance = 50%.

II. Performance Objectives — Based on the total number of projects planned to be funded for the fiscal year.
   A. 50%: 4 = all portfolio projects are consistently force ranked strategically by corporate governance throughout the fiscal year using enterprise-wide PMO prioritization standard; 3 = 95%; 2 = 90%; 1 = <90%.
   B. 50%: 4 = corporate governance members own portfolio delivery commitment for all funded/sponsored entities in the project/asset/resource/corporate objective portfolios, and most critical initiative, asset, or resource is always known based on portfolio data; 3 = 95%; 2 = 90%; 1 = <90%.
III. Performance Scorecard
IV. Performance Factors
V. Training Objectives
   A. Short Term
   B. Long Term

IMPROVE PROFITABILITY

I. Key Value Areas Weighting (%)
   A. Avoid costs = 50%.
   B. Increase revenues = 50%.
II. Performance Objectives — Based on the total number of projects planned to be funded for the fiscal year.
   A. 50%: 4 = all projects are delivered on time and on budget, and remaining projects are delivered below budget and on time; 3 = 95%; 2 = all projects delivered on budget and on time; 1 = <90%.
   B. 50%: 4 = corporate governance members own portfolio delivery commitment for all funded/sponsored entities in the project/asset/resource/corporate objective portfolios, and most critical initiative, asset, or resource is always known based on portfolio data; 3 = 95% or more; 2 = 90% or more; 1 = less than 90%.
III. Performance Scorecard
IV. Performance Factors
V. Training Objectives
   A. Short Term
   B. Long Term

SUMMARY

Management oversight has become more of a strategic weapon than ever. Those businesses that can manage project delivery more effectively than their competitors will be the big winners. This is true even in government and nonprofit organizations. New visibility into uncollected opportunities brought about by internal projects can propel a business into the stratosphere. The reverse is also true: poor visibility into pending project threats can drop a business like a rock. The landscape is littered with companies that have failed to understand this model — Packard, Edsel, Studebaker, and now Oldsmobile are just a few real examples!

A well-structured metrics program can vastly aid corporate governance at any level of a business. It is imperative that "we know that we know," or maybe you would rather be like the fellow in a recent television commercial who said, "I don't even know enough to know that I don't know."

Management oversight must be a viable entity in project delivery for the overall welfare of the business. Stated another way, the absence of corporate governance is a strong signal that the executive team is not interested in the positive evolution of the business.

QUESTIONS

16-1. Corporate governance establishes work priority for strategic projects for the benefit of the business. True or false?
16-2. Corporate governance membership is derived from:
   a. Project teams
   b. Other businesses
   c. Internal auditing
   d. Business unit leaders or their delegates
16-3. There is no direct relationship between strategic projects and corporate objectives. True or false?
16-4. It is best for a business if supply-side leadership makes most of the business decisions. True or false?
16-5. In forming the corporate governance team, which of the following is not critical:
   a. All suborganizations should be represented
   b. All project work should be prioritized in force-ranked fashion by corporate governance
   c. Each strategic project must have a corporate governance sponsor
   d. The most achievable corporate objective must be known
16-6. The fiscal year strategic plan defines what projects must be worked in the fiscal year. True or false?
16-7. The fiscal year strategic plan establishes the baseline expectations for growing the business. True or false?
16-8. Management action by the corporate governance team often can be determined by the results published by the PMO in its monthly report to key stakeholders. True or false?
16-9. Project fraud can be prevented by reducing the opportunity to commit project fraud. True or false?
16-10. Most businesses prosper from a supply-side business approach. True or false?
16-11. Corporate governance provides the balance between market-side leadership and supply-side leadership in helping the business achieve its mission. True or false?

16-12. Most project teams should not care about the health of the corporate objectives during the fiscal year. True or false?
16-13. Corporate governance owns the responsibility for the achievement of each corporate objective during the fiscal year. True or false?
16-14. Corporate governance must manage for fraud. True or false?
16-15. Project fraud only exists in the supply-side organization of a business. True or false?

This book has free materials available for download from the
Web Added Value™ Resource Center at www.jrosspub.com.

17

PROJECT INTEGRATION MANAGEMENT

Project Integration Management knowledge area includes the processes and the activities needed to identify, define, combine, unify, and coordinate the various processes and project management activities within the project management process groups.

In the context of project management, it is the integrative actions of the processes performed during the project life cycle that bring out the value proposition of project management to the business. Without integration to synergize project management processes, true intrinsic value is diminished for the funding organization because of lost value in time. We know that time is money and thus, we submit, is the basic justification for project integration management.

The requirement for integration in project management becomes evident in situations where individual processes often become dependent upon each other. Consider the cost estimate required for a contingency plan that involves integrating the planning processes as described in Chapter 20 on project cost management, Chapter 19 on project time management, and Chapter 24 on project risk management.

We must become predictive as project management professionals to ensure we gain every potential grain of intrinsic value to be wrought from project integration management. The following 3Ms metric profiles are offered to assist you in your journey.

Project Integration Management PMBOK® area of knowledge includes the following processes and deliverables:

1. Develop Project Charter
    a. Project Charter
2. Develop Project Scope Statement (Preliminary)
    a. Project Scope Statement (Preliminary)

3. Develop Project Management Plan
   a. Project Management Plan
4. Direct and Manage Project Execution
   a. Deliverables
   b. Requested Changes
   c. Implemented Change Requests
   d. Implemented Corrective Actions
   e. Implemented Preventive Actions
   f. Implemented Defect Repair
   g. Work Performance Information
5. Monitor and Control Project Work
   a. Recommended Corrective Actions
   b. Recommended Preventive Actions
   c. Forecasts
   d. Recommended Defect Repair
   e. Requested Changes
6. Integrated Change Control
   a. Approved Change Requests
   b. Rejected Change Requests
   c. Project Management Plan (Approved Updates)
   d. Project Scope Statement (Approved Updates)
   e. Approved Corrective Actions
   f. Approved Preventive Actions
   g. Approved Defect Repair
   h. Validated Defect Repair
   i. Deliverables
7. Close Project
   a. Administrative Closure Procedure
   b. Contract Closure Procedure
   c. Final Product, Service, or Result
   d. Organizational Process Assets (Updates)

These discrete process components integrate with each other and with other processes from other areas of knowledge within the PMBOK®. In addition, these process components may impact other successor dependent program and/or project initiatives in a manner not visible to the project team.

In the 3Ms metric key value area models that follow in this chapter, each metric model contains rules that require acceptance from the receiving user and, in this manner, ensures that visibility to the deliverable is confirmed by the primary receiving user and other project-related stakeholders. Another benefit from this approach is project fraud prevention and detection. By ensuring that visibility to the specific metric is confirmed, the opportunity for project fraud is reduced, thereby improving project fraud prevention and detection. This action also implies that the artifact has been scrutinized by the receiving user and that this user does not detect project fraud within the artifact(s) or those circumstances surrounding the artifact.

The following 3Ms-oriented metrics support the Project Integration Management PMBOK® area of knowledge:

1. Develop Project Charter — Project Charter
2. Develop Project Scope Statement (Preliminary) — Project Scope Statement (Preliminary)
3. Develop Project Management Plan — Project Management Plan
4. Direct and Manage Project Execution — Deliverables
5. Direct and Manage Project Execution — Requested Changes
6. Direct and Manage Project Execution — Implemented Change Requests
7. Direct and Manage Project Execution — Implemented Corrective Actions
8. Direct and Manage Project Execution — Implemented Preventive Actions
9. Direct and Manage Project Execution — Implemented Defect Repair
10. Direct and Manage Project Execution — Work Performance Information
11. Monitor and Control Project Work — Recommended Corrective Actions
12. Monitor and Control Project Work — Recommended Preventive Actions
13. Monitor and Control Project Work — Forecasts
14. Monitor and Control Project Work — Recommended Defect Repair
15. Monitor and Control Project Work — Requested Changes
16. Integrated Change Control — Approved Change Requests
17. Integrated Change Control — Rejected Change Requests
18. Integrated Change Control — Project Management Plan (Approved Updates)
19. Integrated Change Control — Project Scope Statement (Approved Updates)
20. Integrated Change Control — Approved Corrective Actions
21. Integrated Change Control — Approved Preventive Actions
22. Integrated Change Control — Approved Defect Repair
23. Integrated Change Control — Validated Defect Repair
24. Integrated Change Control — Deliverables
25. Close Project — Administrative Closure Procedure
26. Close Project — Contract Closure Procedure
27. Close Project — Final Product, Service, or Result
28. Close Project — Organizational Process Assets (Updates)

Scoring for Section III: Performance Scorecard for these metrics is as follows: 4 = Excellent; 3 = Very Good; 2 = Satisfactory; 1 = Unsatisfactory.

DEVELOP PROJECT CHARTER — PROJECT CHARTER

This is the document that formally authorizes a project. The project charter provides the project manager with the authority to apply organizational resources to project activities.

I. Key Value Areas Weighting (%)
   A. Completion of process preparation and implementation of project charter = 50%.
   B. Approved by customer = 50%.
II. Performance Objectives — Based on all projects linked to specific corporate objectives.
   A. 50%: 4 = completed early and under budget ≥10%; 3 = ≥5%; 2 = completed on time and on budget; 1 = completed late and/or over budget.
   B. 50%: 4 = approved by all key stakeholders and customers early and under budget ≥10%; 3 = approved early and under budget ≥5%; 2 = approved on time and on budget; 1 = approved late and/or over budget.
III. Performance Scorecard
IV. Performance Factors
   A. Project Team Members — Help construct project charter by providing information relevant to areas of the project within project team delivery expectations for time and cost.
   B. Stakeholders — Review and/or approve various versions of project charter within project team delivery expectations for time and cost.
   C. Customers — Review and/or approve various versions of project charter within project team delivery expectations for time and cost.
   D. Project Manager — Leads and/or performs construction of project charter within project team delivery expectations for time and cost.
V. Training Objectives
   A. Short Term — Project manager conducts meetings with stakeholder(s), customer(s), and team member(s) on the creation and completion of the project charter regarding what is involved and who is performing certain tasks within schedule expectations for performance.
   B. Long Term — Team members become trained in the process to develop and complete a project charter as a means to improve total effort to complete task.

DEVELOP PROJECT SCOPE STATEMENT (PRELIMINARY) — PROJECT SCOPE STATEMENT (PRELIMINARY)

The initial definition of the project as to what needs to be accomplished. The project boundaries and characteristics of the project and its associated products and services are stated.

I. Key Value Areas Weighting (%)
   A. Completion of process preparation and implementation of project scope statement (preliminary) = 50%.
   B. Approved by project initiator and project sponsor = 50%.
II. Performance Objectives — Based on all projects linked to specific corporate objectives.
   A. 50%: 4 = completed early and under budget ≥10%; 3 = ≥5%; 2 = completed on time and on budget; 1 = completed late and/or over budget.
   B. 50%: 4 = approved by all key stakeholders and customers early and under budget ≥10%; 3 = approved early and under budget ≥5%; 2 = approved on time and on budget; 1 = approved late and/or over budget.

III. Performance Scorecard
IV. Performance Factors
   A. Project Team Members — Help construct project scope statement (preliminary) while providing information relevant to areas of the project within project team delivery expectations for time and cost.
   B. Project Initiator(s) — Reviews and/or approves various versions of project scope statement (preliminary) within project team delivery expectations for time and cost.
   C. Project Sponsor(s) — Reviews and/or approves various versions of project scope statement (preliminary) within project team delivery expectations for time and cost.
   D. Project Manager — Leads and/or performs construction of project scope statement (preliminary) within project team delivery expectations for time and cost.
V. Training Objectives
   A. Short Term — Project manager conducts meetings with project initiator, sponsor, and team member(s) on the creation and completion of the project scope statement (preliminary) regarding what is involved and who is performing certain tasks within schedule expectations for performance.
   B. Long Term — Team members become trained in the process to develop and complete a project scope statement (preliminary) as a means to improve total effort to complete task.

DEVELOP PROJECT MANAGEMENT PLAN — PROJECT MANAGEMENT PLAN

Includes the actions necessary to define, integrate, and coordinate all subsidiary plans into a project management plan. Defines how the project is executed, monitored, controlled, and closed.

I. Key Value Areas Weighting (%)
   A. Completion of process preparation and implementation of project management plan = 50%.
   B. Approved by project initiator and project sponsor = 50%.
II. Performance Objectives — Based on all projects linked to specific corporate objectives.
   A. 50%: 4 = completed early and under budget ≥10%; 3 = ≥5%; 2 = completed on time and on budget; 1 = completed late and/or over budget.
   B. 50%: 4 = approved by project initiator and project sponsor early and under budget ≥10%; 3 = approved early and under budget ≥5%; 2 = approved on time and on budget; 1 = approved late and/or over budget.
III. Performance Scorecard
IV. Performance Factors
   A. Project Team Members — Help construct project management plan while providing information relevant to areas of the project within project team delivery expectations for time and cost.
   B. Project Initiator(s) — Reviews and/or approves various versions of project management plan within project team delivery expectations for time and cost.

C. Project Sponsor(s) — Reviews and/or approves various versions of project management plan within project team delivery expectations for time and cost.
  D. Project Manager — Leads and/or performs construction of project management plan within project team delivery expectations for time and cost.
V. Training Objectives
  A. Short Term — Project manager conducts meeting with project initiator, project sponsor, and team member(s) on the creation and completion of the project management plan regarding what is involved and who is performing certain tasks within schedule expectations for performance.
  B. Long Term — Team members become trained in the process to develop and complete a project management plan as a means to improve total effort to complete task.

DIRECT AND MANAGE PROJECT EXECUTION — DELIVERABLES

A deliverable is any unique and verifiable product, result, or capability to perform a service that is identified in the project management planning documentation and must be produced and provided to complete the project.

I. Key Value Areas Weighting (%)
  A. Completion of process preparation and implementation of project deliverables = 50%.
  B. Approved by project initiator and project sponsor = 50%.
II. Performance Objectives — Based on all projects linked to specific corporate objectives.
  A. 50%: 4 = completed early and under budget ≥10%; 3 = ≥5%; 2 = completed on time and on budget; 1 = completed late and/or over budget.
  B. 50%: 4 = approved by project initiator and project sponsor early and under budget ≥10%; 3 = approved early and under budget ≥5%; 2 = approved on time and on budget; 1 = approved late and/or over budget.
III. Performance Scorecard
IV. Performance Factors
  A. Project Team Members — Help construct project deliverables while providing information relevant to specific aspects of the project within project team delivery expectations for time and cost.
  B. Project Initiator(s) — Reviews and/or approves project deliverables within project team delivery expectations for time and cost.
  C. Project Sponsor(s) — Reviews and/or approves project deliverables within project team delivery expectations for time and cost.
  D. Project Manager — Leads and/or performs construction of project deliverables within project team delivery expectations for time and cost.
V. Training Objectives
  A. Short Term — Project manager conducts meetings with project initiator, project sponsor, and team member(s) on the creation and completion of project deliverables regarding what is involved and who is performing certain tasks within schedule expectations for performance.
  B. Long Term — Team members become trained in the process to develop and complete project deliverables as a means to improve total effort to complete task.

DIRECT AND MANAGE PROJECT EXECUTION — REQUESTED CHANGES

Changes requested to expand or reduce project scope, to modify policies or procedures, to modify project cost or budget, or to revise the project schedule often are identified while project work is performed. Requests for a change can be direct or indirect, externally or internally initiated, and optional or legally required.

   I. Key Value Areas Weighting (%)
      A. Completion of process preparation and implementation of project requested change = 50%.
      B. Approved by project initiator and project sponsor = 50%.
  II. Performance Objectives — Based on all projects linked to specific corporate objectives.
      A. 50%: 4 = completed early and under budget ≥10%; 3 = ≥5%; 2 = completed on time and on budget; 1 = completed late and/or over budget.
      B. 50%: 4 = approved by project initiator and project sponsor early and under budget ≥10%; 3 = approved early and under budget ≥5%; 2 = approved on time and on budget; 1 = approved late and/or over budget.
 III. Performance Scorecard
  IV. Performance Factors
      A. Project Team Members — Help construct requested change to project by providing information relevant to specific aspects of the project requested change within project team delivery expectations for time and cost.
      B. Project Initiator(s) — Reviews and/or approves project requested change within project team delivery expectations for time and cost.
      C. Project Sponsor(s) — Reviews and/or approves project requested change within project team delivery expectations for time and cost.
      D. Project Manager — Leads and/or performs construction of project requested change within project team delivery expectations for time and cost.
   V. Training Objectives
      A. Short Term — Project manager conducts meetings with project initiator, project sponsor, and team member(s) on the creation and completion of the project requested change regarding what is involved and who is performing certain tasks within schedule expectations for performance.
      B. Long Term — Team members become trained in the process to develop and complete project requested changes as a means to improve total effort to complete task.

DIRECT AND MANAGE PROJECT EXECUTION — IMPLEMENTED CHANGE REQUESTS

Approved change requests that have been implemented by the project management team during project execution.

   I. Key Value Areas Weighting (%)
      A. Completion of process preparation and implementation of change requests = 50%.
      B. Approved by project initiator and project sponsor = 50%.

II. Performance Objectives — Based on all projects linked to specific corporate objectives.
   A. 50%: 4 = completed early and under budget ≥10%; 3 = ≥5%; 2 = completed on time and on budget; 1 = completed late and/or over budget.
   B. 50%: 4 = approved by project initiator and project sponsor early and under budget ≥10%; 3 = approved early and under budget ≥5%; %: 2 = approved on time and on budget; 1 = approved late and/or over budget.
III. Performance Scorecard
IV. Performance Factors
   A. Project Team Members — Help implement project change request by providing information relevant to specific aspects of the project implemented change request within project team delivery expectations for time and cost.
   B. Project Initiator(s) — Reviews and/or approves project implemented change request within project team delivery expectations for time and cost.
   C. Project Sponsor(s) — Reviews and/or approves project implemented change request within project team delivery expectations for time and cost.
   D. Project Manager — Leads and/or performs project implemented change request within project team delivery expectations for time and cost.
V. Training Objectives
   A. Short Term — Project manager conducts meetings with project initiator(s), project sponsor(s), and team member(s) on the implementation of the project change request regarding what is involved and who is performing certain tasks within schedule expectations for performance.
   B. Long Term — Team members become trained in the process to develop and complete project change request as a means to improve total effort to complete task.

DIRECT AND MANAGE PROJECT EXECUTION — IMPLEMENTED CORRECTIVE ACTIONS

The approved corrective actions that have been implemented by the project management team to bring expected future project performance into conformance with the project management plan.

I. Key Value Areas Weighting (%)
   A. Completion of process preparation and implementation of requested corrective action = 50%.
   B. Approved by project sponsor and project manager = 50%.
II. Performance Objectives — Based on all projects linked to specific corporate objectives.
   A. 50%: 4 = completed early and under budget ≥10%; 3 = ≥5%; 2 = completed on time and on budget; 1 = completed late and/or over budget.
   B. 50%: 4 = approved by project sponsor and project manager early and under budget ≥10%; 3 = approved early and under budget ≥5%; 2 = approved on time and on budget; 1 = approved late and/or over budget.
III. Performance Scorecard
IV. Performance Factors
   A. Project Team Members — Help implement corrective action by providing information relevant to specific aspects of the project implemented corrective action within project team delivery expectations for time and cost.

B. Project Sponsor(s) — Reviews and/or approves project implemented corrective action within project team delivery expectations for time and cost.
C. Project Manager — Leads and/or performs project implemented corrective action within project team delivery expectations for time and cost.

V. Training Objectives
A. Short Term — Project manager conducts meetings with project sponsor and team member(s) on the implementation of the project corrective action regarding what is involved and who is performing certain tasks within schedule expectations for performance.
B. Long Term — Team members become trained in the process to develop and complete project corrective actions as a means to improve total effort to complete task.

DIRECT AND MANAGE PROJECT EXECUTION — IMPLEMENTED PREVENTIVE ACTIONS

The approved preventive actions that have been implemented by the project management team to reduce the consequence of project risks.

I. Key Value Areas Weighting (%)
A. Completion of process preparation and implementation of preventive action = 50%.
B. Approved by project manager and project sponsor = 50%.

II. Performance Objectives — Based on all projects linked to specific corporate objectives.
A. 50%: 4 = completed early and under budget ≥10%; 3 = ≥5%; 2 = completed on time and on budget; 1 = completed late and/or over budget.
B. 50%: 4 = approved by project manager and project sponsor early and under budget ≥10%; 3 = approved early and under budget ≥5%; 2 = approved on time and on budget; 1 = approved late and/or over budget.

III. Performance Scorecard

IV. Performance Factors
A. Project Team Members — Help implement preventive action by providing information relevant to specific aspects of the project implemented preventive action within project team delivery expectations for time and cost.
B. Project Sponsor(s) — Reviews and/or approves project implemented preventive action within project team delivery expectations for time and cost.
C. Project Manager — Leads and/or performs project implemented preventive action within project team delivery expectations for time and cost.

V. Training Objectives
A. Short Term — Project manager conducts meetings with project sponsor and team member(s) on the implementation of the project preventive action regarding what is involved and who is performing certain tasks within schedule expectations for performance.
B. Long Term — Team members become trained in the process to develop and complete a project implemented preventive action as a means to improve total effort to complete task.

DIRECT AND MANAGE PROJECT EXECUTION — IMPLEMENTED DEFECT REPAIR

During project execution, the project management team has implemented approved product defect corrections.

I. Key Value Areas Weighting (%)
   A. Completion of process preparation and implementation of product defect repair = 50%.
   B. Approved by project manager and project sponsor = 50%.
II. Performance Objectives — Based on all projects linked to specific corporate objectives.
   A. 50%: 4 = completed early and under budget ≥10%; 3 = ≥5%; 2 = completed on time and on budget; 1 = completed late and/or over budget.
   B. 50%: 4 = approved by project manager and project sponsor early and under budget ≥10%; 3 = approved early and under budget ≥5%; 2 = approved on time and on budget; 1 = approved late and/or over budget.
III. Performance Scorecard
IV. Performance Factors
   A. Project Team Members — Help implement defect repair by providing information relevant to specific aspects of the project product implemented defect repair within project team delivery expectations for time and cost.
   B. Project Sponsor(s) — Reviews and/or approves project product implemented defect repair within project team delivery expectations for time and cost.
   C. Project Manager — Leads and/or performs project product implemented defect repair within project team delivery expectations for time and cost.
V. Training Objectives
   A. Short Term — Project manager conducts meetings with project sponsor and team member(s) on the implementation of the project product defect repair regarding what is involved and who is performing certain tasks within schedule expectations for performance.
   B. Long Term — Team members become trained in the process to develop and complete a project product defect repair as a means to improve total effort to complete task.

DIRECT AND MANAGE PROJECT EXECUTION — WORK PERFORMANCE INFORMATION

Information on the status of the project activities being performed to accomplish the project work is routinely collected as part of the project management plan execution.

I. Key Value Areas Weighting (%)
   A. Completion of process preparation and implementation of work performance information = 50%.
   B. Approved by project manager and internal auditing = 50%.
II. Performance Objectives — Based on all projects linked to specific corporate objectives.
   A. 50%: 4 = completed early and under budget ≥10%; 3 = ≥5%; 2 = completed on time and on budget; 1 = completed late and/or over budget.

B. 50%: 4 = approved by project manager and internal auditing early and under budget ≥10%; 3 = approved early and under budget ≥5%; 2 = approved on time and on budget; 1 = approved late and/or over budget.
III. Performance Scorecard
IV. Performance Factors
   A. Project Team Members — Help construct work performance information relevant to specific aspects of the project progress within project team delivery expectations for time and cost.
   B. Internal Auditing — Reviews work performance information for project fraud policy compliance.
   C. Project Manager — Leads and/or performs reporting of project work performance information within project team delivery expectations for time and cost on a cyclical basis.
V. Training Objectives
   A. Short Term — Project manager conducts meetings with project sponsor and team member(s) on the implementation of the project work performance information regarding what is involved and who is performing certain tasks within schedule expectations for performance.
   B. Long Term — Team members become trained in the process to develop and complete project work performance information as a means to improve total effort to complete task.

MONITOR AND CONTROL PROJECT WORK — RECOMMENDED CORRECTIVE ACTIONS

Corrective actions are documented recommendations required to bring expected future project performance into conformance with the project management plan.

I. Key Value Areas Weighting (%)
   A. Completion of process preparation and implementation of recommended corrective actions = 50%.
   B. Approved by project manager and project sponsor = 50%.
II. Performance Objectives — Based on all projects linked to specific corporate objectives.
   A. 50%: 4 = completed early and under budget ≥10%; 3 = ≥5%; 2 = completed on time and on budget; 1 = completed late and/or over budget.
   B. 50%: 4 = approved by project manager and project sponsor early and under budget ≥10%; 3 = approved early and under budget ≥5%; 2 = approved on time and on budget; 1 = approved late and/or over budget.
III. Performance Scorecard
IV. Performance Factors
   A. Project Team Members — Help identify recommended corrective actions by providing information relevant to specific aspects of the project recommended corrective actions within project team delivery expectations for time and cost.
   B. Project Sponsor — Reviews and/or approves project recommended corrective actions within project team delivery expectations for time and cost.
   C. Project Manager — Leads and/or performs project recommended corrective actions within project team delivery expectations for time and cost.

V. Training Objectives
   A. Short Term — Project manager conducts meetings with project sponsor and team member(s) on the determination of the project recommended corrective actions regarding what is involved and who is performing certain tasks within schedule expectations for performance.
   B. Long Term — Team members become trained in the process to develop and complete a project recommended corrective action as a means to improve total effort to complete task.

MONITOR AND CONTROL PROJECT WORK — RECOMMENDED PREVENTIVE ACTIONS

Preventive actions are documented recommendations that reduce the probability of negative consequences associated with project risks.

   I. Key Value Areas Weighting (%)
      A. Completion of process preparation and implementation of recommended preventive actions = 50%.
      B. Approved by project manager and project sponsor = 50%.
   II. Performance Objectives — Based on all projects linked to specific corporate objectives.
      A. 50%: 4 = completed early and under budget $\geq$10%; 3 = $\geq$5%; 2 = completed on time and on budget; 1 = completed late and/or over budget.
      B. 50%: 4 = approved by project manager and project sponsor early and under budget $\geq$10%; 3 = approved early and under budget $\geq$5%; 2 = approved on time and on budget; 1 = approved late and/or over budget.
   III. Performance Scorecard
   IV. Performance Factors
      A. Project Team Members — Help identify recommended preventive actions by providing information relevant to specific aspects of the project recommended preventive actions within project team delivery expectations for time and cost.
      B. Project Sponsor(s) — Reviews and/or approves project recommended preventive actions within project team delivery expectations for time and cost.
      C. Project Manager — Leads and/or performs project recommended preventive actions within project team delivery expectations for time and cost.
   V. Training Objectives
      A. Short Term — Project manager conducts meetings with project sponsor and team member(s) on the determination of the project recommended preventive actions regarding what is involved and who is performing certain tasks within schedule expectations for performance.
      B. Long Term — Team members become trained in the process to develop and complete a project recommended preventive action as a means to improve total effort to complete task.

MONITOR AND CONTROL PROJECT WORK — FORECASTS

Forecasts include estimates or predictions of conditions and events in the project's future, based on information and knowledge available at the time of the forecast.

I. Key Value Areas Weighting (%)
   A. Completion of process preparation and implementation of project forecasts = 50%.
   B. Approved by project manager and project sponsor = 50%.
II. Performance Objectives — Based on all projects linked to specific corporate objectives.
   A. 50%: 4 = completed early and under budget ≥10%; 3 = ≥5%; 2 = completed on time and on budget; 1 = completed late and/or over budget.
   B. 50%: 4 = approved by project manager and project sponsor early and under budget ≥10%; 3 = approved early and under budget ≥5%; 2 = approved on time and on budget; 1 = approved late and/or over budget.
III. Performance Scorecard
IV. Performance Factors
   A. Project Team Members — Help identify project forecasts by providing information relevant to specific aspects of the project forecasts within project team delivery expectations for time and cost.
   B. Project Sponsor(s) — Reviews and/or approves project forecasts within project team delivery expectations for time and cost.
   C. Project Manager — Leads and/or performs project forecasts within project team delivery expectations for time and cost.
   D. Project Management Office — Provides uniform project forecast policy standard.
V. Training Objectives
   A. Short Term — Project manager conducts meetings with project sponsor and team member(s) on the provisioning of the project forecasts regarding what is involved and who is performing certain tasks within schedule expectations for performance.
   B. Long Term — Team members become trained in the process to develop and complete project forecasts as a means to improve total effort to complete task.

MONITOR AND CONTROL PROJECT WORK — RECOMMENDED DEFECT REPAIR

Some defects which are found during the quality inspection and audit process are recommended for correction.

I. Key Value Areas Weighting (%)
   A. Completion of process preparation and implementation of recommended defect repair = 50%.
   B. Approved by project manager, project sponsor, and quality assurance = 50%.
II. Performance Objectives — Based on all projects linked to specific corporate objectives.
   A. 50%: 4 = completed early and under budget ≥10%; 3 = ≥5%; 2 = completed on time and on budget; 1 = completed late and/or over budget.
   B. 50%: 4 = approved by project manager, project sponsor, and quality assurance early and under budget ≥10%; 3 = approved early and under budget ≥5%; 2 = approved on time and on budget; 1 = approved late and/or over budget.
III. Performance Scorecard
IV. Performance Factors
   A. Project Team Members — Help identify information relevant to specific aspects of the project to quality assurance for recommended defect repair within project team delivery expectations for time and cost.

B. Project Sponsor(s)— Reviews and/or approves project recommended defect repair within project team delivery expectations for time and cost.
C. Project Manager — Leads and/or performs project recommended defect repair within project team delivery expectations for time and cost.
D. Quality Assurance — Provides uniform project quality standard for project work.

V. Training Objectives
A. Short Term — Project manager conducts meetings with project sponsor and team member(s) on the determination of project work defects by quality assurance for the project regarding what is involved and who is performing certain tasks within schedule expectations for performance.
B. Long Term — Team members become trained in the process to assist quality assurance in defect repair recommendation as a means to improve total effort to complete task.

MONITOR AND CONTROL PROJECT WORK — REQUESTED CHANGES

Changes requested to expand or reduce project scope, to modify policies or procedures, to modify project cost or budget, or to revise the project schedule often are identified when project work is performed.

I. Key Value Areas Weighting (%)
A. Completion of process preparation and implementation of requested changes = 50%.
B. Approved by project manager and project sponsor = 50%.

II. Performance Objectives — Based on all projects linked to specific corporate objectives.
A. 50%: 4 = completed early and under budget $\geq 10\%$; 3 = $\geq 3\%$; 2 = completed on time and on budget; 1 = completed late and/or over budget.
B. 50%: 4 = approved by project manager and project sponsor early and under budget $\geq 10\%$; 3 = approved early and under budget $\geq 5\%$; 2 = approved on time and on budget; 1 = approved late and/or over budget.

III. Performance Scorecard

IV. Performance Factors
A. Project Team Members — Help identify requested project work change by providing information relevant to specific aspects of the project requested change within project team delivery expectations for time and cost.
B. Project Sponsor(s) — Reviews and/or approves project requested changes within project team delivery expectations for time and cost.
C. Project Manager — Leads and/or performs project requested changes corrective action within project team delivery expectations for time and cost.

V. Training Objectives
A. Short Term — Project manager conducts meetings with project sponsor and team member(s) on the determination of the project requested changes regarding what is involved and who is performing certain tasks within schedule expectations for performance.
B. Long Term — Team members become trained in the process to develop and complete a project requested change as a means to improve total effort to complete task.

INTEGRATED CHANGE CONTROL — APPROVED CHANGE REQUESTS

Approved change requests are the documented, authorized changes to expand or contract project scope. The approved change requests can also modify policies, project management plans, procedures, costs, or budgets or revise schedules.

I. Key Value Areas Weighting (%)
   A. Completion of process preparation and implementation of approved change requests = 50%.
   B. Approved by project manager and project sponsor = 50%.
II. Performance Objectives — Based on all projects linked to specific corporate objectives.
   A. 50%: 4 = completed early and under budget ≥10%; 3 = ≥5%; 2 = completed on time and on budget; 1 = completed late and/or over budget.
   B. 50%: 4 = approved by project manager and project sponsor early and under budget ≥10%; 3 = approved early and under budget ≥5%; 2 = approved on time and on budget; 1 = approved late and/or over budget.
III. Performance Scorecard
IV. Performance Factors
   A. Project Team Members — Help identify information relevant to specific approved change request within project team delivery expectations for time and cost.
   B. Project Sponsor(s) — Reviews and/or approves project approved change requests within project team delivery expectations for time and cost.
   C. Project Manager — Leads and/or performs project approved change requests within project team delivery expectations for time and cost.
V. Training Objectives
   A. Short Term — Project manager conducts meetings with project sponsor and team member(s) on the determination of the project approved change requests regarding what is involved and who is performing certain tasks within schedule expectations for performance.
   B. Long Term — Team members become trained in the process to develop and complete a project approved change request as a means to improve total effort to complete task.

INTEGRATED CHANGE CONTROL — REJECTED CHANGE REQUESTS

Includes the change requests, their supporting documentation, and their change review status indicating a disposition of rejected change requests.

I. Key Value Areas Weighting (%)
   A. Completion of process preparation and disposition of rejected change requests = 50%.
   B. Approved by project manager and project sponsor = 50%.
II. Performance Objectives — Based on all projects linked to specific corporate objectives.
   A. 50%: 4 = completed early and under budget ≥10%; 3 = ≥5%; 2 = completed on time and on budget; 1 = completed late and/or over budget.

B. 50%: 4 = approved by project manager and project sponsor early and under budget ≥10%; 3 = approved early and under budget ≥5%; 2 = approved on time and on budget; 1 = approved late and/or over budget.
III. Performance Scorecard
IV. Performance Factors
   A. Project Team Members — Help identify information relevant to specific aspects of the project rejected change request within project team delivery expectations for time and cost.
   B. Project Sponsor(s) — Reviews and/or approves project rejected change requests action within project team delivery expectations for time and cost.
   C. Project Manager — Leads and/or performs project rejected change requests within project team delivery expectations for time and cost.
V. Training Objectives
   A. Short Term — Project manager conducts meetings with project sponsor and team member(s) on the determination of the project rejected change requests regarding what is involved and who is performing certain tasks within schedule expectations for performance.
   B. Long Term — Team members become trained in the process to develop and complete a project rejected change request as a means to improve total effort to complete task.

INTEGRATED CHANGE CONTROL — PROJECT MANAGEMENT PLAN (APPROVED UPDATES)

Updates to the project management plan include actions that improve definition, integration, and coordination of all subsidiary management plans.

I. Key Value Areas Weighting (%)
   A. Completion of process preparation and implementation of approved updates to the project management plan = 50%.
   B. Approved by project manager and project sponsor = 50%.
II. Performance Objectives — Based on all projects linked to specific corporate objectives.
   A. 50%: = completed early and under budget ≥10%; 3 = ≥5%; 2 = completed on time and on budget; 1 = completed late and/or over budget.
   B. 50%: 4 = approved by project manager and project sponsor early and under budget ≥10%; 3 = approved early and under budget ≥5%; 2 = approved on time and on budget; 1 = approved late and/or over budget.
III. Performance Scorecard
IV. Performance Factors
   A. Project Team Members — Help apply approved updates by providing information relevant to specific aspects of the project management plan within project team delivery expectations for time and cost.
   B. Project Sponsor(s) — Reviews and/or approves project management plan updates within project team delivery expectations for time and cost.

C. Project Manager — Leads and/or performs project management plan improvement from approved updates within project team delivery expectations for time and cost.
V. Training Objectives
  A. Short Term — Project manager conducts meetings with project sponsor and team member(s) on the approval of project management plan updates regarding what is involved and who is performing certain tasks within schedule expectations for performance.
  B. Long Term — Team members become trained in the process to develop and complete implementation of an approved project management plan update as a means to improve total effort to complete task.

INTEGRATED CHANGE CONTROL — PROJECT SCOPE STATEMENT (APPROVED UPDATES)

If approved change requests result from the create work breakdown structure process, then the project scope statement is updated to include those approved changes.

I. Key Value Areas Weighting (%)
  A. Completion of process preparation and implementation to updates to project scope statement = 50%.
  B. Approved by project manager and project sponsor = 50%.
II. Performance Objectives — Based on all projects linked to specific corporate objectives.
  A. 50%: 4 = completed early and under budget $\geq 10\%$; 3 = $\geq 5\%$; 2 = completed on time and on budget; 1 = completed late and/or over budget.
  B. 50%: 4 = approved by project manager and project sponsor early and under budget $\geq 10\%$; 3 = approved early and under budget $\geq 5\%$; 2 = approved on time and on budget; 1 = approved late and/or over budget.
III. Performance Scorecard
IV. Performance Factors
  A. Project Teams — Help apply approved updates by providing information relevant to specific approved updates to the project scope statement within project team delivery expectations for time and cost.
  B. Project Sponsor(s) — Reviews and/or approves updates to project scope statement.
  C. Project Manager — Leads and/or applies approved updates to project scope statement.
V. Training Objectives
  A. Short Term — Project manager conducts meetings with project sponsor and team member(s) on the determination of approved updates to the project scope statement regarding what is involved and who is performing certain tasks within schedule expectations for performance.
  B. Long Term — Team members become trained in the process to develop and complete an approved update to the project scope statement as a means to improve total effort to complete task.

INTEGRATED CHANGE CONTROL — APPROVED CORRECTIVE ACTIONS

Approved corrective actions are documented, authorized directions required to bring expected future project performance into conformance with the project management plan.

I. Key Value Areas Weighting (%)
   A. Completion of process preparation and implementation of corrective action = 50%.
   B. Approved by project manager and project sponsor = 50%.
II. Performance Objectives — Based on all projects linked to specific corporate objectives.
   A. 50%: 4 = completed early and under budget ≥10%; 3 = ≥5%; 2 = completed on time and on budget; 1 = completed late and/or over budget.
   B. 50%: 4 = approved by project manager and project sponsor early and under budget ≥10%; 3 = approved early and under budget ≥5%; 2 = approved on time and on budget; 1 = approved late and/or over budget.
III. Performance Scorecard
IV. Performance Factors
   A. Project Team Members — Help identify information relevant to specific aspects of the project corrective action within project team delivery expectations for time and cost.
   B. Project Sponsor(s) — Reviews and/or approves project corrective actions within project team delivery expectations for time and cost.
   C. Project Manager — Leads and/or performs project corrective actions within project team delivery expectations for time and cost.
V. Training Objectives
   A. Short Term — Project manager conducts meetings with project sponsor and team member(s) on the determination of project corrective actions regarding what is involved and who is performing certain tasks within schedule expectations for performance.
   B. Long Term — Team members become trained in the process to develop and complete a project corrective action as a means to improve total effort to complete task.

INTEGRATED CHANGE CONTROL — APPROVED PREVENTIVE ACTIONS

Approved preventive actions are documented, authorized directions that reduce the probability of negative consequences associated with project risks.

I. Key Value Areas Weighting (%)
   A. Completion of process preparation and implementation of approved preventive actions = 50%.
   B. Approved by project manager and project sponsor = 50%.
II. Performance Objectives — Based on all projects linked to specific corporate objectives.
   A. 50%: 4 = completed early and under budget ≥10%; 3 = ≥5%; 2 = completed on time and on budget; 1 = completed late and/or over budget.

B. 50%: 4 = approved by project manager and project sponsor early and under budget ≥10%; 3 = approved early and under budget ≥5%; 2 = approved on time and on budget; 1 = approved late and/or over budget.
III. Performance Scorecard
IV. Performance Factors
   A. Project Team Members — Help identify information relevant to specific aspects of the project to validate possible preventive action(s) within project team delivery expectations for time and cost.
   B. Project Sponsor(s) — Reviews and/or approves project preventive action(s) within project team delivery expectations for time and cost.
   C. Project Manager — Leads and/or performs project development of approved preventive actions within project team delivery expectations for time and cost.
V. Training Objectives
   A. Short Term — Project manager conducts meetings with project sponsor and team member(s) on the determination of project risk preventive actions regarding what is involved and who is performing certain tasks within schedule expectations for performance.
   B. Long Term — Team members become trained in the process to develop and complete a project risk preventive action(s) as a means to improve total effort to complete task.

INTEGRATED CHANGE CONTROL — APPROVED DEFECT REPAIR

The documented, authorized request for product correction of a defect found during the quality inspection or audit process.

I. Key Value Areas Weighting (%)
   A. Completion of process preparation and implementation of defect repair = 50%.
   B. Approved by project manager, project sponsor, and quality assurance = 50%.
II. Performance Objectives — Based on all projects linked to specific corporate objectives.
   A. 50%: 4 = completed early and under budget ≥10%; 3 = ≥5%; 2 = completed on time and on budget; 1 = completed late and/or over budget.
   B. 50%: 4 = approved by project manager, project sponsor, and quality assurance early and under budget ≥10%; 3 = approved early and under budget ≥5%; 2 = approved on time and on budget; 1 = approved late and/or over budget.
III. Performance Scorecard
IV. Performance Factors
   A. Project Team Members — Help identify information relevant to specific aspects of project requested defect repairs within project team delivery expectations for time and cost.
   B. Project Sponsor(s) — Reviews and/or approves project requests for defect repair within project team delivery expectations for time and cost.
   C. Project Manager — Leads and/or performs project requests for defect repair within project team delivery expectations for time and cost.
   D. Quality Assurance — Identifies project defect repair scenarios for project team.

V. Training Objectives
   A. Short Term — Project manager conducts meetings with project sponsor and team member(s) on the standards for quality assurance for project deliverables regarding what is involved and who is performing certain tasks within schedule expectations for performance.
   B. Long Term — Team members become trained in the process to develop defect repair documentation and gain approval as a means to improve total effort to complete task.

INTEGRATED CHANGE CONTROL — VALIDATED DEFECT REPAIR

Notification that reinspected repaired items have been either accepted or rejected.

I. Key Value Areas Weighting (%)
   A. Completion of process preparation and implementation of validated defect repair = 50%.
   B. Approved by project manager, project sponsor, and quality assurance = 50%.
II. Performance Objectives — Based on all projects linked to specific corporate objectives.
   A. 50%: 4 = completed early and under budget ≥10%; 3 = ≥5%; 2 = completed on time and on budget; 1 = completed late and/or over budget.
   B. 50%: 4 = approved by project manager, project sponsor, and quality assurance early and under budget ≥10%; 3 = approved early and under budget ≥5%; 2 = approved on time and on budget; 1 = approved late and/or over budget.
III. Performance Scorecard
IV. Performance Factors
   A. Project Team Members — Help identify information relevant to specific aspects of project defect repair within project team delivery expectations for time and cost.
   B. Project Sponsor(s) — Reviews and/or validates project defect repair within project team delivery expectations for time and cost.
   C. Project Manager — Leads and/or performs project defect repair within project team delivery expectations for time and cost.
   D. Quality Assurance — Identifies nonconformance to project defect repair work for project team and provides approval to project manager and project sponsor that this work meets quality assurance standards.
V. Training Objectives
   A. Short Term — Project manager conducts meetings with project sponsor and team member(s) on the standards for quality assurance for project deliverables regarding what is involved and who is performing certain tasks within schedule expectations for performance.
   B. Long Term — Team members become trained in the process to develop defect repair documentation and gain approval as a means to improve total effort to complete task.

INTEGRATED CHANGE CONTROL — DELIVERABLES

Any unique and verifiable product, result, or capability to perform a service that is identified in the project management planning documentation and must be produced and provided to complete the project.

I. Key Value Areas Weighting (%)
   A. Completion of process preparation and implementation of an approved deliverable derived from change control = 50%.
   B. Approved by project manager and project sponsor = 50%.
II. Performance Objectives — Based on all projects linked to specific corporate objectives.
   A. 50%: 4 = completed early and under budget ≥10%; 3 = ≥5%; 2 = completed on time and on budget; 1 = completed late and/or over budget.
   B. 50%: 4 = approved by project manager and project sponsor early and under budget ≥10%; 3 = approved early and under budget ≥5%; 2 = approved on time and on budget; 1 = approved late and/or over budget.
III. Performance Scorecard
IV. Performance Factors
   A. Project Team Members— Help identify information relevant to specific project deliverables derived from change control within project team delivery expectations for time and cost.
   B. Project Sponsor(s) — Reviews and/or approves project change control deliverables within project team delivery expectations for time and cost.
   C. Project Manager — Leads and/or performs project change control deliverable submission within project team delivery expectations for time and cost.
V. Training Objectives
   A. Short Term — Project manager conducts meetings with project sponsor and team member(s) on the development and submission process of the project deliverables derived from project change control regarding what is involved and who is performing certain tasks within schedule expectations for performance.
   B. Long Term — Team members become trained in the process to develop and submit a project deliverable derived from project change control process as a means to improve total effort to complete task.

CLOSE PROJECT — ADMINISTRATIVE CLOSURE PROCEDURE

Contains all the activities and the related roles and responsibilities of the project team members involved in executing the administrative closure procedure.

I. Key Value Areas Weighting (%)
   A. Completion of process preparation and implementation of actions and activities to define the stakeholder approval requirements for all levels of deliverables and changes = 30%.
   B. 30% = completion of actions and activities in other required project processes that are necessary to:
      1. Confirm that the project has met all stakeholders' mandatory requirements
      2. Verify that all deliverables have been provided and accepted
      3. Validate that any completion and exit criteria have been met
   C. Completion of actions and activities necessary to satisfy completion or exit criteria for the project or its phases = 20%.
   D. Approved by project manager and project sponsor = 20%
II. Performance Objectives — Based on all projects linked to specific corporate objectives.
   A. 30%: 4 = completed early and under budget ≥10%; 3 = ≥5%; 2 = completed on time and on budget; 1 = completed late and/or over budget.

B. 30%: 4 = completed early and under budget ≥10%; 3 = ≥5%; 2 = completed on time and on budget; 1 = completed late and/or over budget.
  C. 20%: 4 = completed early and under budget ≥10%; 3 = ≥5%; 2 = completed on time and on budget; 1 = completed late and/or over budget.
  D. 20%: 4 = approved by project manager and project sponsor early and under budget ≥10%; 3 = approved early and under budget ≥5%; 2 = approved on time and on budget; 1 = approved late and/or over budget.
III. Performance Scorecard
IV. Performance Factors
  A. Project Team Members — Help identify open tasks while providing information relevant to specific aspects of the project administrative closure within project team delivery expectations for time and cost.
  B. Project Sponsor(s) — Reviews and/or approves project administrative closure action within project team delivery expectations for time and cost.
  C. Project Manager — Leads and/or performs project administrative closure procedure within project team delivery expectations for time and cost.
V. Training Objectives
  A. Short Term — Project manager conducts meetings with project sponsor and team member(s) on the administrative closure of the project regarding what is involved and who is performing certain tasks within schedule expectations for performance.
  B. Long Term — Team members become trained in the process to administratively close project work as a means to improve total effort to complete task.

CLOSE PROJECT — CONTRACT CLOSURE PROCEDURE

Developed to provide a step-by-step method that addresses the terms and conditions of the contracts and any required completion or exit criteria for contract closure.

I. Key Value Areas Weighting (%)
  A. Completion of process preparation and implementation of actions to close project-related contracts = 50%.
  B. Approved by project manager and project sponsor = 50%.
II. Performance Objectives — Based on all projects linked to specific corporate objectives.
  A. 50%: 4 = completed early and under budget ≥10%; 3 = ≥5%; 2 = completed on time and on budget; 1 = completed late and/or over budget.
  B. 50%: 4 = approved by project manager and project sponsor early and under budget ≥10%; 3 = approved early and under budget ≥5%; 2 = approved on time and on budget; 1 = approved late and/or over budget.
III. Performance Scorecard
IV. Performance Factors
  A. Project Sponsor(s) — Reviews and/or approves project contract closure action within project team delivery expectations for time and cost.
  B. Project Manager — Leads and/or performs project contract closure procedure within project team delivery expectations for time and cost.
V. Training Objectives
  A. Short Term — Project manager conducts meetings with project sponsor on contract closure of the project regarding what is involved and who is performing certain tasks within schedule expectation for performance.

B. Long Term — Project manager becomes trained in the process to close project contracts as a means to improve total effort to complete task.

CLOSE PROJECT — FINAL PRODUCT, SERVICE, OR RESULT

Formal acceptance and handover of the final product, service, or result that the project was authorized to produce. The acceptance includes receipt of a formal statement that the terms of the contract have been met.

I. Key Value Areas Weighting (%)
   A. Completion of process preparation and implementation for final delivery of project deliverable = 50%.
   B. Approved by project manager and project sponsor = 50%.
II. Performance Objectives — Based on all projects linked to specific corporate objectives.
   A. 50%: 4 = completed early and under budget ≥10%; 3 = ≥5%; 2 = completed on time and on budget; 1 = completed late and/or over budget.
   B. 50%: 4 = approved by project manager and project sponsor early and under budget ≥10%; 3 = approved early and under budget ≥5%; 2 = approved on time and on budget; 1 = approved late and/or over budget.
III. Performance Scorecard
IV. Performance Factors
   A. Project Sponsor(s) — Reviews and/or approves project administrative closure action within project team delivery expectations for time and cost.
   B. Project Manager — Leads and/or performs project deliverable turnover within project team delivery expectations for time and cost.
V. Training Objectives
   A. Short Term — Project manager conducts meetings with project sponsor on the deliverables of the project regarding what is involved and who is performing certain tasks within schedule expectations for performance.
   B. Long Term — Project manager becomes trained in the process to turnover project deliverables as a means to improve total effort to complete task.

CLOSE PROJECT — ORGANIZATIONAL PROCESS ASSETS (UPDATES)

Closure will include the development of the index and location of project documentation using the configuration management systems. It includes formal acceptance documentation, project files, project closure documents, and historical information.

I. Key Value Areas Weighting (%)
   A. Completion of process preparation and implementation for turnover of all project documentation to PMO knowledge library = 30%.
   B. Completion of process preparation and implementation for turnover of all project closure documentation to PMO knowledge library = 30%.
   C. Completion of process preparation and implementation for turnover of all project historical information to PMO knowledge library = 20%.
   D. Approved by customer and project sponsor = 20%.

II. Performance Objectives — Based on all projects linked to specific corporate objectives.
   A. 30%: 4 = completed early and under budget ≥10%; 3 = ≥5%; 2 = completed on time and on budget; 1 = completed late and/or over budget.
   B. 30%: 4 = completed early and under budget ≥10%; 3 = ≥5%; 2 = completed on time and on budget; 1 = completed late and/or over budget.
   C. 20%: 4 = completed early and under budget ≥10%; 3 = ≥5%; 2 = completed on time and on budget; 1 = completed late and/or over budget.
   D. 20%: 4 = approved by customer and project sponsor early and under budget ≥10%; 3 = approved early and under budget ≥5%; 2 = approved on time and on budget; 1 = approved late and/or over budget.
III. Performance Scorecard
IV. Performance Factors
   A. Customer — Has been appropriately prepped to accept project deliverables within project team delivery expectations for time and cost.
   B. Project Sponsor(s) — Reviews and/or approves project turnover action within project team delivery expectations for time and cost.
   C. Project Manager — Leads and/or performs project closure within project team delivery expectations for time and cost.
V. Training Objectives
   A. Short Term — Project manager conducts meetings with customer and project sponsor on closure of the project and its acceptance regarding what is involved and who is performing certain tasks within schedule expectations for performance.
   B. Long Term — Team members become trained in the process to administratively close project work as a means to improve total effort to complete task.

SUMMARY

Project Integration Management essentially defines why the world needs project managers. The project manager value proposition rests on the capability of the project manager to deliver project work on time and on budget or better. Failure to do so is not necessarily an indictment of the individual but more likely an indictment of the low level of project management skills as practiced by the business and an indictment of the poor alignment of corporate objectives to projects and vice versa. Without the project manager, who would bring out the cross-collaboration typically necessary to complete any project?

When considered in the aggregate, the 3Ms metric profiles presented in this chapter can be processed to produce a measurable assessment of any completed project with sufficient inspection given to the competency of the project manager and the project sponsor. That said, it should be inferred that the success of the project manager is strongly dependent on the success of the project sponsor in the results delivered by the project sponsor role. A project manager never fails or succeeds by himself or herself.

In addition to the content specific to the Project Integration Management area of knowledge from the Project Management Institute PMBOK®, a critical benefit of these processes is improved visibility of project opportunity and threat to project delivery. Again, this supports the value proposition of the project manager. However, when the 3Ms Project Integration Management metrics are applied to a project, the visibility of the project becomes exponentially clearer throughout the project life cycle. This includes project delivery acceleration opportunities and related project threats. This additional vision is vital to the success of the project given the constraints that projects typically endure, such as resources, time, and scope.

We believe that the project delivery decision value can be augmented further and greater when the answer to the question is already known (more visibility). It is hard to be wrong when you are always right because you know that you know! This is what the application of 3Ms can do for you.

We encourage your practice and experimentation with these 3Ms PMBOK®-related metrics. You can only prosper.

QUESTIONS

17-1. Which of the following 3Ms metrics is *not* part of the develop project management plan process:
  a. Project management plan
  b. Configuration management system
  c. Project charter
  d. Change control system

17-2. If a project management plan was completed 6% ahead of schedule and cost, then the resulting performance would be a 2. True or false?

17-3. A performance rating of 4 usually indicates:
  a. Nothing
  b. Satisfactory
  c. Poor
  d. Excellent

17-4. In the administrative closure 3Ms metric, it is required that project team members are involved. True or false?

17-5. Which of the following 3Ms metrics is part of the direct and manage project execution process:
  a. Requested changes
  b. Configuration management system
  c. Deliverables (approved)
  d. Contract closure procedure

17-6. The 3Ms metric for organizational process assets contains four key value areas. True or false?

17-7. In the 3Ms metric for integrated change control — rejected change request, a critical performance factor is the project sponsor approving every project rejected change request action within project team delivery expectations for time and cost. True or false?

17-8. In the 3Ms metric for integrated change control — approved corrective action, the short-term training objective is to ensure the work completed is reviewed by the customer. True or false?

17-9. When considered in the aggregate, the 3Ms metric profiles presented in this chapter can be processed to produce a quantifiable assessment of any completed project with sufficient inspection given to the competency of the project manager and the project sponsor. True or false?

17-10. A standard of 3Ms metrics is that no more than five key value areas should be allowed. True or false?

18

PROJECT SCOPE MANAGEMENT

Project Scope Management includes the processes required to ensure that the project includes all the work required and the work to complete the project successfully. It is primarily concerned with defining and controlling what is and is not included in the project.

Scope planning, scope definition, create work breakdown structure, scope verification, and scope control are the processes associated with project scope management and as such contain 21 output-related 3Ms metric profiles.

Project Scope Management PMBOK® area of knowledge includes the following processes and deliverables:

1. Scope Planning
   a. Scope Management Plan
2. Scope Definition
   a. Project Scope Statement
   b. Project Objectives
   c. Product Scope Description
   d. Project Requirements
   e. Project Boundaries
   f. Project Deliverables
   g. Project Acceptance Criteria
   h. Project Constraints
   i. Project Assumptions
   j. Requested Changes
   k. Project Scope Management Plan (Updates)
3. Create Work Breakdown Structure
   a. Project Scope Statement (Updates)
   b. Work Breakdown Structure

      c. Work Breakdown Structure Dictionary
      d. Scope Baseline
      e. Project Scope Management Plan (Updates)
      f. Requested Changes
4. Scope Verification
      a. Accepted Deliverables
      b. Requested Changes
      c. Recommended Corrective Actions
5. Scope Control
      a. Project Scope Statement (Updates)
      b. Work Breakdown Structure (Updates)
      c. Work Breakdown Structure Dictionary (Updates)
      d. Scope Baseline (Updates)
      e. Requested Changes
      f. Recommended Corrective Action
      g. Organizational Process Assets (Updates)
      h. Project Management Plan (Updates)

These discrete process components integrate with each other and with other processes from other areas of knowledge within the PMBOK®. In addition, these process components may impact other successor dependent program and/or project initiatives in a manner not visible to the project team. A valid source for the project team to consider is the relationship of ongoing project events to other interproject related initiatives regarding the cause and effect created by realized opportunities and threats within the project. These relationships can be located through organizations that are managing project portfolios, such as the business governance entities or Project Management Offices.

Often, a project will fail if the project scope is not well managed. Project fraud opportunity can be reduced significantly by raising visibility to project-scope-related work products and deliverables among the key stakeholders and team members. In addition, the application of project schedule critical path techniques within the project team is an absolute minimum that forces visibility to the most important aspects of project scope control. Remember, "if you can't measure, you can't control, and if you can't control, then you can't manage!"

In the 3Ms metric models that follow in this chapter, each metric model contains rules that require validation that the expected work has been performed. In this manner, visibility to the project scope is confirmed, resulting in opportunity for the key stakeholders and team members to further cross-collaborate.

The following 3Ms-oriented metrics support the Project Scope Management PMBOK® area of knowledge:

1. Scope Planning — Scope Management Plan
2. Scope Definition — Project Scope Statement (Detailed)
3. Scope Definition — Project Objectives

4. Scope Definition — Product Scope Description
5. Scope Definition — Project Requirements
6. Scope Definition — Project Boundaries
7. Scope Definition — Project Deliverables
8. Scope Definition — Project Acceptance Criteria
9. Scope Definition — Project Constraints
10. Scope Definition — Project Assumptions
11. Scope Definition — Requested Changes
12. Scope Definition — Project Scope Management Plan (Updates)
13. Create Work Breakdown Structure — Project Scope Statement (Updates)
14. Create Work Breakdown Structure — Work Breakdown Structure
15. Create Work Breakdown Structure — Work Breakdown Structure Dictionary
16. Create Work Breakdown Structure — Scope Baseline
17. Create Work Breakdown Structure — Project Scope Management Plan (Updates)
18. Create Work Breakdown Structure — Requested Changes
19. Scope Verification — Accepted Deliverables
20. Scope Verification — Requested Changes
21. Scope Verification — Recommended Corrective Actions
22. Scope Control — Project Scope Management Plan (Updates)
23. Scope Control — Work Breakdown Structure (Updates)
24. Scope Control — Work Breakdown Structure Dictionary (Updates)
25. Scope Control — Scope Baseline (Updates)
26. Scope Control — Requested Changes
27. Scope Control — Recommended Corrective Action
28. Scope Control — Organizational Process Assets (Updates)
29. Scope Control — Project Management Plan (Updates)

Scoring for Section II: Performance Objectives for these metrics is as follows:

A. 50%: 4 = completed early and under budget ≥10%; 3 = ≥5%; 2 = completed on time and on budget; 1 = completed late and/or over budget.
B. 50%: 4 = approved by all key stakeholders, customers, project initiator, and/or project sponsor early and under budget ≥10%; 3 = approved early and under budget ≥5%; 2 = approved on time and on budget; 1 = approved late and/or over budget.

Scoring for Section III: Performance Scorecard for these metrics is as follows: 4 = Excellent; 3 = Very Good; 2 = Satisfactory; 1 = Unsatisfactory.

SCOPE PLANNING — SCOPE MANAGEMENT PLAN

Provides guidance on how project scope will be defined, documented, verified, managed, and controlled by the project management team.

I. Key Value Areas Weighting (%)
   A. Completion of process preparation and implementation of scope management plan = 50%.
   B. Approved by project initiator and/or project sponsor = 50%.
II. Performance Objectives — Based on project management plan.
III. Performance Scorecard
IV. Performance Factors
   A. Project Team Members — Help construct project scope management plan by providing information relevant to areas of the project scope statement (preliminary) within project team delivery expectations for time and cost.
   B. Project Initiator(s) — Reviews and/or approves various versions of project scope management plan within project team delivery expectations for time and cost.
   C. Project Sponsor(s) — Reviews and/or approves various versions of project scope management plan within project team delivery expectations for time and cost.
   D. Project Manager — Leads and/or performs construction of project scope management plan within project team delivery expectations for time and cost.
V. Training Objectives
   A. Short Term — Project manager conducts meetings with project initiator, sponsor, and team member(s) on the creation and completion of the project scope management plan regarding what is involved and who is performing certain tasks within schedule expectations for performance.
   B. Long Term — Team members become trained in the process to develop and complete a project scope management plan as a means to improve total effort to complete task.

SCOPE DEFINITION — PROJECT SCOPE STATEMENT (DETAILED)

Describes in detail the project's deliverables and the work required to create those deliverables.

I. Key Value Areas Weighting (%)
   A. Completion of process preparation and implementation of project scope statement = 50%.
   B. Approved by project sponsor = 50%.
II. Performance Objectives — Based on project scope management plan.
III. Performance Scorecard
IV. Performance Factors
   A. Project Team Members — Help construct project scope statement (detailed) by providing information relevant to areas of the project within project team delivery expectations for time and cost.
   B. Project Sponsor(s) — Reviews and/or approves various versions of project scope statement (detailed) within project team delivery expectations for time and cost.
   C. Project Manager — Leads and/or performs construction of project scope statement (detailed) within project team delivery expectations for time and cost.
V. Training Objectives
   A. Short Term — Project manager conducts meetings with sponsor and team member(s) on the creation and completion of the project scope statement (detailed) regarding

what is involved and who is performing certain tasks within schedule expectations for performance.
B. Long Term — Team members become trained in the process to develop and complete a project scope statement (detailed) as a means to improve total effort to complete task.

SCOPE DEFINITION — PROJECT OBJECTIVES

Includes the measurable success criteria of the project.

I. Key Value Areas Weighting (%)
   A. Completion of process preparation and implementation of project objectives = 50%.
   B. Approved by project initiator and/or project sponsor = 50%.
II. Performance Objectives — Based on project scope management plan.
III. Performance Scorecard
IV. Performance Factors
   A. Project Team Members — Help construct project objectives by providing information relevant to areas of the project scope management plan within project team delivery expectations for time and cost.
   B. Project Sponsor(s) — Reviews and/or approves various versions of project objectives within project team delivery expectations for time and cost.
   C. Project Manager — Leads and/or performs construction of project objectives within project team delivery expectations for time and cost.
V. Training Objectives
   A. Short Term — Project manager conducts meetings with project sponsor and team member(s) on the creation of the project objectives regarding what is involved and who is performing certain tasks within schedule expectations for performance.
   B. Long Term — Team members become trained in the process to develop and complete project objectives as a means to improve total effort to complete task.

SCOPE DEFINITION — PRODUCT SCOPE DESCRIPTION

Describes the characteristics of the product, service, or result that the project was undertaken to create.

I. Key Value Areas Weighting (%)
   A. Completion of process preparation and implementation of product scope description = 50%.
   B. Approved by project initiator and/or project sponsor = 50%.
II. Performance Objectives — Based on project scope management plan.
III. Performance Scorecard
IV. Performance Factors
   A. Project Team Members — Help construct product scope description by providing information relevant to areas of the project scope management plan within project team delivery expectations for time and cost.
   B. Project Sponsor(s) — Reviews and/or approves various versions of product scope description within project team delivery expectations for time and cost.

C. Project Manager — Leads and/or performs construction of product scope description within project team delivery expectations for time and cost.
V. Training Objectives
   A. Short Term — Project manager conducts meetings with project sponsor and team member(s) on the creation and completion of the product scope description regarding what is involved and who is performing certain tasks within schedule expectations for performance.
   B. Long Term — Team members become trained in the process to develop and complete product scope description as a means to improve total effort to complete task.

SCOPE DEFINITION — PROJECT REQUIREMENTS

Describes the conditions or capabilities that must be met or processed by the deliverables of the project to satisfy a contract, standard, specification, or other formally imposed documents.

I. Key Value Areas Weighting (%)
   A. Completion of process preparation and implementation of project requirements = 50%.
   B. Approved by project initiator and/or project sponsor = 50%.
II. Performance Objectives — Based on project scope management plan.
III. Performance Scorecard
IV. Performance Factors
   A. Project Team Members — Help construct project requirements by providing information relevant to areas of the project scope management plan within project team delivery expectations for time and cost.
   B. Project Sponsor(s) — Reviews and/or approves various versions of project requirements within project team delivery expectations for time and cost.
   C. Project Manager — Leads and/or performs construction of project requirements within project team delivery expectations for time and cost.
V. Training Objectives
   A. Short Term — Project manager conducts meetings with project sponsor and team member(s) on the creation and completion of the project requirements regarding what is involved and who is performing certain tasks within schedule expectations for performance.
   B. Long Term — Team members become trained in the process to develop and complete project requirements as a means to improve total effort to complete task.

SCOPE DEFINITION — PROJECT BOUNDARIES

Identifies generally what is included within the project and what is excluded from the project.

I. Key Value Areas Weighting (%)
   A. Completion of process preparation and implementation of project boundaries = 50%.
   B. Approved by project initiator and/or project sponsor = 50%.
II. Performance Objectives — Based on project scope management plan.

III. Performance Scorecard
IV. Performance Factors
   A. Project Team Members — Help construct project boundaries by providing information relevant to areas of the project scope management plan within project team delivery expectations for time and cost.
   B. Project Sponsor(s) — Reviews and/or approves various versions of project boundaries within project team delivery expectations for time and cost.
   C. Project Manager — Leads and/or performs construction of project boundaries within project team delivery expectations for time and cost.
V. Training Objectives
   A. Short Term — Project manager conducts meetings with project sponsor and team member(s) on the creation and completion of the project boundaries regarding what is involved and who is performing certain tasks within schedule expectations for performance.
   B. Long Term — Team members become trained in the process to develop and complete project boundaries as a means to improve total effort to complete task.

SCOPE DEFINITION — PROJECT DELIVERABLES

Deliverables include both the outputs that comprise the product or service of the project as well as ancillary results such as project management reports and documentation.

   I. Key Value Areas Weighting (%)
      A. Completion of process preparation and implementation of project deliverables = 50%.
      B. Approved by project initiator and/or project sponsor = 50%.
  II. Performance Objectives — Based on project scope management plan.
 III. Performance Scorecard
  IV. Performance Factors
      A. Project Team Members — Help construct project deliverables by providing information relevant to areas of the project scope management plan within project team delivery expectations for time and cost.
      B. Project Sponsor(s) — Reviews and/or approves various versions of project deliverables within project team delivery expectations for time and cost.
      C. Project Manager — Leads and/or performs construction of project deliverables within project team delivery expectations for time and cost.
   V. Training Objectives
      A. Short Term — Project manager conducts meetings with project sponsor and team member(s) on the creation and completion of the project deliverables regarding what is involved and who is performing certain tasks within schedule expectations for performance.
      B. Long Term — Team members become trained in the process to develop and complete project deliverables as a means to improve total effort to complete task.

SCOPE DEFINITION — PROJECT ACCEPTANCE CRITERIA

Defines the process and criteria for accepting completed products.

I. Key Value Areas Weighting (%)
   A. Completion of process preparation and implementation of project acceptance criteria = 50%.
   B. Approved by project initiator and/or project sponsor = 50%.
II. Performance Objectives — Based on project scope management plan.
III. Performance Scorecard
IV. Performance Factors
   A. Project Team Members — Help construct project acceptance criteria by providing information relevant to areas of the project scope management plan within project team delivery expectations for time and cost.
   B. Project Sponsor(s) — Reviews and/or approves various versions of project acceptance criteria within project team delivery expectations for time and cost.
   C. Project Manager — Leads and/or performs construction of project acceptance criteria within project team delivery expectations for time and cost.
V. Training Objectives
   A. Short Term — Project manager conducts meetings with project sponsor and team member(s) on the creation and completion of the project acceptance criteria regarding what is involved and who is performing certain tasks within schedule expectations for performance.
   B. Long Term — Team members become trained in the process to develop and complete project acceptance criteria as a means to improve total effort to complete task.

SCOPE DEFINITION — PROJECT CONSTRAINTS

Lists and describes the specific project constraints associated with the project scope that limit the team's options.

I. Key Value Areas Weighting (%)
   A. Completion of process preparation and implementation of project constraints = 50%.
   B. Approved by project initiator and/or project sponsor = 50%.
II. Performance Objectives — Based on project scope management plan.
III. Performance Scorecard
IV. Performance Factors
   A. Project Team Members — Help construct project constraints by providing information relevant to areas of the project scope management plan within project team delivery expectations for time and cost.
   B. Project Sponsor(s) — Reviews and/or approves various versions of project constraints within project team delivery expectations for time and cost.
   C. Project Manager — Leads and/or performs construction of project constraints within project team delivery expectations for time and cost.
V. Training Objectives
   A. Short Term — Project manager conducts meetings with project sponsor and team member(s) on the creation and completion of the project constraints regarding what is involved and who is performing certain tasks within schedule expectations for performance.

B. Long Term — Team members become trained in the process to develop and complete project constraints as a means to improve total effort to complete task.

SCOPE DEFINITION — PROJECT ASSUMPTIONS

Lists and describes the specific project assumptions associated with the project scope and the potential impact of those assumptions if they prove to be false.

   I. Key Value Areas Weighting (%)
      A. Completion of process preparation and implementation of project assumptions = 50%.
      B. Approved by project initiator and/or project sponsor = 50%.
  II. Performance Objectives — Based on project scope management plan.
 III. Performance Scorecard
  IV. Performance Factors
      A. Project Team Members — Help construct project assumptions by providing information relevant to areas of the project scope management plan within project team delivery expectations for time and cost.
      B. Project Sponsor(s) — Reviews and/or approves various versions of project assumptions within project team delivery expectations for time and cost.
      C. Project Manager — Leads and/or performs construction of project assumptions within project team delivery expectations for time and cost.
   V. Training Objectives
      A. Short Term — Project manager conducts meetings with project sponsor and team member(s) on the creation and completion of the project assumptions regarding what is involved and who is performing certain tasks within schedule expectations for performance.
      B. Long Term — Team members become trained in the process to develop and complete project assumptions as a means to improve total effort to complete task.

SCOPE DEFINITION — REQUESTED CHANGES

Requested changes to the project management plan and its subsidiary plans may be developed during the scope definition process. Requested changes are processed for review and disposition through the integrated change control process.

   I. Key Value Areas Weighting (%)
      A. Completion of process preparation and implementation of requested changes = 50%.
      B. Approved by project initiator and/or project sponsor = 50%.
  II. Performance Objectives — Based on project scope management plan.
 III. Performance Scorecard
  IV. Performance Factors
      A. Project Team Members — Help construct requested changes by providing information relevant to areas of the project scope management plan within project team delivery expectations for time and cost.

B. Project Sponsor(s) — Reviews and/or approves various versions of requested changes within project team delivery expectations for time and cost.
   C. Project Manager — Leads and/or performs construction of requested changes within project team delivery expectations for time and cost.
V. Training Objectives
   A. Short Term — Project manager conducts meetings with project sponsor and team member(s) on the creation and completion of requested changes regarding what is involved and who is performing certain tasks within schedule expectations for performance.
   B. Long Term — Team members become trained in the process to develop and complete requested changes as a means to improve total effort to complete task.

SCOPE DEFINITION — PROJECT SCOPE MANAGEMENT PLAN (UPDATES)

The project scope management plan component of the project management plan may need to be updated to include approved change requests resulting from the project's scope definition process.

I. Key Value Areas Weighting (%)
   A. Completion of process preparation and implementation of project scope management plan updates = 50%.
   B. Approved by project initiator and/or project sponsor = 50%.
II. Performance Objectives — Based on project scope management plan.
III. Performance Scorecard
IV. Performance Factors
   A. Project Team Members — Help construct project scope management plan updates by providing information relevant to areas of the project scope management plan within project team delivery expectations for time and cost.
   B. Project Sponsor(s) — Reviews and/or approves various versions of project scope management plan updates within project team delivery expectations for time and cost.
   C. Project Manager — Leads and/or performs construction of project scope management plan updates within project team delivery expectations for time and cost.
V. Training Objectives
   A. Short Term — Project manager conducts meetings with project sponsor and team member(s) on the creation and completion of project scope management plan updates regarding what is involved and who is performing certain tasks within schedule expectations for performance.
   B. Long Term — Team members become trained in the process to develop and complete project scope management plan updates as a means to improve total effort to complete task.

CREATE WORK BREAKDOWN STRUCTURE — PROJECT SCOPE STATEMENT (UPDATES)

If approved change requests result from the create work breakdown structure process, then the project scope statement is updated to include those approved changes.

I. Key Value Areas Weighting (%)
   A. Completion of process preparation and implementation of project scope statement updates = 50%.
   B. Approved by project sponsor = 50%.
II. Performance Objectives — Based on project scope statement.
III. Performance Scorecard
IV. Performance Factors
   A. Project Team Members — Help construct project scope statement updates by providing information relevant to areas of the project scope within project team delivery expectations for time and cost.
   B. Project Sponsor(s) — Reviews and/or approves project scope statement updates within project team delivery expectations for time and cost.
   C. Project Manager — Leads and/or performs construction of project scope statement updates within project team delivery expectations for time and cost.
V. Training Objectives
   A. Short Term — Project manager conducts meetings with project initiator, sponsor, and team member(s) on the creation and completion of project scope statement updates regarding what is involved and who is performing certain tasks within schedule expectations for performance.
   B. Long Term — Team members become trained in the process to develop and complete project scope statement updates as a means to improve total effort to complete task.

CREATE WORK BREAKDOWN STRUCTURE — WORK BREAKDOWN STRUCTURE

The key document generated by the create work breakdown structure process is the actual work breakdown structure. Each work breakdown structure component, including work package and control accounts within a work breakdown structure, is generally a unique identifier from a code of accounts. These identifiers provide a structure for hierarchical summarization of costs, schedule, and resource information.

I. Key Value Areas Weighting (%)
   A. Completion of process preparation and implementation of work breakdown structure = 50%.
   B. Approved by project sponsor = 50%.
II. Performance Objectives — Based on project scope statement.

III. Performance Scorecard
IV. Performance Factors
   A. Project Team Members — Help construct work breakdown structure by providing information relevant to areas of the project scope within project team delivery expectations for time and cost.
   B. Project Sponsor(s) — Reviews and/or approves work breakdown structure within project team delivery expectations for time and cost.
   C. Project Manager — Leads and/or performs construction of work breakdown structure within project team delivery expectations for time and cost.
V. Training Objectives
   A. Short Term — Project manager conducts meetings with project initiator, sponsor, and team member(s) on the creation and completion of the work breakdown structure regarding what is involved and who is performing certain tasks within schedule expectations for performance.
   B. Long Term — Team members become trained in the process to develop and complete a work breakdown structure as a means to improve total effort to complete task.

CREATE WORK BREAKDOWN STRUCTURE — WORK BREAKDOWN STRUCTURE DICTIONARY

The document created by the create work breakdown structure process that supports the work breakdown structure is called the work breakdown structure dictionary and is a comparison document to the work breakdown structure.

I. Key Value Areas Weighting (%)
   A. Completion of process preparation and implementation of work breakdown structure dictionary = 50%.
   B. Approved by project sponsor = 50%.
II. Performance Objectives — Based on project scope statement.
III. Performance Scorecard
IV. Performance Factors
   A. Project Team Members — Help construct work breakdown structure dictionary by providing information relevant to areas of the project scope within project team delivery expectations for time and cost.
   B. Project Manager — Leads and/or performs construction of work breakdown structure dictionary within project team delivery expectations for time and cost.
V. Training Objectives
   A. Short Term — Project manager conducts meetings with project initiator, sponsor, and team member(s) on the creation and completion of the work breakdown structure dictionary regarding what is involved and who is performing certain tasks within schedule expectations for performance.
   B. Long Term — Team members become trained in the process to develop and complete a work breakdown structure dictionary as a means to improve total effort to complete task.

CREATE WORK BREAKDOWN STRUCTURE — SCOPE BASELINE

The approved detailed project scope statement and its associated work breakdown structure and work breakdown structure dictionary are the scope baseline for the project.

   I. Key Value Areas Weighting (%)
      A. Completion of process preparation and implementation of scope baseline = 50%.
      B. Approved by project sponsor = 50%.
  II. Performance Objectives — Based on project scope statement.
 III. Performance Scorecard
  IV. Performance Factors
      A. Project Team Members — Help construct scope baseline by providing information relevant to areas of the project scope within project team delivery expectations for time and cost.
      B. Project Sponsor(s) — Reviews and/or approves scope baseline within project team delivery expectations for time and cost.
      C. Project Manager — Leads and/or performs construction of scope baseline within project team delivery expectations for time and cost.
   V. Training Objectives
      A. Short Term — Project manager conducts meetings with project initiator, sponsor, and team member(s) on the creation and completion of the scope baseline regarding what is involved and who is performing certain tasks within schedule expectations for performance.
      B. Long Term — Team members become trained in the process to develop and complete a scope baseline as a means to improve total effort to complete task.

CREATE WORK BREAKDOWN STRUCTURE — PROJECT SCOPE MANAGEMENT PLAN (UPDATES)

If approved change requests result from the create work breakdown structure process, then the project scope management plan may need to be updated to include approved changes.

   I. Key Value Areas Weighting (%)
      A. Completion of process preparation and implementation of project scope management plan updates = 50%.
      B. Approved by project sponsor = 50%.
  II. Performance Objectives — Based on project scope management plan.
 III. Performance Scorecard
  IV. Performance Factors
      A. Project Team Members — Help construct project scope management plan updates by providing information relevant to areas of the project scope within project team delivery expectations for time and cost.
      B. Project Sponsor(s) — Reviews and/or approves project scope management plan updates within project team delivery expectations for time and cost.

C. Project Manager — Leads and/or performs construction of project scope management plan updates within project team delivery expectations for time and cost.
V. Training Objectives
   A. Short Term — Project manager conducts meetings with project initiator, sponsor, and team member(s) on the creation and completion of project scope management plan updates regarding what is involved and who is performing certain tasks within schedule expectations for performance.
   B. Long Term — Team members become trained in the process to develop and complete project scope management plan updates as a means to improve total effort to complete task.

CREATE WORK BREAKDOWN STRUCTURE — REQUESTED CHANGES

Requested changes to the project scope statement and its components may be generated from the create work breakdown structure process and are processed for review and approved through the integrated change control process.

I. Key Value Areas Weighting (%)
   A. Completion of process preparation and implementation of requested changes = 50%.
   B. Approved by project sponsor = 50%.
II. Performance Objectives — Based on project scope statement.
III. Performance Scorecard
IV. Performance Factors
   A. Project Team Members — Help construct requested changes by providing information relevant to areas of the project scope within project team delivery expectations for time and cost.
   B. Project Sponsor(s) — Reviews and/or approves requested changes within project team delivery expectations for time and cost.
   C. Project Manager — Leads and/or performs construction of requested changes within project team delivery expectations for time and cost.
V. Training Objectives
   A. Short Term — Project manager conducts meetings with project initiator, sponsor, and team member(s) on the creation and completion of requested changes regarding what is involved and who is performing certain tasks within schedule expectations for performance.
   B. Long Term — Team members become trained in the process to develop and complete requested changes as a means to improve total effort to complete task.

SCOPE VERIFICATION — ACCEPTED DELIVERABLES

The process documents those completed deliverables that have been accepted. The completed deliverables that have not been accepted are also documented, along with the reasons for nonacceptance.

I. Key Value Areas Weighting (%)
   A. Completion of process preparation and implementation of accepted deliverables = 50%.
   B. Approved by project sponsor = 50%.
II. Performance Objectives — Based on project scope statement.
III. Performance Scorecard
IV. Performance Factors
   A. Project Team Members — Help construct accepted deliverables by providing information relevant to areas of the project scope within project team delivery expectations for time and cost.
   B. Project Sponsor(s) — Reviews and/or approves accepted deliverables within project team delivery expectations for time and cost.
   C. Project Manager — Leads and/or performs identification of accepted deliverables within project team delivery expectations for time and cost.
V. Training Objectives
   A. Short Term — Project manager conducts meetings with project initiator, sponsor, and team member(s) on identifying accepted deliverables regarding what is involved and who is performing certain tasks within schedule expectations for performance.
   B. Long Term — Team members become trained in the process to identify accepted deliverables as a means to improve total effort to complete task.

SCOPE VERIFICATION — REQUESTED CHANGES

May be generated from the scope verification process and are processed for review and disposition through the integrated change control process.

I. Key Value Areas Weighting (%)
   A. Completion of process preparation and implementation of requested changes = 50%.
   B. Approved by project sponsor = 50%.
II. Performance Objectives — Based on project scope statement.
III. Performance Scorecard
IV. Performance Factors
   A. Project Team Members — Help construct requested changes by providing information relevant to areas of the project scope within project team delivery expectations for time and cost.
   B. Project Sponsor(s) — Reviews and/or approves requested changes within project team delivery expectations for time and cost.
   C. Project Manager — Leads and/or performs identification of requested changes within project team delivery expectations for time and cost.
V. Training Objectives
   A. Short Term — Project manager conducts meetings with project initiator, sponsor, and team member(s) on the creation and completion of requested changes regarding what is involved and who is performing certain tasks within schedule expectations for performance.

B. Long Term — Team members become trained in the process to develop and complete requested changes as a means to improve total effort to complete task.

SCOPE VERIFICATION — RECOMMENDED CORRECTIVE ACTIONS

Corrective actions are documented recommendations required to bring expected future project performance into conformance with the project management plan.

  I. Key Value Areas Weighting (%)
     A. Completion of process preparation and implementation of recommended corrective actions = 50%.
     B. Approved by project sponsor = 50%.
 II. Performance Objectives — Based on project scope statement.
III. Performance Scorecard
 IV. Performance Factors
     A. Project Team Members — Help construct recommended corrective actions by providing information relevant to areas of the project scope within project team delivery expectations for time and cost.
     B. Project Sponsor(s) — Reviews and/or approves recommended corrective actions within project team delivery expectations for time and cost.
     C. Project Manager — Leads and/or performs development and implementation of recommended corrective actions within project team delivery expectations for time and cost.
  V. Training Objectives
     A. Short Term — Project manager conducts meetings with project initiator, sponsor, and team member(s) on identifying recommended corrective actions regarding what is involved and who is performing certain tasks within schedule expectations for performance.
     B. Long Term — Team members become trained in the process to identify and implement recommended corrective actions as a means to improve total effort to complete task.

SCOPE CONTROL — PROJECT SCOPE MANAGEMENT PLAN (UPDATES)

If the approved change requests have an effect on the project scope, then the project scope statement is revised and reissued to reflect the approved changes. The updated project scope statement becomes the new project scope baseline for future changes.

  I. Key Value Areas Weighting (%)
     A. Completion of process preparation and implementation of project scope statement updates = 50%.
     B. Approved by project sponsor = 50%.
 II. Performance Objectives — Based on project scope statement.

III. Performance Scorecard
IV. Performance Factors
   A. Project Team Members — Help construct updates to the project scope statement by providing information relevant to areas of the project scope within project team delivery expectations for time and cost.
   B. Project Sponsor(s) — Reviews and/or approves updates to the project scope statement within project team delivery expectations for time and cost.
   C. Project Manager — Leads and/or performs updates to the project scope statement within project team delivery expectations for time and cost.
V. Training Objectives
   A. Short Term — Project manager conducts meetings with project initiator, sponsor, and team member(s) on the creation and completion of updates to the project scope statement regarding what is involved and who is performing certain tasks within schedule expectations for performance.
   B. Long Term — Team members become trained in the process to develop and complete updates to the project scope statement as a means to improve total effort to complete task.

SCOPE CONTROL — WORK BREAKDOWN STRUCTURE (UPDATES)

If the approved change requests have an effect on the project scope, then the work breakdown structure is revised and reissued to reflect the approved changes.

I. Key Value Areas Weighting (%)
   A. Completion of process preparation and implementation of work breakdown structure updates = 50%.
   B. Approved by project sponsor = 50%.
II. Performance Objectives — Based on project scope statement.
III. Performance Scorecard
IV. Performance Factors
   A. Project Team Members — Help construct updates to the work breakdown structure by providing information relevant to areas of the project scope within project team delivery expectations for time and cost.
   B. Project Sponsor(s) — Reviews and/or approves updates to the work breakdown structure within project team delivery expectations for time and cost.
   C. Project Manager — Leads and/or performs updates to the work breakdown structure within project team delivery expectations for time and cost.
V. Training Objectives
   A. Short Term — Project manager conducts meetings with project initiator, sponsor, and team member(s) on the creation and completion of work breakdown structure updates regarding what is involved and who is performing certain tasks within schedule expectations for performance.
   B. Long Term — Team members become trained in the process to develop and complete updates to the work breakdown structure as a means to improve total effort to complete task.

SCOPE CONTROL — WORK BREAKDOWN STRUCTURE DICTIONARY (UPDATES)

If the approved change requests have an effect on the project scope, then the work breakdown structure dictionary is revised and reissued to reflect the approved changes.

   I. Key Value Areas Weighting (%)
      A. Completion of process preparation and implementation of work breakdown structure dictionary updates = 50%.
      B. Approved by project sponsor = 50%.
  II. Performance Objectives — Based on project scope statement.
 III. Performance Scorecard
  IV. Performance Factors
      A. Project Team Members — Help construct updates to the work breakdown structure dictionary by providing information relevant to areas of the project scope within project team delivery expectations for time and cost.
      B. Project Sponsor(s) — Reviews and/or approves updates to the work breakdown structure dictionary within project team delivery expectations for time and cost.
      C. Project Manager — Leads and/or performs updates to the work breakdown structure dictionary within project team delivery expectations for time and cost.
   V. Training Objectives
      A. Short Term — Project manager conducts meetings with project initiator, sponsor, and team member(s) on the creation and completion of work breakdown structure dictionary updates regarding what is involved and who is performing certain tasks within schedule expectations for performance.
      B. Long Term — Team members become trained in the process to develop and complete updates to the work breakdown structure dictionary as a means to improve total effort to complete task.

SCOPE CONTROL — SCOPE BASELINE (UPDATES)

The approved detailed project scope statement and its associated work breakdown structure and work breakdown structure dictionary are the scope baseline for which updates are applied for the project to remain in conformance.

   I. Key Value Areas Weighting (%)
      A. Completion of process preparation and implementation of scope baseline updates = 50%.
      B. Approved by project sponsor = 50%.
  II. Performance Objectives — Based on project scope statement.
 III. Performance Scorecard
  IV. Performance Factors
      A. Project Team Members — Help construct updates to the scope baseline by providing information relevant to areas of the project scope within project team delivery expectations for time and cost.

B. Project Sponsor(s) — Reviews and/or approves updates to the scope baseline within project team delivery expectations for time and cost.
   C. Project Manager — Leads and/or performs updates to the scope baseline within project team delivery expectations for time and cost.
V. Training Objectives
   A. Short Term — Project manager conducts meetings with project initiator, sponsor, and team member(s) on the creation and completion of updates to the scope baseline regarding what is involved and who is performing certain tasks within schedule expectations for performance.
   B. Long Term — Team members become trained in the process to develop and complete updates to the scope baseline as a means to improve total effort to complete task.

SCOPE CONTROL — REQUESTED CHANGES

The result of proper scope control can generate requested changes, which are processed for review and disposition according to the project integrated change control process.

   I. Key Value Areas Weighting (%)
      A. Completion of process preparation and implementation of requested changes = 50%.
      B. Approved by project sponsor = 50%.
   II. Performance Objectives — Based on project scope statement.
   III. Performance Scorecard
   IV. Performance Factors
      A. Project Team Members — Help construct requested changes by providing information relevant to areas of the project scope within project team delivery expectations for time and cost.
      B. Project Sponsor(s) — Reviews and/or approves requested changes within project team delivery expectations for time and cost.
      C. Project Manager — Leads and/or performs requested changes within project team delivery expectations for time and cost.
   V. Training Objectives
      A. Short Term — Project manager conducts meetings with project initiator, sponsor, and team member(s) on the creation and completion of requested changes regarding what is involved and who is performing certain tasks within schedule expectations for performance.
      B. Long Term — Team members become trained in the process to develop and complete requested changes as a means to improve total effort to complete task.

SCOPE CONTROL — RECOMMENDED CORRECTIVE ACTION

A recommended corrective action is any step recommended to bring expected future project performance in line with the project management plan and project scope statement.

I. Key Value Areas Weighting (%)
     A. Completion of process preparation and implementation of recommended corrective action = 50%.
     B. Approved by project sponsor = 50%.
 II. Performance Objectives — Based on project scope statement.
III. Performance Scorecard
 IV. Performance Factors
     A. Project Team Members — Help construct recommended corrective actions by providing information relevant to areas of the project scope within project team delivery expectations for time and cost.
     B. Project Sponsor(s) — Reviews and/or approves recommended corrective actions within project team delivery expectations for time and cost.
     C. Project Manager — Leads and/or performs recommended corrective actions within project team delivery expectations for time and cost.
  V. Training Objectives
     A. Short Term — Project manager conducts meetings with project initiator, sponsor, and team member(s) on the creation and completion of recommended corrective actions regarding what is involved and who is performing certain tasks within schedule expectations for performance.
     B. Long Term — Team members become trained in the process to develop and complete recommended corrective actions as a means to improve total effort to complete task.

SCOPE CONTROL — ORGANIZATIONAL PROCESS ASSETS (UPDATES)

The causes of variances, the reasons behind the corrective action chosen, and other types of lessons learned from project scope change control are documented and updated in the historical database of the organizational process assets.

  I. Key Value Areas Weighting (%)
     A. Completion of process preparation and implementation of organizational process assets updates = 50%.
     B. Approved by project sponsor = 50%.
 II. Performance Objectives — Based on project scope statement.
III. Performance Scorecard
 IV. Performance Factors
     A. Project Team Members — Help construct updates to the organizational process assets by providing information relevant to areas of the project scope within project team delivery expectations for time and cost.
     B. Project Sponsor(s) — Reviews and/or approves updates to the organizational process assets within project team delivery expectations for time and cost.
     C. Project Manager — Leads and/or performs updates to the organizational process assets within project team delivery expectations for time and cost.
  V. Training Objectives
     A. Short Term — Project manager conducts meetings with project initiator, sponsor, and team member(s) on the creation and completion of updates to the organizational

process assets regarding what is involved and who is performing certain tasks within schedule expectations for performance.
B. Long Term — Team members become trained in the process to develop and complete updates to the organizational process assets as a means to improve total effort to complete task.

SCOPE CONTROL — PROJECT MANAGEMENT PLAN (UPDATES)

If the approved change requests have an effect on the project scope, then the corresponding component documents and cost baseline and schedule baselines of the project management plan are revised and reissued to reflect the approved changes.

I. Key Value Areas Weighting (%)
   A. Completion of process preparation and implementation of project management plan updates = 50%.
   B. Approved by project sponsor = 50%.
II. Performance Objectives — Based on project scope statement.
III. Performance Scorecard
IV. Performance Factors
   A. Project Team Members — Help construct updates to the project management plan by providing information relevant to areas of the project scope within project team delivery expectations for time and cost.
   B. Project Sponsor(s) — Reviews and/or approves updates to the project management plan within project team delivery expectations for time and cost.
   C. Project Manager — Leads and/or performs updates to the project management plan within project team delivery expectation for time and cost.
V. Training Objectives
   A. Short Term — Project manager conducts meetings with project initiator, sponsor, and team member(s) on the creation and completion of updates to the project management plan regarding what is involved and who is performing certain tasks within schedule expectations for performance.
   B. Long Term — Team members become trained in the process to develop and complete updates to the project management plan as a means to improve total effort to complete task.

SUMMARY

Project Scope Management is certainly a critical component for project delivery. Project requirements are derived from the project scope. Project delivery speed, project fraud, and project value can be greatly impacted by how well or how poorly project scope is defined, controlled, and achieved. Lessening the management of project controls over project scope will lessen the project potential for delivery success.

Oftentimes, business requirements developed for the project consume more project effort than was expected. Poorly defined project scope can lead to this situation, thus causing project delivery failure.

QUESTIONS

18-1. Work breakdown structure creation does not produce which of the following outputs:
   a. Work breakdown structure
   b. Work breakdown structure dictionary
   c. Project management plan (updates)
   d. Work breakdown structure (updates)

18-2. A key performance factor for the project sponsor(s) is review and/or approval of various versions of recommended corrective project scope action within project team delivery expectations for time and cost. True or false?

18-3. Short-term training objective for scope verification is the project manager conducts meetings with project sponsor and team member(s) on updating the project scope from the work breakdown structure information regarding what is involved and who is performing certain tasks within schedule expectations for performance. True or false?

18-4. The project sponsor has approval authority for the detailed project scope statement in scope planning. True or false?

18-5. Work breakdown structure updates are not an output of scope control. True or false?

18-6. Approval by the project initiator is a key value area for scope control updates of the organizational process assets. True or false?

18-7. Satisfactory performance for approving applied work breakdown structure updates to project scope can be late in time and/or over budget. True or false?

18-8. In scope planning for the scope management plan, this document must be approved by the project sponsor. True or false?

18-9. Project scope development does not contain which of the following processes:
   a. Scope planning
   b. Scope definition
   c. Scope change control
   d. Scope verification

18-10. Project Scope Management is a critical component in effectively managing project governance and reporting. True or false?

This book has free materials available for download from the
Web Added Value™ Resource Center at www.jrosspub.com.

19

PROJECT TIME MANAGEMENT

Project Time Management PMBOK® area of knowledge includes the processes required to accomplish timely completion of the project. The following processes are included in Project Time Management:

- **Activity Definition** — Identify the specific schedule activities that need to be performed to produce the various project deliverables
- **Activity Sequencing** — Identify and document dependencies among schedule activities
- **Activity Resource Estimating** — Estimate the type and quantities of resources required to perform each schedule activity
- **Activity Duration Estimating** — Estimate the number of work periods that will be needed to complete individual schedule activities
- **Schedule Development** — Analyze activity sequences, durations, resource requirements, and schedule constraints to create the project schedule
- **Schedule Control** — Control changes to the project schedule

Project Time Management PMBOK® area of knowledge includes the following outputs:

1. Activity Definition
    a. Activity List
    b. Activity List Attributes
    c. Milestone List
    d. Requested Changes
2. Activity Sequencing
    a. Project Schedule Network Diagrams
    b. Activity List (Updates)
    c. Activity Attributes (Updates)
    d. Requested Changes

3. Activity Resource Estimating
   a. Activity Resource Requirements
   b. Activity Attributes (Updates)
   c. Resource Breakdown Structure
   d. Resource Calendars (Updates)
   e. Requested Changes
4. Activity Duration Estimating
   a. Activity Duration Estimates
   b. Activity Attributes (Updates)
5. Schedule Development
   a. Project Schedule
   b. Schedule Model Data
   c. Schedule Baseline
   d. Resource Requirement (Updates)
   e. Activity Attributes (Updates)
   f. Project Calendar (Updates)
   g. Requested Changes
   h. Project Management Plan (Updates)
6. Schedule Control
   a. Schedule Model Data (Updates)
   b. Schedule Baseline (Updates)
   c. Performance Measurements
   d. Requested Changes
   e. Recommended Corrective Actions
   f. Organizational Process Assets
   g. Activity List (Updates)
   h. Activity Attributes (Updates)
   i. Project Management Plan (Updates)

These discrete process components integrate with each other and with other processes from other areas of knowledge within the PMBOK®. In addition, these process components may impact other successor dependent program and/or project initiatives in a manner not visible to the project team.

The following 3Ms-oriented metrics support the Project Time Management PMBOK® area of knowledge:

1. Activity Definition — Activity List
2. Activity Definition — Activity List Attributes
3. Activity Definition — Milestone List
4. Activity Definition — Requested Changes
5. Activity Sequencing — Project Schedule Network Diagrams
6. Activity Sequencing — Activity List (Updates)
7. Activity Sequencing — Activity Attributes (Updates)
8. Activity Sequencing — Requested Changes

9. Activity Resource Estimating — Activity Resource Requirements
10. Activity Resource Estimating — Activity Attributes (Updates)
11. Activity Resource Estimating — Resource Breakdown Structure
12. Activity Resource Estimating — Resource Calendars (Updates)
13. Activity Resource Estimating — Requested Changes
14. Activity Duration Estimating — Activity Duration Estimates
15. Activity Duration Estimating — Activity Attributes (Updates)
16. Schedule Development — Project Schedule
17. Schedule Development — Schedule Model Data
18. Schedule Development — Schedule Baseline
19. Schedule Development — Resource Requirement (Updates)
20. Schedule Development — Activity Attributes (Updates)
21. Schedule Development — Project Calendar (Updates)
22. Schedule Development — Requested Changes
23. Schedule Development — Project Management Plan (Updates)
24. Schedule Control — Schedule Model Data (Updates)
25. Schedule Control — Schedule Baseline (Updates)
26. Schedule Control — Performance Measurements
27. Schedule Control — Requested Changes
28. Schedule Control — Recommended Corrective Actions
29. Schedule Control — Organizational Process Assets (Updates)
30. Schedule Control — Activity List (Updates)
31. Schedule Control — Activity Attributes (Updates)
32. Schedule Control — Project Management Plan (Updates)

Scoring for Section II: Performance Objectives for these metrics is as follows:

A. 50%: 4 = completed early and under budget ≥10%; 3 = ≥5%; 2 = completed on time and on budget; 1 = completed late and/or over budget.
B. 50%: 4 = approved by project initiator and/or project sponsor early and under budget ≥10%; 3 = approved early and under budget ≥5%; 2 = approved on time and on budget; 1 = approved late and/or over budget.

Scoring for Section III: Performance Scorecard for these metrics is as follows: 4 = Excellent; 3 = Very Good; 2 = Satisfactory; 1 = Unsatisfactory.

ACTIVITY DEFINITION — ACTIVITY LIST

The activity list is a comprehensive list that includes all schedule activities that are planned to be performed on the project. The activity list does not include any scheduled activities that are not required as part of the project scope.

I. Key Value Areas Weighting (%)
   A. Completion of process preparation and implementation of activity list = 50%.
   B. Approved by project manager = 50%.

II. Performance Objectives — Based on project management plan.
III. Performance Scorecard
IV. Performance Factors
   A. Project Team Members — Help construct activity list by providing information relevant to areas of the project within project team delivery expectations for time and cost.
   B. Project Manager — Leads and/or performs construction of activity list within project team delivery expectations for time and cost.
V. Training Objectives
   A. Short Term — Project manager conducts meetings with project team member(s) on the creation and completion of the activity list regarding what is involved and who is performing certain tasks within schedule expectations for performance.
   B. Long Term — Team members become trained in the process to develop a project activity list as a means to improve total effort to complete task.

ACTIVITY DEFINITION — ACTIVITY LIST ATTRIBUTES

The activity attributes are an extension of the identified activity in the activity list and identify the multiple attributes associated with each schedule activity.

I. Key Value Areas Weighting (%)
   A. Completion of process preparation and creation of the attributes of each project activity = 50%.
   B. Approved by project initiator and/or project sponsor = 50%.
II. Performance Objectives — Based on project management plan.
III. Performance Scorecard
IV. Performance Factors
   A. Project Team Members — Help construct activity list attributes by providing information relevant to areas of the project scope statement (preliminary) within project team delivery expectations for time and cost.
   B. Project Manager — Leads and/or performs construction of activity list attributes within project team delivery expectations for time and cost.
V. Training Objectives
   A. Short Term — Project manager conducts meetings with project initiator, sponsor, and team member(s) on the creation and completion of activity list attributes regarding what is involved and who is performing certain tasks within schedule expectations for performance.
   B. Long Term — Team members become trained in the process to develop and complete activity list attributes as a means to improve total effort to complete task.

ACTIVITY DEFINITION — MILESTONE LIST

The list of schedule milestones identifies all milestones and indicates whether a milestone is mandatory or optional.

I. Key Value Areas Weighting (%)
   A. Completion of process preparation and creation of the milestone list for the project schedule = 50%.
   B. Approved by project initiator and/or project sponsor = 50%.
II. Performance Objectives — Based on project management plan.
III. Performance Scorecard
IV. Performance Factors
   A. Project Team Members — Help construct milestone list by providing information relevant to areas of the project scope statement (preliminary) within project team delivery expectations for time and cost.
   B. Project Initiator(s) — Reviews and/or approves various versions of milestone list within project team delivery expectations for time and cost.
   C. Project Sponsor(s) — Reviews and/or approves various versions of milestone list within project team delivery expectations for time and cost.
   D. Project Manager — Leads and/or performs construction of milestone list within project team delivery expectations for time and cost.
V. Training Objectives
   A. Short Term — Project manager conducts meetings with project initiator, sponsor, and team member(s) on the creation and completion of the milestone list regarding what is involved and who is performing certain tasks within schedule expectations for performance.
   B. Long Term — Team members become trained in the process to develop and complete a milestone list as a means to improve total effort to complete task.

ACTIVITY DEFINITION — REQUESTED CHANGES

The activity definition process can generate requested changes that can affect the project scope statement and the work breakdown structure.

I. Key Value Areas Weighting (%)
   A. Completion of process preparation and determination of content of activity definition requested changes = 50%.
   B. Approved by project initiator and/or project sponsor = 50%.
II. Performance Objectives — Based on project management plan.
III. Performance Scorecard
IV. Performance Factors
   A. Project Team Members — Help construct activity definition requested changes by providing information relevant to areas of the project scope statement (preliminary) within project team delivery expectations for time and cost.
   B. Project Initiator(s) — Reviews and/or approves various versions of activity definition requested changes within project team delivery expectations for time and cost.
   C. Project Sponsor(s) — Reviews and/or approves various versions of activity definition requested changes within project team delivery expectations for time and cost.
   D. Project Manager — Leads and/or performs construction of activity definition requested changes within project team delivery expectations for time and cost.

V. Training Objectives
   A. Short Term — Project manager conducts meetings with project initiator, sponsor, and team member(s) on the creation and completion of activity definition requested changes regarding what is involved and who is performing certain tasks within schedule expectations for performance.
   B. Long Term — Team members become trained in the process to develop and complete activity definition requested changes as a means to improve total effort to complete task.

ACTIVITY SEQUENCING — PROJECT SCHEDULE NETWORK DIAGRAMS

Project schedule network diagrams are schematic displays of the project's schedule activities and the logical relationships.

I. Key Value Areas Weighting (%)
   A. Completion of process preparation and creation of the project schedule network diagrams = 50%.
   B. Approved by project initiator and/or project sponsor = 50%.
II. Performance Objectives — Based on project management plan.
III. Performance Scorecard
IV. Performance Factors
   A. Project Team Members — Help construct project schedule network diagrams by providing information relevant to areas of the project management plan within project team delivery expectations for time and cost.
   B. Project Manager — Leads and/or performs construction of project schedule network diagrams within project team delivery expectations for time and cost.
V. Training Objectives
   A. Short Term — Project manager conducts meetings with project initiator, sponsor, and team member(s) on the creation and completion of the project schedule network diagrams regarding what is involved and who is performing certain tasks within schedule expectations for performance.
   B. Long Term — Team members become trained in the process to develop and complete a project schedule network diagram as a means to improve total effort to complete task.

ACTIVITY SEQUENCING — ACTIVITY LIST (UPDATES)

If approved change requests result from the activity sequencing process, the activity list is updated to include these approved changes.

I. Key Value Areas Weighting (%)
   A. Completion of process preparation and implementation of updates to the activities list = 50%.
   B. Approved by project initiator and/or project sponsor = 50%.
II. Performance Objectives — Based on project management plan.
III. Performance Scorecard

IV. Performance Factors
   A. Project Team Members — Help construct updates to the activity list by providing information relevant to areas of the project management plan within project team delivery expectations for time and cost.
   B. Project Initiator(s) — Reviews and/or approves various updates to the activity list within project team delivery expectations for time and cost.
   C. Project Sponsor(s) — Reviews and/or approves various updates to the activity list within project team delivery expectations for time and cost.
   D. Project Manager — Leads and/or performs updates to the activity list within project team delivery expectations for time and cost.
V. Training Objectives
   A. Short Term — Project manager conducts meetings with project initiator, sponsor, and team member(s) on the creation and completion of updates to the activity list regarding what is involved and who is performing certain tasks within schedule expectations for performance.
   B. Long Term — Team members become trained in the process to develop and complete updates to the activity list as a means to improve total effort to complete task.

ACTIVITY SEQUENCING — ACTIVITY ATTRIBUTES (UPDATES)

The activity attributes are updated to include the defined logical relationships and any associated leads and lags. If approved change requests resulting from the activity sequencing process affect the activity list, then the related items in the activity attributes are updated to include those approved changes.

   I. Key Value Areas Weighting (%)
      A. Completion of process preparation and implementation of updates to activity attributes = 50%.
      B. Approved by project initiator and/or project sponsor = 50%.
  II. Performance Objectives — Based on project management plan.
 III. Performance Scorecard
  IV. Performance Factors
      A. Project Team Members — Help construct updates to activity attributes by providing information relevant to areas of the project management plan within project team delivery expectations for time and cost.
      B. Project Initiator(s) — Reviews and/or approves various updates to activity attributes of the project management plan within project team delivery expectations for time and cost.
      C. Project Sponsor(s) — Reviews and/or approves various updates to activity attributes within project team delivery expectations for time and cost.
      D. Project Manager — Leads and/or performs updates to activity attributes within project team delivery expectations for time and cost.
   V. Training Objectives
      A. Short Term — Project manager conducts meetings with project initiator, sponsor, and team member(s) on the creation and completion of updates to activity attributes regarding what is involved and who is performing certain tasks within schedule expectations for performance.

B. Long Term — Team members become trained in the process to develop and complete updates to activity attributes as a means to improve total effort to complete task.

ACTIVITY SEQUENCING — REQUESTED CHANGES

Preparation of project logical relationships, leads and lags might reveal instances that can generate change to the activity list or the activity attributes.

I. Key Value Areas Weighting (%)
   A. Completion of process preparation and implementation of requested changes = 50%.
   B. Approved by project initiator and/or project sponsor = 50%.
II. Performance Objectives — Based on project management plan.
III. Performance Scorecard
IV. Performance Factors
   A. Project Team Members — Help construct requested changes by providing information relevant to areas of the project management plan within project team delivery expectations for time and cost.
   B. Project Initiator(s) — Reviews and/or approves various requested changes within project team delivery expectations for time and cost.
   C. Project Sponsor(s) — Reviews and/or approves various requested changes within project team delivery expectations for time and cost.
   D. Project Manager — Leads and/or performs construction of requested changes within project team delivery expectations for time and cost.
V. Training Objectives
   A. Short Term — Project manager conducts meetings with project initiator, sponsor, and team member(s) on the creation and completion of requested changes regarding what is involved and who is performing certain tasks within schedule expectations for performance.
   B. Long Term — Team members become trained in the process to develop and complete requested changes as a means to improve total effort to complete task.

ACTIVITY RESOURCE ESTIMATING — ACTIVITY RESOURCE REQUIREMENTS

The output of the activity resource estimating process is identification and description of the types and quantities required for each schedule activity in a work package. These requirements can then be aggregated to determine the estimated resources for each work package.

I. Key Value Areas Weighting (%)
   A. Completion of process preparation and implementation of activity resource requirements = 50%.
   B. Approved by project initiator and/or project sponsor = 50%.
II. Performance Objectives — Based on project scope statement.

III. Performance Scorecard
IV. Performance Factors
   A. Project Team Members — Help construct activity resource requirements by providing information relevant to areas of the project scope statement within project team delivery expectations for time and cost.
   B. Project Initiator(s) — Reviews and/or approves various versions of activity resource requirements for the project scope statement within project team delivery expectations for time and cost.
   C. Project Sponsor(s) — Reviews and/or approves various versions of activity resource requirements for the project scope statement within project team delivery expectations for time and cost.
   D. Project Manager — Leads and/or performs construction of activity resource requirements within project team delivery expectations for time and cost.
V. Training Objectives
   A. Short Term — Project manager conducts meetings with project initiator, sponsor, and team member(s) on the creation and completion of activity resource requirements for the project scope statement regarding what is involved and who is performing certain tasks within schedule expectations for performance.
   B. Long Term — Team members become trained in the process to develop and complete activity resource requirements as a means to improve total effort to complete task.

ACTIVITY RESOURCE ESTIMATING — ACTIVITY ATTRIBUTES (UPDATES)

The types and quantities of resources required for each schedule activity are incorporated into the activity attributes.

I. Key Value Areas Weighting (%)
   A. Completion of process preparation and implementation of updates to activity attributes = 50%.
   B. Approved by project initiator and/or project sponsor = 50%.
II. Performance Objectives — Based on project scope statement.
III. Performance Scorecard
IV. Performance Factors
   A. Project Team Members — Help construct updates to activity attributes by providing information relevant to areas of the project scope statement within project team delivery expectations for time and cost.
   B. Project Manager — Leads and/or performs updates to activity attributes within project team delivery expectations for time and cost.
V. Training Objectives
   A. Short Term — Project manager conducts meetings with project initiator, sponsor, and team member(s) on the creation and completion of updates to activity attributes regarding what is involved and who is performing certain tasks within schedule expectations for performance.

B. Long Term — Team members become trained in the process to develop and complete updates to activity attributes as a means to improve total effort to complete task.

ACTIVITY RESOURCE ESTIMATING — RESOURCE BREAKDOWN STRUCTURE

The resource breakdown structure is a hierarchical structure of the identified resources by resource category and resource type.

I. Key Value Areas Weighting (%)
   A. Completion of process preparation and implementation of resource breakdown structure = 50%.
   B. Approved by project initiator and/or project sponsor = 50%.
II. Performance Objectives — Based on project scope statement.
III. Performance Scorecard
IV. Performance Factors
   A. Project Team Members — Help construct resource breakdown structure by providing information relevant to areas of the project scope statement within project team delivery expectations for time and cost.
   B. Project Manager — Leads and/or performs construction of resource breakdown structure within project team delivery expectations for time and cost.
V. Training Objectives
   A. Short Term — Project manager conducts meetings with project initiator, sponsor, and team member(s) on the creation and completion of the resource breakdown structure regarding what is involved and who is performing certain tasks within schedule expectations for performance.
   B. Long Term — Team members become trained in the process to develop and complete a resource breakdown structure as a means to improve total effort to complete task.

ACTIVITY RESOURCE ESTIMATING — RESOURCE CALENDARS (UPDATES)

A composite resource calendar for the project that documents working days and nonworking days to determine those dates on which a specific resource, whether a person or material, can be active or idle.

I. Key Value Areas Weighting (%)
   A. Completion of process preparation and implementation of updates to resource calendars for activity resources = 50%.
   B. Approved by project initiator and/or project sponsor = 50%.
II. Performance Objectives — Based on project scope statement.
III. Performance Scorecard

IV. Performance Factors
  A. Project Team Members — Help construct updates to resource calendars by providing information relevant to areas of the project scope statement within project team delivery expectations for time and cost.
  B. Project Initiator(s) — Reviews and/or approves various updates to resource calendars within project team delivery expectations for time and cost.
  C. Project Sponsor(s) — Reviews and/or approves various updates to resource calendars within project team delivery expectations for time and cost.
  D. Project Manager — Leads and/or performs updates to resource calendars within project team delivery expectations for time and cost.
V. Training Objectives
  A. Short Term — Project manager conducts meetings with project initiator, sponsor, and team member(s) on the creation and completion of updates to resource calendars regarding what is involved and who is performing certain tasks within schedule expectations for performance.
  B. Long Term — Team members become trained in the process to develop and complete updates to resource calendars as a means to improve total effort to complete task.

ACTIVITY RESOURCE ESTIMATING — REQUESTED CHANGES

The activity resource estimating process can result in requested changes to add or delete planned schedule activities within the activity list.

I. Key Value Areas Weighting (%)
  A. Completion of process preparation and implementation of requested changes = 50%.
  B. Approved by project initiator and/or project sponsor = 50%.
II. Performance Objectives — Based on project scope statement.
III. Performance Scorecard
IV. Performance Factors
  A. Project Team Members — Help construct requested changes by providing information relevant to areas of the project scope statement within project team delivery expectations for time and cost.
  B. Project Initiator(s) — Reviews and/or approves various versions of requested changes within project team delivery expectations for time and cost.
  C. Project Sponsor(s) — Reviews and/or approves various versions of requested changes within project team delivery expectations for time and cost.
  D. Project Manager — Leads and/or performs requested changes within project team delivery expectations for time and cost.
V. Training Objectives
  A. Short Term — Project manager conducts meetings with project initiator, sponsor, and team member(s) on the creation and completion of requested changes regarding what is involved and who is performing certain tasks within schedule expectations for performance.

B. Long Term — Team members become trained in the process to develop and complete requested changes as a means to improve total effort to complete task.

ACTIVITY DURATION ESTIMATING — ACTIVITY DURATION ESTIMATES

Activity duration estimates are quantitative assessments of the likely number of work periods that will be required to complete a schedule activity.

I. Key Value Areas Weighting (%)
   A. Completion of process preparation of creation of activity duration estimates for the project schedule = 50%.
   B. Approved by project initiator and/or project sponsor = 50%.
II. Performance Objectives — Based on project scope statement.
III. Performance Scorecard
IV. Performance Factors
   A. Project Team Members — Help construct activity duration estimates by providing information relevant to areas of the project scope statement within project team delivery expectations for time and cost.
   B. Project Initiator(s) — Reviews and/or approves various versions of activity duration estimates within project team delivery expectations for time and cost.
   C. Project Sponsor(s) — Reviews and/or approves various versions of activity duration estimates within project team delivery expectations for time and cost.
   D. Project Manager — Leads and/or performs construction of activity duration estimates within project team delivery expectations for time and cost.
V. Training Objectives
   A. Short Term — Project manager conducts meetings with project initiator, sponsor, and team member(s) on the creation and completion of activity duration estimates regarding what is involved and who is performing certain tasks within schedule expectations for performance.
   B. Long Term — Team members become trained in the process to develop and complete activity duration estimates as a means to improve total effort to complete task.

ACTIVITY DURATION ESTIMATING — ACTIVITY ATTRIBUTES (UPDATES)

The activity attributes are updated to include the duration for each schedule activity, the assumption made in developing the activity duration estimates, and any contingency reserves.

I. Key Value Areas Weighting (%)
   A. Completion of process preparation and implementation of updates to activity attributes for activity duration estimating = 50%.
   B. Approved by project initiator and/or project sponsor = 50%.
II. Performance Objectives — Based on project scope statement.
III. Performance Scorecard

IV. Performance Factors
   A. Project Team Members — Help construct updates to activity attributes by providing information relevant to areas of the project scope statement within project team delivery expectations for time and cost.
   B. Project Initiator(s) — Reviews and/or approves various updates to activity attributes of project scope management within project team delivery expectations for time and cost.
   C. Project Sponsor(s) — Reviews and/or approves various updates to activity attributes within project team delivery expectations for time and cost.
   D. Project Manager — Leads and/or performs updates to activity attributes within project team delivery expectations for time and cost.
V. Training Objectives
   A. Short Term — Project manager conducts meetings with project initiator, sponsor, and team member(s) on the creation and completion of updates to activity attributes regarding what is involved and who is performing certain tasks within schedule expectations for performance.
   B. Long Term — Team members become trained in the process to develop and complete updates to activity attributes as a means to improve total effort to complete task.

SCHEDULE DEVELOPMENT — PROJECT SCHEDULE

This process usually happens no later than the completion of the project management plan.

I. Key Value Areas Weighting (%)
   A. Completion of process preparation and implementation of project schedule = 50%.
   B. Approved by project initiator and/or project sponsor = 50%.
II. Performance Objectives — Based on project management plan.
III. Performance Scorecard
IV. Performance Factors
   A. Project Team Members — Help construct project schedule by providing information relevant to areas of the project management plan within project team delivery expectations for time and cost.
   B. Project Initiator(s) — Reviews and/or approves various versions of project schedule within project team delivery expectations for time and cost.
   C. Project Sponsor(s) — Reviews and/or approves various versions of project schedule within project team delivery expectations for time and cost.
   D. Project Manager — Leads and/or performs construction of project schedule within project team delivery expectations for time and cost.
V. Training Objectives
   A. Short Term — Project manager conducts meetings with project initiator, sponsor, and team member(s) on the creation and completion of the project schedule regarding what is involved and who is performing certain tasks within schedule expectations for performance.
   B. Long Term — Team members become trained in the process to develop and complete a project schedule as a means to improve total effort to complete task.

SCHEDULE DEVELOPMENT — SCHEDULE MODEL DATA

Supporting data for the project schedule include schedule milestones, schedule activities, activity attributes, and documentation of all identified assumptions and constraints.

I. Key Value Areas Weighting (%)
   A. Completion of process preparation and implementation of schedule model data = 50%.
   B. Approved by project initiator and/or project sponsor = 50%.
II. Performance Objectives — Based on project management plan.
III. Performance Scorecard
IV. Performance Factors
   A. Project Team Members — Help construct schedule model data by providing information relevant to areas of the project management plan within project team delivery expectations for time and cost.
   B. Project Initiator(s) — Reviews and/or approves various versions of schedule model data within project team delivery expectations for time and cost.
   C. Project Sponsor(s) — Reviews and/or approves various versions of schedule model data within project team delivery expectations for time and cost.
   D. Project Manager — Leads and/or performs creation of schedule model data within project team delivery expectations for time and cost.
V. Training Objectives
   A. Short Term — Project manager conducts meetings with project initiator, sponsor, and team member(s) on the creation and completion of the schedule model data regarding what is involved and who is performing certain tasks within schedule expectations for performance.
   B. Long Term — Team members become trained in the process to develop and complete the schedule model data as a means to improve total effort to complete task.

SCHEDULE DEVELOPMENT — SCHEDULE BASELINE

A specific version of the project schedule developed from the schedule network analysis of the schedule model.

I. Key Value Areas Weighting (%)
   A. Completion of process preparation and implementation of schedule baseline = 50%.
   B. Approved by project initiator and/or project sponsor = 50%.
II. Performance Objectives — Based on project management plan.
III. Performance Scorecard
IV. Performance Factors
   A. Project Team Members — Help construct schedule baseline by providing information relevant to areas of the project management plan within project team delivery expectations for time and cost.
   B. Project Initiator(s) — Reviews and/or approves various versions of schedule baseline within project team delivery expectations for time and cost.

C. Project Sponsor(s) — Reviews and/or approves various versions of schedule baseline within project team delivery expectations for time and cost.
D. Project Manager — Leads and/or performs construction of schedule baseline within project team delivery expectations for time and cost.

V. Training Objectives
  A. Short Term — Project manager conducts meetings with project initiator, sponsor, and team member(s) on the creation and completion of the schedule baseline regarding what is involved and who is performing certain tasks within schedule expectations for performance.
  B. Long Term — Team members become trained in the process to develop and complete a schedule baseline as a means to improve total effort to complete task.

SCHEDULE DEVELOPMENT — RESOURCE REQUIREMENT (UPDATES)

Resource leveling can have a significant effect on preliminary estimates of the types and quantities of resources required. If the resource-leveling analysis changes the project resource requirements, then the resource requirements are updated.

I. Key Value Areas Weighting (%)
  A. Completion of process preparation and implementation of updates to resource requirements = 50%.
  B. Approved by project initiator and/or project sponsor = 50%.
II. Performance Objectives — Based on project management plan.
III. Performance Scorecard
IV. Performance Factors
  A. Project Team Members — Help construct updates to resource requirements by providing information relevant to areas of the project management plan within project team delivery expectations for time and cost.
  B. Project Initiator(s) — Reviews and/or approves various updates to resource requirements of project management plan within project team delivery expectations for time and cost.
  C. Project Sponsor(s) — Reviews and/or approves various updates to resource requirements of project management plan within project team delivery expectations for time and cost.
  D. Project Manager — Leads and/or performs updates to resource requirements within project team delivery expectations for time and cost.
V. Training Objectives
  A. Short Term — Project manager conducts meetings with project initiator, sponsor, and team member(s) on the creation and completion of updates to resource requirements regarding what is involved and who is performing certain tasks within schedule expectations for performance.
  B. Long Term — Team members become trained in the process to develop and complete updates to resource requirements as a means to improve total effort to complete task.

SCHEDULE DEVELOPMENT — ACTIVITY ATTRIBUTES (UPDATES)

Activity attributes are updated to include any revised resource requirements and any other approved changes generated by the schedule development process.

I. Key Value Areas Weighting (%)
   A. Completion of process preparation and implementation of updates to activity attributes for project schedule = 50%.
   B. Approved by project initiator and/or project sponsor = 50%.
II. Performance Objectives — Based on project management plan.
III. Performance Scorecard
IV. Performance Factors
   A. Project Team Members — Help construct updates to activity attributes by providing information relevant to areas of the project management plan within project team delivery expectations for time and cost.
   B. Project Manager — Leads and/or performs updates to activity attributes within project team delivery expectations for time and cost.
V. Training Objectives
   A. Short Term — Project manager conducts meetings with project initiator, sponsor, and team member(s) on the creation and completion of updates to activity attributes regarding what is involved and who is performing certain tasks within schedule expectations for performance.
   B. Long Term — Team members become trained in the process to develop and complete updates to activity attributes as a means to improve total effort to complete task.

SCHEDULE DEVELOPMENT — PROJECT CALENDAR (UPDATES)

A project calendar is a calendar of working days or shifts that establishes those dates on which schedule activities are worked. It also establishes the nonworking days that determine dates on which schedule activities are idle, such as holidays, weekends, and nonshift hours.

I. Key Value Areas Weighting (%)
   A. Completion of process preparation and implementation of updates to project calendar = 50%.
   B. Approved by project initiator and/or project sponsor = 50%.
II. Performance Objectives — Based on project management plan.
III. Performance Scorecard
IV. Performance Factors
   A. Project Team Members — Help construct updates to the project calendar by providing information relevant to areas of the project management plan within project team delivery expectations for time and cost.
   B. Project Initiator(s) — Reviews and/or approves various updates to the project calendar within project team delivery expectations for time and cost.
   C. Project Sponsor(s) — Reviews and/or approves various updates to the project calendar within project team delivery expectations for time and cost.

D. Project Manager — Leads and/or performs updates to the project calendar within project team delivery expectations for time and cost.
V. Training Objectives
A. Short Term — Project manager conducts meetings with project initiator, sponsor, and team member(s) on the creation and completion of updates to the project calendar regarding what is involved and who is performing certain tasks within schedule expectations for performance.
B. Long Term — Team members become trained in the process to develop and complete updates to the project calendar as a means to improve total effort to complete task.

SCHEDULE DEVELOPMENT — REQUESTED CHANGES

The schedule development process can create requested changes that are submitted for review and processing through the integrated change control process.

I. Key Value Areas Weighting (%)
A. Completion of process preparation and implementation of requested changes to project schedule = 50%.
B. Approved by project initiator and/or project sponsor = 50%.
II. Performance Objectives — Based on project management plan.
III. Performance Scorecard
IV. Performance Factors
A. Project Team Members — Help construct requested changes by providing information relevant to areas of the project management plan within project team delivery expectations for time and cost.
B. Project Initiator(s) — Reviews and/or approves various versions of requested changes within project team delivery expectations for time and cost.
C. Project Sponsor(s) — Reviews and/or approves various versions of requested changes within project team delivery expectations for time and cost.
D. Project Manager — Leads and/or performs construction of requested changes within project team delivery expectations for time and cost.
V. Training Objectives
A. Short Term — Project manager conducts meetings with project initiator, sponsor, and team member(s) on the creation and completion of requested changes regarding what is involved and who is performing certain tasks within schedule expectations for performance.
B. Long Term — Team members become trained in the process to develop and complete requested changes as a means to improve total effort to complete task.

SCHEDULE DEVELOPMENT — PROJECT MANAGEMENT PLAN (UPDATES)

Throughout the project execution, the development process creates variance to the project management plan expectations. As this variance is dealt with, the project management plan must be updated.

I. Key Value Areas Weighting (%)
   A. Completion of process preparation and implementation of project management plan updates = 50%.
   B. Approved by project initiator and/or project sponsor = 50%.
II. Performance Objectives — Based on project management plan.
III. Performance Scorecard
IV. Performance Factors
   A. Project Team Members — Help construct updates to the project management plan by providing information relevant to areas of the project within project team delivery expectations for time and cost.
   B. Project Initiator(s) — Reviews and/or approves various updates to project management plan within project team delivery expectations for time and cost.
   C. Project Sponsor(s) — Reviews and/or approves various updates to project management plan within project team delivery expectations for time and cost.
   D. Project Manager — Leads and/or performs updates to the project management plan within project team delivery expectations for time and cost.
V. Training Objectives
   A. Short Term — Project manager conducts meetings with project initiator, sponsor, and team member(s) on the creation and completion of updates to the project management plan regarding what is involved and who is performing certain tasks within schedule expectations for performance.
   B. Long Term — Team members become trained in the process to develop and complete updates to the project management plan as a means to improve total effort to complete task.

SCHEDULE CONTROL — SCHEDULE MODEL DATA (UPDATES)

A project schedule update is any modification to the project schedule model information that is used to manage the project.

I. Key Value Areas Weighting (%)
   A. Completion of process preparation and implementation of updates to schedule data model = 50%.
   B. Approved by project initiator and/or project sponsor = 50%.
II. Performance Objectives — Based on schedule management plan.
III. Performance Scorecard
IV. Performance Factors
   A. Project Team Members — Help construct updates to the project schedule model data by providing information relevant to areas of the project within project team delivery expectations for time and cost.
   B. Project Initiator(s) — Reviews and/or approves various updates to the schedule model data within project team delivery expectations for time and cost.
   C. Project Sponsor(s) — Reviews and/or approves various updates to the schedule model data within project team delivery expectations for time and cost.
   D. Project Manager — Leads and/or performs updates to the schedule model data within project team delivery expectations for time and cost.

V. Training Objectives
   A. Short Term — Project manager conducts meetings with project initiator, sponsor, and team member(s) on the creation and completion of updates to the schedule model data regarding what is involved and who is performing certain tasks within schedule expectations for performance.
   B. Long Term — Team members become trained in the process to develop and complete updates to the schedule model data as a means to improve total effort to complete task.

SCHEDULE CONTROL — SCHEDULE BASELINE (UPDATES)

Schedule revisions are a special category of project schedule updates. Revisions are changes to the schedule's start and finish dates in the approved schedule baseline.

I. Key Value Areas Weighting (%)
   A. Completion of process preparation and implementation of updates to schedule baseline = 50%.
   B. Approved by project initiator and/or project sponsor = 50%.
II. Performance Objectives — Based on schedule management plan.
III. Performance Scorecard
IV. Performance Factors
   A. Project Team Members — Help construct updates to the schedule baseline by providing information relevant to areas of the project schedule management plan within project team delivery expectations for time and cost.
   B. Project Initiator(s) — Reviews and/or approves various updates to the schedule baseline within project team delivery expectations for time and cost.
   C. Project Sponsor(s) — Reviews and/or approves various updates to the schedule baseline within project team delivery expectations for time and cost.
   D. Project Manager — Leads and/or performs updates to the schedule baseline within project team delivery expectations for time and cost.
V. Training Objectives
   A. Short Term — Project manager conducts meetings with project initiator, sponsor, and team member(s) on the creation and completion of updates to the schedule baseline regarding what is involved and who is performing certain tasks within schedule expectations for performance.
   B. Long Term — Team members become trained in the process to develop and complete updates to the schedule baseline as a means to improve total effort to complete task.

SCHEDULE CONTROL — PERFORMANCE MEASUREMENTS

The calculated schedule variance and schedule performance index values for work breakdown structure components are documented and communicated to stakeholders.

I. Key Value Areas Weighting (%)
   A. Completion of process preparation and implementation of performance measurements = 50%.
   B. Approved by project initiator and/or project sponsor = 50%.

II. Performance Objectives — Based on schedule management plan.
III. Performance Scorecard
IV. Performance Factors
   A. Project Team Members — Help construct performance measurements by providing information relevant to areas of the project schedule management plan within project team delivery expectations for time and cost.
   B. Project Initiator(s) — Reviews and/or approves various versions of performance measurements within project team delivery expectations for time and cost.
   C. Project Sponsor(s) — Reviews and/or approves various versions of performance measurements within project team delivery expectations for time and cost.
   D. Project Manager — Leads and/or performs performance measurements within project team delivery expectations for time and cost.
V. Training Objectives
   A. Short Term — Project manager conducts meetings with project initiator, sponsor, and team member(s) on the creation and completion of performance measurements regarding what is involved and who is performing certain tasks within schedule expectations for performance.
   B. Long Term — Team members become trained in the process to develop and complete performance measurements as a means to improve total effort to complete task.

SCHEDULE CONTROL — REQUESTED CHANGES

Schedule variance analysis along with review of progress reports, results of performance measures, and modification to the project schedule model can result in requested changes to the project baseline.

I. Key Value Areas Weighting (%)
   A. Completion of process preparation and implementation of requested changes = 50%.
   B. Approved by project initiator and/or project sponsor = 50%.
II. Performance Objectives — Based on schedule management plan.
III. Performance Scorecard
IV. Performance Factors
   A. Project Team Members — Help construct requested changes by providing information relevant to areas of the project schedule management plan within project team delivery expectations for time and cost.
   B. Project Initiator(s) — Reviews and/or approves various versions of requested changes within project team delivery expectations for time and cost.
   C. Project Sponsor(s) — Reviews and/or approves various versions of requested changes within project team delivery expectations for time and cost.
   D. Project Manager — Leads and/or performs requested changes within project team delivery expectations for time and cost.
V. Training Objectives
   A. Short Term — Project manager conducts meetings with project initiator, sponsor, and team member(s) on the updating and completion of requested changes regarding what is involved and who is performing certain tasks within schedule expectations for performance.

B. Long Term — Team members become trained in the process to develop and complete requested changes as a means to improve total effort to complete task.

SCHEDULE CONTROL — RECOMMENDED CORRECTIVE ACTIONS

A corrective action is anything that will bring expected future project schedule performance in line with the approved project schedule baseline.

I. Key Value Areas Weighting (%)
   A. Completion of process preparation and implementation of requested corrective actions = 50%.
   B. Approved by project initiator and/or project sponsor = 50%.
II. Performance Objectives — Based on schedule management plan.
III. Performance Scorecard
IV. Performance Factors
   A. Project Team Members — Help construct recommended corrective actions by providing information relevant to areas of the project schedule management plan within project team delivery expectations for time and cost.
   B. Project Initiator(s) — Reviews and/or approves various versions of recommended corrective actions within project team delivery expectations for time and cost.
   C. Project Sponsor(s) — Reviews and/or approves various versions of recommended corrective actions within project team delivery expectations for time and cost.
   D. Project Manager — Leads and/or performs recommended corrective actions within project team delivery expectations for time and cost.
V. Training Objectives
   A. Short Term — Project manager conducts meetings with project initiator, sponsor, and team member(s) on the creation and completion of recommended corrective actions regarding what is involved and who is performing certain tasks within schedule expectations for performance.
   B. Long Term — Team members become trained in the process to develop and complete recommended corrective actions as a means to improve total effort to complete task.

SCHEDULE CONTROL — ORGANIZATIONAL PROCESS ASSETS (UPDATES)

Documentation of the causes of variance, the reasoning behind the corrective actions chosen, and other types of lessons learned from schedule control are documented in the organizational process assets.

I. Key Value Areas Weighting (%)
   A. Completion of process of preparation and implementation of updates to organizational process assets = 50%.
   B. Approved by project initiator and/or project sponsor = 50%.
II. Performance Objectives — Based on schedule management plan.
III. Performance Scorecard

IV. Performance Factors
   A. Project Team Members — Help construct updates to the organizational process assets by providing information relevant to areas of the project schedule management plan within project team delivery expectations for time and cost.
   B. Project Initiator(s) — Reviews and/or approves various updates to the organizational process assets within project team delivery expectations for time and cost.
   C. Project Sponsor(s) — Reviews and/or approves various updates to the organizational process assets within project team delivery expectations for time and cost.
   D. Project Manager — Leads and/or performs updates to the organizational process assets within project team delivery expectations for time and cost.
V. Training Objectives
   A. Short Term — Project manager conducts meetings with project initiator, sponsor, and team member(s) on the creation and completion of updates to the organizational process assets regarding what is involved and who is performing certain tasks within schedule expectations for performance.
   B. Long Term — Team members become trained in the process to develop and complete updates to the organizational process assets as a means to improve total effort to complete task.

SCHEDULE CONTROL — ACTIVITY LIST (UPDATES)

A comprehensive list of activity changes for all schedule activities that are planned to be performed on the project.

I. Key Value Areas Weighting (%)
   A. Completion of process preparation and implementation of updates to the activity list = 50%.
   B. Approved by project initiator and/or project sponsor = 50%.
II. Performance Objectives — Based on schedule management plan.
III. Performance Scorecard
IV. Performance Factors
   A. Project Team Members — Help construct updates to the activity list relevant to areas of the project schedule management plan within project team delivery expectations for time and cost.
   B. Project Initiator(s) — Reviews and/or approves various updates to the activity list within project team delivery expectations for time and cost.
   C. Project Sponsor(s) — Reviews and/or approves various updates to the activity list within project team delivery expectations for time and cost.
   D. Project Manager — Leads and/or performs updates to the activity list of the project schedule management plan within project team delivery expectations for time and cost.
V. Training Objectives
   A. Short Term — Project manager conducts meetings with project initiator, sponsor, and team member(s) on the creation and completion of the updates to the activity list regarding what is involved and who is performing certain tasks within schedule expectations for performance.

B. Long Term — Team members become trained in the process to develop and complete updates to the activity list as a means to improve total effort to complete task.

SCHEDULE CONTROL — ACTIVITY ATTRIBUTES (UPDATES)

The updates to the activity attributes are an extension of the activity attributes in the activity list and identify the multiple attributes associated with each schedule activity.

I. Key Value Areas Weighting (%)
   A. Completion of process preparation and implementation of updates to the activity attributes = 50%.
   B. Approved by project initiator and/or project sponsor = 50%.
II. Performance Objectives — Based on schedule management plan.
III. Performance Scorecard
IV. Performance Factors
   A. Project Team Members — Help construct updates to the activity attributes by providing information relevant to areas of the schedule management plan within project team delivery expectations for time and cost.
   B. Project Initiator(s) — Reviews and/or approves various updates to the activity attributes within project team delivery expectations for time and cost.
   C. Project Sponsor(s) — Reviews and/or approves various updates to the activity attributes within project team delivery expectations for time and cost.
   D. Project Manager — Leads and/or performs various updates to the activity attributes within project team delivery expectations for time and cost.
V. Training Objectives
   A. Short Term — Project manager conducts meetings with project initiator, sponsor, and team member(s) on the creation and completion of updates to the activity attributes regarding what is involved and who is performing certain tasks within schedule expectations for performance.
   B. Long Term — Team members become trained in the process to develop and complete updates to the activity attributes as a means to improve total effort to complete task.

SCHEDULE CONTROL — PROJECT MANAGEMENT PLAN (UPDATES)

The project management plan is updated to reflect any approved changes resulting from the schedule control process and how the project schedule will be managed.

I. Key Value Areas Weighting (%)
   A. Completion of process preparation and implementation of updates to the project management plan = 50%.
   B. Approved by project initiator and/or project sponsor = 50%.
II. Performance Objectives — Based on schedule management plan.

III. Performance Scorecard
IV. Performance Factors
   A. Project Team Members — Help construct updates to the project management plan by providing information relevant to areas of the project schedule management plan within project team delivery expectations for time and cost.
   B. Project Initiator(s) — Reviews and/or approves various updates to the project management plan within project team delivery expectations for time and cost.
   C. Project Sponsor(s) — Reviews and/or approves various updates to the project management plan within project team delivery expectations for time and cost.
   D. Project Manager — Leads and/or performs updates to the project management plan within project team delivery expectations for time and cost.
V. Training Objectives
   A. Short Term — Project manager conducts meetings with project initiator, sponsor, and team member(s) on the creation and completion of updates to the project management plan regarding what is involved and who is performing certain tasks within schedule expectations for performance.
   B. Long Term — Team members become trained in the process to develop and complete updates to the project management plan as a means to improve total effort to complete task.

SUMMARY

Project time management has long been an essential component of project measurement. Without it, project measurement and performance measurement are much weaker in value. Today, many businesses are wrestling with the issue of capturing this information at the employee level in sufficient detail to bring value through performance analysis. There are many good reasons to do so, but most important is the implication that everyone is accountable. To not be so fosters fraudulent behavior and activity because the expectation is that "no one is watching." One of the basic tenets of project management is the requirement for internal control. Project time management is an internal control mechanism that should not be disregarded. Choosing not to collect employee project time increases the risk of project failure because the project manager can only guess at the level of effort performed without it.

Furthermore, tracking by project milestones is not a substitute for tracking work effort by project team members. Has it come to this for your team? How will you quantify future staff changes without it? How will you forecast estimate-to-complete or estimate-at-completion without it?

QUESTIONS

19-1. Project Time Management PMBOK® area of knowledge includes the processes required to accomplish timely completion of the project. True or false?

19-2. Project Time Management does not include which of the following significant process:
   a. Activity definition
   b. Activity sequencing
   c. Schedule development
   d. Schedule reporting
19-3. The activity list is a comprehensive list that includes all schedule activities that are planned to be performed on the project. True or false?
19-4. Preparation of project logical relationships, leads and lags might reveal instances that can generate change to the activity list or the activity attributes. True or false?
19-5. Which of the following is not an output of the schedule control process:
   a. Schedule model data (updates)
   b. Schedule baseline (updates)
   c. Performance measurements
   d. Activity list

This book has free materials available for download from the Web Added Value™ Resource Center at www.jrosspub.com.

20

PROJECT COST MANAGEMENT

Project Cost Management includes the processes involved in planning, estimating, budgeting, and controlling costs so the project can be completed within the approved budget. These processes interact with each other and with other processes in the other knowledge areas as well. Each process can involve effort from one or more persons or groups based upon the needs of the project.

Project Cost Management PMBOK® area of knowledge includes the following processes and deliverables:

1. Cost Estimating
    a. Activity Cost Estimates
    b. Activity Cost Supporting Detail
    c. Requested Changes
    d. Cost Management Plan (Updates)
2. Cost Budgeting
    a. Cost Baseline
    b. Project Funding Requirements
    c. Project Management Plan (Updates)
    d. Requested Changes
3. Cost Control
    a. Cost Updates (Estimates)
    b. Cost Baseline (Updates)
    c. Performance Measurements
    d. Forecasted Completion
    e. Requested Changes
    f. Recommended Corrective Actions
    g. Organizational Process Assets (Updates)
    h. Project Management Plan (Updates)

These discrete process components integrate with each other and with other processes from other areas of knowledge within the PMBOK®. In addition, these process components may impact other successor dependent program and/or project initiatives in a manner not visible to the project team.

In the 3Ms metric key value area models that follow in this chapter, each metric model contains rules that require acceptance from the receiving user. This ensures that visibility to the deliverable is confirmed by the primary receiving user and other project-related stakeholders. Another benefit of this approach is project fraud prevention and detection. By ensuring that visibility to the specific deliverable is confirmed, opportunity for project fraud is reduced, thereby improving project fraud prevention. This action also implies that the artifact has been scrutinized by the receiving user and that this user does not detect project fraud within the artifact or those circumstances surrounding the artifact.

The following 3Ms-oriented metrics support the Project Cost Management PMBOK® area of knowledge:

1. Cost Estimating — Activity Cost Estimates
2. Cost Estimating — Activity Cost Supporting Detail
3. Cost Estimating — Requested Changes
4. Cost Estimating — Cost Management Plan (Updates)
5. Cost Budgeting — Cost Baseline
6. Cost Budgeting — Project Funding Requirements
7. Cost Budgeting — Cost Management Plan (Updates)
8. Cost Budgeting — Requested Changes
9. Cost Control — Cost Estimates (Updates)
10. Cost Control — Cost Baseline (Updates)
11. Cost Control — Performance Measurements
12. Cost Control — Forecasted Completion
13. Cost Control — Requested Changes
14. Cost Control — Recommended Corrective Action
15. Cost Control — Organizational Process Assets (Updates)
16. Cost Control — Project Management Plan (Updates)

Scoring for Section II: Performance Objectives for these metrics is as follows:

A. 50%: 4 = completed early and under budget ≥10%; 3 = ≥5%; 2 = completed on time and on budget; 1 = completed late and/or over budget.
B. 50%: 4 = approved by project initiator and project sponsor early and under budget ≥10%; 3 = approved early and under budget ≥5%; 2 = approved on time and on budget; 1 = approved late and/or over budget.

Scoring for Section III: Performance Scorecard for these metrics is as follows: 4 = Excellent; 3 = Very Good; 2 = Satisfactory; 1 = Unsatisfactory.

COST ESTIMATING — ACTIVITY COST ESTIMATES

An activity cost estimate is a quantitative measure of the most probable costs of the resources required to complete schedule activities. This specific type of metric can be presented in summary or detail form. Costs are estimated for all resources that are applied to the activity cost estimate. This includes but is not limited to labor, materials, equipment, services, facilities, information technology, and special categories such as an inflation allowance or cost contingency reserve.

I. Key Value Area Weighting (%)
   A. Completion of process preparation for all identified activity cost estimates = 50%.
   B. Approved by project initiator and/or project sponsor = 50%.
II. Performance Objectives — Based on all requested activity cost estimates.
III. Performance Scorecard
IV. Performance Factors
   A. Project Team Members — Help construct activity cost estimates by providing information relevant to areas of the project management plan within project team delivery expectations for project completion.
   B. Project Initiator(s) — Reviews and/or approves various versions of activity cost estimates within project team delivery expectations for project completion.
   C. Project Sponsor(s) — Reviews and/or approves various versions of activity cost estimates within project team delivery expectations for project completion.
   D. Project Manager — Leads and/or performs construction of activity cost estimates within project team delivery expectation for project completion.
V. Training Objectives
   A. Short Term — Project manager conducts meetings with project initiator, sponsor, and team member(s) on the creation and completion of the project activity cost estimates regarding what is involved and who is performing certain tasks within schedule expectations for performance.
   B. Long Term — Team members become trained in the process to develop and complete activity cost estimates as a means to improve total effort to complete task.

COST ESTIMATING — ACTIVITY COST SUPPORTING DETAIL

The amount and type of additional details supporting the schedule activity cost estimate. The supporting documentation should provide a clear, professional, and complete picture of how cost estimates are derived. Supporting detail for activity cost should include the following items:

- Activity scope of work
- Documentation of the genesis for the activity cost estimate
- Documentation of assumptions for the activity cost estimate
- Documentation of constraints for the activity cost estimate
- Activity cost estimate range (high to low)

I. Key Value Area Weighting (%)
   A. Completion of process preparation of activity cost estimates = 50%.
   B. Approved by project initiator and/or project sponsor = 50%.
II. Performance Objectives — Based on all activity cost estimates requested.
III. Performance Scorecard
IV. Performance Factors
   A. Project Team Members — Help provide activity cost estimate supporting detail by providing information relevant to areas of the project within project team delivery expectations for project completion.
   B. Project Manager — Leads and/or performs the collection/construction of activity cost estimate supporting detail within project team delivery expectations for project completion.
V. Training Objectives
   A. Short Term — Project manager conducts meetings with project team member(s) on the creation and completion of activity costs estimate supporting detail regarding what is involved and who is performing certain tasks within schedule expectations for performance.
   B. Long Term — Team members become trained in the process to develop and complete activity cost estimate supporting detail as a means to improve total effort to complete task.

COST ESTIMATING — REQUESTED CHANGES

The cost estimating process often generates requested changes that may only be relevant to the cost management plan, activity resource requirements, and other components of the project management plan. Requested changes are processed for review and disposition through the integrated change control process.

I. Key Value Areas Weighting (%)
   A. Completion of process preparation for requested changes = 50%.
   B. Approved by project initiator and/or project sponsor = 50%.
II. Performance Objectives — Based on all requested changes to the project management plan.
III. Performance Scorecard
IV. Performance Factors
   A. Project Team Members — Help construct requested changes by providing information relevant to areas of the project management plan within project team delivery expectations for project completion.
   B. Project Initiator(s) — Reviews and/or approves various versions of requested changes within project team delivery expectations for project completion.
   C. Project Sponsor(s) — Reviews and/or approves various versions of requested changes within project team delivery expectations for project completion.
   D. Project Manager — Leads and/or performs construction of requested change(s) within project team delivery expectations for project completion.
V. Training Objectives
   A. Short Term — Project manager conducts meetings with project initiator, sponsor, and team member(s) on the creation and completion of requested changes regarding

what is involved and who is performing certain tasks within schedule expectations for performance.
   B. Long Term — Team members become trained in the process to develop and complete requested changes as a means to improve total effort to complete task.

COST ESTIMATING — COST MANAGEMENT PLAN (UPDATES)

As the requested change(s) are approved, the cost management plan of the project management plan is updated if the approved change(s) impacts the management of costs.

   I. Key Value Areas Weighting (%)
      A. Completion of process preparation and implementation of updates to the cost management plan from requested change(s) = 50%.
      B. Approved by project initiator and/or project sponsor = 50%.
   II. Performance Objectives — Based on all requested change(s) approved for project management plan.
   III. Performance Scorecard
   IV. Performance Factors
      A. Project Team Members — Help construct cost management plan updates by providing information relevant to areas of the project management plan within project team delivery expectations for time and cost.
      B. Project Initiator(s) — Reviews and/or approves various versions of updates to the cost management plan within project team delivery expectations for time and cost.
      C. Project Sponsor(s) — Reviews and/or approves various versions of updates to the cost management plan within project team delivery expectations for time and cost.
      D. Project Manager — Leads and/or performs construction of updates to the cost management plan within project team delivery expectations for time and cost.
   V. Training Objectives
      A. Short Term — Project manager conducts meetings with project initiator, sponsor, and team member(s) on the creation and completion of updates to the cost management plan regarding what is involved and who is performing certain tasks within schedule expectations for performance.
      B. Long Term — Team members become trained in the process to develop and complete updates to the cost management plan as a means to improve total effort to complete task.

COST BUDGETING — COST BASELINE

The cost baseline is a time-segmented budget that is used as a comparative means against which to measure overall cost performance on the project. The cost baseline is developed by aggregating estimated costs by period of time. The cost baseline is a component of the project management plan.

   I. Key Value Areas Weighting (%)
      A. Completion of process preparation and implementation of the cost baseline = 50%.
      B. Approved by project initiator and/or project sponsor = 50%.

II. Performance Objectives — Based on all costs determined as necessary to complete the project.
III. Performance Scorecard
IV. Performance Factors
   A. Project Team Members — Help construct cost baseline by providing information relevant to areas of the project management plan within project team delivery expectations for time and cost.
   B. Project Initiator(s) — Reviews and/or approves various versions of cost baseline within project team delivery expectations for time and cost.
   C. Project Sponsor(s) — Reviews and/or approves various versions of cost baseline within project team delivery expectations for time and cost.
   D. Project Manager — Leads and/or performs construction of cost baseline within project team delivery expectations for time and cost.
V. Training Objectives
   A. Short Term — Project manager conducts meetings with project initiator, sponsor, and team member(s) on the creation and completion of the project cost baseline regarding what is involved and who is performing certain tasks within schedule expectations for performance.
   B. Long Term — Team members become trained in the process to develop and complete a project cost baseline as a means to improve total effort to complete task.

COST BUDGETING — PROJECT FUNDING REQUIREMENTS

Total and periodic funding requirements for the project are derived from the cost baseline. Funding usually occurs in incremental amounts that are sporadic and different. Total funds required are those included in the cost baseline plus the management contingency reserve amount. Some portion of the management contingency reserve can be included incrementally in each funding step or funded as required, depending on organizational and/or project management policies.

I. Key Value Areas Weighting (%)
   A. Completion of process preparation and implementation of project funding requirements = 50%.
   B. Approved by project initiator and/or project sponsor = 50%.
II. Performance Objectives — Based on project management plan and cost baseline.
III. Performance Scorecard
IV. Performance Factors
   A. Project Team Members — Help construct project funding requirements by providing information relevant to areas of the project cost baseline and project management plan within project team delivery expectations for time and cost.
   B. Project Initiator(s) — Reviews and/or approves various versions of project funding requirements within project team delivery expectations for time and cost.
   C. Project Sponsor(s) — Reviews and/or approves various versions of project funding requirements within project team delivery expectations for time and cost.

D. Project Manager — Leads and/or performs construction of project funding requirements within project team delivery expectations for time and cost.
V. Training Objectives
   A. Short Term — Project manager conducts meetings with project initiator, sponsor, and team member(s) on the creation and completion of the project funding requirements regarding what is involved and who is performing certain tasks within schedule expectations for performance.
   B. Long Term — Team members become trained in the process to develop and complete project funding requirements as a means to improve total effort to complete task.

COST BUDGETING — COST MANAGEMENT PLAN (UPDATES)

Change requests are created, approved, and applied to the cost management plan if these changes are expected to impact the management of costs.

I. Key Value Areas Weighting (%)
   A. Completion of process preparation and implementation of cost management plan updates = 50%.
   B. Approved by project initiator and/or project sponsor = 50%.
II. Performance Objectives — Based on project management plan and existing cost management plan.
III. Performance Scorecard
IV. Performance Factors
   A. Project Team Members — Help construct cost management plan updates by providing information relevant to areas of the project management plan within project team delivery expectations for time and cost.
   B. Project Initiator(s) — Reviews and/or approves various versions updates to the of cost management plan within project team delivery expectations for time and cost.
   C. Project Sponsor(s) — Reviews and/or approves various versions of updates to the cost management plan within project team delivery expectations for time and cost.
   D. Project Manager — Leads and/or performs construction of updates to the cost management plan within project team delivery expectations for time and cost.
V. Training Objectives
   A. Short Term — Project manager conducts meetings with project initiator, sponsor, and team member(s) on the creation and completion of updates to the cost management plan (updates) regarding what is involved and who is performing certain tasks within schedule expectations for performance.
   B. Long Term — Team members become trained in the process to develop and complete updates to the cost management plan as a means to improve total effort to complete task.

COST BUDGETING — REQUESTED CHANGES

The cost budgeting process can generate requested changes to the cost management plan or other components of the project management plan.

I. Key Value Areas Weighting (%)
   A. Completion of process preparation and implementation of cost control requested changes = 50%.
   B. Approved by project initiator and/or project sponsor = 50%.
II. Performance Objectives — Based on current cost management plan.
III. Performance Scorecard
IV. Performance Factors
   A. Project Team Members — Help construct requested changes to cost management plan by providing information relevant to areas of the project management plan within project team delivery expectations for time and cost.
   B. Project Initiator(s) — Reviews and/or approves various versions of requested changes to the cost management plan within project team delivery expectations for time and cost.
   C. Project Sponsor(s) — Reviews and/or approves various versions of requested changes to the cost management plan within project team delivery expectations for time and cost.
   D. Project Manager — Leads and/or performs requested changes to the cost management plan within project team delivery expectations for time and cost.
V. Training Objectives
   A. Short Term — Project manager conducts meetings with project initiator, sponsor, and team member(s) on the creation and completion of requested changes to the cost management plan regarding what is involved and who is performing certain tasks within schedule expectations for performance.
   B. Long Term — Team members become trained in the process to develop and complete requested changes to the cost management plan as a means to improve total effort to complete task.

COST CONTROL — COSTS ESTIMATES (UPDATES)

Costs estimates for revised schedule activities are changes to the cost information used to manage the project. Revised cost estimates may require adjustments to other aspects of the project management plan.

I. Key Value Areas Weighting (%)
   A. Completion of process preparation and implementation of cost estimate updates to the project management plan = 50%.
   B. Approved by project initiator and/or project sponsor = 50%.
II. Performance Objectives — Based on current project management plan.
III. Performance Scorecard
IV. Performance Factors
   A. Project Team Members — Help construct cost estimate updates by providing information relevant to areas of the project management plan within project team delivery expectations for time and cost.
   B. Project Initiator(s) — Reviews and/or approves various versions of cost estimate updates within project team delivery expectations for time and cost.

C. Project Sponsor(s) — Reviews and/or approves various versions of cost estimate updates within project team delivery expectations for time and cost.
　　D. Project Manager — Leads and/or performs construction of cost estimate updates within project team delivery expectations for time and cost.
　V. Training Objectives
　　A. Short Term — Project manager conducts meetings with project initiator, sponsor, and team member(s) on the creation and completion of cost estimate updates regarding what is involved and who is performing certain tasks within schedule expectations for performance.
　　B. Long Term — Team members become trained in the process to develop and complete cost estimate updates to the project management plan as a means to improve total effort to complete task.

COST CONTROL — COST BASELINE (UPDATES)

The cost baseline is updated through approved budget updates. These changes are generally implemented as a result of changes to the project scope.

　I. Key Value Areas Weighting (%)
　　A. Completion of process preparation and implementation of budget updates to the cost baseline = 50%.
　　B. Approved by project initiator and/or project sponsor = 50%.
　II. Performance Objectives — Based on changes in project scope.
　III. Performance Scorecard
　IV. Performance Factors
　　A. Project Team Members — Help construct cost baseline updates by providing information relevant to areas of the project scope statement within project team delivery expectations for time and cost.
　　B. Project Initiator(s) — Reviews and/or approves various versions of cost baseline updates within project team delivery expectations for time and cost.
　　C. Project Sponsor(s) — Reviews and/or approves various versions of cost baseline updates within project team delivery expectations for time and cost.
　　D. Project Manager — Leads and/or performs construction of cost baseline updates within project team delivery expectations for time and cost.
　V. Training Objectives
　　A. Short Term — Project manager conducts meetings with project initiator, sponsor, and team member(s) on the creation and completion of cost baseline updates regarding what is involved and who is performing certain tasks within schedule expectations for performance.
　　B. Long Term — Team members become trained in the process to develop and complete cost baseline updates as a means to improve total effort to complete task.

COST CONTROL — PERFORMANCE MEASUREMENTS

The calculated cost variance, schedule variance, cost performance index, and schedule performance index for the work breakdown structure of the project are documented and communicated to stakeholders.

I. Key Value Areas Weighting (%)
   A. Completion of process preparation and implementation for performance measurement = 50%.
   B. Approved by project initiator and/or project sponsor = 50%.
II. Performance Objectives — Based on project management plan.
III. Performance Scorecard
IV. Performance Factors
   A. Project Team Members — Help construct performance measurements by providing information relevant to areas of the project management plan within project team delivery expectations for time and cost.
   B. Project Initiator(s) — Reviews and/or approves various versions of performance measurements within project team delivery expectations for time and cost.
   C. Project Sponsor(s) — Reviews and/or approves various versions of performance measurements within project team delivery expectations for time and cost.
   D. Project Manager — Leads and/or performs construction of performance measurements within project team delivery expectations for time and cost.
V. Training Objectives
   A. Short Term — Project manager conducts meetings with project initiator, sponsor, and team member(s) on the creation and completion of performance measurements regarding what is involved and who is performing certain tasks within schedule expectations for performance.
   B. Long Term — Team members become trained in the process to develop and complete performance measurements as a means to improve total effort to complete task.

COST CONTROL — FORECASTED COMPLETION

An estimate-to-complete value or a reported estimate-at-completion value is provided by the performing organization and the value is reported to the stakeholders.

I. Key Value Areas Weighting (%)
   A. Completion of process preparation and implementation of estimate-at-completion and estimate-to-complete = 50%.
   B. Approved by project initiator and/or project sponsor = 50%.
II. Performance Objectives — Based on project management plan.
III. Performance Scorecard
IV. Performance Factors
   A. Project Team Members — Help construct estimate-at-completion and estimate-to-complete by providing information relevant to areas of the project management plan within project team delivery expectations for time and cost.
   B. Project Initiator(s) — Reviews and/or approves various versions of estimate-at-completion and estimate-to-complete within project team delivery expectations for time and cost.
   C. Project Sponsor(s) — Reviews and/or approves various versions of estimate-at-completion and estimate-to-complete within project team delivery expectations for time and cost.

D. Project Manager — Leads and/or performs construction of estimate-at-completion and estimate-to-complete within project team delivery expectations for time and cost.
V. Training Objectives
   A. Short Term — Project manager conducts meetings with project initiator, sponsor, and team member(s) on the creation and completion of estimate-at-completion and estimate-to-complete regarding what is involved and who is performing certain tasks within schedule expectations for performance.
   B. Long Term — Team members become trained in the process to develop and complete estimate-at-completion and estimate-to-complete as a means to improve total effort to complete task.

COST CONTROL — REQUESTED CHANGES

Analysis of project performance can generate a request for a change to some aspect of the project. Identified changes can require increasing or decreasing the budget.

I. Key Value Areas Weighting (%)
   A. Completion of process preparation and implementation of requested change(s) = 50%.
   B. Approved by project initiator and/or project sponsor = 50%.
II. Performance Objectives — Based on project management plan.
III. Performance Scorecard
IV. Performance Factors
   A. Project Team Members — Help construct requested change(s) by providing information relevant to areas of the project management plan within project team delivery expectations for time and cost.
   B. Project Initiator(s) — Reviews and/or approves various versions of requested change(s) within project team delivery expectations for time and cost.
   C. Project Sponsor(s) — Reviews and/or approves various versions of requested change(s) within project team delivery expectations for time and cost.
   D. Project Manager — Leads and/or performs construction of requested change(s) within project team delivery expectations for time and cost.
V. Training Objectives
   A. Short Term — Project manager conducts meetings with project initiator, sponsor, and team member(s) on the creation and completion of requested change(s) regarding what is involved and who is performing certain tasks within schedule expectations for performance.
   B. Long Term — Team members become trained in the process to develop and complete requested change(s) as a means to improve total effort to complete task.

COST CONTROL — RECOMMENDED CORRECTIVE ACTION

A corrective action is work performed to bring expected future performance of the project in line with the project management plan. Corrective action in cost management often involves adjusting schedule activity budgets.

I. Key Value Areas Weighting (%)
    A. Completion of process preparation and implementation of recommended corrective action = 50%.
    B. Approved by project initiator and/or project sponsor = 50%.
II. Performance Objectives — Based on project management plan.
III. Performance Scorecard
IV. Performance Factors
    A. Project Team Members — Help implement recommended corrective action by providing information relevant to areas of the project management plan within project team delivery expectations for time and cost.
    B. Project Initiator(s) — Reviews and/or approves various versions of recommended corrective action within project team delivery expectations for time and cost.
    C. Project Sponsor(s) — Reviews and/or approves various versions of recommended corrective action within project team delivery expectations for time and cost.
    D. Project Manager — Leads and/or performs recommended corrective action within project team delivery expectations for time and cost.
V. Training Objectives
    A. Short Term — Project manager conducts meetings with project initiator, sponsor, and team member(s) on the creation and completion of recommended corrective action regarding what is involved and who is performing certain tasks within schedule expectations for performance.
    B. Long Term — Team members become trained in the process to develop and complete a recommended corrective action as a means to improve total effort to complete task.

COST CONTROL — ORGANIZATIONAL PROCESS ASSETS (UPDATES)

Lessons learned are documented so they can become part of the historical databases for both the project and the performing organization. Documentation includes the root causes of variances, the reasoning behind the corrective action chosen, and other types of lessons learned from cost, resource, or resource production control.

I. Key Value Areas Weighting (%)
    A. Completion of process preparation and implementation of updates to organizational process assets = 50%.
    B. Approved by project initiator and/or project sponsor = 50%.
II. Performance Objectives — Based on identified lessons learned documentation.
III. Performance Scorecard
IV. Performance Factors
    A. Project Team Members — Help construct updates to organizational process assets by providing information relevant to areas of the project management plan within project team delivery expectations for time and cost.
    B. Project Initiator(s) — Reviews and/or approves various versions of organizational process assets updates within project team delivery expectations for time and cost.

C. Project Sponsor(s) — Reviews and/or approves various versions of organizational process assets updates within project team delivery expectations for time and cost.
   D. Project Manager — Leads and/or performs construction of organizational process assets updates within project team delivery expectations for time and cost.
V. Training Objectives
   A. Short Term — Project manager conducts meetings with project initiator, sponsor, and team member(s) on the creation and completion of organizational process assets updates regarding what is involved and who is performing certain tasks within schedule expectations for performance.
   B. Long Term — Team members become trained in the process to develop and complete organizational process assets updates as a means to improve total effort to complete task.

COST CONTROL — PROJECT MANAGEMENT PLAN (UPDATES)

Schedule activity, work package, planning package cost estimates, cost baseline, cost management plan, and project budget documents can be updated to reflect changes to the project management plan.

   I. Key Value Areas Weighting (%)
      A. Completion of process preparation and implementation of project management plan updates = 50%.
      B. Approved by project initiator and/or project sponsor = 50%.
  II. Performance Objectives — Based on project management plan component need to change.
 III. Performance Scorecard
  IV. Performance Factors
      A. Project Team Members — Help construct project management plan updates by providing information relevant to areas of the project management plan within project team delivery expectations for time and cost.
      B. Project Initiator(s) — Reviews and/or approves various versions of project management plan updates within project team delivery expectations for time and cost.
      C. Project Sponsor(s) — Reviews and/or approves various versions of project management plan updates within project team delivery expectations for time and cost.
      D. Project Manager — Leads and/or performs construction of project management plan updates within project team delivery expectations for time and cost.
   V. Training Objectives
      A. Short Term — Project manager conducts meetings with project initiator, sponsor, and team member(s) on the creation and completion of the project management plan updates regarding what is involved and who is performing certain tasks within schedule expectations for performance.
      B. Long Term — Team members become trained in the process to develop and complete project management plan updates as a means to improve total effort to complete task.

SUMMARY

Project Cost Management is primarily concerned with the cost of the resources required to complete schedule activities. It also considers the effect of project decisions on the cost of using, maintaining, and supporting the product, service, or result of the project. The broader perspective of Project Cost Management is frequently known as life cycle costing. When applied holistically with recognition of acceleration opportunities and threats to project delivery/completion, life cycle costing can have significant incremental intrinsic value to the project team.

QUESTIONS

20-1. Project Cost Management does not include which of the following processes:
   a. Cost estimating
   b. Cost budgeting
   c. Cost control
   d. Cost management

20-2. Cost estimating process does not include which of the following outputs:
   a. Activity cost estimates
   b. Activity cost estimates supporting detail
   c. Cost management plan update(s)
   d. Cost baseline

20-3. Cost budgeting process does not include which of the following outputs:
   a. Cost baseline
   b. Project funding requirements
   c. Requested changes
   d. Forecasted completion

20-4. Cost control process does not include which of the following outputs:
   a. Cost estimate (updates)
   b. Performance measurements
   c. Requested changes
   d. Cost management plan (updates)

20-5. In performing cost estimating, activity cost estimates do not rely on which of the following inputs:
   a. Labor
   b. Material
   c. Equipment
   d. Requested changes

20-6. Requested changes to cost estimating are processed for review and disposition through:
   a. Project management plan processes
   b. Cost management plan processes

Project Cost Management **273**

      c. Integrated change control processes
      d. Risk management plan processes
20-7. Cost baseline is a time-based budget that is not used as a basis to:
      a. Measure
      b. Monitor
      c. Control
      d. Add resources
20-8. Project funding requirements usually are supported best by the:
      a. Management contingency reserve
      b. Cost management plan
      c. Project management plan
      d. Requested changes
20-9. Cost management plan updates result from the:
      a. Cost budgeting process
      b. Cost estimating process
      c. Cost control process
      d. Risk management process
20-10. Which of the following is not an output of cost control:
      a. Cost estimate updates
      b. Activity cost estimate supporting detail
      c. Forecasted completion
      d. Organizational process assets (updates)
20-11. Organizational process assets updates does not include:
      a. Root causes of variances
      b. The reasoning behind the corrective action chosen
      c. Resource production control updates
      d. Stakeholder approval
20-12. Cost control process for recommended corrective action enables expected future performance of the project to be in line with the project management plan. True or false?
20-13. Cost baseline measures overall performance of the project. True or false?
20-14. Activity cost estimates supporting detail often includes the risk response plan. True or false?
20-15. Project cost management involves planning, estimating, budgeting, and controlling costs. True or false?

This book has free materials available for download from the
Web Added Value™ Resource Center at www.jrosspub.com.

PROJECT QUALITY MANAGEMENT

Project Quality Management processes include all the activities of the performing organization that determine quality policies, objectives, and responsibilities so the project will meet the needs for which it was created.

Project Quality Management consists of three processes:

1. **Quality Planning** — Identify the quality standards appropriate to the project and how to satisfy them
2. **Perform Quality Assurance** — Ensure that the project applies all processes necessary to meet requirements
3. **Perform Quality Control** — Measure quality compliance within the project, as well as how to eliminate unsatisfactory quality results

Project Quality Management PMBOK® area of knowledge includes the following processes and deliverables:

1. Quality Planning
   a. Quality Management Plan
   b. Quality Metrics
   c. Quality Checklists
   d. Process Improvement Plan
   e. Quality Baseline
   f. Project Management Plan (Updates)
2. Perform Quality Assurance
   a. Requested Changes
   b. Recommended Corrective Actions
   c. Organizational Process Assets (Updates)
   d. Project Management Plan (Updates)

3. Perform Quality Control
   a. Quality Control Measurements
   b. Validated Defect Repair
   c. Quality Baseline (Updates)
   d. Recommended Corrective Actions
   e. Recommended Preventive Actions
   f. Requested Changes
   g. Recommended Defect Repair
   h. Organizational Process Assets (Updates)
   i. Validated Deliverables
   j. Project Management Plan (Updates)

These discrete process components integrate with each other and with other processes from other areas of knowledge within the PMBOK®. In addition, these process components may impact other successor dependent program and/or project initiatives in a manner not visible to the project team.

In the 3Ms metric profiles that follow in this chapter, each metric profile contains rules that require acceptance from the receiving user. This ensures that visibility to the deliverable is confirmed by the primary receiving user and other project-related stakeholders. Another benefit of this approach is project fraud prevention and detection. By ensuring that visibility to the specific deliverable is confirmed, opportunity for project fraud is reduced, thereby improving project fraud prevention. This action also implies that the artifact has been scrutinized by the receiving user and that this user does not detect project fraud within the artifact or those circumstances surrounding the artifact.

The following 3Ms-oriented metrics support the Project Quality Management PMBOK® area of knowledge:

1. Quality Planning — Quality Management Plan
2. Quality Planning — Quality Metrics
3. Quality Planning — Quality Checklists
4. Quality Planning — Process Improvement Plan
5. Quality Planning — Quality Baseline
6. Quality Planning — Project Management Plan (Updates)
7. Perform Quality Assurance — Requested Changes
8. Perform Quality Assurance — Recommended Corrective Actions
9. Perform Quality Assurance — Organizational Process Assets (Updates)
10. Perform Quality Assurance — Project Management Plan (Updates)
11. Perform Quality Control — Quality Control Measurements
12. Perform Quality Control — Validated Defect Repair
13. Perform Quality Control — Quality Baseline (Updates)
14. Perform Quality Control — Recommended Corrective Actions
15. Perform Quality Control — Recommended Preventive Actions
16. Perform Quality Control — Requested Changes

17. Perform Quality Control — Recommended Defect Repair
18. Perform Quality Control — Organizational Process Assets (Updates)
19. Perform Quality Control — Validated Deliverables
20. Perform Quality Control — Project Management Plan (Updates)

Scoring for Section II: Performance Objectives for these metrics is as follows:

A. 50%: 4 = completed early and under budget ≥10%; 3 = ≥5%; 2 = completed on time and on budget; 1 = completed late and/or over budget.
B. 50%: 4 = approved by project initiator and/or project sponsor early and under budget ≥10%; 3 = approved early and under budget ≥5%; 2 = approved on time and on budget; 1 = approved late and/or over budget.

Scoring for Section III: Performance Scorecard for these metrics is as follows: 4 = Excellent; 3 = Very Good; 2 = Satisfactory; 1 = Unsatisfactory.

QUALITY PLANNING — QUALITY MANAGEMENT PLAN

Describes how the project team will implement the performing organization's quality policy. The quality management plan provides input to the project management plan and must include the quality control, quality assurance, and continuous process improvement processes for the project.

I. Key Value Areas Weighting (%)
   A. Completion of process preparation and implementation of quality management plan = 50%.
   B. Approved by project initiator and/or project sponsor = 50%.
II. Performance Objectives — Based on all projects linked to specific corporate objectives.
III. Performance Scorecard
IV. Performance Factors
   A. Project Team Members — Help construct quality management plan by providing information relevant to areas of the project management plan within project team delivery expectations for time and cost.
   B. Project Initiator(s) — Reviews and/or approves various versions of the quality management plan within project team delivery expectations for time and cost.
   C. Project Sponsor(s) — Reviews and/or approves various versions of the quality management plan within project team delivery expectations for time and cost.
   D. Project Manager — Leads and/or performs construction of quality management plan within project team delivery expectations for time and cost.
V. Training Objectives
   A. Short Term — Project manager conducts meetings with project initiator, sponsor, and team member(s) on the creation and completion of the quality management plan regarding what is involved and who is performing certain tasks within schedule expectations for performance.
   B. Long Term — Team members become trained in the process to develop and complete a quality management plan as a means to improve total effort to complete task.

QUALITY PLANNING — QUALITY METRICS

A metric is an operational definition that describes an entity and how the control processes measures that entity. A measurement is an actual value. Examples of quality metrics include defect density, failure rate, availability, reliability, and test coverage.

I. Key Value Areas Weighting (%)
   A. Completion of process preparation for developing and implementing quality metrics = 50%.
   B. Approved by project initiator and/or project sponsor = 50%.
II. Performance Objectives — Based on project management plan.
III. Performance Scorecard
IV. Performance Factors
   A. Project Team Members — Help construct quality metrics by providing information relevant to areas of the project within project team delivery expectations for time and cost.
   B. Project Initiator(s) — Reviews and/or approves various versions of quality metrics within project team delivery expectations for time and cost.
   C. Project Sponsor(s) — Reviews and/or approves various versions of quality metrics within project team delivery expectations for time and cost.
   D. Project Manager — Leads and/or performs development and implementation of quality metrics within project team delivery expectations for time and cost.
V. Training Objectives
   A. Short Term — Project manager conducts meetings with project initiator, sponsor, and team member(s) on the creation and completion of the project quality metrics regarding what is involved and who is performing certain tasks within schedule expectations for performance.
   B. Long Term — Team members become trained in the process to develop and implement quality metrics as a means to improve total effort to complete task.

QUALITY PLANNING — QUALITY CHECKLISTS

A checklist is a structured tool, normally component specific, used to verify that a set of required steps has been performed.

I. Key Value Areas Weighting (%)
   A. Completion of process preparation and implementation of project quality checklists = 50%.
   B. Approved by project initiator and/or project sponsor = 50%.
II. Performance Objectives — Based on project management plan.
III. Performance Scorecard
IV. Performance Factors
   A. Project Team Members — Help construct project-related quality checklists by providing information relevant to areas of the project within project team delivery expectations for time and cost.

B. Project Initiator(s) — Reviews and/or approves various versions of project quality checklists within project team delivery expectations for time and cost.
   C. Project Sponsor(s) — Reviews and/or approves various versions of project quality checklists within project team delivery expectations for time and cost.
   D. Project Manager — Leads and/or performs construction of project quality checklists within project team delivery expectations for time and cost.
V. Training Objectives
   A. Short Term — Project manager conducts meetings with project initiator, sponsor, and team member(s) on the creation and completion of the project quality checklists regarding what is involved and who is performing certain tasks within schedule expectations for performance.
   B. Long Term — Team members become trained in the process to develop and complete project quality checklists as a means to improve total effort to complete task.

QUALITY PLANNING — PROCESS IMPROVEMENT PLAN

A subsidiary of the project management plan that details the steps for analyzing processes to facilitate the identification of waste and nonvalue-added activity, leading to increased customer value. These activities include process boundaries, process configuration, process metrics, and targets for improved performance.

   I. Key Value Areas Weighting (%)
      A. Completion of process preparation and implementation of the process improvement plan = 50%.
      B. Approved by project initiator and/or project sponsor = 50%.
   II. Performance Objectives — Based on project management plan.
   III. Performance Scorecard
   IV. Performance Factors
      A. Project Team Members — Help construct process improvement plan by providing information relevant to areas of the project management plan within project team delivery expectations for time and cost.
      B. Project Initiator(s) — Reviews and/or approves various versions of project process improvement plan within project team delivery expectations for time and cost.
      C. Project Sponsor(s) — Reviews and/or approves various versions of project process improvement plan within project team delivery expectations for time and cost.
      D. Project Manager — Leads and/or performs construction of project process improvement plan within project team delivery expectations for time and cost.
   V. Training Objectives
      A. Short Term — Project manager conducts meetings with project initiator, sponsor, and team member(s) on the creation and completion of the project process improvement plan regarding what is involved and who is performing certain tasks within schedule expectations for performance.
      B. Long Term — Team members become trained in the process to develop and complete a project process improvement plan as a means to improve total effort to complete task.

QUALITY PLANNING — QUALITY BASELINE

Records the quality objectives of the project. The quality baseline is the basis for measuring and reporting quality performance as part of the performance measurement baseline.

   I. Key Value Areas Weighting (%)
      A. Completion of process preparation to establish the quality baseline for the project management plan = 50%.
      B. Approved by project initiator and/or project sponsor = 50%.
  II. Performance Objectives — Based on the project management plan.
 III. Performance Scorecard
  IV. Performance Factors
      A. Project Team Members — Help construct quality baseline by providing information relevant to areas of the project within project team delivery expectations for time and cost.
      B. Project Initiator(s) — Reviews and/or approves various versions of quality baseline within project team delivery expectations for time and cost.
      C. Project Sponsor(s) — Reviews and/or approves various versions of quality baseline within project team delivery expectations for time and cost.
      D. Project Manager — Leads and/or performs construction of quality baseline within project team delivery expectations for time and cost.
   V. Training Objectives
      A. Short Term — Project manager conducts meetings with project initiator, sponsor, and team member(s) on the creation and completion of the quality baseline regarding what is involved and who is performing certain tasks within schedule expectations for performance.
      B. Long Term — Team members become trained in the process to develop and complete a quality baseline as a means to improve total effort to complete task.

QUALITY PLANNING — PROJECT MANAGEMENT PLAN (UPDATES)

The project management plan will be updated through the inclusion of a supporting quality management plan and process improvement plan. Requested changes to the project management plan and its supporting plans are processed by project management review through the integrated change control process.

   I. Key Value Areas Weighting (%)
      A. Completion of process preparation and implementation of updates to the project management plan = 50%.
      B. Approved by project initiator and/or project sponsor = 50%.
  II. Performance Objectives — Based on project management plan.
 III. Performance Scorecard
  IV. Performance Factors
      A. Project Team Members — Help construct quality planning updates to the project management plan by providing information relevant to areas of the project within project team delivery expectations for time and cost.

B. Project Initiator(s) — Reviews and/or approves various versions of quality planning updates to the project management plan within project team delivery expectations for time and cost.
C. Project Sponsor(s) — Reviews and/or approves various versions of quality planning updates to the project management plan within project team delivery expectations for time and cost.
D. Project Manager — Leads and/or performs construction of quality planning updates to the project management plan within project team delivery expectations for time and cost.

V. Training Objectives
A. Short Term — Project manager conducts meetings with project initiator, sponsor, and team member(s) on the creation and completion of quality planning updates to the project management plan regarding what is involved and who is performing certain tasks within schedule expectations for performance.
B. Long Term — Team members become trained in the process to develop and complete quality planning updates to the project management plan as a means to improve total effort to complete task.

PERFORM QUALITY ASSURANCE — REQUESTED CHANGES

Quality improvement through validation includes taking action to increase the effectiveness and efficiency of the policies, processes, and procedures of the performing organization.

I. Key Value Areas Weighting (%)
   A. Completion of process preparation and implementation of requested changes to the performing organization's processes, policies, and procedures = 50%.
   B. Approved by project initiator and/or project sponsor = 50%.
II. Performance Objectives — Based on project management plan.
III. Performance Scorecard
IV. Performance Factors
   A. Project Team Members — Help construct requested changes to performing organization's processes, policies, and procedures by providing information relevant to areas of the project within project team delivery expectations for time and cost.
   B. Project Initiator(s) — Reviews and/or approves various versions of requested changes to performing organization's processes, policies, and procedures within project team delivery expectations for time and cost.
   C. Project Sponsor(s) — Reviews and/or approves various versions of requested changes to performing organization's processes, policies, and procedures within project team delivery expectations for time and cost.
   D. Project Manager — Leads and/or performs project requested changes to performing organization's processes, policies, and procedures within project team delivery expectations for time and cost.
V. Training Objectives
   A. Short Term — Project manager conducts meetings with project initiator, sponsor, and team member(s) on the creation and completion of the project requested changes to performing organization's processes, policies, and procedures regarding what is

involved and who is performing certain tasks within schedule expectations for performance.
B. Long Term — Team members become trained in the process to develop and complete requested changes to performing organization's processes, policies, and procedures as a means to improve total effort to complete task.

PERFORM QUALITY ASSURANCE — RECOMMENDED CORRECTIVE ACTIONS

Includes recommending actions to increase the effectiveness and efficiency of the performing organization. Corrective actions are recommended immediately as a result of quality assurance activities such as audits and process analysis.

I. Key Value Areas Weighting (%)
   A. Completion of process preparation and implementation of recommended corrective actions = 50%.
   B. Approved by project initiator and/or project sponsor = 50%.
II. Performance Objectives — Based on project management plan.
III. Performance Scorecard
IV. Performance Factors
   A. Project Team Members — Help to implement recommended corrective actions for project by providing information relevant to areas of the project within project team delivery expectations for time and cost.
   B. Project Initiator(s) — Reviews and/or approves various versions of recommended corrective actions for the project within project team delivery expectations for time and cost.
   C. Project Sponsor(s) — Reviews and/or approves various versions of recommended corrective actions for the project within project team delivery expectations for time and cost.
   D. Project Manager — Leads and/or performs recommended corrective actions for project within project team delivery expectations for time and cost.
V. Training Objectives
   A. Short Term — Project manager conducts meetings with project initiator, sponsor, and team member(s) on the creation and completion of recommended corrective actions for the project regarding what is involved and who is performing certain tasks within schedule expectations for performance.
   B. Long Term — Team members become trained in the process to develop and complete recommended corrective actions for a project as a means to improve total effort to complete task.

PERFORM QUALITY ASSURANCE — ORGANIZATIONAL PROCESS ASSETS (UPDATES)

Updated quality standards provide validation of the effectiveness and efficiency of the performing organization's quality standards and processes to meet requirements. These quality standards are used during the perform quality control process.

I. Key Value Areas Weighting (%)
   A. Completion of process preparation and implementation of updates to the performing organization's quality processes and standards = 50%.
   B. Approved by project initiator and/or project sponsor = 50%.
II. Performance Objectives — Based on project management plan.
III. Performance Scorecard
IV. Performance Factors
   A. Project Team Members — Help construct updates to the performing organization's quality processes and standards by providing information relevant to areas of the project within project team delivery expectations for time and cost.
   B. Project Initiator(s) — Reviews and/or approves various versions of updates to the performing organization's quality processes and standards within project team delivery expectations for time and cost.
   C. Project Sponsor(s) — Reviews and/or approves various versions of updates to the performing organization's quality processes and standards within project team delivery expectations for time and cost.
   D. Project Manager — Leads and/or performs updates to the performing organization's quality processes and standards within project team delivery expectations for time and cost.
V. Training Objectives
   A. Short Term — Project manager conducts meetings with project initiator, sponsor, and team member(s) on the creation and completion of updates to the performing organization's quality processes and standards regarding what is involved and who is performing certain tasks within schedule expectations for performance.
   B. Long Term — Team members become trained in the process to develop and complete updates to the performing organization's quality processes and standards as a means to improve total effort to complete task.

PERFORM QUALITY ASSURANCE — PROJECT MANAGEMENT PLAN (UPDATES)

The project management plan is updated from changes to the quality management plan that are the result of changes to the perform quality assurance process. These updates can include incorporation of processes that have been through continuous process improvement and are ready to repeat the cycle and improvements to the processes that have been identified and measured and are ready to be implemented.

I. Key Value Areas Weighting (%)
   A. Completion of process preparation and implementation of updates to the project management plan from changes to the quality management plan = 50%.
   B. Approved by project initiator and/or project sponsor = 50%.
II. Performance Objectives — Based on all projects linked to specific corporate objectives.
III. Performance Scorecard
IV. Performance Factors
   A. Project Team Members — Help construct project management plan updates by providing information relevant to areas of the project management plan within project team delivery expectations for time and cost.

B. Project Initiator(s) — Reviews and/or approves various versions of updates to the project management plan within project team delivery expectations for time and cost.
C. Project Sponsor(s) — Reviews and/or approves various versions of updates to the project management plan within project team delivery expectations for time and cost.
D. Project Manager — Leads and/or performs updates to the project management plan within project team delivery expectations for time and cost.

V. Training Objectives
A. Short Term — Project manager conducts meetings with project initiator, sponsor, and team member(s) on updates to the project management plan regarding what is involved and who is performing certain tasks within schedule expectations for performance.
B. Long Term — Team members become trained in the process to develop and complete updates to the project management plan as a means to improve total effort to complete task.

PERFORM QUALITY CONTROL — QUALITY CONTROL MEASUREMENTS

Represent the results of the quality control activities that are fed back to quality assurance to re-evaluate and analyze the quality standards and processes of the performing organization.

I. Key Value Areas Weighting (%)
A. Completion of process preparation and implementation of quality control measurements of the project = 50%.
B. Approved by project initiator and/or project sponsor = 50%.

II. Performance Objectives — Based on project management plan.

III. Performance Scorecard

IV. Performance Factors
A. Project Team Members — Help implement quality control measurements by providing information and support relevant to areas of the project within project team delivery expectations for time and cost.
B. Project Initiator(s) — Reviews and/or approves various versions of quality control measurements within project team delivery expectations for time and cost.
C. Project Sponsor(s) — Reviews and/or approves various versions of quality control measurements within project team delivery expectations for time and cost.
D. Project Manager — Leads and/or performs construction of quality control measurements within project team delivery expectations for time and cost.

V. Training Objectives
A. Short Term — Project manager conducts meetings with project initiator, sponsor, and team member(s) on the creation and completion of quality control measurements regarding what is involved and who is performing certain tasks within schedule expectations for performance.

B. Long Term — Team members become trained in the process to develop and complete quality control measurements as a means to improve total effort to complete task.

PERFORM QUALITY CONTROL — VALIDATED DEFECT REPAIR

Repaired items are reinspected and will either be accepted or rejected before notification of the decision is provided. Rejected items may require further defect repair.

  I. Key Value Areas Weighting (%)
     A. Completion of process preparation and implementation of validated defect repair = 50%.
     B. Approved by project initiator and/or project sponsor = 50%.
 II. Performance Objectives — Based on project management plan.
III. Performance Scorecard
 IV. Performance Factors
     A. Project Team Members — Help perform inspection of repaired defect by providing information and support relevant to areas of the project within project team delivery expectations for time and cost.
     B. Project Initiator(s) — Reviews and/or approves various versions of repaired defects within project team delivery expectations for time and cost.
     C. Project Sponsor(s) — Reviews and/or approves various versions of repaired defects within project team delivery expectations for time and cost.
     D. Project Manager — Leads and/or performs validation of repaired defects within project team delivery expectations for time and cost.
  V. Training Objectives
     A. Short Term — Project manager conducts meetings with project initiator, sponsor, and team member(s) on how to validate repaired defects regarding what is involved and who is performing certain tasks within schedule expectations for performance.
     B. Long Term — Team members become trained in the process to develop and complete validation of repaired defects as a means to improve total effort to complete task.

PERFORM QUALITY CONTROL — QUALITY BASELINE (UPDATES)

Records the quality objectives update(s) of the project. Also is the basis for measuring and reporting quality performance update(s) as part of the performance measurement baseline.

  I. Key Value Areas Weighting (%)
     A. Completion of process preparation and implementation of updates to the quality baseline = 50%.
     B. Approved by project initiator and/or project sponsor = 50%.
 II. Performance Objectives — Based on project management plan.

III. Performance Scorecard
IV. Performance Factors
   A. Project Team Members — Help implement quality baseline updates to the project by providing information and support relevant to areas of the project within project team delivery expectations for time and cost.
   B. Project Initiator(s) — Reviews and/or approves various versions of updates to the quality baseline within project team delivery expectations for time and cost.
   C. Project Sponsor(s) — Reviews and/or approves various versions of updates to the quality baseline within project team delivery expectations for time and cost.
   D. Project Manager — Leads and/or performs updates to the quality baseline within project team delivery expectations for time and cost.
V. Training Objectives
   A. Short Term — Project manager conducts meetings with project initiator, sponsor, and team member(s) on the creation and completion of quality baseline updates regarding what is involved and who is performing certain tasks within schedule expectations for performance.
   B. Long Term — Team members become trained in the process to develop and complete quality baseline updates derived from quality control measurements as a means to improve total effort to complete task.

PERFORM QUALITY CONTROL — RECOMMENDED CORRECTIVE ACTIONS

Involves actions taken as a result of a quality control measurement that indicates the process exceeds established parameters.

I. Key Value Areas Weighting (%)
   A. Completion of process preparation and implementation of recommended corrective action(s) = 50%.
   B. Approved by project initiator and/or project sponsor = 50%.
II. Performance Objectives — Based on project management plan.
III. Performance Scorecard
IV. Performance Factors
   A. Project Team Members — Help implement recommended corrective action(s) by providing information and support relevant to areas of the project within project team delivery expectations for time and cost.
   B. Project Initiator(s) — Reviews and/or approves various versions of recommended corrective action(s) within project team delivery expectations for time and cost.
   C. Project Sponsor(s) — Reviews and/or approves various versions of recommended corrective action(s) within project team delivery expectations for time and cost.
   D. Project Manager — Leads and/or performs recommended corrective action(s) within project team delivery expectations for time and cost.
V. Training Objectives
   A. Short Term — Project manager conducts meetings with project initiator, sponsor, and team member(s) on the creation and completion of recommended corrective

action(s) regarding what is involved and who is performing certain tasks within schedule expectations for performance.
   B. Long Term — Team members become trained in the process to develop and complete recommended corrective action(s) derived from quality control measurements as a means to improve total effort to complete task.

PERFORM QUALITY CONTROL — RECOMMENDED PREVENTIVE ACTIONS

Involves action taken to forestall a condition that may exceed established parameters in a manufacturing or development process.

I. Key Value Areas Weighting (%)
   A. Completion of process preparation and implementation of recommended preventive action(s) = 50%.
   B. Approved by project initiator and/or project sponsor = 50%.
II. Performance Objectives — Based on project management plan.
III. Performance Scorecard
IV. Performance Factors
   A. Project Team Members — Help implement recommended preventive action(s) by providing information and support relevant to areas of the project within project team delivery expectations for time and cost.
   B. Project Initiator(s) — Reviews and/or approves various versions of recommended preventive action(s) within project team delivery expectations for time and cost.
   C. Project Sponsor(s) — Reviews and/or approves various versions of recommended preventive action(s) within project team delivery expectations for time and cost.
   D. Project Manager — Leads and/or performs recommended preventive action(s) within project team delivery expectations for time and cost.
V. Training Objectives
   A. Short Term — Project manager conducts meetings with project initiator, sponsor, and team member(s) on the creation and completion of recommended preventive action(s) regarding what is involved and who is performing certain tasks within schedule expectations for performance.
   B. Long Term — Team members become trained in the process to develop and complete recommended preventive action(s) derived from quality control measurements as a means to improve total effort to complete task.

PERFORM QUALITY CONTROL — REQUESTED CHANGES

If the recommended corrective or preventive actions require a change to the project, a change request should be initiated in accordance with the defined integrated change control process.

I. Key Value Areas Weighting (%)
   A. Completion of process preparation and implementation of change request(s) = 50%.
   B. Approved by project initiator and/or project sponsor = 50%.

II. Performance Objectives — Based on project management plan.
III. Performance Scorecard
IV. Performance Factors
   A. Project Team Members — Help construct change request(s) by providing information relevant to areas of the project within project team delivery expectations for time and cost.
   B. Project Initiator(s) — Reviews and/or approves various versions of project change request(s) within project team delivery expectations for time and cost.
   C. Project Sponsor(s) — Reviews and/or approves various versions of project change request(s) within project team delivery expectations for time and cost.
   D. Project Manager — Leads and/or performs construction of project change request(s) within project team delivery expectations for time and cost.
V. Training Objectives
   A. Short Term — Project manager conducts meetings with project initiator, sponsor, and team member(s) regarding the creation and completion of project change request(s) regarding what is involved and who is performing certain tasks within schedule expectations for performance.
   B. Long Term — Team members become trained in the process to develop and complete a project change request(s) as a means to improve total effort to complete task.

PERFORM QUALITY CONTROL — RECOMMENDED DEFECT REPAIR

A defect occurs when a component does not meet its requirements or specifications and needs to be repaired or replaced. Defects are identified and recommended for repair by the quality control department.

I. Key Value Areas Weighting (%)
   A. Completion of process preparation and implementation of defect repair(s) = 50%.
   B. Approved by project initiator and/or project sponsor = 50%.
II. Performance Objectives — Based on project management plan.
III. Performance Scorecard
IV. Performance Factors
   A. Project Team Members — Help implement defect repair(s) by providing relevant information within project team delivery expectations for time and cost.
   B. Project Initiator(s) — Reviews and/or approves various defect repair(s) within project team delivery expectations for time and cost.
   C. Project Sponsor(s) — Reviews and/or approves various versions of defect repair(s) within project team delivery expectations for time and cost.
   D. Project Manager — Leads and/or performs project defect repair(s) within project team delivery expectations for time and cost.
V. Training Objectives
   A. Short Term — Project manager conducts meetings with project initiator, sponsor, and team member(s) on the completion of project defect repair(s) regarding what is involved and who is performing certain tasks within schedule expectations for performance.

B. Long Term — Team members become trained in the process to complete defect repair of a project as a means to improve total effort to complete task.

PERFORM QUALITY CONTROL — ORGANIZATIONAL PROCESS ASSETS (UPDATES)

When checklists are used, the completed checklists should become part of the project's records. The causes of variances, the reasoning behind the corrective action chosen, and other types of lessons learned from quality control should be documented so that they become part of the historical database for the project and the performing organization.

I. Key Value Areas Weighting (%)
   A. Completion of process preparation and implementation of updates to organizational process assets = 50%.
   B. Approved by project initiator and/or project sponsor = 50%.
II. Performance Objectives — Based on project management plan.
III. Performance Scorecard
IV. Performance Factors
   A. Project Team Members — Help construct organizational process assets updates by providing information relevant to areas of the project within project team delivery expectations for time and cost.
   B. Project Initiator(s) — Reviews and/or approves various updates to organizational process assets within project team delivery expectations for time and cost.
   C. Project Sponsor(s) — Reviews and/or approves various updates to organizational process assets within project team delivery expectations for time and cost.
   D. Project Manager — Leads and/or performs updates to organizational process assets within project team delivery expectations for time and cost.
V. Training Objectives
   A. Short Term — Project manager conducts meetings with project initiator, sponsor, and team member(s) on updates to the organizational process assets regarding what is involved and who is performing certain tasks within schedule expectations for performance.
   B. Long Term — Team members become trained in the process to update organizational process assets as a means to improve total effort to complete task.

PERFORM QUALITY CONTROL — VALIDATED DELIVERABLES

A goal of quality is to determine the correctness of deliverables. The results of the execution of quality control processes are validated deliverables.

I. Key Value Areas Weighting (%)
   A. Completion of process preparation and implementation of validated project deliverables = 50%.
   B. Approved by project initiator and/or project sponsor = 50%.
II. Performance Objectives — Based on project management plan.

III. Performance Scorecard
IV. Performance Factors
   A. Project Team Members — Help review deliverables for validation by providing information relevant to areas of the project within project team delivery expectations for time and cost.
   B. Project Initiator(s) — Reviews and/or approves deliverables of the project for validation within project team delivery expectations for time and cost.
   C. Project Sponsor(s) — Reviews and/or approves deliverables of the project for validation within project team delivery expectations for time and cost.
   D. Project Manager — Leads and/or performs deliverable validation within project team expectations for time and cost.
V. Training Objectives
   A. Short Term — Project manager conducts meetings with project initiator, sponsor, and team member(s) on deliverable validation regarding what is involved and who is performing certain tasks within schedule expectations for performance.
   B. Long Term — Team members become trained in the process to validate deliverables of the project as a means to improve total effort to complete task.

PERFORM QUALITY CONTROL — PROJECT MANAGEMENT PLAN (UPDATES)

Updated to reflect changes to the quality management plan that result from changes in performing the quality control process.

I. Key Value Areas Weighting (%)
   A. Completion of process preparation and implementation of updates to the project management plan from changes resulting from quality control processes = 50%.
   B. Approved by project initiator and/or project sponsor = 50%.
II. Performance Objectives — Based on project management plan.
III. Performance Scorecard
IV. Performance Factors
   A. Project Team Members — Help create quality control updates to the project management plan by providing information relevant to areas of the project within project team delivery expectations for time and cost.
   B. Project Initiator(s) — Reviews and/or approves various quality control updates to the project management plan within project team delivery expectations for time and cost.
   C. Project Sponsor(s) — Reviews and/or approves various quality control updates to the project management plan within project team delivery expectations for time and cost.
   D. Project Manager — Leads and/or performs quality control updates to the project management plan within project team delivery expectations for time and cost.
V. Training Objectives
   A. Short Term — Project manager conducts meetings with project initiator, sponsor, and team member(s) on the quality control updating of the project management plan regarding what is involved and who is performing certain tasks within schedule expectations for performance.

B. Long Term — Team members become trained in the process to apply quality control updates to a project management plan as a means to improve total effort to complete task.

SUMMARY

Project Quality Management has become more of a critical success factor than ever. Important in this is the value derived from completing work correctly the first time. This requires effective processes and standards that are well understood among project teams. If your project teams are expending more time and money than expected, time and cost savings can be achieved by improving project team member understanding through training and/or improvement in the current standards and processes for Project Quality Management. This training should be given to all members of the project team, including the project sponsor.

QUESTIONS

21-1. The quality management plan is a deliverable of the perform quality assurance process. True or false?

21-2. Validated defect repair is a deliverable of the perform quality control process. True or false?

21-3. In measuring the quality management plan, project team members help construct the quality management plan by providing information relevant to areas of the project quality management plan within project team delivery expectations for time and cost. True or false?

21-4. A long-term training objective for team members in updating a project management plan is to become trained in the process to develop and complete updates to a project management plan as a means to improve total effort to complete task. True or false?

21-5. In the perform quality control — validated defect repair deliverable, the project sponsor and the project initiator are not critical performance factors. True or false?

21-6. The fiscal year strategic plan defines what projects must be worked in the fiscal year. True or false?

21-7. In the perform quality control process, project team members help construct quality control measurements by providing information relevant to areas of the project within project team delivery expectations for time and cost. True or false?

21-8. Process deliverables are measurable for time and cost. True or false?

21-9. Satisfactory performance is dependent on critical performance factors. True or false?

21-10. Project Quality Management is the most important area of knowledge within the Project Management Institute's PMBOK®. True or false?

22

PROJECT HUMAN RESOURCE MANAGEMENT

Often human resources is the area considered least in resolving project issues. Many times, a "tool" solution is chosen when the answer could have been a better understanding of what is essential or satisfactory in performance.

Project Human Resource Management includes the processes that organize and manage the project team. The project team is comprised of the people who have assigned roles and responsibilities for completing the project. The incremental value added by the involvement of the project human resources correlates to their comprehension of current and future opportunities for and threats to delivery of completed work. As in baseball, if you can't see the pitch, you can't hit it! The same is true for the project human resources. The project human resources must have visibility to measurable accountabilities in order to apply their competency in a meaningful manner.

Project Human Resource Management PMBOK® area of knowledge includes the following processes and deliverables:

1. Human Resource Planning
   a. Roles and Responsibilities
   b. Project Organization Charts
   c. Staffing Management Plan
2. Acquire Project Team
   a. Project Staff Assignments
   b. Resource Availability
   c. Staff Management Plan (Updates)
3. Develop Project Team
   a. Team Performance Assessment

4. Manage Project Team
   a. Requested Changes
   b. Recommended Corrective Actions
   c. Recommended Preventive Actions
   d. Organizational Process Assets (Updates)
   e. Project Management Plan (Updates)

These discrete process components integrate with each other and with other processes from other areas of knowledge within the PMBOK®. In addition, these process components may impact other successor dependent program and/or project initiatives in a manner not visible to the project team.

In the 3Ms metric key value area models that follow in this chapter, each metric model contains rules that require acceptance from the receiving user. This ensures that visibility to the deliverable is confirmed by the primary receiving user and other project-related stakeholders. Another benefit of this approach is project fraud prevention and detection. By ensuring that visibility to the specific deliverable is confirmed, opportunity for project fraud is reduced, thereby improving project fraud prevention. This action also implies that the artifact has been scrutinized by the receiving user and that this user does not detect project fraud within the artifact or those circumstances surrounding the artifact.

The following 3Ms-oriented metrics support the Project Human Resource Management PMBOK® area of knowledge:

1. Human Resource Planning — Roles and Responsibilities
2. Human Resource Planning — Project Organization Charts
3. Human Resource Planning — Staffing Management Plan
4. Acquire Project Team — Project Staff Assignments
5. Acquire Project Team — Resource Availability
6. Acquire Project Team — Staffing Management Plan (Updates)
7. Develop Project Team — Team Performance Assessment
8. Manage Project Team — Requested Changes
9. Manage Project Team — Recommended Corrective Actions
10. Manage Project Team — Recommended Preventive Actions
11. Manage Project Team — Organizational Process Assets (Updates)
12. Manage Project Team — Project Management Plan (Updates)

Scoring for Section II: Performance Objectives for these metrics is as follows:

A. 50%: 4 = completed early and under budget ≥10%; 3 = ≥5%; 2 = completed on time and on budget; 1 = completed late and/or over budget.
B. 50%: 4 = approved by project initiator and/or project sponsor early and under budget ≥10%; 3 = approved early and under budget ≥5%; 2 = approved on time and on budget; 1 = approved late and/or over budget.

Scoring for Section III: Performance Scorecard for these metrics is as follows: 4 = Excellent; 3 = Very Good; 2 = Satisfactory; 1 = Unsatisfactory.

HUMAN RESOURCE PLANNING — ROLES AND RESPONSIBILITIES

The following items should be addressed when listing the roles and responsibilities required to complete the project: role, authority, responsibility, and competency.

I. Key Value Areas Weighting (%)
   A. Completion of process preparation and implementation of planned roles and responsibilities = 50%.
   B. Approved by project initiator and/or project sponsor = 50%.
II. Performance Objectives — Based on project management plan.
III. Performance Scorecard
IV. Performance Factors
   A. Project Initiator(s) — Reviews and/or approves various versions of project roles and responsibilities plan within project team delivery expectations for time and cost.
   B. Project Sponsor(s) — Reviews and/or approves various versions of project roles and responsibilities plan within project team delivery expectations for time and cost.
   C. Project Manager — Leads and/or performs planning of project roles and responsibilities within project team delivery expectations for time and cost.
V. Training Objectives
   A. Short Term — Project manager conducts meetings with project initiator, sponsor, and team member(s) on the creation and completion of the project roles and responsibilities regarding what is involved and who is performing certain tasks within schedule expectations for performance.
   B. Long Term — Team members become trained in the process to develop and complete planning of project roles and responsibilities as a means to improve total effort to complete task.

HUMAN RESOURCE PLANNING — PROJECT ORGANIZATION CHARTS

A project organization chart is a graphical display of the project team members and their reporting relationships. It can be formal or informal and highly detailed or broadly framed, based on the needs of the project.

I. Key Value Areas Weighting (%)
   A. Completion of process preparation and implementation of project organization charts = 50%.
   B. Approved by project initiator and/or project sponsor = 50%.
II. Performance Objectives — Based on project management plan.
III. Performance Scorecard
IV. Performance Factors
   A. Project Initiator(s) — Reviews and/or approves various versions of project organization charts within project team delivery expectations for time and cost.
   B. Project Sponsor(s) — Reviews and/or approves various versions of project organization charts within project team delivery expectations for time and cost.

C. Project Manager — Leads and/or performs construction of project organization charts within project team delivery expectations for time and cost.
V. Training Objectives
   A. Short Term — Project manager conducts meetings with project initiator, sponsor, and team member(s) on the creation and completion of the project organization charts regarding what is involved and who is performing certain tasks within schedule expectations for performance.
   B. Long Term — Team members become trained in the process to develop and complete project organization charts as a means to improve total effort to complete task.

HUMAN RESOURCE PLANNING — STAFFING MANAGEMENT PLAN

The staffing management plan is a subset of the project management plan and describes when and how human resource requirements will be met. This plan is updated continually during the project to direct ongoing team member acquisition and development actions.

   I. Key Value Areas Weighting (%)
      A. Completion of process preparation and implementation of staffing management plan = 50%.
      B. Approved by project initiator and/or project sponsor = 50%.
  II. Performance Objectives — Based on project management plan.
 III. Performance Scorecard
  IV. Performance Factors
      A. Project Initiator(s) — Reviews and/or approves various versions of staffing management plan within project team delivery expectations for time and cost.
      B. Project Sponsor(s) — Reviews and/or approves various versions of staffing management plan within project team delivery expectations for time and cost.
      C. Project Manager — Leads and/or performs construction of staffing management plan within project team delivery expectations for time and cost.
   V. Training Objectives
      A. Short Term — Project manager conducts meetings with project initiator, sponsor, and team member(s) on the creation and completion of the staffing management plan regarding what is involved and who is performing certain tasks within schedule expectations for performance.
      B. Long Term — Team members become trained in the process to develop and complete the staffing management plan as a means to improve total effort to complete task.

ACQUIRE PROJECT TEAM — PROJECT STAFF ASSIGNMENTS

The project is staffed when appropriate people have been assigned to work on the project. Documentation can include a project team directory, memos to team members, and names inserted into other parts of the project management plan such as organization charts and project schedules.

I. Key Value Areas Weighting (%)
   A. Completion of process preparation and implementation of project staff assignments = 50%.
   B. Approved by project initiator and/or project sponsor = 50%.
II. Performance Objectives — Based on project management plan.
III. Performance Scorecard
IV. Performance Factors
   A. Project Initiator(s) — Reviews and/or approves various versions of project staff assignments within project team delivery expectations for time and cost.
   B. Project Sponsor(s) — Reviews and/or approves various versions of project staff assignments within project team delivery expectations for time and cost.
   C. Project Manager — Leads and/or performs completion of project staff assignments within project team delivery expectations for time and cost.
V. Training Objectives
   A. Short Term — Project manager conducts meetings with project initiator, sponsor, and team member(s) on the creation and completion of the project staff assignments regarding what is involved and who is performing certain tasks within schedule expectations for performance.
   B. Long Term — Team members become trained in the process to develop and complete project staff assignments as a means to improve total effort to complete task.

ACQUIRE PROJECT TEAM — RESOURCE AVAILABILITY

Documents the time periods each project team member can work on the project. Creating a reliable final schedule depends on having a good understanding of each person's schedule conflicts, including vacation time and commitments to other projects.

I. Key Value Areas Weighting (%)
   A. Completion of process preparation and implementation of planned resource availability = 50%.
   B. Approved by project initiator and/or project sponsor = 50%.
II. Performance Objectives — Based on project management plan.
III. Performance Scorecard
IV. Performance Factors
   A. Project Initiator(s) — Reviews and/or approves various versions of project resource availability plan within project team delivery expectations for time and cost.
   B. Project Sponsor(s) — Reviews and/or approves various versions of project resource availability plan within project team delivery expectations for time and cost.
   C. Project Manager — Leads and/or performs planning of project resource availability within project team delivery expectations for time and cost.

V. Training Objectives
  A. Short Term — Project manager conducts meetings with project initiator, sponsor, and team member(s) on the creation and completion of the project resource availability plan regarding what is involved and who is performing certain tasks within schedule expectations for performance.
  B. Long Term — Team members become trained in the process to develop and complete planning of project resource availability as a means to improve total effort to complete task.

ACQUIRE PROJECT TEAM — STAFFING MANAGEMENT PLAN (UPDATES)

As specific people fill the project roles and responsibilities, changes in the staffing management plan may be needed, because people seldom fit the exact staffing requirements that are planned. Other reasons for changing the staffing management plan include promotion, retirement, illness, performance issues, and workload changes.

I. Key Value Areas Weighting (%)
  A. Completion of process preparation and implementation of staffing management plan updates = 50%.
  B. Approved by project initiator and/or project sponsor = 50%.
II. Performance Objectives — Based on project management plan.
III. Performance Scorecard
IV. Performance Factors
  A. Project Initiator(s) — Reviews and/or approves various versions of staffing management plan updates within project team delivery expectations for time and cost.
  B. Project Sponsor(s) — Reviews and/or approves various versions of staffing management plan updates within project team delivery expectations for time and cost.
  C. Project Manager — Leads and/or performs updates to staffing management plan within project team delivery expectations for time and cost.
V. Training Objectives
  A. Short Term — Project manager conducts meetings with project initiator, sponsor, and team member(s) on the creation and completion of updates to the staffing management plan regarding what is involved and who is performing certain tasks within schedule expectations for performance.
  B. Long Term — Team members become trained in the process to develop and complete updates to the staffing management plan as a means to improve total effort to complete task.

DEVELOP PROJECT TEAM — TEAM PERFORMANCE ASSESSMENT

As development efforts such as training, team building, and co-location are completed, the project management team makes informal or formal assessments of the project team's effectiveness. The evaluation of a team's effectiveness can include indicators such as skills improvements, group dynamics, staff turnover rate, etc.

I. Key Value Areas Weighting (%)
   A. Completion of process preparation and implementation of team performance assessment = 50%.
   B. Approved by project initiator and/or project sponsor = 50%.
II. Performance Objectives — Based on project management plan.
III. Performance Scorecard
IV. Performance Factors
   A. Project Initiator(s) — Reviews and/or approves various versions of team performance assessment within project team delivery expectations for time and cost.
   B. Project Sponsor(s) — Reviews and/or approves various versions of team performance assessment within project team delivery expectations for time and cost.
   C. Project Manager — Leads and/or performs planning of team performance assessment within project team delivery expectations for time and cost.
V. Training Objectives
   A. Short Term — Project manager conducts meetings with project initiator, sponsor, and team member(s) on the creation and completion of the team performance assessment regarding what is involved and who is performing certain tasks within schedule expectations for performance.
   B. Long Term — Team members become trained in the process to develop and complete a team performance assessment as a means to improve total effort to complete task.

MANAGE PROJECT TEAM — REQUESTED CHANGES

Staffing changes, whether by choice or due to uncontrollable events, can affect the rest of the project plan. When staffing issues will disrupt the project plan, such as causing the schedule to be extended or the budget to be exceeded, a change request can be processed through the integrated change control process.

I. Key Value Areas Weighting (%)
   A. Completion of process preparation and implementation of requested changes = 50%.
   B. Approved by project initiator and/or project sponsor = 50%.
II. Performance Objectives — Based on project management plan.
III. Performance Scorecard
IV. Performance Factors
   A. Project Initiator(s) — Reviews and/or approves various versions of requested changes within project team delivery expectations for time and cost.
   B. Project Sponsor(s) — Reviews and/or approves various versions of requested changes within project team delivery expectations for time and cost.
   C. Project Manager — Leads and/or performs requested changes within project team delivery expectations for time and cost.
V. Training Objectives
   A. Short Term — Project manager conducts meetings with project initiator, sponsor, and team member(s) on the creation and completion of requested changes regarding what is involved and who is performing certain tasks within schedule expectations for performance.

B. Long Term — Team members become trained in the process to develop and complete requested changes as a means to improve total effort to complete task.

MANAGE PROJECT TEAM — RECOMMENDED CORRECTIVE ACTIONS

Corrective action for human resource management includes items such as staffing changes, additional training, and disciplinary actions. Staffing changes can include moving people to different assignments, outsourcing some work, and replacing team members who leave.

I. Key Value Areas Weighting (%)
   A. Completion of process preparation and implementation of recommended corrective actions = 50%.
   B. Approved by project initiator and/or project sponsor = 50%.
II. Performance Objectives — Based on project management plan.
III. Performance Scorecard
IV. Performance Factors
   A. Project Initiator(s) — Reviews and/or approves various versions of recommended corrective actions within project team delivery expectations for time and cost.
   B. Project Sponsor(s) — Reviews and/or approves various versions of recommended corrective actions within project team delivery expectations for time and cost.
   C. Project Manager — Leads and/or performs recommended corrective actions within project team delivery expectations for time and cost.
V. Training Objectives
   A. Short Term — Project manager conducts meetings with project initiator, sponsor, and team member(s) on the creation and completion of recommended corrective actions regarding what is involved and who is performing certain tasks within schedule expectations for performance.
   B. Long Term — Team members become trained in the process to develop and complete recommended corrective actions as a means to improve total effort to complete task.

MANAGE PROJECT TEAM — RECOMMENDED PREVENTIVE ACTIONS

When the project management team identifies potential or emerging human resources issues, preventive actions can be developed to reduce the probability and/or impact of problems before they occur. Preventive actions can include cross-training in order to reduce problems before they occur.

I. Key Value Areas Weighting (%)
   A. Completion of process preparation and implementation of recommended preventive actions = 50%.
   B. Approved by project initiator and/or project sponsor = 50%.

II. Performance Objectives — Based on project management plan.
III. Performance Scorecard
IV. Performance Factors
   A. Project Initiator(s) — Reviews and/or approves various versions of recommended preventive actions within project team delivery expectations for time and cost.
   B. Project Sponsor(s) — Reviews and/or approves various versions of recommended preventive actions within project team delivery expectations for time and cost.
   C. Project Manager — Leads and/or performs recommended preventive actions within project team delivery expectations for time and cost.
V. Training Objectives
   A. Short Term — Project manager conducts meetings with project initiator, sponsor, and team member(s) on the creation and completion of recommended preventive actions regarding what is involved and who is performing certain tasks within schedule expectations for performance.
   B. Long Term — Team members become trained in the process to develop and complete recommended preventive actions as a means to improve total effort to complete task.

MANAGE PROJECT TEAM — ORGANIZATIONAL PROCESS ASSETS (UPDATES)

Project staff should generally be prepared to provide input for regular organizational performance appraisals of any project team member with whom they interact in a significant way. Also, all knowledge learned during the project should be documented so that it becomes part of the historical database of the organization.

I. Key Value Areas Weighting (%)
   A. Completion of process preparation and implementation of organizational process assets updates = 50%.
   B. Approved by project initiator and/or project sponsor = 50%.
II. Performance Objectives — Based on project management plan.
III. Performance Scorecard
IV. Performance Factors
   A. Project Initiator(s) — Reviews and/or approves various versions of updates to organizational process assets within project team delivery expectations for time and cost.
   B. Project Sponsor(s) — Reviews and/or approves various versions of updates to organizational process asset within project team delivery expectations for time and cost.
   C. Project Manager — Leads and/or performs updates to organizational process assets within project team delivery expectations for time and cost.
V. Training Objectives
   A. Short Term — Project manager conducts meetings with project initiator, sponsor, and team member(s) on the creation and completion of updates to organizational process assets regarding what is involved and who is performing certain tasks within schedule expectations for performance.

B. Long Term — Team members become trained in the process to develop and complete updates to organizational process assets as a means to improve total effort to complete task.

MANAGE PROJECT TEAM — PROJECT MANAGEMENT PLAN (UPDATES)

Approved change requests and corrective actions can result in updates to the staffing management plan, which is part of the project management plan.

I. Key Value Areas Weighting (%)
   A. Completion of process preparation and implementation of project management plan updates = 50%.
   B. Approved by project initiator and/or project sponsor = 50%.
II. Performance Objectives — Based on project management plan.
III. Performance Scorecard
IV. Performance Factors
   A. Project Initiator(s) — Reviews and/or approves various versions of updates to the project management plan within project team delivery expectations for time and cost.
   B. Project Sponsor(s) — Reviews and/or approves various versions of updates to the project management plan within project team delivery expectations for time and cost.
   C. Project Manager — Leads and/or performs updates to the project management plan within project team expectations for time and cost.
V. Training Objectives
   A. Short Term — Project manager conducts meetings with project initiator, sponsor, and team member(s) on the creation and completion of updates to the project management plan regarding what is involved and who is performing certain tasks within schedule expectations for performance.
   B. Long Term — Team members become trained in the process to develop and complete updates to the project management plan as a means to improve total effort to complete task.

SUMMARY

The project management team is a component of the overall project team. This component group is responsible for project management activities such as planning, controlling, and closing. These activities lead to interactions with other knowledge areas in the PMBOK® and as such require constant vigilance to identify results that could fall short of expectations.

As the 3Ms metric profiles are applied to the project team, great care should be exercised to ensure accurate measurement. The standard model we have employed in this book allows for you to modify key parameters at your choosing. If you choose to apply these metrics in a modified manner, be careful to be holistic in scope because there is nothing worse than comparing apples to oranges.

QUESTIONS

22-1. Project Human Resource Management include the processes that organize and manage the project team. True or false?

22-2. Which of the following is not an output of the human resource planning process:
   a. Resource availability
   b. Roles and responsibilities
   c. Project organization charts
   d. Staffing management plan

22-3. There is no direct relationship between project organization charts and organizational process assets. True or false?

22-4. Manage program team is a process within Project Human Resource Management. True or false?

22-5. Which of the following is not an output of the manage project team process:
   a. Project staff assignments
   b. Requested changes
   c. Recommended corrective actions
   d. Project management plan (updates)

22-6. Which of the following processes are not included in Project Human Resource Management:
   a. Manage project team
   b. Develop project team
   c. Human resource planning
   d. Roles and responsibilities

22-7. A project organization chart is a graphic display of project team members and their reporting relationship. True or false?

22-8. Acquire project team is the process of obtaining the human resources needed to complete the project. True or false?

22-9. Team performance assessment is an output of the develop project team process. True or false?

22-10. Project staff assignments is an output of the acquire project team process. True or false?

This book has free materials available for download from the Web Added Value™ Resource Center at www.jrosspub.com.

23

PROJECT COMMUNICATIONS MANAGEMENT

Project Communications Management is a knowledge area that processes project information for the benefit of the project team and key stakeholders, the sponsor, and customers.

Included within the Project Communications Management area of knowledge are the following processes:

1. **Communications Planning** — Determine the information and communications needs of the project stakeholders, sponsor, and customers
2. **Information Distribution** — Make required information available to project stakeholders, sponsor, and customers in a timely manner
3. **Performance Reporting** — Collect and distribute performance information about project progress past, present, and forecasted.
4. **Manage Stakeholders** — Manage communications to satisfy the requirements of and resolve issues with project stakeholders, sponsor, and customers

Everyone involved in a project should understand the need for communications, as reporting progress is a basic tenet of project management internal control. To not report progress of project work when it is expected is a failure of the project management leadership to manage potential abuse within the internal and/or external team. Communications raises awareness that induces more positive pressure on the key stakeholders to not be tempted to direct project outcomes for their personal benefit, since everyone will be cognizant of their activity if they do. In this manner, essential communications can improve project internal integrity, including trust and honesty, which can improve project delivery speed for project team members.

Project Communications Management PMBOK® area of knowledge includes the following processes and deliverables:

1. Communications Planning
   a. Communications Management Plan
2. Information Distribution
   a. Performance Reports
   b. Forecasts
   c. Requested Changes
   d. Recommended Corrective Actions
   e. Organizational Process Assets
3. Performance Reporting
   a. Performance Reports
   b. Forecasts
   c. Requested Changes
   d. Recommended Corrective Actions
   e. Organizational Process Assets (Updates)
4. Manage Stakeholders
   a. Resolved Issues
   b. Approved Change Requests
   c. Approved Corrective Actions
   d. Organizational Process Assets (Updates)
   e. Project Management Plan (Updates)

The following 3Ms-oriented metrics support the Project Communications Management PMBOK® area of knowledge:

1. Communications Planning — Communications Management Plan
2. Information Distribution — Organizational Process Assets (Updates)
3. Information Distribution — Requested Changes
4. Performance Reporting — Performance Reports
5. Performance Reporting — Forecasts
6. Performance Reporting — Requested Changes
7. Performance Reporting — Recommended Corrective Actions
8. Performance Reporting — Organizational Process Assets (Updates)
9. Manage Stakeholders — Resolved Issues
10. Manage Stakeholders — Approved Change Requests
11. Manage Stakeholders — Approved Corrective Actions
12. Manage Stakeholders — Organizational Process Assets (Updates)
13. Manage Stakeholders — Project Management Plan (Updates)

Scoring for Section II: Performance Objectives for these metrics is as follows:

A. 50%: 4 = completed early and under budget $\geq 10\%$; 3 = $\geq 5\%$; 2 = completed on time and on budget; 1 = completed late and/or over budget.

B. 50%: 4 = approved by project initiator and/or project sponsor early and under budget ≥10%; 3 = approved early and under budget ≥5%; 2 = approved on time and on budget; 1 = approved late and/or over budget.

Scoring for Section III: Performance Scorecard for these metrics is as follows: 4 = Excellent; 3 = Very Good; 2 = Satisfactory; 1 = Unsatisfactory.

COMMUNICATIONS PLANNING — COMMUNICATIONS MANAGEMENT PLAN

The communications management plan is a subsidiary plan of the project management plan and provides essential information such as stakeholder communication requirements, information to be communicated, person accountable for communicating, person or groups receiving information, methods or technologies used to convey information, frequency of information, escalation processes, methods for updating the communications management plan, and a glossary of terms.

I. Key Value Areas Weighting (%)
   A. Completion of process preparation and implementation of communications management plan = 50%.
   B. Approved by project initiator and/or project sponsor = 50%.
II. Performance Objectives — Based on project management plan.
III. Performance Scorecard
IV. Performance Factors
   A. Project Initiator(s) — Reviews and/or approves various versions of communications management plan within project team delivery expectations for time and cost.
   B. Project Sponsor(s) — Reviews and/or approves various versions of communications management plan within project team delivery expectations for time and cost.
   C. Project Manager — Leads and/or performs construction of communications management plan within project team delivery expectations for time and cost.
V. Training Objectives
   A. Short Term — Project manager conducts meetings with project initiator, sponsor, and team member(s) on the creation and completion of the communications management plan regarding what is involved and who is performing certain tasks within schedule expectations for performance.
   B. Long Term — Team members become trained in the process to develop and complete the communications management plan as a means to improve total effort to complete task.

INFORMATION DISTRIBUTION — ORGANIZATIONAL PROCESS ASSETS (UPDATES)

Includes lessons learned documentation, project records, project reports, project presentations, feedback from stakeholders, and stakeholder notifications.

I. Key Value Areas Weighting (%)
   A. Completion of process preparation and implementation of updates to organizational process assets = 50%.
   B. Approved by project initiator and/or project sponsor = 50%.
II. Performance Objectives — Based on project management plan.
III. Performance Scorecard
IV. Performance Factors
   A. Project Initiator(s) — Reviews and/or approves various versions of updates to organizational process assets within project team delivery expectations for time and cost.
   B. Project Sponsor(s) — Reviews and/or approves various versions of updates to organizational process assets within project team delivery expectations for time and cost.
   C. Project Manager — Leads and/or performs construction of updates to organizational process assets within project team delivery expectations for time and cost.
V. Training Objectives
   A. Short Term — Project manager conducts meetings with project initiator, sponsor, and team member(s) on the creation and completion of updates to the organizational process assets regarding what is involved and who is performing certain tasks within schedule expectations for performance.
   B. Long Term — Team members become trained in the process to develop and complete updates to the organizational process assets as a means to improve total effort to complete task.

INFORMATION DISTRIBUTION — REQUESTED CHANGES

Changes to the information distribution process should result in changes to the project management plan and the communications management plan. Requested changes are managed through the integrated change control process.

I. Key Value Areas Weighting (%)
   A. Completion of process preparation and implementation of requested changes = 50%.
   B. Approved by project initiator and/or project sponsor = 50%.
II. Performance Objectives — Based on project management plan.
III. Performance Scorecard
IV. Performance Factors
   A. Project Initiator(s) — Reviews and/or approves various versions of requested changes within project team delivery expectations for time and cost.
   B. Project Sponsor(s) — Reviews and/or approves various versions of requested changes within project team delivery expectations for time and cost.
   C. Project Manager — Leads and/or performs construction of requested changes within project team delivery expectations for time and cost.
V. Training Objectives
   A. Short Term — Project manager conducts meetings with project initiator, sponsor, and team member(s) on the creation and completion of requested changes regarding what is involved and who is performing certain tasks within schedule expectations for performance.

B. Long Term — Team members become trained in the process to develop and complete requested changes as a means to improve total effort to complete task.

PERFORMANCE REPORTING — PERFORMANCE REPORTS

Organize and summarize the information gathered and present the results of any analysis as compared to the performance measurement baseline. Reports should provide the status and progress information and the level of detail required by stakeholders as documented in the communications management plan.

   I. Key Value Areas Weighting (%)
      A. Completion of process preparation and implementation of performance reports = 50%.
      B. Approved by project initiator and/or project sponsor = 50%.
  II. Performance Objectives — Based on project management plan.
 III. Performance Scorecard
  IV. Performance Factors
      A. Project Initiator(s) — Reviews and/or approves various versions of performance reports within project team delivery expectations for time and cost.
      B. Project Sponsor(s) — Reviews and/or approves various versions of performance reports within project team delivery expectations for time and cost.
      C. Project Manager — Leads and/or performs construction of performance reports within project team delivery expectations for time and cost.
   V. Training Objectives
      A. Short Term — Project manager conducts meetings with project initiator, sponsor, and team member(s) on the creation and completion of performance reports regarding what is involved and who is performing certain tasks within schedule expectations for performance.
      B. Long Term — Team members become trained in the process to develop and complete performance reports as a means to improve total effort to complete task.

PERFORMANCE REPORTING — FORECASTS

Forecasts are updated and reissued based on work performance information provided as the project is executed. This information is about past performance that could impact the project in the future.

   I. Key Value Areas Weighting (%)
      A. Completion of process preparation and implementation of forecasts = 50%.
      B. Approved by project initiator and/or project sponsor = 50%.
  II. Performance Objectives — Based on project management plan.
 III. Performance Scorecard
  IV. Performance Factors
      A. Project Initiator(s) — Reviews and/or approves various versions of forecasts within project team delivery expectations for time and cost.
      B. Project Sponsor(s) — Reviews and/or approves various versions of forecasts within project team delivery expectations for time and cost.

C. Project Manager — Leads and/or performs construction of forecasts within project team delivery expectations for time and cost.
V. Training Objectives
   A. Short Term — Project manager conducts meetings with project initiator, sponsor, and team member(s) on the creation and completion of forecasts regarding what is involved and who is performing certain tasks within schedule expectations for performance.
   B. Long Term — Team members become trained in the process to develop and complete forecasts as a means to improve total effort to complete task.

PERFORMANCE REPORTING — REQUESTED CHANGES

Analysis of project performance often generates requested changes to some area of the project. These changes are processed through the integrated change control process.

   I. Key Value Areas Weighting (%)
      A. Completion of process preparation and implementation of requested changes = 50%.
      B. Approved by project initiator and/or project sponsor = 50%.
  II. Performance Objectives — Based on project management plan.
 III. Performance Scorecard
  IV. Performance Factors
      A. Project Initiator(s) — Reviews and/or approves various versions of requested changes within project team delivery expectations for time and cost.
      B. Project Sponsor(s) — Reviews and/or approves various versions of requested changes within project team delivery expectations for time and cost.
      C. Project Manager — Leads and/or performs construction of requested changes within project team delivery expectations for time and cost.
   V. Training Objectives
      A. Short Term — Project manager conducts meetings with project initiator, sponsor, and team member(s) on the creation and completion of requested changes regarding what is involved and who is performing certain tasks within schedule expectations for performance.
      B. Long Term — Team members become trained in the process to develop and complete requested changes as a means to improve total effort to complete task.

PERFORMANCE REPORTING — RECOMMENDED CORRECTIVE ACTIONS

Includes changes that induce the expected future performance of the project plan to be in line with the project management plan.

   I. Key Value Areas Weighting (%)
      A. Completion of process preparation and implementation of recommended corrective actions = 50%.
      B. Approved by project initiator and/or project sponsor = 50%.
  II. Performance Objectives — Based on project management plan.

III. Performance Scorecard
IV. Performance Factors
   A. Project Initiator(s) — Reviews and/or approves various versions of recommended corrective actions within project team delivery expectations for time and cost.
   B. Project Sponsor(s) — Reviews and/or approves various versions of recommended corrective actions within project team delivery expectations for time and cost.
   C. Project Manager — Leads and/or performs construction of recommended corrective actions within project team delivery expectations for time and cost.
V. Training Objectives
   A. Short Term — Project manager conducts meetings with project initiator, sponsor, and team member(s) on the creation and completion of recommended corrective actions regarding what is involved and who is performing certain tasks within schedule expectations for performance.
   B. Long Term — Team members become trained in the process to develop and complete recommended corrective actions as a means to improve total effort to complete task.

PERFORMANCE REPORTING — ORGANIZATIONAL PROCESS ASSETS (UPDATES)

Documentation includes the causes of issues, reasoning behind the corrective action chosen, and other types of lessons learned regarding performance reporting.

I. Key Value Areas Weighting (%)
   A. Completion of process preparation and implementation of updates to organizational process assets = 50%.
   B. Approved by project initiator and/or project sponsor = 50%.
II. Performance Objectives — Based on project management plan.
III. Performance Scorecard
IV. Performance Factors
   A. Project Initiator(s) — Reviews and/or approves various versions of updates to organizational process assets within project team delivery expectations for time and cost.
   B. Project Sponsor(s) — Reviews and/or approves various versions of updates to organizational process assets within project team delivery expectations for time and cost.
   C. Project Manager — Leads and/or performs construction of updates to organizational process assets within project team delivery expectations for time and cost.
V. Training Objectives
   A. Short Term — Project manager conducts meetings with project initiator, sponsor, and team member(s) on the creation and completion of updates to organizational process assets regarding what is involved and who is performing certain tasks within schedule expectations for performance.
   B. Long Term — Team members become trained in the process to develop and complete updates to organizational process assets as a means to improve total effort to complete task.

MANAGE STAKEHOLDERS — RESOLVED ISSUES

As stakeholder requirements are identified and resolved, the issues log will document concerns that have been raised and/or addressed and completed.

I. Key Value Areas Weighting (%)
   A. Completion of process preparation and implementation of resolved issues = 50%.
   B. Approved by project initiator and/or project sponsor = 50%.
II. Performance Objectives — Based on project management plan.
III. Performance Scorecard
IV. Performance Factors
   A. Project Initiator(s) — Reviews and/or approves various versions of resolved issues within project team delivery expectations for time and cost.
   B. Project Sponsor(s) — Reviews and/or approves various versions of resolved issues within project team delivery expectations for time and cost.
   C. Project Manager — Leads and/or performs construction of resolved issues within project team delivery expectations for time and cost.
V. Training Objectives
   A. Short Term — Project manager conducts meetings with project initiator, sponsor, and team member(s) on the creation and completion of resolved issues regarding what is involved and who is performing certain tasks within schedule expectations for performance.
   B. Long Term — Team members become trained in the process to develop and complete resolved issues as a means to improve total effort to complete task.

MANAGE STAKEHOLDERS — APPROVED CHANGE REQUESTS

Includes stakeholder issue status changes in the staffing management plan that reflect changes in how communications are made to stakeholders.

I. Key Value Areas Weighting (%)
   A. Completion of process preparation and implementation of approved change requests = 50%.
   B. Approved by project initiator and/or project sponsor = 50%.
II. Performance Objectives — Based on project management plan.
III. Performance Scorecard
IV. Performance Factors
   A. Project Initiator(s) — Reviews and/or approves various versions of approved change requests within project team delivery expectations for time and cost.
   B. Project Sponsor(s) — Reviews and/or approves various versions of approved change requests within project team delivery expectations for time and cost.
   C. Project Manager — Leads and/or performs construction of approved change requests within project team delivery expectations for time and cost.
V. Training Objectives
   A. Short Term — Project manager conducts meetings with project initiator, sponsor, and team member(s) on the creation and completion of approved change requests

regarding what is involved and who is performing certain tasks within schedule expectations for performance.
B. Long Term — Team members become trained in the process to develop and complete approved change requests as a means to improve total effort to complete task.

MANAGE STAKEHOLDERS — APPROVED CORRECTIVE ACTIONS

Includes changes that bring the expected future performance of the project in line with the project management plan.

I. Key Value Areas Weighting (%)
   A. Completion of process preparation and implementation of approved corrective actions = 50%.
   B. Approved by project initiator and/or project sponsor = 50%.
II. Performance Objectives — Based on project management plan.
III. Performance Scorecard
IV. Performance Factors
   A. Project Initiator(s) — Reviews and/or approves various versions of approved corrective actions within project team delivery expectations for time and cost.
   B. Project Sponsor(s) — Reviews and/or approves various versions of approved corrective actions within project team delivery expectations for time and cost.
   C. Project Manager — Leads and/or performs construction of approved corrective actions within project team delivery expectations for time and cost.
V. Training Objectives
   A. Short Term — Project manager conducts meetings with project initiator, sponsor, and team member(s) on the creation and completion of approved corrective actions regarding what is involved and who is performing certain tasks within schedule expectations for performance.
   B. Long Term — Team members become trained in the process to develop and complete approved corrective actions as a means to improve total effort to complete task.

MANAGE STAKEHOLDERS — ORGANIZATIONAL PROCESS ASSETS (UPDATES)

Includes documentation of lessons learned as a result of project issues and other types of lessons learned in completing project work.

I. Key Value Areas Weighting (%)
   A. Completion of process preparation and implementation of updates to organizational process assets = 50%.
   B. Approved by project initiator and/or project sponsor = 50%.
II. Performance Objectives — Based on project management plan.
III. Performance Scorecard

IV. Performance Factors
   A. Project Initiator(s) — Reviews and/or approves various versions of updates to organizational process assets within project team delivery expectations for time and cost.
   B. Project Sponsor(s) — Reviews and/or approves various versions of updates to organizational process assets within project team delivery expectations for time and cost.
   C. Project Manager — Leads and/or performs construction of updates to organizational process assets within project team delivery expectations for time and cost.
V. Training Objectives
   A. Short Term — Project manager conducts meetings with project initiator, sponsor, and team member(s) on the creation and completion of updates to the organizational process assets regarding what is involved and who is performing certain tasks within schedule expectations for performance.
   B. Long Term — Team members become trained in the process to develop and complete updates to the organizational process assets as a means to improve total effort to complete task.

MANAGE STAKEHOLDERS — PROJECT MANAGEMENT PLAN (UPDATES)

The project management plan is updated to reflect the changes made to the communications plan.

I. Key Value Areas Weighting (%)
   A. Completion of process preparation and implementation of updates to the project management plan = 50%.
   B. Approved by project initiator and/or project sponsor = 50%.
II. Performance Objectives — Based on communications plan.
III. Performance Scorecard
IV. Performance Factors
   A. Project Initiator(s) — Reviews and/or approves various versions of updates to the project management plan within project team delivery expectations for time and cost.
   B. Project Sponsor(s) — Reviews and/or approves various versions of updates to the project management plan within project team delivery expectations for time and cost.
   C. Project Manager — Leads and/or performs construction of updates to the project management plan within project team delivery expectations for time and cost.
V. Training Objectives
   A. Short Term — Project manager conducts meetings with project initiator, sponsor, and team member(s) on the creation and completion of updates to the project management plan regarding what is involved and who is performing certain tasks within schedule expectations for performance.
   B. Long Term — Team members become trained in the process to develop and complete updates to the project management plan as a means to improve total effort to complete task.

SUMMARY

Project communication is an important and vital ingredient in the success of a project. People are influenced through communications in their decision making to support the project life cycle toward completion. As a result, a holistic approach must be sought to receive the most benefit. Measuring project progress and reporting that analysis is the key enabler that can raise universal awareness and visibility to the opportunities and threats incrementally in project delivery performance as seen by the project stakeholders.

The improved capability of cross-collaboration can be the difference between failure and success, and the price of doing this well is minuscule compared to the benefit success brings to everyone involved.

QUESTIONS

23-1. Project Communications Management includes the processes that ensure timely and appropriate generation, collection, distribution, storage, retrieval, and the ultimate disposition of project information. True or false?

23-2. Which of the following is an output of the communications planning process:
   a. Communications management plan
   b. Requested changes
   c. Project organization charts
   d. Staffing management plan

23-3. The communications management plan is a subsidiary of the project management plan. True or false?

23-4. Manage stakeholders is a process in Project Communications Management. True or false?

23-5. Which of the following is not an output of the performance reporting process:
   a. Performance reports
   b. Forecasts
   c. Recommended corrective actions
   d. Project management plan (updates)

23-6. Which of the following processes are not included in Project Communications Management?:
   a. Communications planning
   b. Develop project team
   c. Manage stakeholders
   d. Information distribution

23-7. Requested changes to information distribution should be made in the project management plan. True or false?

23-8. Performance reports organize and summarize information gathered and present the results of any project analysis as compared to the performance measurement baseline. True or false?

23-9. Forecasts are updated based on work performance information provided after project work has been executed. True or false?

23-10. Resolved issues will document concerns about expected project work. True or false?

24

PROJECT RISK MANAGEMENT

Project Risk Management PMBOK® area of knowledge is the cornerstone to essential project governance and as such includes processes concerned with managing project risk for failure and success. Improving the probability and impact of success while reducing the probability and impact of project work failure requires the project team members to become more cognitive than they are today, at the beginning of a project and/or during the project life cycle, of delivery acceleration opportunities and/or delivery threats to work progress that may fail the project.

The following 3Ms metric profiles can be employed to be predictive or detective in nature when applied to the object of measurement. Detective measures are those that reveal evidence to explain why certain events occurred. Predictive measures are those that indicate probability and impact will occur to a degree of certainty if recommended actions are applied to the objective under measurement. The 3Ms metric profiles that follow in this chapter are detective in nature. If you are interested in implementing predictive measures in your organization, we encourage you to contact us directly. In these situations, an assessment of your environment is often required to implement these types of measures. What is the worth of telling the future for your organization's projects?

Project Risk Management PMBOK® area of knowledge includes the following processes and deliverables:

1. Risk Management Planning
    a. Risk Management Plan
2. Risk Identification
    a. Risk Register
    b. Project Management Plan (Updates)
3. Qualitative Risk Analysis
    a. Risk Register (Updates)

4. Quantitative Risk Analysis
   a. Risk Register (Updates)
5. Risk Response Planning
   a. Risk Register (Updates)
   b. Risk-Related Contractual Agreements
6. Risk Monitoring and Control
   a. Recommended Corrective Actions
   b. Requested Changes
   c. Risk Register (Updates)
   d. Organizational Process Assets (Updates)

The following 3Ms-oriented metrics inventory supports the Project Risk Management PMBOK® area of knowledge:

1. Risk Management Planning — Risk Management Plan
2. Risk Identification — Risk Register
3. Qualitative Risk Analysis — Risk Register (Updates)
4. Quantitative Risk Analysis — Risk Register (Updates)
5. Risk Response Planning — Risk Register (Updates)
6. Risk Response Planning — Project Management Plan (Updates)
7. Risk Response Planning — Risk-Related Contractual Agreements
8. Risk Monitoring and Control — Risk Register (Updates)
9. Risk Monitoring and Control — Requested Changes
10. Risk Monitoring and Control — Recommended Corrective Actions
11. Risk Monitoring and Control — Recommended Preventive Actions
12. Risk Monitoring and Control — Organizational Process Assets (Updates)
13. Risk Monitoring and Control — Project Management Plan (Updates)

Scoring for Section II: Performance Objectives for these metrics is as follows:

A. 50%: 4 = completed early and under budget ≥10%; 3 = ≥5%; 2 = completed on time and on budget; 1 = completed late and/or over budget.
B. 50%: 4 = approved by project initiator and/or project sponsor early and under budget ≥10%; 3 = approved early and under budget ≥5%; 2 = approved on time and on budget; 1 = approved late and/or over budget.

Scoring for Section III: Performance Scorecard for these metrics is as follows: 4 = Excellent; 3 = Very Good; 2 = Satisfactory; 1 = Unsatisfactory.

RISK MANAGEMENT PLANNING — RISK MANAGEMENT PLAN

The risk management plan describes how risk management will be structured and performed on the project. The risk management plan is a subsidiary of the project management plan and contains information related to methodology, roles and responsibilities, budgeting, timing, risk categories, definition of probability and impact, and the probability and impact matrix, along with revised stakeholders' tolerance, reporting formats, and tracking.

I. Key Value Areas Weighting (%)
   A. Completion of process preparation and implementation of the risk management plan = 50%.
   B. Approved by project initiator and/or project sponsor = 50%.
II. Performance Objectives — Based on project management plan.
III. Performance Scorecard
IV. Performance Factors
   A. Project Team Members — Help construct risk management plan by providing information relevant to areas of the project scope statement (preliminary) within project team delivery expectations for time and cost.
   B. Project Initiator(s) — Reviews and/or approves various versions of project risk management plan within project team delivery expectations for time and cost.
   C. Project Sponsor(s) — Reviews and/or approves various versions of project risk management plan within project team delivery expectations for time and cost.
   D. Project Manager — Leads and/or performs project risk management plan construction within project team delivery expectations for time and cost.
V. Training Objectives
   A. Short Term — Project manager conducts meetings with project initiator, sponsor, and team member(s) on the creation and completion of the project risk management plan regarding what is involved and who is performing certain tasks within schedule expectations for performance.
   B. Long Term — Team members become trained in the process to develop and complete a project risk management plan as a means to improve total effort to complete task.

RISK IDENTIFICATION — RISK REGISTER

The risk register is a component of the project management plan and contains the following information: list of identified risks, list of potential responses, root causes of risk, and updated risk categories.

I. Key Value Areas Weighting (%)
   A. Completion of process preparation and implementation of the risk register = 50%.
   B. Approved by project initiator and/or project sponsor = 50%.
II. Performance Objectives — Based on project management plan.
III. Performance Scorecard
IV. Performance Factors
   A. Project Team Members — Help construct risk register by providing information relevant to areas of the project scope statement (preliminary) within project team delivery expectations for time and cost.
   B. Project Initiator(s) — Reviews and/or approves various versions of project risk register within project team delivery expectations for time and cost.

C. Project Sponsor(s) — Reviews and/or approves various versions of project risk register within project team delivery expectations for time and cost.
D. Project Manager — Leads and/or performs project risk register construction within project team delivery expectations for time and cost.

V. Training Objectives
A. Short Term — Project manager conducts meetings with project initiator, sponsor, and team member(s) on the creation and completion of the project risk register regarding what is involved and who is performing certain tasks within schedule expectations for performance.
B. Long Term — Team members become trained in the process to develop and complete a project risk register as a means to improve total effort to complete task.

QUALITATIVE RISK ANALYSIS — RISK REGISTER (UPDATES)

The risk register is updated with information from the qualitative risk analysis, and the updated risk register is included in the project management plan. It contains the following information: relative ranking of project risks, risks grouped by categories, list of risks requiring response in the near term, list of risks requiring additional analysis and response, watch lists of low-priority risks, and trends in qualitative risk analysis results.

I. Key Value Areas Weighting (%)
   A. Completion of process preparation and implementation of the risk register = 50%.
   B. Approved by project initiator and/or project sponsor = 50%.
II. Performance Objectives — Based on project management plan.
III. Performance Scorecard
IV. Performance Factors
   A. Project Team Members — Help construct updates to risk register by providing information relevant to areas of the project scope statement (preliminary) within project team delivery expectations for time and cost.
   B. Project Initiator(s) — Reviews and/or approves various versions of updates to project risk register within project team delivery expectations for time and cost.
   C. Project Sponsor(s) — Reviews and/or approves various versions of updates to project risk register within project team delivery expectations for time and cost.
   D. Project Manager — Leads and/or performs construction of updates to project risk register within project team delivery expectation for time and cost.
V. Training Objectives
   A. Short Term — Project manager conducts meetings with project initiator, sponsor, and team member(s) on the creation and completion of updates to the project risk register regarding what is involved and who is performing certain tasks within schedule expectations for performance.
   B. Long Term — Team members become trained in the process to develop and complete updates to the project risk register as a means to improve total effort to complete task.

QUANTITATIVE RISK ANALYSIS — RISK REGISTER (UPDATES)

The risk register is further updated with information from the quantitative risk analysis, and the updated risk register is included in the project management plan. It contains the following information: probabilistic analysis of the project, probability of achieving cost and time objectives, prioritized list of quantified risks, and trends in quantitative risk analysis results.

I. Key Value Areas Weighting (%)
   A. Completion of process preparation and implementation of updates to the risk register = 50%.
   B. Approved by project initiator and/or project sponsor = 50%.
II. Performance Objectives — Based on project management plan.
III. Performance Scorecard
IV. Performance Factors
   A. Project Team Members — Help construct updates to risk register by providing information relevant to areas of the project scope statement (preliminary) within project team delivery expectations for time and cost.
   B. Project Initiator(s) — Reviews and/or approves various versions of updates to project risk register within project team delivery expectations for time and cost.
   C. Project Sponsor(s) — Reviews and/or approves various versions of updates to project risk register within project team delivery expectations for time and cost.
   D. Project Manager — Leads and/or performs construction of updates to project risk register within project team delivery expectations for time and cost.
V. Training Objectives
   A. Short Term — Project manager conducts meetings with project initiator, sponsor, and team member(s) on the creation and completion of updates to the project risk register regarding what is involved and who is performing certain tasks within schedule expectations for performance.
   B. Long Term — Team members become trained in the process to develop and complete updates to the project risk register as a means to improve total effort to complete task.

RISK RESPONSE PLANNING — RISK REGISTER (UPDATES)

In the risk response planning process, appropriate responses are chosen, agreed upon, and included in the risk register.

I. Key Value Areas Weighting (%)
   A. Completion of process preparation and implementation of updates to the risk register = 50%.
   B. Approved by project initiator and/or project sponsor = 50%.
II. Performance Objectives — Based on project management plan.
III. Performance Scorecard

IV. Performance Factors
   A. Project Team Members — Help construct updates to risk register by providing information relevant to areas of the project scope statement (preliminary) within project team delivery expectations for time and cost.
   B. Project Initiator(s) — Reviews and/or approves various versions of updates to project risk register within project team delivery expectations for time and cost.
   C. Project Sponsor(s) — Reviews and/or approves various versions of updates to project risk register within project team delivery expectations for time and cost.
   D. Project Manager — Leads and/or performs construction of updates to project risk register within project team delivery expectations for time and cost.
V. Training Objectives
   A. Short Term — Project manager conducts meetings with project initiator, sponsor, and team member(s) on the creation and completion of updates to the project risk register regarding what is involved and who is performing certain tasks within schedule expectations for performance.
   B. Long Term — Team members become trained in the process to develop and complete updates to the project risk register as a means to improve total effort to complete task.

RISK RESPONSE PLANNING — PROJECT MANAGEMENT PLAN (UPDATES)

The project management plan is updated as response activities are added after review and handling through the integrated change control process.

I. Key Value Areas Weighting (%)
   A. Completion of process preparation and implementation of updates to the project management plan = 50%.
   B. Approved by project initiator and/or project sponsor = 50%.
II. Performance Objectives — Based on project management plan.
III. Performance Scorecard
IV. Performance Factors
   A. Project Team Members — Help construct updates to project management plan by providing information relevant to areas of the project scope statement (preliminary) within project team delivery expectations for time and cost.
   B. Project Initiator(s) — Reviews and/or approves various versions of updates to project management plan within project team delivery expectations for time and cost.
   C. Project Sponsor(s) — Reviews and/or approves various versions of updates to project management plan within project team delivery expectations for time and cost.
   D. Project Manager — Leads and/or performs construction of updates to project management plan within project team delivery expectations for time and cost.
V. Training Objectives
   A. Short Term — Project manager conducts meetings with project initiator, sponsor, and team member(s) on the creation and completion of updates to the project management plan regarding what is involved and who is performing certain tasks within schedule expectations for performance.

B. Long Term — Team members become trained in the process to develop and complete updates to the project management plan as a means to improve total effort to complete task.

RISK RESPONSE PLANNING — RISK-RELATED CONTRACTUAL AGREEMENTS

Contractual agreements, such as those for insurance, services, and other items, can be prepared for specificity for each party's accountabilities for defined risks should they occur.

I. Key Value Areas Weighting (%)
   A. Completion of process preparation and implementation of risk-related contractual agreements = 50%.
   B. Approved by project initiator and/or project sponsor = 50%.
II. Performance Objectives — Based on project management plan.
III. Performance Scorecard
IV. Performance Factors
   A. Project Team Members — Help construct updates to risk-related contractual agreements by providing information relevant to areas of the project scope statement (preliminary) within project team delivery expectations for time and cost.
   B. Project Initiator(s) — Reviews and/or approves various versions of risk-related contractual agreements within project team delivery expectations for time and cost.
   C. Project Sponsor(s) — Reviews and/or approves various versions of risk-related contractual agreements within project team delivery expectations for time and cost.
   D. Project Manager — Leads and/or performs construction of risk-related contractual agreements within project team delivery expectations for time and cost.
V. Training Objectives
   A. Short Term — Project manager conducts meetings with project initiator, sponsor, and team member(s) on the creation and completion of risk-related contractual agreements regarding what is involved and who is performing certain tasks within schedule expectations for performance.
   B. Long Term — Team members become trained in the process to develop and complete risk-related contractual agreements as a means to improve total effort to complete task.

RISK MONITORING AND CONTROL — RISK REGISTER (UPDATES)

An updated risk register contains the following updates: outcomes of risk assessments, risk audits, and periodic risk reviews and actual outcomes of the project's risks and of risk responses that can help plan for risk throughout the project.

I. Key Value Areas Weighting (%)
   A. Completion of process preparation and implementation of updates to the risk register = 50%.
   B. Approved by project initiator and/or project sponsor = 50%.

II. Performance Objectives — Based on project management plan.
III. Performance Scorecard
IV. Performance Factors
   A. Project Team Members — Help construct updates to risk register by providing information relevant to areas of the project scope statement (preliminary) within project team delivery expectations for time and cost.
   B. Project Initiator(s) — Reviews and/or approves various versions of updates to project risk register within project team delivery expectations for time and cost.
   C. Project Sponsor(s) — Reviews and/or approves various versions of updates to project risk register within project team delivery expectations for time and cost.
   D. Project Manager — Leads and/or performs construction of updates to project risk register within project team delivery expectations for time and cost.
V. Training Objectives
   A. Short Term — Project manager conducts meetings with project initiator, sponsor, and team member(s) on the creation and completion of updates to the project risk register regarding what is involved and who is performing certain tasks within schedule expectations for performance.
   B. Long Term — Team members become trained in the process to develop and complete updates to the project risk register as a means to improve total effort to complete task.

RISK MONITORING AND CONTROL — REQUESTED CHANGES

Implementing contingency plans or workarounds often results in a requirement to change the project management plan to respond to risks.

I. Key Value Areas Weighting (%)
   A. Completion of process preparation and implementation of requested changes = 50%.
   B. Approved by project initiator and/or project sponsor = 50%.
II. Performance Objectives — Based on project management plan.
III. Performance Scorecard
IV. Performance Factors
   A. Project Team Members — Help construct requested changes by providing information relevant to areas of the project management plan within project team delivery expectations for time and cost.
   B. Project Initiator(s) — Reviews and/or approves various versions of requested changes within project team delivery expectations for time and cost.
   C. Project Sponsor(s) — Reviews and/or approves various versions of requested changes within project team delivery expectations for time and cost.
   D. Project Manager — Leads and/or performs construction of requested changes within project team delivery expectations for time and cost.
V. Training Objectives
   A. Short Term — Project manager conducts meetings with project initiator, sponsor, and team member(s) on the creation and completion of requested changes regarding what is involved and who is performing certain tasks within schedule expectations for performance.

B. Long Term — Team members become trained in the process to develop and complete requested changes as a means to improve total effort to complete task.

RISK MONITORING AND CONTROL — RECOMMENDED CORRECTIVE ACTIONS

Includes contingency plans and workaround plans. The latter are responses that were not initially planned, but are required to deal with emerging risks that were previously unidentified.

   I. Key Value Areas Weighting (%)
      A. Completion of process preparation and implementation of recommended corrective actions = 50%.
      B. Approved by project initiator and/or project sponsor = 50%.
  II. Performance Objectives — Based on project management plan.
 III. Performance Scorecard
  IV. Performance Factors
      A. Project Team Members — Help construct recommended corrective actions by providing information relevant to areas of the project within project team delivery expectations for time and cost.
      B. Project Initiator(s) — Reviews and/or approves various versions of recommended corrective actions within project team delivery expectations for time and cost.
      C. Project Sponsor(s) — Reviews and/or approves various versions of recommended corrective actions within project team delivery expectations for time and cost.
      D. Project Manager — Leads and/or performs recommended corrective actions within project team delivery expectations for time and cost.
   V. Training Objectives
      A. Short Term — Project manager conducts meetings with project initiator, sponsor, and team member(s) on the creation and completion of recommended corrective actions regarding what is involved and who is performing certain tasks within schedule expectations for performance.
      B. Long Term — Team members become trained in the process to develop and complete recommended corrective actions as a means to improve total effort to complete task.

RISK MONITORING AND CONTROL — RECOMMENDED PREVENTIVE ACTIONS

Used to bring the project into compliance with the project management plan.

   I. Key Value Areas Weighting (%)
      A. Completion of process preparation and implementation of recommended preventive actions = 50%.
      B. Approved by project initiator and/or project sponsor = 50%.
  II. Performance Objectives — Based on project management plan.
 III. Performance Scorecard

IV. Performance Factors
   A. Project Team Members — Help construct recommended preventive actions by providing information relevant to areas of the project within project team delivery expectations for time and cost.
   B. Project Initiator(s) — Reviews and/or approves various versions of recommended preventive actions within project team delivery expectations for time and cost.
   C. Project Sponsor(s) — Reviews and/or approves various versions of recommended preventive actions within project team delivery expectations for time and cost.
   D. Project Manager — Leads and/or performs recommended preventive actions within project team delivery expectation for time and cost.
V. Training Objectives
   A. Short Term — Project manager conducts meetings with project initiator, sponsor, and team member(s) on the creation and completion of recommended preventive actions regarding what is involved and who is performing certain tasks within schedule expectations for performance.
   B. Long Term — Team members become trained in the process to develop and complete recommended preventive actions as a means to improve total effort to complete task.

RISK MONITORING AND CONTROL — ORGANIZATIONAL PROCESS ASSETS (UPDATES)

The six project risk management processes produce information that can be used for future projects and should be captured in the organizational process assets.

I. Key Value Areas Weighting (%)
   A. Completion of process preparation and implementation of updates to the organizational process assets = 50%.
   B. Approved by project initiator and/or project sponsor = 50%.
II. Performance Objectives — Based on project management plan.
III. Performance Scorecard
IV. Performance Factors
   A. Project Team Members — Help construct recommended updates to the organizational process assets relevant to areas of the project within project team delivery expectations for time and cost.
   B. Project Initiator(s) — Reviews and/or approves various versions of updates to the organizational process assets within project team delivery expectations for time and cost.
   C. Project Sponsor(s) — Reviews and/or approves various versions of updates to the organizational process assets within project team delivery expectations for time and cost.
   D. Project Manager — Leads and/or performs updates to the organizational process assets within project team delivery expectations for time and cost.
V. Training Objectives
   A. Short Term — Project manager conducts meetings with project initiator, sponsor, and team member(s) on the creation and completion of updates to the organizational

process assets regarding what is involved and who is performing certain tasks within schedule expectations for performance.
B. Long Term — Team members become trained in the process to develop and complete updates to the organizational process assets as a means to improve total effort to complete task.

RISK MONITORING AND CONTROL — PROJECT MANAGEMENT PLAN (UPDATES)

If the approved change requests have an effect on the risk management processes, then the corresponding component documents of the project management plan are revised and reissued to reflect the approved changes.

I. Key Value Areas Weighting (%)
   A. Completion of process preparation and implementation of the updates to the project management plan = 50%.
   B. Approved by project initiator and/or project sponsor = 50%.
II. Performance Objectives — Based on project management plan.
III. Performance Scorecard
IV. Performance Factors
   A. Project Team Members — Help construct updates to the project management plan by providing information relevant to areas of the project within project team delivery expectations for time and cost.
   B. Project Initiator(s) — Reviews and/or approves various versions of updates to the project management plan within project team delivery expectations for time and cost.
   C. Project Sponsor(s) — Reviews and/or approves various versions of updates to the project management plan within project team delivery expectations for time and cost.
   D. Project Manager — Leads and/or performs updates to the project management plan within project team delivery expectations for time and cost.
V. Training Objectives
   A. Short Term — Project manager conducts meetings with project initiator, sponsor, and team member(s) on the creation and completion of updates to the project management plan regarding what is involved and who is performing certain tasks within schedule expectations for performance.
   B. Long Term — Team members become trained in the process to develop and complete updates to the project management plan as a means to improve total effort to complete task.

SUMMARY

Risk management is a key cornerstone to any project, for any organization. Failure to manage risk in the project investment space of a business is a recipe for failure. Through practice in project management, you must become sufficiently skilled in preventing and detecting risk in every project you are involved with, as it is this competency that states to your employer your personal value in the job you do. Those who are best at this competency will continue. The rest of us will have to work at becoming better and will have to settle for the leftover benefits that come from just getting the job done.

Our job in this book is to provide metrics correlation to the PMBOK® areas of knowledge outputs and to offer examples. This focus places emphasis on the single project environment specifically, although the metric profiles presented in this chapter allow for common measure of all risk activities and their identified outputs as standardized by the PMBOK® for risk management in projects.

QUESTIONS

24-1. The risk management plan describes how risk management will be structured and performed on the project. True or false?

24-2. Which of the following processes is not a risk management process:
   a. Risk management planning
   b. Risk identification
   c. Risk response planning
   d. Risk measurement

24-3. The risk register is further updated with information from the quantitative risk analysis, and the updated risk register is included in the project management plan. True or false?

24-4. In the risk response planning process, appropriate responses are chosen, agreed upon, and included in the risk register. True or false?

24-5. Which of the following is not an output of the risk response planning process:
   a. Risk register (updates)
   b. Project management plan (updates)
   c. Risk-related contractual agreements
   d. Risk performance measurement identification

24-6. Risk monitoring and control — recommended corrective actions includes contingency plans and workaround plans. The latter are responses that were not initially planned, but are required to deal with emerging risks that were previously unidentified. True or false?

24-7. Risk monitoring and control — requested changes involves implementing contingency plans or workarounds that often result in a requirement to change the project management plan to respond to risks. True or false?

24-8. Risk monitoring and control — recommended preventive actions are used to bring the project into compliance with the project management plan. True or false?

24-9. Risk monitoring and control — organizational process assets (updates) involves the six project risk management processes that produce information that can be used for future projects and should be captured in the organizational process assets. True or false?

24-10. Risk performance measurement is the most important process in risk management. True or false?

This book has free materials available for download from the Web Added Value™ Resource Center at www.jrosspub.com.

25

PROJECT PROCUREMENT MANAGEMENT

Project Procurement Management area of knowledge includes the processes to purchase or acquire the products, services, or results needed from outside the project team to perform the work. This area of knowledge also includes the contract management and change control processes required to administer contracts or purchase orders issued by authorized team members.

The following processes are included in Project Procurement Management:

- **Plan Purchases and Acquisitions** — Determine what to purchase or acquire and when and how
- **Plan Contracting** — Document products, services, quotations, bids, offers, or proposals as appropriate
- **Request Seller Responses** — Obtain information, quotations, bids, or offers of proposals
- **Select Sellers** — Review offers, choose among potential sellers, and negotiate a written contract with each seller
- **Contract Administration** — Manage the contract and relationship between the buyer and seller, review and document how a seller is performing or has performed to establish required corrective actions and provide a basis for feature relationships with the seller, manage contract-related changes, and when appropriate manage the contractual relationship with the outside buyer of the project
- **Contract Closure** — Complete and sell each contract, including the resolution of any open items and closing each contract applicable to the project or a project phase

Project Procurement Management PMBOK® area of knowledge includes the following processes and deliverables:

1. Plan Purchases and Acquisitions
   a. Procurement Management Plan
   b. Contract Statement of Work
   c. Make-or-Buy Decisions
   d. Requested Changes
2. Plan Contracting
   a. Procurement Documents
   b. Evaluation Criteria
   c. Contract Statement of Work (Updates)
3. Request Seller Responses
   a. Qualified Sellers List
   b. Procurement Document Package
   c. Proposals
4. Select Sellers
   a. Selected Sellers
   b. Contract
   c. Contract Management Plan
   d. Resource Availability
   e. Procurement Management Plan (Updates)
   f. Requested Changes
5. Contract Administration
   a. Contract Documentation
   b. Requested Changes
   c. Recommended Corrective Actions
   d. Organizational Process Assets (Updates)
   e. Project Management Plan (Updates)
6. Contract Closure
   a. Closed Contracts
   b. Organizational Process Assets (Updates)

The following 3Ms-oriented metrics support the Project Procurement Management PMBOK® area of knowledge:

1. Plan Purchases and Acquisitions — Procurement Management Plan
2. Plan Purchases and Acquisitions — Contract Statement of Work
3. Plan Purchases and Acquisitions — Make-or-Buy Decisions
4. Plan Purchases and Acquisitions — Requested Changes
5. Plan Contracting — Procurement Documents
6. Plan Contracting — Evaluation Criteria
7. Plan Contracting — Contract Statement of Work (Updates)
8. Request Seller Responses — Qualified Sellers List
9. Request Seller Responses — Procurement Document Package
10. Request Seller Responses — Proposals
11. Select Sellers — Selected Sellers

12. Select Sellers — Contract
13. Select Sellers — Contract Management Plan
14. Select Sellers — Resource Availability
15. Select Sellers — Procurement Management Plan (Updates)
16. Select Sellers — Requested Changes
17. Contract Administration — Contract Documentation
18. Contract Administration — Requested Changes
19. Contract Administration — Recommended Corrective Actions
20. Contract Administration — Organizational Process Assets (Updates)
21. Contract Administration — Project Management Plan (Updates)
22. Contract Closure — Closed Contracts
23. Contract Closure — Organizational Process Assets (Updates)

Scoring for Section II: Performance Objectives for these metrics is as follows:

A. 50%: 4 = completed early and under budget ≥10%; 3 = ≥5%; 2 = completed on time and on budget; 1 = completed late and/or over budget.
B. 50%: 4 = approved by project initiator and/or project sponsor early and under budget ≥10%; 3 = approved early and under budget ≥5%; 2 = approved on time and on budget; 1 = approved late and/or over budget.

Scoring for Section III: Performance Scorecard for these metrics is as follows:
4 = Excellent; 3 = Very Good; 2 = Satisfactory; 1 = Unsatisfactory.

PLAN PURCHASES AND ACQUISITIONS — PROCUREMENT MANAGEMENT PLAN

The procurement management plan describes how the procurement processes will be managed from developing procurement documentation through contract closure.

I. Key Value Areas Weighting (%)
   A. Completion of process preparation and implementation of procurement management plan = 50%.
   B. Approved by project initiator and/or project sponsor = 50%.
II. Performance Objectives — Based on project scope statement.
III. Performance Scorecard
IV. Performance Factors
   A. Project Team Members — Help construct procurement management plan by providing information relevant to areas of the project management plan within project team delivery expectations for time and cost.
   B. Project Initiator(s) — Reviews and/or approves various versions of procurement management plan within project team delivery expectations for time and cost.
   C. Project Sponsor(s) — Reviews and/or approves various versions of procurement management plan within project team delivery expectations for time and cost.
   D. Project Manager — Leads and/or performs construction of procurement management plan within project team delivery expectations for time and cost.

V. Training Objectives
   A. Short Term — Project manager conducts meetings with project initiator, sponsor, and team member(s) on the creation and completion of the procurement management plan regarding what is involved and who is performing certain tasks within schedule expectations for performance.
   B. Long Term — Team members become trained in the process to develop and complete a procurement management plan as a means to improve total effort to complete task.

PLAN PURCHASES AND ACQUISITIONS — CONTRACT STATEMENT OF WORK

Each contract statement of work defines what is being purchased or acquired for the related section of work in the project.

I. Key Value Areas Weighting (%)
   A. Completion of process preparation and implementation of contract statement of work = 50%.
   B. Approved by project initiator and/or project sponsor = 50%.
II. Performance Objectives — Based on project scope statement.
III. Performance Scorecard
IV. Performance Factors
   A. Project Team Members — Help construct contract statement of work by providing information relevant to areas of the project management plan within project team delivery expectations for time and cost.
   B. Project Initiator(s) — Reviews and/or approves various versions of contract statement of work within project team delivery expectations for time and cost.
   C. Project Sponsor(s) — Reviews and/or approves various versions of contract statement of work within project team delivery expectations for time and cost.
   D. Project Manager — Leads and/or performs contract statement of work construction within project team delivery expectations for time and cost.
V. Training Objectives
   A. Short Term — Project manager conducts meetings with project initiator, sponsor, and team member(s) on the creation and completion of the contract statement of work regarding what is involved and who is performing certain tasks within schedule expectations for performance.
   B. Long Term — Team members become trained in the process to develop and complete a contract statement of work as a means to improve total effort to complete task.

PLAN PURCHASES AND ACQUISITIONS — MAKE-OR-BUY DECISIONS

The documented decisions of what project products, services, or results will be either acquired or developed by the project team.

I. Key Value Areas Weighting (%)
   A. Completion of process preparation and implementation of make-or-buy decisions = 50%.
   B. Approved by project initiator and/or project sponsor = 50%.
II. Performance Objectives — Based on project scope statement.
III. Performance Scorecard
IV. Performance Factors
   A. Project Team Members — Help construct make-or-buy decisions by providing information relevant to areas of the project scope statement within project team delivery expectations for time and cost.
   B. Project Initiator(s) — Reviews and/or approves various versions of make-or-buy decisions within project team delivery expectations for time and cost.
   C. Project Sponsor(s) — Reviews and/or approves various versions of make-or-buy decisions within project team delivery expectations for time and cost.
   D. Project Manager — Leads and/or performs make-or-buy decisions within project team delivery expectations for time and cost.
V. Training Objectives
   A. Short Term — Project manager conducts meetings with project initiator, sponsor, and team member(s) on the creation and completion of make-or-buy decisions regarding what is involved and who is performing certain tasks within schedule expectations for performance.
   B. Long Term — Team members become trained in the process to develop and complete make-or-buy decisions as a means to improve total effort to complete task.

PLAN PURCHASES AND ACQUISITIONS — REQUESTED CHANGES

Requested changes to the project management plan and its subsidiary plans may result from the plan purchases and acquisitions process.

I. Key Value Areas Weighting (%)
   A. Completion of process preparation and implementation of requested changes = 50%.
   B. Approved by project initiator and/or project sponsor = 50%.
II. Performance Objectives — Based on project scope statement.
III. Performance Scorecard
IV. Performance Factors
   A. Project Team Members — Help construct requested changes by providing information relevant to areas of the project management plan within project team delivery expectations for time and cost.
   B. Project Initiator(s) — Reviews and/or approves various versions of requested changes within project team delivery expectations for time and cost.
   C. Project Sponsor(s) — Reviews and/or approves various versions of requested changes within project team delivery expectations for time and cost.
   D. Project Manager — Leads and/or performs requested changes within project team delivery expectations for time and cost.

V. Training Objectives
   A. Short Term — Project manager conducts meetings with project initiator, sponsor, and team member(s) on the creation and completion of the requested changes regarding what is involved and who is performing certain tasks within schedule expectations for performance.
   B. Long Term — Team members become trained in the process to develop and complete requested changes as a means to improve total effort to complete task.

PLAN CONTRACTING — PROCUREMENT DOCUMENTS

The buyer creates procurement documents to facilitate an accurate and complete response from each prospective seller and to facilitate easy evaluation of the bids.

I. Key Value Areas Weighting (%)
   A. Completion of process preparation and implementation of procurement documents = 50%.
   B. Approved by project initiator and/or project sponsor = 50%.
II. Performance Objectives — Based on project scope statement.
III. Performance Scorecard
IV. Performance Factors
   A. Project Team Members — Help construct procurement documents by providing information relevant to areas of the project management plan within project team delivery expectations for time and cost.
   B. Project Initiator(s) — Reviews and/or approves various versions of procurement documents within project team delivery expectations for time and cost.
   C. Project Sponsor(s) — Reviews and/or approves various versions of procurement documents within project team delivery expectations for time and cost.
   D. Project Manager — Leads and/or performs construction of procurement documents within project team delivery expectations for time and cost.
V. Training Objectives
   A. Short Term — Project manager conducts meetings with project initiator, sponsor, and team member(s) on the creation and completion of the procurement documents regarding what is involved and who is performing certain tasks within schedule expectations for performance.
   B. Long Term — Team members become trained in the process to develop and complete procurement documents as a means to improve total effort to complete task.

PLAN CONTRACTING — EVALUATION CRITERIA

Developed and used to rate and score proposals.

I. Key Value Areas Weighting (%)
   A. Completion of process preparation and implementation of evaluation criteria = 50%.
   B. Approved by project initiator and/or project sponsor = 50%.
II. Performance Objectives — Based on project scope statement.
III. Performance Scorecard

IV. Performance Factors
   A. Project Team Members — Help construct evaluation criteria by providing information relevant to areas of the project management plan within project team delivery expectations for time and cost.
   B. Project Initiator(s) — Reviews and/or approves various versions of evaluation criteria within project team delivery expectations for time and cost.
   C. Project Sponsor(s) — Reviews and/or approves various versions of evaluation criteria within project team delivery expectations for time and cost.
   D. Project Manager — Leads and/or performs construction of evaluation criteria within project team delivery expectations for time and cost.
V. Training Objectives
   A. Short Term — Project manager conducts meetings with project initiator, sponsor, and team member(s) on the creation and completion of the evaluation criteria regarding what is involved and who is performing certain tasks within schedule expectations for performance.
   B. Long Term — Team members become trained in the process to develop and complete evaluation criteria as a means to improve total effort to complete task.

PLAN CONTRACTING — CONTRACT STATEMENT OF WORK (UPDATES)

Updates to one or more contract statements of work can be identified during the development of procurement documentation.

I. Key Value Areas Weighting (%)
   A. Completion of process preparation and implementation of updates to the contract statement(s) of work procurement documents = 50%.
   B. Approved by project initiator and/or project sponsor = 50%.
II. Performance Objectives — Based on project scope statement.
III. Performance Scorecard
IV. Performance Factors
   A. Project Team Members — Help construct updates to various contract statement(s) of work by providing information relevant to areas of the procurement management plan within project team delivery expectations for time and cost.
   B. Project Initiator(s) — Reviews and/or approves various versions of updates to contract statement(s) of work within project team delivery expectations for time and cost.
   C. Project Sponsor(s) — Reviews and/or approves various versions of updates to contract statement(s) of work within project team delivery expectations for time and cost.
   D. Project Manager — Leads and/or performs updates to contract statement(s) of work within project team delivery expectation for time and cost.
V. Training Objectives
   A. Short Term — Project manager conducts meetings with project initiator, sponsor, and team member(s) on the creation and completion of updates to contract statement(s) of work regarding what is involved and who is performing certain tasks within schedule expectations for performance.

B. Long Term — Team members become trained in the process to develop and complete updates to contract statement(s) of work as a means to improve total effort to complete task.

REQUEST SELLER RESPONSES — QUALIFIED SELLERS LIST

Those sellers that are asked to submit a proposal or quotation.

  I. Key Value Areas Weighting (%)
     A. Completion of process preparation and implementation of the qualified sellers list = 50%.
     B. Approved by project initiator and/or project sponsor = 50%.
  II. Performance Objectives — Based on project scope statement.
  III. Performance Scorecard
  IV. Performance Factors
     A. Project Team Members — Help construct the qualified sellers list by providing information relevant to areas of the procurement management plan within project team delivery expectations for time and cost.
     B. Project Initiator(s) — Reviews and/or approves various versions of qualified sellers list within project team delivery expectations for time and cost.
     C. Project Sponsor(s) — Reviews and/or approves various versions of qualified sellers list within project team delivery expectations for time and cost.
     D. Project Manager — Leads and/or performs construction of qualified sellers list within project team delivery expectations for time and cost.
  V. Training Objectives
     A. Short Term — Project manager conducts meetings with project initiator, sponsor, and team member(s) on the creation and completion of the qualified sellers list regarding what is involved and who is performing certain tasks within schedule expectations for performance.
     B. Long Term — Team members become trained in the process to develop and complete a qualified sellers list as a means to improve total effort to complete task.

REQUEST SELLER RESPONSES — PROCUREMENT DOCUMENT PACKAGE

The procurement document package is a buyer-prepared formal request sent to each seller and is the basis upon which a seller prepares a bid for the requested product, service, or results that are defined in the procurement documentation.

  I. Key Value Areas Weighting (%)
     A. Completion of process preparation and implementation of the procurement document package = 50%.
     B. Approved by project initiator and/or project sponsor = 50%.
  II. Performance Objectives — Based on project scope statement.
  III. Performance Scorecard

IV. Performance Factors
   A. Project Team Members — Help construct the qualified sellers list by providing information relevant to areas of the procurement document package within project team delivery expectations for time and cost.
   B. Project Initiator(s) — Reviews and/or approves various versions of procurement document package within project team delivery expectations for time and cost.
   C. Project Sponsor(s) — Reviews and/or approves various versions of procurement document package within project team delivery expectations for time and cost.
   D. Project Manager — Leads and/or performs construction of procurement document package within project team delivery expectation for time and cost.
V. Training Objectives
   A. Short Term — Project manager conducts meetings with project initiator, sponsor, and team member(s) on the creation and completion of the procurement document package regarding what is involved and who is performing certain tasks within schedule expectations for performance.
   B. Long Term — Team members become trained in the process to develop and complete a procurement document package as a means to improve total effort to complete task.

REQUEST SELLER RESPONSES — PROPOSALS

Seller-prepared documents that define the seller's ability and willingness to provide the requested product, service, or results defined in the procurement documentation.

I. Key Value Areas Weighting (%)
   A. Completion of process preparation and implementation of the proposals = 50%.
   B. Approved by project initiator and/or project sponsor = 50%.
II. Performance Objectives — Based on project scope statement.
III. Performance Scorecard
IV. Performance Factors
   A. Project Sponsor(s) — Reviews and/or approves various versions of proposals within project team delivery expectations for time and cost.
   B. Project Manager — Leads and/or performs approval of proposals within project team delivery expectations for time and cost.
V. Training Objectives
   A. Short Term — Project manager conducts meetings with project initiator, sponsor, and team member(s) on the completion of the proposals regarding what is involved and who is performing certain tasks within schedule expectations for performance.
   B. Long Term — Team members become trained in the process to develop and complete proposals as a means to improve total effort to complete task.

SELECT SELLERS — SELECTED SELLERS

Those sellers that have been judged to be in a competitive range based upon the outcome of the proposal or bid evaluation and that have negotiated a draft contract, which becomes the final contract when the award is made.

I. Key Value Areas Weighting (%)
   A. Completion of process preparation and implementation of the selected sellers = 50%.
   B. Approved by project initiator and/or project sponsor = 50%.
II. Performance Objectives — Based on procurement management plan.
III. Performance Scorecard
IV. Performance Factors
   A. Project Sponsor(s) — Reviews and/or approves selected sellers within project team delivery expectations for time and cost.
   B. Project Manager — Leads and/or performs selection of sellers within project team delivery expectation for time and cost.
V. Training Objectives
   A. Short Term — Project manager conducts meetings with project initiator, sponsor, and team member(s) on the selection of sellers regarding what is involved and who is performing certain tasks within schedule expectations for performance.
   B. Long Term — Team members become trained in the process to develop and complete selection of sellers as a means to improve total effort to complete task.

SELECT SELLERS — CONTRACT

A contract is awarded to each selected seller.

I. Key Value Areas Weighting (%)
   A. Completion of process preparation and implementation of the selected contract(s) = 50%.
   B. Approved by project initiator and/or project sponsor = 50%.
II. Performance Objectives — Based on procurement management plan.
III. Performance Scorecard
IV. Performance Factors
   A. Project Sponsor(s) — Reviews and/or approves various seller contracts within project team delivery expectations for time and cost.
   B. Project Manager — Leads and/or performs seller contract award within project team delivery expectations for time and cost.
V. Training Objectives
   A. Short Term — Project manager conducts meetings with project initiator, sponsor, and team member(s) on the creation and completion of awarding seller contracts regarding what is involved and who is performing certain tasks within schedule expectations for performance.
   B. Long Term — Team members become trained in the process to develop and complete awarding seller contracts as a means to improve total effort to complete task.

SELECT SELLERS — CONTRACT MANAGEMENT PLAN

For significant purchases or acquisitions, a plan to administer the contract is prepared based upon the specific buyer-specified items within the contract, such as documentation and delivery and performance requirements, that the buyer and the seller must meet.

I. Key Value Areas Weighting (%)
   A. Completion of process preparation and implementation of the contract management plan = 50%.
   B. Approved by project initiator and/or project sponsor = 50%.
II. Performance Objectives — Based on procurement management plan.
III. Performance Scorecard
IV. Performance Factors
   A. Project Team Members — Help construct contract management plan by providing information relevant to areas of the procurement management plan within project team delivery expectations for time and cost.
   B. Project Initiator(s) — Reviews and/or approves various versions of the contract management plan within project team delivery expectations for time and cost.
   C. Project Sponsor(s) — Reviews and/or approves various versions of the contract management plan within project team delivery expectations for time and cost.
   D. Project Manager — Leads and/or performs construction of the contract management plan within project team delivery expectations for time and cost.
V. Training Objectives
   A. Short Term — Project manager conducts meetings with project initiator, sponsor, and team member(s) on the creation and completion of the contract management plan regarding what is involved and who is performing certain tasks within schedule expectations for performance.
   B. Long Term — Team members become trained in the process to develop and complete a contract management plan as a means to improve total effort to complete task.

SELECT SELLERS — RESOURCE AVAILABILITY

The quantity and availability of resources and the dates on which each specific resource can be active or idle are documented.

I. Key Value Areas Weighting (%)
   A. Completion of process preparation and implementation of resource availability = 50%.
   B. Approved by project initiator and/or project sponsor = 50%.
II. Performance Objectives — Based on procurement management plan.
III. Performance Scorecard
IV. Performance Factors
   A. Project Team Members — Help construct resource availability by providing information relevant to areas of the procurement management plan within project team delivery expectations for time and cost.
   B. Project Initiator(s) — Reviews and/or approves various versions of resource availability within project team delivery expectations for time and cost.
   C. Project Sponsor(s) — Reviews and/or approves various versions of resource availability within project team delivery expectations for time and cost.
   D. Project Manager — Leads and/or performs determination of resource availability within project team delivery expectations for time and cost.

V. Training Objectives
   A. Short Term — Project manager conducts meetings with project initiator, sponsor, and team member(s) on the creation and completion of resource availability determination regarding what is involved and who is performing certain tasks within schedule expectations for performance.
   B. Long Term — Team members become trained in the process to develop and complete resource availability determination plan as a means to improve total effort to complete task.

SELECT SELLERS — PROCUREMENT MANAGEMENT PLAN (UPDATES)

The procurement management plan is updated to reflect any approved change requests that affect procurement management.

I. Key Value Areas Weighting (%)
   A. Completion of process preparation and implementation of updates to the procurement management plan = 50%.
   B. Approved by project initiator and/or project sponsor = 50%.
II. Performance Objectives — Based on procurement management plan.
III. Performance Scorecard
IV. Performance Factors
   A. Project Team Members — Help construct updates to the procurement management plan by providing information relevant to areas of the selected sellers list within project team delivery expectations for time and cost.
   B. Project Initiator(s) — Reviews and/or approves various versions of updates to the procurement management plan within project team delivery expectations for time and cost.
   C. Project Sponsor(s) — Reviews and/or approves various versions of updates to the procurement management plan within project team delivery expectations for time and cost.
   D. Project Manager — Leads and/or performs updates to the procurement management plan within project team delivery expectations for time and cost.
V. Training Objectives
   A. Short Term — Project manager conducts meetings with project initiator, sponsor, and team member(s) on the creation and completion of updates to the procurement management plan regarding what is involved and who is performing certain tasks within schedule expectations for performance.
   B. Long Term — Team members become trained in the process to develop and complete updates to the procurement management plan as a means to improve total effort to complete task.

SELECT SELLERS — REQUESTED CHANGES

Requested changes to the project management plan and its subsidiary plans may result from the select sellers process. Requested changes are processed for review and completion through the integrated change control process.

I. Key Value Areas Weighting (%)
   A. Completion of process preparation and implementation of requested changes = 50%.
   B. Approved by project initiator and/or project sponsor = 50%.
II. Performance Objectives — Based on procurement management plan.
III. Performance Scorecard
IV. Performance Factors
   A. Project Team Members — Help construct requested changes by providing information relevant to areas of the procurement management plan within project team delivery expectations for time and cost.
   B. Project Initiator(s) — Reviews and/or approves various versions of requested changes within project team delivery expectations for time and cost.
   C. Project Sponsor(s) — Reviews and/or approves various versions of requested changes within project team delivery expectations for time and cost.
   D. Project Manager — Leads and/or performs requested changes within project team delivery expectations for time and cost.
V. Training Objectives
   A. Short Term — Project manager conducts meetings with project initiator, sponsor, and team member(s) on the creation and completion of requested changes regarding what is involved and who is performing certain tasks within schedule expectations for performance.
   B. Long Term — Team members become trained in the process to develop and complete requested changes as a means to improve total effort to complete task.

CONTRACT ADMINISTRATION — CONTRACT DOCUMENTATION

Includes but is not limited to the contract along with the supporting schedules, requested unapproved contract changes, and approved change requests.

I. Key Value Areas Weighting (%)
   A. Completion of process preparation and implementation of the contract documentation = 50%.
   B. Approved by project initiator and/or project sponsor = 50%.
II. Performance Objectives — Based on contract management plan.
III. Performance Scorecard
IV. Performance Factors
   A. Project Team Members — Help construct contract documentation by providing information relevant to areas of the procurement management plan within project team delivery expectations for time and cost.
   B. Project Initiator(s) — Reviews and/or approves various versions of the contract documentation within project team delivery expectations for time and cost.
   C. Project Sponsor(s) — Reviews and/or approves various versions of the contract documentation within project team delivery expectations for time and cost.
   D. Project Manager — Leads and/or performs construction of the contract documentation within project team delivery expectations for time and cost.
V. Training Objectives
   A. Short Term — Project manager conducts meetings with project initiator, sponsor, and team member(s) on the creation and completion of the contract documentation

regarding what is involved and who is performing certain tasks within schedule expectations for performance.
  B. Long Term — Team members become trained in the process to develop and complete contract documentation as a means to improve total effort to complete task.

CONTRACT ADMINISTRATION — REQUESTED CHANGES

Requested changes to the project management plan and its subsidiary plans and other components may result from the contract administration process. Requested changes are processed for review and approval through the integrated change control process.

I. Key Value Areas Weighting (%)
   A. Completion of process preparation and implementation of the requested changes = 50%.
   B. Approved by project initiator and/or project sponsor = 50%.
II. Performance Objectives — Based on contract management plan.
III. Performance Scorecard
IV. Performance Factors
   A. Project Team Members — Help construct requested changes by providing information relevant to areas of the project management plan within project team delivery expectations for time and cost.
   B. Project Initiator(s) — Reviews and/or approves various versions of the requested changes within project team delivery expectations for time and cost.
   C. Project Sponsor(s) — Reviews and/or approves various versions of the requested changes within project team delivery expectations for time and cost.
   D. Project Manager — Leads and/or performs requested changes within project team delivery expectations for time and cost.
V. Training Objectives
   A. Short Term — Project manager conducts meetings with project initiator, sponsor, and team member(s) on the creation and completion of the requested changes regarding what is involved and who is performing certain tasks within schedule expectations for performance.
   B. Long Term — Team members become trained in the process to develop and complete requested changes as a means to improve total effort to complete task.

CONTRACT ADMINISTRATION — RECOMMENDED CORRECTIVE ACTIONS

A recommended corrective action is anything that needs to be done to bring the seller in compliance with the terms of the contract.

I. Key Value Areas Weighting (%)
   A. Completion of process preparation and implementation of the recommended corrective actions = 50%.
   B. Approved by project initiator and/or project sponsor = 50%.
II. Performance Objectives — Based on contract management plan.

III. Performance Scorecard
IV. Performance Factors
   A. Project Team Members — Help construct recommended corrective actions by providing information relevant to areas of the procurement management plan within project team delivery expectations for time and cost.
   B. Project Initiator(s) — Reviews and/or approves various versions of recommended corrective actions within project team delivery expectations for time and cost.
   C. Project Sponsor(s) — Reviews and/or approves various versions of recommended corrective actions within project team delivery expectations for time and cost.
   D. Project Manager — Leads and/or performs the recommended corrective actions within project team delivery expectations for time and cost.
V. Training Objectives
   A. Short Term — Project manager conducts meetings with project initiator, sponsor, and team member(s) on the creation and completion of the recommended corrective actions regarding what is involved and who is performing certain tasks within schedule expectations for performance.
   B. Long Term — Team members become trained in the process to develop and complete recommended corrective actions as a means to improve total effort to complete task.

CONTRACT ADMINISTRATION — ORGANIZATIONAL PROCESS ASSETS (UPDATES)

Includes but is not limited to correspondence, payment schedules and requests, and seller performance evaluation documentation.

I. Key Value Areas Weighting (%)
   A. Completion of process preparation and implementation of updates to the organizational process assets = 50%.
   B. Approved by project initiator and/or project sponsor = 50%.
II. Performance Objectives — Based on contract management plan.
III. Performance Scorecard
IV. Performance Factors
   A. Project Team Members — Help construct updates to the organizational process assets by providing information relevant to areas of the procurement management plan within project team delivery expectations for time and cost.
   B. Project Initiator(s) — Reviews and/or approves various versions of updates to the organizational process assets within project team delivery expectations for time and cost.
   C. Project Sponsor(s) — Reviews and/or approves various versions of updates to the organizational process assets within project team delivery expectations for time and cost.
   D. Project Manager — Leads and/or performs updates to the organizational process assets within project team delivery expectations for time and cost.
V. Training Objectives
   A. Short Term — Project manager conducts meetings with project initiator, sponsor, and team member(s) on the creation and completion of updates to the organizational

process assets regarding what is involved and who is performing certain tasks within schedule expectations for performance.
B. Long Term — Team members become trained in the process to develop and complete updates to organizational process assets as a means to improve total effort to complete task.

CONTRACT ADMINISTRATION — PROJECT MANAGEMENT PLAN (UPDATES)

Includes change requests that affect the procurement and contract management plans.

I. Key Value Areas Weighting (%)
    A. Completion of process preparation and implementation of updates to the project management plan = 50%.
    B. Approved by project initiator and/or project sponsor = 50%.
II. Performance Objectives — Based on procurement and contract management plans.
III. Performance Scorecard
IV. Performance Factors
    A. Project Team Members — Help construct updates to the project management plan by providing information relevant to areas of the procurement management plan within project team delivery expectations for time and cost.
    B. Project Initiator(s) — Reviews and/or approves various updates to the project management plan within project team delivery expectations for time and cost.
    C. Project Sponsor(s) — Reviews and/or approves various updates to the project management plan within project team delivery expectations for time and cost.
    D. Project Manager — Leads and/or performs updates to the project management plan within project team delivery expectations for time and cost.
V. Training Objectives
    A. Short Term — Project manager conducts meetings with project initiator, sponsor, and team member(s) on the creation and completion of updates to the project management plan regarding what is involved and who is performing certain tasks within schedule expectations for performance.
    B. Long Term — Team members become trained in the process to develop and complete updates to the project management plan as a means to improve total effort to complete task.

CONTRACT CLOSURE — CLOSED CONTRACTS

The buyer provides the seller with formal written notice that the contract has been completed.

I. Key Value Areas Weighting (%)
    A. Completion of process preparation and implementation of the closed contract = 50%.
    B. Approved by project initiator and/or project sponsor = 50%.
II. Performance Objectives — Based on procurement and contract management plans.

III. Performance Scorecard
IV. Performance Factors
   A. Project Team Members — Help perform contract closure by providing information relevant to areas of the procurement and contract management plans within project team delivery expectations for time and cost.
   B. Project Initiator(s) — Reviews and/or approves seller notification of contract closure within project team delivery expectations for time and cost.
   C. Project Sponsor(s) — Reviews and/or approves seller notification of contract closure within project team delivery expectations for time and cost.
   D. Project Manager — Leads and/or performs seller notification of contract closure within project team delivery expectations for time and cost.
V. Training Objectives
   A. Short Term — Project manager conducts meetings with project initiator, sponsor, and team member(s) on the creation and completion of contract closure regarding what is involved and who is performing certain tasks within schedule expectations for performance.
   B. Long Term — Team members become trained in the process to develop and complete contract closure as a means to improve total effort to complete task.

CONTRACT CLOSURE — ORGANIZATIONAL PROCESS ASSETS (UPDATES)

Includes but is not limited to the contract file, deliverable acceptance, and lessons learned documentation.

I. Key Value Areas Weighting (%)
   A. Completion of process preparation and implementation of updates to the organizational process assets = 50%.
   B. Approved by project initiator and/or project sponsor = 50%.
II. Performance Objectives — Based on procurement and contract management plans.
III. Performance Scorecard
IV. Performance Factors
   A. Project Team Members — Help construct updates to the organizational process assets by providing information relevant to areas of the procurement management plan within project team delivery expectations for time and cost.
   B. Project Initiator(s) — Reviews and/or approves various versions of updates to the organizational process assets within project team delivery expectations for time and cost.
   C. Project Sponsor(s) — Reviews and/or approves various versions of updates to the organizational process assets within project team delivery expectations for time and cost.
   D. Project Manager — Leads and/or performs updates to the organizational process assets within project team delivery expectations for time and cost.
V. Training Objectives
   A. Short Term — Project manager conducts meetings with project initiator, sponsor, and team member(s) on the creation and completion of updates to the organizational

process assets regarding what is involved and who is performing certain tasks within schedule expectations for performance.
B. Long Term — Team members become trained in the process to develop and complete updates to the organizational process assets as a means to improve total effort to complete task.

SUMMARY

The Project Procurement Management processes involve contracts that are legal documents between the buyer and the seller. A contract is a mutually binding agreement that obligates the seller to provide specified products, services, or results and obligates the buyer to provide monetary or other valuable compensation for these provisions.

In today's world, procurement and contracting are as important as they ever have been. More and more project work is supported by off-shore companies that can provide low-cost value in their products and services or other media. Because of these relationships in particular, more emphasis than every before is placed on procurement management to manage contract risk. The risk is often very high in this type of contract where the seller is located far away. The buyer may not be able to simply walk down the hall to determine the adequacy of progress. Thus this task falls to the procurement area, where specificity is a critical success factor for contract and procurement management. Being late half a day in your time zone can mean a two-day loss in progress because of significant distances communications must travel to be heard, understood, and worked with. Late resolution in procurement management has doomed many a project.

QUESTIONS

25-1. Project Procurement Management area of knowledge includes the processes to purchase or acquire the products, services, or results needed from outside the project team to perform the work. True or false?

25-2. Which of the following is not an output of the plan contracting process:
  a. Procurement documents
  b. Expert judgment
  c. Evaluation criteria
  d. Updates to the contract statement of work

25-3. Plan contracting is the documenting of products, services, quotations, bids, offers, or proposals as appropriate. True or false?

25-4. Each contract statement of work defines what is being purchased or acquired for the related section of work in the project. True or false?

25-5. Which of the following is not an output of the select sellers process:
  a. Proposals
  b. Selected sellers

c. Contract
d. Contract management plan

25-6. In plan contracting for procurement documents, the buyer creates procurement documents to facilitate an accurate and complete response from each prospective seller and to facilitate easy evaluation of the bids. True or false?

25-7. In the output select sellers — contract management plan, for significant purchases or acquisitions, a plan to administer the contract is prepared based upon the specific buyer-specified items within the contract, such as documentation and delivery and performance requirements, that the buyer and the seller must meet. True or false?

25-8. The output request seller responses — proposals includes the seller-prepared documents that define the seller's ability and willingness to provide the requested product, service, or results defined in the procurement documentation. True or false?

25-9. The output select sellers — selected sellers identifies those sellers that have been judged to be in a competitive range based upon the outcome of the proposal or bid evaluation and that have negotiated a draft contract, which becomes the final contract when the award is made. True or false?

25-10. The output contract administration — contract documentation includes but is not limited to the contract along with the supporting schedules, requested unapproved contract changes, and approved change requests. True or false?

This book has free materials available for download from the
Web Added Value™ Resource Center at www.jrosspub.com.

26

PROJECT FRAUD MANAGEMENT

Project Fraud Management is not a PMBOK® area of knowledge, but it should be. The focus of Project Fraud Management is on the proper execution of project team internal controls as the ways and means to optimize team performance and to prevent project abuse.

Project Fraud Management encompasses the following processes:

- **Fraud Management Planning** — Identify the policy and procedure for the project team to perform prevention and detection of project fraud
- **Project Fraud Auditing** — Perform the project assessment of project health
- **Transparent Reporting** — Identify project progress to all stakeholders pertinent to each project team member and the project team as a whole
- **Internal Controls** — Management mechanisms that provide evidence of management intent to prevent and detect project fraud within the project team

Given these considerations, the following 3Ms-oriented metric profiles support Project Fraud Management:

1. Fraud Management Planning — Fraud Management Plan
2. Project Fraud Auditing — Project Fraud Identification
3. Project Fraud Auditing — Project Fraud Audit
4. Transparent Reporting — Team Member Status Reports
5. Transparent Reporting — Project Team Status Report
6. Internal Controls — Critical Path Scheduling
7. Internal Controls — Project Team Member Status Reports Publishing
8. Internal Controls — Project Status Reports Publishing
9. Internal Controls — Team Member Code of Conduct

10. Internal Controls — Activity Estimating
11. Internal Controls — Materiality Risk
12. Internal Controls — Project Management Plan
13. Internal Controls — Internal Control Management Plan
14. Internal Controls — Project Schedule
15. Internal Controls — Team Member Time Entry
16. Internal Controls — Issue Management
17. Internal Controls — Risk Management
18. Internal Controls — Acceptance Criteria

Scoring for Section II: Performance Objectives for these metrics is as follows:

A. 50%: 4 = completed early and under budget ≥10%; 3 = ≥5%; 2 = completed on time and on budget; 1 = completed late and/or over budget.
B. 50%: 4 = approved early and under budget ≥10%; 3 = approved early and under budget ≥5%; 2 = approved on time and on budget; 1 = approved late and/or over budget.

Scoring for Section III: Performance Scorecard for these metrics is as follows: 4 = Excellent; 3 = Very Good; 2 = Satisfactory; 1 = Unsatisfactory.

FRAUD MANAGEMENT PLANNING — FRAUD MANAGEMENT PLAN

The fraud management plan details how the project team will prevent and detect fraud.

I. Key Value Areas Weighting (%)
   A. Completion of process preparation and implementation of fraud management plan = 50%.
   B. Approved by project initiator and/or project sponsor = 50%.
II. Performance Objectives — Based on project management plan.
III. Performance Scorecard
IV. Performance Factors
   A. Project Team Members — Help construct fraud management plan by providing information relevant to areas of the project management plan within project team delivery expectations for time and cost.
   B. Project Initiator(s) — Reviews and/or approves various versions of fraud management plan within project team delivery expectations for time and cost.
   C. Project Sponsor(s) — Reviews and/or approves various versions of fraud management plan within project team delivery expectations for time and cost.
   D. Project Manager — Leads and/or performs fraud management plan construction within project team delivery expectations for time and cost.
V. Training Objectives
   A. Short Term — Project manager conducts meetings with project initiator, sponsor, and team member(s) on the creation and completion of the fraud management plan

regarding what is involved and who is performing certain tasks within schedule expectations for performance.
B. Long Term — Team members become trained in the process to develop and complete a fraud management plan as a means to improve total effort to complete task.

PROJECT FRAUD AUDITING — PROJECT FRAUD IDENTIFICATION

Documents and details how project fraud could be committed within the project team based on the project management plan.

I. Key Value Areas Weighting (%)
   A. Completion of process preparation and implementation of project fraud identification = 50%.
   B. Approved by project initiator and/or project sponsor = 50%.
II. Performance Objectives — Based on project management plan.
III. Performance Scorecard
IV. Performance Factors
   A. Project Team Members — Help identify potential project fraud by providing information relevant to areas of the project management plan within project team delivery expectations for time and cost.
   B. Project Manager — Leads and/or performs project fraud identification construction within project team delivery expectations for time and cost.
V. Training Objectives
   A. Short Term — Project manager conducts meetings with project initiator, sponsor, and team member(s) on the creation and completion of project fraud identification regarding what is involved and who is performing certain tasks within schedule expectations for performance.
   B. Long Term — Team members become trained in the process to develop and complete project fraud identification as a means to improve total effort to complete task.

PROJECT FRAUD AUDITING — PROJECT FRAUD AUDIT

The process of actually inspecting project records and conducting interviews to assess project health.

I. Key Value Areas Weighting (%)
   A. Completion of process preparation and implementation of project fraud audit = 50%.
   B. Approved by project initiator and/or project sponsor = 50%.
II. Performance Objectives — Based on project management plan.
III. Performance Scorecard
IV. Performance Factors
   A. Project Team Members — Help support project fraud audit by providing information relevant to areas of the project management plan within project team delivery expectations for time and cost.
   B. Project Manager — Supports project fraud audit within project team delivery expectations for time and cost.

V. Training Objectives
  A. Short Term — Project manager conducts meetings with project initiator, sponsor, and team member(s) on the creation and completion of the project fraud audit regarding what is involved and who is performing certain tasks within schedule expectations for performance.
  B. Long Term — Team members become trained in the process to develop and complete project fraud audit as a means to improve total effort to complete task.

TRANSPARENT REPORTING — TEAM MEMBER STATUS REPORTS

Documents and details how project team members are progressing on their assignments regarding issues, risks, what work they have completed, and what work they will complete next reporting period.

  I. Key Value Areas Weighting (%)
     A. Completion of process preparation and implementation of team member status report = 50%.
     B. Approved by project manager = 50%.
  II. Performance Objectives — Based on project management plan.
  III. Performance Scorecard
  IV. Performance Factors
     A. Project Team Members — Complete project status report for their assigned accountabilities by providing information relevant to areas of the project management plan within project team delivery expectations for time and cost.
     B. Project Manager — Accepts team member status report and approves or rejects based on content within project team delivery expectations for time and cost.
  V. Training Objectives
     A. Short Term — Project manager conducts meetings with project initiator, sponsor, and team member(s) on the creation and completion of the team member status reporting requirements regarding what is involved and who is performing certain tasks within schedule expectations for performance.
     B. Long Term — Team members become trained in the process to develop and complete team member status reports as a means to improve total effort to complete task.

TRANSPARENT REPORTING — PROJECT TEAM STATUS REPORT

Documents and details how project team is progressing on assignments regarding issues, risks, what work has been completed, and what work will be completed next reporting period.

  I. Key Value Areas Weighting (%)
     A. Completion of process preparation and implementation of project team status report = 50%.
     B. Approved by project initiator and/or project sponsor = 50%.
  II. Performance Objectives — Based on project management plan.
  III. Performance Scorecard

IV. Performance Factors
  A. Project Team Members — Help construct project team status report by providing information relevant to areas of the project management plan within project team delivery expectations for time and cost.
  B. Project Manager — Leads and/or performs project team status report construction within project team delivery expectations for time and cost.
V. Training Objectives
  A. Short Term — Project manager conducts meetings with project initiator, sponsor, and team member(s) on the creation and completion of the project team status report regarding what is involved and who is performing certain tasks within schedule expectations for performance.
  B. Long Term — Team members become trained in the process to develop and complete a project team status report as a means to improve total effort to complete task.

INTERNAL CONTROLS — CRITICAL PATH SCHEDULING

Documents and details what the critical path of work is for the project through the schedule baseline. Also requires that all team members comprehend this process and are trained to find opportunities and threats to their work and that of their peers on the project team that impact the project completion date.

  I. Key Value Areas Weighting (%)
    A. Completion of process preparation and implementation of critical path scheduling = 50%.
    B. Approved by project initiator and/or project sponsor = 50%.
  II. Performance Objectives — Based on schedule baseline.
  III. Performance Scorecard
  IV. Performance Factors
    A. Project Team Members — Help construct critical path by providing information relevant to areas of the schedule baseline within project team delivery expectations for time and cost.
    B. Project Manager — Leads and/or performs critical path scheduling construction within project team delivery expectations for time and cost.
  V. Training Objectives
    A. Short Term — Project manager conducts meetings with project initiator, sponsor, and team member(s) on the creation and completion of critical path scheduling regarding what is involved and who is performing certain tasks within schedule expectations for performance.
    B. Long Term — Team members become trained in the process to develop and complete critical path scheduling as a means to improve total effort to complete task.

INTERNAL CONTROLS — PROJECT TEAM MEMBER STATUS REPORTS PUBLISHING

Are shared with all members of the project team and stakeholders. This process raises visibility to the results reported and enables others to improve their collaboration efforts while deterring abuse from occurring.

I. Key Value Areas Weighting (%)
   A. Completion of process preparation and implementation of project team member status reports publishing = 50%.
   B. Approved by project initiator and/or project sponsor = 50%.
II. Performance Objectives — Based on schedule baseline.
III. Performance Scorecard
IV. Performance Factors
   A. Project Team Members — Help publish their status report to stakeholders by providing information relevant to areas of the schedule baseline within project team delivery expectations for time and cost.
   B. Project Manager — Leads and/or performs team member status report publishing to stakeholders within project team delivery expectations for time and cost.
V. Training Objectives
   A. Short Term — Project manager conducts meetings with project initiator, sponsor, and team member(s) on the creation and completion of team member status report publishing regarding what is involved and who is performing certain tasks within schedule expectations for performance.
   B. Long Term — Team members become trained in the process to develop and complete the publishing of team member status reports as a means to improve total effort to complete task.

INTERNAL CONTROLS — PROJECT STATUS REPORTS PUBLISHING

Are shared with all members of the project team and stakeholders. This process raises visibility to the results reported and enables others to improve their collaboration efforts while deterring abuse from occurring.

I. Key Value Areas Weighting (%)
   A. Completion of process preparation and implementation of project status reports publishing = 50%.
   B. Approved by project initiator and/or project sponsor = 50%.
II. Performance Objectives — Based on schedule baseline.
III. Performance Scorecard
IV. Performance Factors
   A. Project Team Members — Help publish the project status reports to stakeholders by providing information relevant to areas of the schedule baseline within project team delivery expectations for time and cost.
   B. Project Manager — Leads and/or performs project status reports publishing to stakeholders within project team delivery expectations for time and cost.
V. Training Objectives
   A. Short Term — Project manager conducts meetings with project initiator, sponsor, and team member(s) on the creation and completion of project status reports publishing regarding what is involved and who is performing certain tasks within schedule expectations for performance.
   B. Long Term — Team members become trained in the process to develop and complete the publishing of project status reports as a means to improve total effort to complete task.

INTERNAL CONTROLS — TEAM MEMBER CODE OF CONDUCT

All project team members are expected to formally sign documentation of their acceptance of project code of conduct that details project fraud policy.

I. Key Value Areas Weighting (%)
    A. Completion of process preparation and signature approval of team member code of conduct = 50%.
    B. Approved by project initiator and/or project sponsor = 50%.
II. Performance Objectives — Based on schedule baseline.
III. Performance Scorecard
IV. Performance Factors
    A. Project Team Members — Provide their signature approval of project code of conduct relevant to areas of the schedule baseline within project team delivery expectations for time and cost.
    B. Project Manager — Leads team member signature approval of project code of conduct within project team delivery expectations for time and cost.
V. Training Objectives
    A. Short Term — Project manager conducts meetings with project initiator, sponsor, and team member(s) on the creation and completion of a project code of conduct for project fraud prevention and detection regarding what is involved and who is performing certain tasks within schedule expectations for performance.
    B. Long Term — Team members become trained in the process to develop the project code of conduct for team member signature approval as a means to improve total effort to complete task.

INTERNAL CONTROLS — ACTIVITY ESTIMATING

All estimated work is contained within whichever is lesser of 80 hours or 2 weeks of effort.

I. Key Value Areas Weighting (%)
    A. Completion of process preparation and implementation of internal control for activity estimating = 50%.
    B. Approved by project initiator and/or project sponsor = 50%.
II. Performance Objectives — Based on schedule baseline.
III. Performance Scorecard
IV. Performance Factors
    A. Project Team Members — Help control work estimates by providing information relevant to areas of the schedule baseline within project team delivery expectations for time and cost.
    B. Project Manager — Leads and/or performs internal control for activity estimating within project team delivery expectations for time and cost.
V. Training Objectives
    A. Short Term — Project manager conducts meetings with project initiator, sponsor, and team member(s) on the creation and completion of internal control for activity estimating regarding what is involved and who is performing certain tasks within schedule expectations for performance.

B. Long Term — Team members become trained in the process to develop internal control for activity estimating as a means to improve total effort to complete task.

INTERNAL CONTROLS — MATERIALITY RISK

All budgeted project work is considered as material. Specific requirements that consume 10% or more of the project budget are considered to be of material risk for failure. This process determines which portion of the project has material risk that requires specific project management attention so as to prevent project failure.

I. Key Value Areas Weighting (%)
   A. Completion of process preparation and implementation of internal control for determining materiality risk = 50%.
   B. Approved by project initiator and/or project sponsor = 50%.
II. Performance Objectives — Based on schedule baseline.
III. Performance Scorecard
IV. Performance Factors
   A. Project Team Members — Help control work materiality by providing information relevant to areas of the schedule baseline within project team delivery expectations for time and cost.
   B. Project Manager — Leads and/or performs materiality risk assessments for budgeted areas of the project within project team delivery expectations for time and cost.
V. Training Objectives
   A. Short Term — Project manager conducts meetings with project initiator, sponsor, and team member(s) on the creation and completion of internal control for materiality risk regarding what is involved and who is performing certain tasks within schedule expectations for performance.
   B. Long Term — Team members become trained in the process to develop the internal control for materiality risk assessments as a means to improve total effort to complete task.

INTERNAL CONTROLS — PROJECT MANAGEMENT PLAN

A required document for any project that details how the project will be completed.

I. Key Value Areas Weighting (%)
   A. Completion of process preparation and implementation of internal control for project management plan = 50%.
   B. Approved by project initiator and/or project sponsor = 50%.
II. Performance Objectives — Based on schedule baseline.
III. Performance Scorecard
IV. Performance Factors
   A. Project Team Members — Help construct the project management plan by providing relevant information within project team delivery expectations for time and cost.

B. Project Manager — Leads and/or performs internal control for project management plan development within project team delivery expectations for time and cost.
V. Training Objectives
  A. Short Term — Project manager conducts meetings with project initiator, sponsor, and team member(s) on the creation and completion of internal control for the project management plan regarding what is involved and who is performing certain tasks within schedule expectations for performance.
  B. Long Term — Team members become trained in the process to develop internal control for the project management plan as a means to improve total effort to complete task.

INTERNAL CONTROLS — INTERNAL CONTROL MANAGEMENT PLAN

A required document for any project that details how the project will be controlled for fraud prevention and detection.

I. Key Value Areas Weighting (%)
  A. Completion of process preparation and implementation of internal control management plan = 50%.
  B. Approved by project initiator and/or project sponsor = 50%.
II. Performance Objectives — Based on project management plan.
III. Performance Scorecard
IV. Performance Factors
  A. Project Team Members — Help construct the internal control management plan by providing relevant information within project team delivery expectations for time and cost.
  B. Project Manager — Leads and/or performs internal control management plan development within project team delivery expectations for time and cost.
V. Training Objectives
  A. Short Term — Project manager conducts meetings with project initiator, sponsor, and team member(s) on the creation and completion of internal control management plan regarding what is involved and who is performing certain tasks within schedule expectations for performance.
  B. Long Term — Team members become trained in the process to develop the internal control management plan as a means to improve total effort to complete task.

INTERNAL CONTROLS — PROJECT SCHEDULE

A required document for any project that details how the project will be completed according to the schedule.

I. Key Value Areas Weighting (%)
  A. Completion of process preparation and implementation of internal control for project schedule = 50%.
  B. Approved by project initiator and/or project sponsor = 50%.

II. Performance Objectives — Based on schedule baseline.
III. Performance Scorecard
IV. Performance Factors
   A. Project Team Members — Help construct the project schedule by providing relevant information within project team delivery expectations for time and cost.
   B. Project Manager — Leads and/or performs internal control for project schedule development within project team delivery expectations for time and cost.
V. Training Objectives
   A. Short Term — Project manager conducts meetings with project initiator, sponsor, and team member(s) on the creation and completion of internal control for the project schedule regarding what is involved and who is performing certain tasks within schedule expectations for performance.
   B. Long Term — Team members become trained in the process to develop internal control for the project schedule as a means to improve total effort to complete task.

INTERNAL CONTROLS — TEAM MEMBER TIME ENTRY

A required process for all project team members to report their work effort on project assignments for which are accountable.

I. Key Value Areas Weighting (%)
   A. Completion of process preparation and implementation of internal control for team member time entry = 50%.
   B. Approved by project initiator and/or project sponsor = 50%.
II. Performance Objectives — Based on schedule baseline.
III. Performance Scorecard
IV. Performance Factors
   A. Project Team Members — Post their cyclical time entry by providing relevant information within project team delivery expectations for their accountabilities.
   B. Project Manager — Leads and/or performs internal control for team member time entry development within project team delivery expectations for team member time entry.
V. Training Objectives
   A. Short Term — Project manager conducts meetings with project initiator, sponsor, and team member(s) on the creation and completion of internal control for team member time entry regarding what is involved and who is performing certain tasks within schedule expectations for performance.
   B. Long Term — Team members become trained in the process to develop the internal control for team member time entry reporting as a means to improve total effort to complete task.

INTERNAL CONTROLS — ISSUE MANAGEMENT

A required process for any project that collects and prioritizes all project work issues that require attention to resolve.

I. Key Value Areas Weighting (%)
   A. Completion of process preparation and implementation of internal control for issue management process = 50%.
   B. Approved by project initiator and/or project sponsor = 50%.
II. Performance Objectives — Based on schedule baseline.
III. Performance Scorecard
IV. Performance Factors
   A. Project Team Members — Help construct the project issues by providing relevant information within project team delivery expectations for time and cost.
   B. Project Manager — Leads and/or performs internal control for project issue management development within project team delivery expectations for time and cost.
V. Training Objectives
   A. Short Term — Project manager conducts meetings with project initiator, sponsor, and team member(s) on the creation and completion of internal control for project issue management regarding what is involved and who is performing certain tasks within schedule expectations for performance.
   B. Long Term — Team members become trained in the process to develop the internal control for project issue management as a means to improve total effort to complete task.

INTERNAL CONTROLS — RISK MANAGEMENT

A required process for any project that collects and prioritizes all project work risks that require attention to mitigate.

I. Key Value Areas Weighting (%)
   A. Completion of process preparation and implementation of internal control for risk management process = 50%.
   B. Approved by project initiator and/or project sponsor = 50%.
II. Performance Objectives — Based on schedule baseline.
III. Performance Scorecard
IV. Performance Factors
   A. Project Team Members — Help construct the project risks by providing relevant information within project team delivery expectations for time and cost.
   B. Project Manager — Leads and/or performs internal control for project risk management development within project team delivery expectations for time and cost.
V. Training Objectives
   A. Short Term — Project manager conducts meetings with project initiator, sponsor, and team member(s) on the creation and completion of internal control for project risk management regarding what is involved and who is performing certain tasks within schedule expectations for performance.
   B. Long Term — Team members become trained in the process to develop the internal control for project risk management as a means to improve total effort to complete task.

INTERNAL CONTROLS — ACCEPTANCE CRITERIA

All project outputs that require approval must have defined acceptance criteria specified in the project management plan.

I. Key Value Areas Weighting (%)
    A. Completion of process preparation and implementation of internal control for acceptance criteria process = 50%.
    B. Approved by project initiator and/or project sponsor = 50%.
II. Performance Objectives — Based on project management plan.
III. Performance Scorecard
IV. Performance Factors
    A. Project Team Members — Help construct the output acceptance criteria by providing relevant information within project team delivery expectations for time and cost.
    B. Project Manager — Leads and/or performs internal control for output acceptance criteria development within project team delivery expectations for time and cost.
V. Training Objectives
    A. Short Term — Project manager conducts meetings with project initiator, sponsor, and team member(s) on the creation and completion of internal control for output acceptance criteria regarding what is involved and who is performing certain tasks within schedule expectations for performance.
    B. Long Term — Team members become trained in the process to develop the internal control for project output acceptance criteria as a means to improve total effort to complete task.

SUMMARY

Project Fraud Management within the project team can reduce personal efforts by the team members to protect themselves from criticism from others by the appropriate insertion of internal controls that protect the team from uncontrolled abuse internally and externally.

By reducing and/or eliminating the defensive mechanisms that team members often build to protect themselves, a project team can gain delivery speed up to 40% of the team member work estimate. The project team will not get there overnight but can improve incrementally during the project life cycle if the selected internal controls are working as expected — for everyone's benefit.

Many other internal controls can easily be developed to control areas of concern. The list of 3Ms metric profiles provided in this chapter is a start and represents essential project governance.

QUESTIONS

26-1. Project Fraud Management is not a PMBOK® area of knowledge but should be. True or false?

26-2. Which of the following is not a process in Project Fraud Management:
a. Fraud management planning
b. Project fraud auditing
c. Internal auditing
d. Transparent reporting

26-3. Fraud management planning identifies the policy and procedure for the project team to perform prevention and detection of project fraud. True or false?

26-4. Project internal controls are management mechanisms that provide evidence of management intent to prevent and detect project fraud within the project team. True or false?

26-5. In enabling project internal controls, which of the following is not a 3Ms metric for internal control:
a. Activity estimating
b. Materiality risk
c. Project schedule
d. Staff acquisition

26-6. Transparent reporting identifies to all stakeholders project progress pertinent to each project team member and the project team as a whole. True or false?

26-7. Project fraud auditing performs the project assessment of project health. True or false?

26-8. Critical path scheduling documents and details what the critical path of work is for the project through the schedule baseline. It also requires that all team members comprehend this process and are trained to find opportunities and threats to their work and that of their peers on the project team that impact the project completion date. True or false?

26-9. Team member code of conduct is a form of internal control. True or false?

26-10. All project outputs that require approval must have defined acceptance criteria specified in the project management plan. True or false?

This book has free materials available for download from the Web Added Value™ Resource Center at www.jrosspub.com.

27

PROJECT MANAGEMENT OFFICE MANAGEMENT

Project Management Office (PMO) Management is not a PMBOK® area of knowledge, but it should be. The PMO has the potential to harness the value proposition of project management for your organization in ways probably not imagined in your environment. The PMO can bring about organization alignment, rescue projects, help project teams with best practices, find available resources, and support senior management tactically while supporting the project teams strategically.

The focus of the PMO should be on delivery excellence in project management. Emphasis should be given to throughput (completing more work when opportunity presents itself) versus cost containment (consuming allocated costs at the expense of completing more work) and on the proper execution of project team internal controls as the ways and means to optimize team performance and to prevent project abuse.

In 3Ms, we see the PMO Management process focusing on the following processes as a means to improve delivery speed:

- **Portfolio Management** — Identify high-value strategic entities in an aggregated collection that can be assessed collectively for delivery optimization within a specific time period
- **Corporate Governance Reporting** — Identify cyclical progress to date while forecasting future progress, opportunities, and threats for projects of strategic value
- **Project Fraud Management** — Enable appropriate internal controls for the project management community that are applied in a consistent and uniform manner
- **Tools** — Provide oversight and guidance on tool application for project teams

- **PMBOK®** — Ensure the PMBOK® standard is followed by every strategic project initiative

There are many other processes that the PMO will perform, but we see these as basic building blocks. It will be assumed that these building blocks are in place for the purpose of this discussion.

The following 3Ms-oriented metrics support PMO Management:

1. Portfolio Management — Project Portfolio
2. Portfolio Management — Corporate Objectives Portfolio
3. Portfolio Management — Resource Portfolio
4. Portfolio Management — Asset Portfolio
5. Portfolio Management — Internal Control Portfolio
6. Corporate Governance Reporting — Monthly Plan of Record
7. Corporate Governance Reporting — Value Proposition Assessment of PMO
8. Project Fraud Management — Fraud Management Plan Policy
9. Project Fraud Management — Project Audits
10. Project Fraud Management — Internal Controls
11. Tools — Project Management Templates
12. Tools — Project Management Information Systems
13. PMBOK® — Methodology
14. PMBOK® — Training

Scoring for Section III: Performance Scorecard is as follows: 4 = Excellent; 3 = Very Good; 2 = Satisfactory; 1 = Unsatisfactory.

PORTFOLIO MANAGEMENT — PROJECT PORTFOLIO

Contains all strategic project initiatives, force ranked in strategic value order. Each initiative is identified by sponsoring business unit, current health status, budget and actual total expenditures, sponsor, project manager, and start and end dates.

I. Key Value Areas Weighting (%)
   A. Completion of process preparation and implementation of the project portfolio to contain all planned fiscal year strategic projects = 50%.
   B. Approved by project initiator and/or project sponsor = 50%.
II. Performance Objectives — Based on all projects linked to specific corporate objectives.
   A. 50%: 4 = completed early and under budget ≥10%; 3 = ≥5%; 2 = completed on time and on budget; 1 = completed late and/or over budget.
   B. 50%: 4 = approved by project initiator and/or project sponsor early and under budget ≥10%; 3 = approved early and under budget ≥5%; 2 = approved on time and on budget; 1 = approved late and/or over budget.
III. Performance Scorecard
IV. Performance Factors
   A. Project Initiator(s) — Reviews and/or approves various versions of project portfolio within delivery expectations for time and cost.

B. Project Sponsor(s) — Reviews and/or approves various versions of project portfolio within delivery expectations for time and cost.
C. PMO Portfolio Manager — Leads and/or performs construction of project portfolio within project team delivery expectations for time and cost.

V. Training Objectives
A. Short Term — Project manager conducts meetings with project initiator, sponsor, and team member(s) on the creation and completion of the project portfolio regarding what is involved and who is performing certain tasks within schedule expectations for performance.
B. Long Term — Team members become trained in the process to develop and complete a project portfolio as a means to improve total effort to complete task.

PORTFOLIO MANAGEMENT — CORPORATE OBJECTIVES PORTFOLIO

Contains all corporate objectives, which are mapped by strategic project initiatives, force ranked in strategic value order within each corporate objective. Each initiative is identified by sponsoring business unit, current health status, budget and actual total expenditures, sponsor, project manager, and start and end dates.

I. Key Value Areas Weighting (%)
A. Completion of process preparation and implementation of the corporate objectives portfolio to contain all planned fiscal year corporate objectives and strategic projects = 50%.
B. Approved by project initiator and/or project sponsor = 50%.

II. Performance Objectives — Based on all projects linked to specific corporate objectives.
A. 50%: 4 = completed early and under budget $\geq 10\%$; 3 = $\geq 5\%$; 2 = completed on time and on budget; 1 = completed late and/or over budget.
B. 50%: 4 = approved by project initiator and/or project sponsor early and under budget $\geq 10\%$; 3 = approved early and under budget $\geq 5\%$; 2 = approved on time and on budget; 1 = approved late and/or over budget.

III. Performance Scorecard

IV. Performance Factors
A. Project Initiator(s) — Reviews and/or approves various versions of corporate objectives portfolio within delivery expectations for time and cost.
B. Project Sponsor(s) — Reviews and/or approves various versions of corporate objectives portfolio within delivery expectations for time and cost.
C. PMO Portfolio Manager — Leads and/or performs construction of corporate objectives portfolio within project team delivery expectations for time and cost.

V. Training Objectives
A. Short Term — Project manager conducts meetings with project initiator, sponsor, and team member(s) on the creation and completion of the corporate objectives portfolio regarding what is involved and who is performing certain tasks within schedule expectations for performance.
B. Long Term — Team members become trained in the process to develop and complete a corporate objectives portfolio as a means to improve total effort to complete task.

PORTFOLIO MANAGEMENT — RESOURCE PORTFOLIO

Contains all strategic resources, force ranked in strategic value order. Each resource is identified by sponsoring business unit, current status, budget and actual total expenditures, sponsor, project manager, and start and end dates per project initiative.

I. Key Value Areas Weighting (%)
   A. Completion of process preparation and implementation of the resource portfolio to contain all planned fiscal year strategic resources = 50%.
   B. Approved by project initiator and/or project sponsor = 50%.
II. Performance Objectives — Based on all projects linked to specific corporate objectives.
   A. 50%: 4 = completed early and under budget ≥10%; 3 = ≥5%; 2 = completed on time and on budget; 1 = completed late and/or over budget.
   B. 50%: 4 = approved by project initiator and/or project sponsor early and under budget ≥10%; 3 = approved early and under budget ≥5%; 2 = approved on time and on budget; 1 = approved late and/or over budget.
III. Performance Scorecard
IV. Performance Factors
   A. Project Initiator(s) — Reviews and/or approves various versions of resource portfolio within delivery expectations for time and cost.
   B. Project Sponsor(s) — Reviews and/or approves various versions of resource portfolio within delivery expectations for time and cost.
   C. PMO Portfolio Manager — Leads and/or performs construction of resource portfolio within project team delivery expectations for time and cost.
V. Training Objectives
   A. Short Term — Project manager conducts meetings with project initiator, sponsor, and team member(s) on the creation and completion of the resource portfolio regarding what is involved and who is performing certain tasks within schedule expectations for performance.
   B. Long Term — Team members become trained in the process to develop and complete a resource portfolio as a means to improve total effort to complete task.

PORTFOLIO MANAGEMENT — ASSET PORTFOLIO

Contains all strategic assets, force ranked in strategic value order. Each asset is identified by sponsoring business unit, current status, budget and actual total expenditures, sponsor, manager, and start and end dates per project initiative.

I. Key Value Areas Weighting (%)
   A. Completion of process preparation and implementation of the asset portfolio to contain all planned fiscal year strategic assets = 50%.
   B. Approved by project initiator and/or project sponsor = 50%.
II. Performance Objectives — Based on all projects linked to specific corporate objectives.
   A. 50%: 4 = completed early and under budget ≥10%; 3 = ≥5%; 2 = completed on time and on budget; 1 = completed late and/or over budget.

B. 50%: 4 = approved by project initiator and/or project sponsor early and under budget ≥10%; 3 = approved early and under budget ≥5%; 2 = approved on time and on budget; 1 = approved late and/or over budget.
III. Performance Scorecard
IV. Performance Factors
   A. Project Initiator(s) — Reviews and/or approves various versions of asset portfolio within delivery expectations for time and cost.
   B. Project Sponsor(s) — Reviews and/or approves various versions of asset portfolio within delivery expectations for time and cost.
   C. PMO Portfolio Manager— Leads and/or performs construction of asset portfolio within project team delivery expectations for time and cost.
V. Training Objectives
   A. Short Term — Project manager conducts meetings with project initiator, sponsor, and team member(s) on the creation and completion of the asset portfolio regarding what is involved and who is performing certain tasks within schedule expectations for performance.
   B. Long Term — Team members become trained in the process to develop and complete an asset portfolio as a means to improve total effort to complete task.

PORTFOLIO MANAGEMENT — INTERNAL CONTROL PORTFOLIO

Contains all material internal controls, force ranked in strategic value order. Each internal control is identified by sponsoring business unit, percentage of materiality relative to general ledger account, current status, sponsor, start and end dates per project initiative, and associated project manager.

I. Key Value Areas Weighting (%)
   A. Completion of process preparation and implementation of the internal control portfolio to contain all planned fiscal year internal controls = 50%.
   B. Approved by project initiator and/or project sponsor = 50%.
II. Performance Objectives — Based on all projects linked to specific corporate objectives.
   A. 50%: 4 = completed early and under budget ≥10%; 3 = ≥5%; 2 = completed on time and on budget; 1 = completed late and/or over budget.
   B. 50%: 4 = approved by project initiator and/or project sponsor early and under budget ≥10%; 3 = approved early and under budget ≥5%; 2 = approved on time and on budget; 1 = approved late and/or over budget.
III. Performance Scorecard
IV. Performance Factors
   A. Project Initiator(s) — Reviews and/or approves various versions of internal control portfolio within delivery expectations for time and cost.
   B. Project Sponsor(s) — Reviews and/or approves various versions of internal control portfolio within delivery expectations for time and cost.
   C. PMO Portfolio Manager — Leads and/or performs construction of internal control portfolio within project team delivery expectations for time and cost.
V. Training Objectives
   A. Short Term — Project manager conducts meetings with project initiator, sponsor, and team member(s) on the creation and completion of the internal control portfolio

regarding what is involved and who is performing certain tasks within schedule expectations for performance.
B. Long Term — Team members become trained in the process to develop and complete an internal control portfolio as a means to improve total effort to complete task.

CORPORATE GOVERNANCE REPORTING — MONTHLY PLAN OF RECORD

Presented monthly to corporate governance to report organizational progress based on previous reporting and forecast future progress for acceleration opportunities and delivery threats. Contains reference to all portfolios: project, corporate objectives, resource, asset, and internal control. Also identifies the over/under of plan to actual expenditures for all projects reporting.

I. Key Value Areas Weighting (%)
   A. Completion of process preparation and implementation of the monthly plan of record = 50%.
   B. Approved by project initiator and/or project sponsor = 50%.
II. Performance Objectives — Based on all projects linked to specific corporate objectives.
   A. 50%: 4 = completed early and under budget ≥10%; 3 = ≥5%; 2 = completed on time and on budget; 1 = completed late and/or over budget.
   B. 50%: 4 = approved by project initiator and/or project sponsor early and under budget ≥10%; 3 = approved early and under budget ≥5%; 2 = approved on time and on budget; 1 = approved late and/or over budget.
III. Performance Scorecard
IV. Performance Factors
   A. Project Initiator(s) — Reviews and/or approves various versions of monthly plan of record within delivery expectations for time and cost.
   B. Project Sponsor(s) — Reviews and/or approves various versions of monthly plan of record within delivery expectations for time and cost.
   C. PMO Portfolio Manager — Leads and/or performs construction of monthly plan of record within project team delivery expectations for time and cost.
V. Training Objectives
   A. Short Term — Project manager conducts meetings with project initiator, sponsor, and team member(s) on the creation and completion of the monthly plan of record regarding what is involved and who is performing certain tasks within schedule expectations for performance.
   B. Long Term — Team members become trained in the process to develop and complete a monthly plan of record as a means to improve total effort to complete task.

CORPORATE GOVERNANCE REPORTING — VALUE PROPOSITION ASSESSMENT OF PMO

The PMO is audited for performance based on the 3Ms metric profile for the PMO value proposition.

I. Key Value Areas Weighting (%)
   A. Completion of process preparation and implementation of the PMO value proposition assessment = 50%.
   B. Approved by project initiator and/or project sponsor = 50%.
II. Performance Objectives — Based on all projects linked to specific corporate objectives and aggregated plan budget.
   A. 50%: 4 = completed early and under budget ≥20%; 3 = ≥15%; 2 = 10% return on investment; 1 = <11% return on investment.
   B. 50%: 4 = approved by project initiator and/or project sponsor early and under budget ≥10%; 3 = approved early and under budget ≥5%; 2 = approved on time and on budget; 1 = approved late and/or over budget.
III. Performance Scorecard
IV. Performance Factors
   A. Project Initiator(s) — Reviews and/or approves assessment of PMO value proposition within delivery expectations for time and cost.
   B. Project Sponsor(s) — Reviews and/or approves assessment of PMO value proposition within delivery expectations for time and cost.
   C. Internal Auditor — Leads and/or performs PMO value proposition assessment within project team delivery expectations for time and cost.
V. Training Objectives
   A. Short Term — Project manager conducts meetings with project initiator, sponsor, and team member(s) on the creation and completion of the PMO value proposition assessment regarding what is involved and who is performing certain tasks within schedule expectations for performance.
   B. Long Term — Team members become trained in the process to develop and complete an assessment of the PMO value proposition as a means to improve total effort to complete task.

PROJECT FRAUD MANAGEMENT — FRAUD MANAGEMENT PLAN POLICY

Contains standard policy for project team application to prevent and detect project fraud during project life cycle.

I. Key Value Areas Weighting (%)
   A. Completion of process preparation and implementation of the fraud management plan policy = 50%.
   B. Approved by project initiator and/or project sponsor = 50%.
II. Performance Objectives — Based on all projects linked to specific corporate objectives.
   A. 50%: 4 = completed early and under budget ≥10%; 3 = ≥5%; 2 = completed on time and on budget; 1 = completed late and/or over budget.
   B. 50%: 4 = approved by project initiator and/or project sponsor early and under budget ≥10%; 3 = approved early and under budget ≥5%; 2 = approved on time and on budget; 1 = approved late and/or over budget.
III. Performance Scorecard

IV. Performance Factors
   A. Project Initiator(s) — Reviews and/or approves various versions of fraud management plan policy within delivery expectations for time and cost.
   B. Project Sponsor(s) — Reviews and/or approves various versions of fraud management plan policy within delivery expectations for time and cost.
   C. PMO Portfolio Manager — Leads and/or performs construction of fraud management plan policy within project team delivery expectations for time and cost.
V. Training Objectives
   A. Short Term — Project manager conducts meetings with project initiator, sponsor, and team member(s) on the creation and completion of the fraud management plan policy regarding what is involved and who is performing certain tasks within schedule expectations for performance.
   B. Long Term — Team members become trained in the process to develop and complete a fraud management plan policy as a means to improve total effort to complete task.

PROJECT FRAUD MANAGEMENT — PROJECT AUDITS

Ensures that all strategic projects are audited in a consistent manner during their life cycle to ensure proper controls are in place to ensure project success.

I. Key Value Areas Weighting (%)
   A. Completion of process preparation and implementation of the project audits = 50%.
   B. Approved by project initiator and/or project sponsor = 50%.
II. Performance Objectives — Based on all projects linked to specific corporate objectives.
   A. 50%: 4 = >95% of all active strategic projects; 3 = ≥90%; 2 = ≥80%; 1 = <80%.
   B. 50%: 4 = approved by project initiator and/or project sponsor early and under budget ≥10%; 3 = approved early and under budget ≥5%; 2 = approved on time and on budget; 1 = approved late and/or over budget.
III. Performance Scorecard
IV. Performance Factors
   A. Project Initiator(s) — Reviews and/or approves various project audits within delivery expectations for time and cost.
   B. Project Sponsor(s) — Reviews and/or approves various project audits within delivery expectations for time and cost.
   C. Project Manager — Leads and/or supports project audits within project team delivery expectations for time and cost.
V. Training Objectives
   A. Short Term — Project manager conducts meetings with project initiator, sponsor, and team member(s) on the creation and completion of project audits regarding what is involved and who is performing certain tasks within schedule expectations for performance.
   B. Long Term — Team members become trained in the process to develop and complete a project audit as a means to improve total effort to complete task.

PROJECT FRAUD MANAGEMENT — INTERNAL CONTROLS

Ensures that all strategic projects are practicing essential internal controls in a consistent manner during their life cycle to ensure project success.

I. Key Value Areas Weighting (%)
   A. Completion of process preparation and implementation of the internal controls = 50%.
   B. Approved by project initiator and/or project sponsor = 50%.
II. Performance Objectives — Based on all projects linked to specific corporate objectives.
   A. 50%: 4 = >95% of all active strategic projects; 3 = ≥90%; 2 = ≥80%; 1 = <80%.
   B. 50%: 4 = approved by project initiator and/or project sponsor early and under budget ≥10%; 3 = approved early and under budget ≥5%; 2 = approved on time and on budget; 1 = approved late and/or over budget.
III. Performance Scorecard
IV. Performance Factors
   A. Project Initiator(s) — Reviews and/or approves various project internal controls within delivery expectations for time and cost.
   B. Project Sponsor(s) — Reviews and/or approves various project internal controls within delivery expectations for time and cost.
   C. Project Manager — Leads and/or performs project internal controls within project team delivery expectations for time and cost.
V. Training Objectives
   A. Short Term — Project manager conducts meetings with project initiator, sponsor, and team member(s) on the creation and completion of project internal controls regarding what is involved and who is performing certain tasks within schedule expectations for performance.
   B. Long Term — Team members become trained in the process to develop and complete project internal controls as a means to improve total effort to complete task.

TOOLS — PROJECT MANAGEMENT TEMPLATES

Ensures that all strategic projects are utilizing PMO-supplied PMBOK® standard templates in a consistent manner during their life cycle to ensure project success.

I. Key Value Areas Weighting (%)
   A. Completion of process preparation and implementation of the project management templates = 50%.
   B. Approved by project initiator and/or project sponsor = 50%.
II. Performance Objectives — Based on all projects linked to specific corporate objectives.
   A. 50%: 4 = >95% of all active strategic projects; 3 = ≥90%; 2 = ≥80%; 1 = <80%.
   B. 50%: 4 = approved by project initiator and/or project sponsor early and under budget ≥10%; 3 = approved early and under budget ≥5%; 2 = approved on time and on budget; 1 = approved late and/or over budget.
III. Performance Scorecard

IV. Performance Factors
   A. Project Team Members — Help apply project management template plan by providing information relevant to areas of the project management plan within project team delivery expectations for time and cost.
   B. Project Manager — Leads and/or performs project management templates construction within project team delivery expectations for time and cost.
V. Training Objectives
   A. Short Term — Project manager conducts meetings with project initiator, sponsor, and team member(s) on the creation and completion of project management templates regarding what is involved and who is performing certain tasks within schedule expectations for performance.
   B. Long Term — Team members become trained in the process to develop and complete project management templates as a means to improve total effort to complete task.

TOOLS — PROJECT MANAGEMENT INFORMATION SYSTEMS

Enables a consistent and automated system for project information collection and reporting.

I. Key Value Areas Weighting (%)
   A. Completion of process preparation and implementation of the project management information system = 50%.
   B. Approved by project initiator and/or project sponsor = 50%.
II. Performance Objectives — Based on all projects linked to specific corporate objectives.
   A. 50%: 4 = >95% of all active strategic projects; 3 = ≥90%; 2 = ≥80%; 1 = <80%.
   B. 50%: 4 = projects approved by project initiator and/or project sponsor early and under budget ≥10%; 3 = ≥5%; 2 = projects approved on time and on budget; 1 = projects approved late and/or over budget.
III. Performance Scorecard
IV. Performance Factors
   A. Project Team Members — Help load project management information into system by providing information relevant to areas of the project management plan within project team delivery expectations for time and cost.
   B. Project Manager — Leads and/or performs project management information loading into system within project team delivery expectations for time and cost.
V. Training Objectives
   A. Short Term — Project manager conducts meetings with project initiator, sponsor, and team member(s) on the creation and completion of project management information system regarding what is involved and who is performing certain tasks within schedule expectations for performance.
   B. Long Term — Team members become trained in the process to develop and complete project management information system as a means to improve total effort to complete task.

PMBOK® — METHODOLOGY

Ensures that all strategic projects are utilizing Project Management Institute PMBOK® standards in project delivery in a consistent manner during their life cycle to ensure project success.

   I. Key Value Areas Weighting (%)
      A. Completion of process preparation and implementation of project management methodology = 50%.
      B. Approved by project initiator and/or project sponsor = 50%.
  II. Performance Objectives — Based on all projects linked to specific corporate objectives.
      A. 50%: 4 = >95% of all active strategic projects; 3 = ≥90%; 2 = ≥80%; 1 = <80%.
      B. 50%: 4 = approved by project initiator and/or project sponsor early and under budget ≥10%; 3 = approved early and under budget ≥5%; 2 = approved on time and on budget; 1 = approved late and/or over budget.
 III. Performance Scorecard
  IV. Performance Factors
      A. Project Team Members — Help apply PMBOK® methodology by providing information relevant to areas of the project management plan within project team delivery expectations for time and cost.
      B. Project Manager — Leads and/or performs PMBOK® methodology within project team delivery expectations for time and cost.
   V. Training Objectives
      A. Short Term — Project manager conducts meetings with project initiator, sponsor, and team member(s) on the creation and completion of PMBOK® methodology regarding what is involved and who is performing certain tasks within schedule expectations for performance.
      B. Long Term — Team members become trained in the process to develop and complete PMBOK® methodology standards as a means to improve total effort to complete task.

PMBOK® — TRAINING

Ensures that organizational resources have been trained in Project Management Institute PMBOK® standards relative to their work roles.

   I. Key Value Areas Weighting (%)
      A. Completion of process preparation and implementation of PMBOK® training = 50%.
      B. Approved by project initiator and/or project sponsor = 50%.
  II. Performance Objectives — Based on all projects linked to specific corporate objectives.
      A. 50%: 4 = >95% of all active strategic projects; 3 = ≥90%; 2 = ≥80%; 1 = <80%.
      B. 50%: 4 = approved by project initiator and/or project sponsor early and under budget ≥10%; 3 = approved early and under budget ≥5%; 2 = approved on time and on budget; 1 = approved late and/or over budget.

III. Performance Scorecard
IV. Performance Factors
   A. Project Team Members — Complete necessary training that applies PMBOK® methodology plan within project team delivery expectations for time and cost.
   B. Project Manager — Completes and/or supports PMBOK® training within project team delivery expectations for time and cost.
V. Training Objectives
   A. Short Term — Project manager conducts meetings with project initiator, sponsor, and team member(s) on the creation and completion of PMBOK® training regarding what is involved and who is performing certain tasks within schedule expectations for performance.
   B. Long Term — Team members become trained in PMBOK® methods.

SUMMARY

The PMO has shown that it can leverage organizational value found in projects to other projects in a manner that leads to accelerated transformation. Important to the value is the recognition that holistic measures are required to make the connection between opportunity or threat and projects, corporate objectives, assets, resources, or internal controls. Uniformity is required in applying project management best practices; otherwise, project teams will think and work in different languages and processes. A critical component of this is the creation of the PMO value proposition, which in itself must be measurable. It is our hope and prayer that we have assisted you in beginning to bring out this value to your business. The real value of project management is out there just for the taking. Your PMO must be diligent in its search to acquire this value.

QUESTIONS

27-1. Portfolio management identifies high-value strategic entities in an aggregated collection that can be assessed collectively for delivery optimization within a specific time period. True or false?

27-2. Which of the following outputs of portfolio management are not PMO related:
   a. Project portfolio
   b. Resource portfolio
   c. Internal control portfolio
   d. Executive portfolio

27-3. Corporate governance reporting identifies cyclical progress to date while forecasting future progress, opportunities, and threats for projects of strategic value. True or false?

27-4. Project fraud management enables appropriate internal controls for the project management community that are applied in a consistent and uniform manner. True or false?

27-5. Which of the following are not outputs of project fraud management:
   a. Fraud management plan policy
   b. Project audits
   c. Internal controls
   d. Project management templates

27-6. The project portfolio contains all strategic project initiatives, force ranked in strategic value order. Each initiative is identified by sponsoring business unit, current health status, budget and actual total expenditures, sponsor, project manager, and start and end dates. True or false?

27-7. The internal controls portfolio contains all material internal controls, force ranked in strategic value order. Each internal control is identified by sponsoring business unit, percentage of materiality relative to general ledger account, current status, sponsor, start and end dates per project initiative, and associated project manager. True or false?

27-8. The fraud management plan policy contains standard policy for project team application to prevent and detect project fraud during the project life cycle. True or false?

27-9. The project audit process ensures that all strategic projects are audited in a consistent manner during their life cycle to ensure proper controls are in place to ensure project success. True or false?

27-10. The project management information systems process enables a consistent and automated system for project information collection and reporting. True or false?

This book has free materials available for download from the
Web Added Value™ Resource Center at www.jrosspub.com.

PART IV:
REALIZING THE VALUE PROPOSITION OF AN IMPLEMENTED MEASUREMENT PROGRAM FOR YOUR ORGANIZATION

28

METRICS MATURITY MODEL

Many businesses today continue to struggle with the measurement process of delivery value. Businesses are projects too. They need to understand how they are performing. Much of the confusion is due to the lack of a well-defined measurable value model that should have been well thought out in the beginning of the business development.

In this chapter, we will focus on measuring the business value and how to measure using a reasonable and easy-to-apply metrics maturity model.

ASSESSING THE METRICS MATURITY LEVEL

The metrics maturity model (Table 28-1) is comprised of eight levels of maturity and is measured across nine knowledge areas of the Project Management Body of Knowledge (PMBOK®) defined by the Project Management Institute. In applying the metrics maturity model, a business must clearly identify the most strategic initiatives that are scheduled to reach completion in the next 12 months. This excludes any canceled projects. Each of these strategic projects is then reviewed for how well it complied with the specifications assigned to each project management knowledge area within the maturity level under assessment.

The delivery speed of each of the strategic projects is also assessed in the same manner as *high, medium,* or *low*. If a project completed (deployed) ahead of schedule by more than two calendar weeks, then this project should be rated as high in delivery speed. If a project completed (deployed) behind schedule by more than two calendar weeks, then this project should be rated as low. Projects that fall in between should be rated as medium. The final scope of the delivered project is not measured against the initial scope of the project, as the final project delivery speed assessment implicates scope delivery quality or the lack thereof. This perspective is protective

Table 28-1. 3Ms Metrics Maturity Model

	Level I: Defining Value	Level II: Metrics Organized	Level III: Searching for Delivery Value
Scope management	Poor definition of in-scope or out-of-scope items	Scope statement developed by supply-side project manager	Defined project requirements for in-scope and out-of-scope items
Time management	Project teams are siloed, not aware of team member utilization	Project managers understand their work order position among all strategic projects	Project managers are using PMO for information source for delivery acceleration opportunities and/or delivery delay threats among strategic projects
Resource management	Resources are sought as tasks begin, and projects start late	Resource portfolio established	Resource utilization rates known for planned, estimate to complete, and actual for 80% of delivery resources
Communications management	Standard reporting process for project delivery status is not implemented	Periodic status meetings; reports as requested by management	Regular project manager community status meetings to raise delivery visibility
Risk management	Risks not considered outside of project manager's informal thought process	Top risks for active projects have been identified	Top project delivery opportunities and delivery threats are known
Quality management	Project teams do not understand who their customers are	PMO mentors are available to help project managers with delivery questions	Project team members are focused on helping each other achieve their project objectives
Cost management	Costs not estimated or tracked; project manager does not receive project reports	Project portfolio budget tracked for fiscal year	Project fiscal health is tracked monthly; total project portfolio cost; costs relative to plan are known throughout the fiscal year
Procurement management	Contracts reviewed and signed by legal staff	Vendors/contractors are managed to end dates only	Subcontractors establish interim milestones and report if they are not met
Project integration	Project manager not involved in project definition	Projects managed on milestone reporting	Project manager assigned early in project identification process

Metrics Maturity Model

	Level IV: Metrics Maturity Achieved	Level V: Community Buy-in Established	Level VI: Project Teams Delivering on Schedule 95%
Scope management	Project scope dependencies with other projects are understood	Executive buy-in and project management community buy-in exist	Projects are completing on schedule most of the time
Time management	All important projects are being tracked; all delivery resources utilization rates are tracked; all assets are known	Governance board is operational and responsible for project portfolio delivery results	Some projects are completing early
Resource management	Resource portfolio applied to plan project delivery dates	Resource labor is electronically entered by resource	Resource assignments are calibrated to project portfolio through resource portfolio
Communications management	Project managers understand the status of other projects in the portfolio and how they relate to their projects	Operational status is published to corporate governance board from the PMO	Operation status reports reflecting delivery results
Risk management	Contingency plans are developed for risks which can be mitigated	Risk management is normal part of status reporting	Project teams are seizing delivery opportunities
Quality management	Project managers know who their interproject customers are	Metrics are established that focus on project delivery benchmarks	Metrics are collected and analyzed on load leveling, skill impacts, etc.
Cost management	Project managers are accountable for meeting project budget	Project vendors understand their impact on project objectives	Project teams are managing their project budget within 10% of budget plan
Procurement management	Contract changes are managed and controlled by project team manager	Project partnering is a normal part of doing business	Subcontractors manage projects using same system as company
Project integration	Procedures developed to manage changes and track performance against planned	Increased number of PMP®; a PMIS is being used throughout life cycle	Planning process always balances scope, schedule, and resources

Table 28-1. 3Ms Metrics Maturity Model (continued)

	Level VII: Project Teams Calibrated with Portfolios, More Projects in Fiscal Year	Level VIII: Organization Delivering
Scope management	Project teams are using their delivery knowledge of their environment to meet scope requirements	All strategic objectives of the organization are achieved in the fiscal year
Time management	Everyone understands their workload and how it relates to order of work	Worst case is projects are completing on time; 10% of projects are completing early
Resource management	Team-based performance process has been implemented	Resource utilization rates are optimized
Communications management	Resource utilization rates are improving and in alignment with project portfolios	Communications reflect fiscal year strategic plan to key stakeholders
Risk management	Project delivery schedule changes based on impact of delivery efforts of other projects	Project teams are able to take advantage of delivery opportunities while avoiding delivery threats
Quality management	Metrics are used to predict delivery acceleration opportunities and/or delivery threats	Delivery organizations strive to improve their processes and metrics, searching for improved project delivery techniques
Cost management	Actual costs of the project portfolio managed through governance board of the project portfolio	Governance board actively reallocates excess project budget to other project work
Procurement management	Business partners are integrated into project planning process and use corporate procedures	Vendors/contractors cannot be differentiated from corporate staff
Project integration	Project selection is a formal process, adhered to by all business leaders	Project management maturity is integrated with all other business processes and is continually reviewed for improvement

from other negative influences because of the visibility of the strategic projects within the business. The delivery speed for each project is summarized and averaged into a final *metrics maturity level* rating of high, medium, or low.

The review process should also assign a high, medium, or low rating for each knowledge area per project. As each project is assessed against the nine knowledge areas, the overall assessment knowledge area for each project is derived as the overall *metrics maturity level*. This value should equal the summation of the knowledge area ratings from each project by knowledge area, and then the summations are averaged to derive the overall knowledge area rating. Thus, if scope management was rated medium for a series of strategic projects, then the rating for those strategic projects in scope management should be medium. In this manner, the remaining eight knowledge areas should be measured similarly.

Thus, if the summarized knowledge areas for the strategic projects are rated high in three knowledge areas, medium in three knowledge areas, and low in the three other knowledge areas, and the averaged metrics maturity level is correspondingly supportive (i.e., Levels IV to VI should not have a low metrics maturity level), then this should be minimally sufficient to enable the metrics maturity level for the business to be assessed at the next higher level for the past 12 months.

Overall assessments that fall below the overall medium rating for five or more knowledge areas indicate that the overall metrics maturity level has declined (once the business has achieved Level II). Also, metrics maturity levels that are assessed at Level VI and higher should not have a metrics maturity level that is less than high; otherwise the metrics maturity is less than Level VI. The same is similarly true for metrics maturity levels that are assessed at Level IV and V; they should not have a project delivery maturity level that is less than medium; otherwise the metrics maturity level would be less than Level IV.

Consistency in how metrics maturity is measured from year to year is dependent upon the acceptance of the criteria requirements from each of the PMBOK® knowledge areas. Normally, the criteria in these areas of knowledge will not change over time.

Measuring metrics maturity is straightforward and easy to apply. This process should be conducted at least once every reporting cycle (monthly) by the Project Management Office (PMO). The PMO can certainly help itself by making this information available to the project management community and to corporate governance so that the project teams can understand what is necessary and sufficient relative to project delivery expectations.

Levels of PMO Maturity

- Level I: Defining value
- Level II: Metrics organized
- Level III: Searching for delivery value
- Level IV: Metrics maturity achieved
- Level V: Community buy-in established

- Level VI: Project teams delivering on schedule 95% or more
- Level VII: Project teams calibrated with portfolios, more projects in fiscal year
- Level VIII: Organization delivering

Knowledge Areas of the PMBOK®
- Scope management
- Time management
- Resource management
- Communications management
- Risk management
- Quality management
- Cost management
- Procurement management
- Project integration

METRICS MATURITY MODEL OVERVIEW

Level I: Defining Value

In this stage, the organization is identifying what the current situation is as it begins to develop the metrics maturity value proposition. Common characteristics include the following: Poor definition of in-scope or out-of-scope items. Project teams are in silos and not aware of team member utilization rates and trends. Resources are allowed to work at their own pace. Resources are sought as tasks begin instead of being preplanned. Projects start late, and most finish late because of the late start. Project and resource managers are constantly fighting over resources, not fully comprehending which project is more critical to the business. Standard reporting processes for project delivery status are not implemented. Risks are not considered outside of the project manager's informal thought process because project managers are so isolated from availability of external project information. Project teams do not understand their customers' needs and do not understand who their customers are and in what circumstances customer status changes. Project costs are not estimated or tracked. Project managers do not give or receive project reports. Vendors and contractors are not considered part of the project team. No standard project definitions, terminology, scheduling, or methodology are used.

How to Move to Level II

Focus on the behavior needed to effect work expectations at the project team level. Build and implement 3Ms metrics profiles that measure this behavior each reporting cycle. Key result information will germinate the motivation needed to cause others to pick up the pace and focus their work on tasks that move the critical path for key projects along at an incremental delivery rate. Project teams must bring consistency to project status reporting that best reflects delivery progress to date. Begin a public relations campaign from within the PMO that places focus on the fiscal year strategic objectives in relation to where each project primarily supports and is mapped to. The PMO should begin identifying predecessors and successors within the project portfolio for all to see and understand. In this manner, additional 3Ms metrics profiles can be implemented that focus on weak spots in project delivery speed. Organize the project management community into regular portfolio review meetings to review these holistic and aggregated 3Ms metrics results.

Pitfalls to Avoid

Stay away from anything that gives the perception that the PMO is too authoritative. The PMO should be selling itself as consultative/facilitative and there to assist the project manager and project team to be successful. The PMO should never force the issue at this point to gain compliance. Use the group peer pressure techniques in a positive manner to effect the information required.

Level II: Metrics Organized

Level II initially focuses on identifying the "as is" of project delivery. Common characteristics include the following: Scope statement is developed by supply-side project manager, often with IT emphasis. Business partner participation is very limited and weak. Functional requirements are poor and not aligned with value to the business. Project managers understand their project's position among all strategic projects at a high level of understanding but do not have sufficient information to anticipate external dependencies with other projects. A high-level resource portfolio is established but normally is not aligned to the force rank order of strategic projects as determined by the business partners. Project team member work assignments are not sufficiently calibrated such that each resource can predict future workload beyond two calendar weeks with a high degree of certainty. Periodic status meetings are just that — periodic.

Top risks for major projects have been identified and are known by the PMO. PMO mentors are available to help project managers determine customer needs and are assigned to the most important strategic projects as project management subject matter experts. The project portfolio budget has been identified for the fiscal year at the project level and baselined. Vendors/contractors are managed to end dates only by project managers. Projects are managed on milestone reporting, and predecessor/successor dependencies are not well known. Many project tasks operate in a serial finish-to-start relationship that is leaving delivery speed opportunity on the floor.

How to Move to the Next Level

Project status reports and project schedules are consistent with business-side initiatives and expectations. The PMO must focus on leveling this process so the business side can contribute. The project manager should be acquiring the client signature for each status report provided. This will force accountability and improve basic internal controls for communication in a closed-loop manner. All strategic objectives should be assigned to a senior executive for strategic and tactical accountability for delivery.

Pitfalls to Avoid

The PMO should begin to receive notice from the business side at this level. Portfolio reporting should bring more visibility to strategic objective run rates to date and related accomplishments so bottlenecks will be identified by people who are more aware.

Level III: Searching for Delivery Value

Level III brings awareness of the potential for project delivery speed improvements. Common characteristics include the following: Functional requirements are better defined and easily translated for development purposes. In-scope and out-of-scope items are identified and planned for. Project work delays that cause rework are documented. Project managers are using the PMO as an information source to learn and develop their own project-level strategy for project delivery acceleration opportunities and/or delivery delay threat avoidance. Resource utilization rates are known for planned, estimate to complete, and actual for 80% of resources for more than 30 calendar days in the future. Strategic resource(s) is identified. 3Ms metrics profiles deemed essential are implemented at all levels of the organizations and related to delivery speed and achievement of the strategic objectives.

Regular project manager community status meetings are normal to raise delivery visibility within the group. The top project delivery acceleration opportunities and delivery threats are known within the project management community at the project manager level for key strategic projects. Project team members are focused on meeting customer needs that affect organization goals. The workforce is aware of the business fiscal year strategic objectives and the primary relationship of the strategic projects to a primary strategic objective. Project financials (plan versus actual) are tracked monthly at the project level by the project team. Total project portfolio baseline and fiscal-year-to-date run rate costs are available. The overall fiscal health of the project portfolio is known to date by the project manager community. Contractors are reporting progress cyclically to the project teams. Earlier delivery is beginning to occur for critical path projects within specific strategic objective portfolios. Project management delivery metrics are inducing project teams to accelerate while avoiding project work delay. Project team members are learning and developing their new attitudes in considering their personal work delivery speed and attempting to stay off the critical path of the project they are working on.

How to Move to the Next Level

Implement 3Ms metrics profiles for asset, strategic, and resource portfolio management and use these tools to help balance overall portfolio management. Force rank these portfolios by business value now and expected by end of the fiscal year.

Organize all strategic projects by their primary strategic objective and identify visible bottlenecks, positive and negative. Identify and establish interdependent relationships among projects so that opportunities and threats can be seen easily by the organization.

Pitfalls to Avoid

Don't worry too much about becoming perfect in collecting project cost data. Use the 80/20 rule for tolerance when calculating project resource costs. Use standard labor resource rates that include overhead when calculating estimate to complete effort and related estimates. Using a common denominator in all cost projections will enable management decision making to cycle in shorter intervals.

Level IV: Metrics Maturity Achieved

Level IV brings more focus on saving delivery time while searching for delivery issues that are in the distance. Common characteristics include the following: Scope interdependencies between projects are understood between project managers so that when the lead project accelerates in delivery, the other dependent projects can as well. All important projects are being tracked within the project portfolio. Projected scheduling delays are identified, and projects are reranked within the project portfolio strategically. The resource portfolio is applied to help plan project delivery dates. Resource portability is beginning to emerge as a key cost PMO value point. Resource labor by project is electronically entered by resource within tolerance by reporting period. Project managers understand the status of other projects in the portfolio and how they relate to their projects. Project team calibration is more enhanced and predictive in status reporting. The project portfolio and related project artifacts and information are available to project managers online. Contingency plans include consideration for external projects and are developed for project risks which can be mitigated. Project managers know the impact of their project on the end customer and the market and have improved vision in predicting project delivery achievement throughout the life cycle. Project managers understand how project acceleration and delay can impact the budget and the aggregate portfolio management processes and take responsibility for it for their project's impact on the total fiscal year work plan relative to related projects. Problem vendors/contractors across projects are identified and dealt with through implemented 3Ms metrics profiles that detect them. Procedures are developed to manage interproject changes, particularly in force ranking, tracking performance against plan, and reporting on all projects, affected assets, and strategic objective compliance within the portfolios.

How to Move to the Next Level

Project mentoring is in full swing for all key strategic projects. The PMO mentors are instructed to coach team member cognitive skills and techniques to assist teams in developing faster delivery solutions ahead of delivery expectations. The PMO drives the quality of delivery data through the portfolio processes in a manner that begins to identify real business growth in the form of less realized project costs. Project sponsor training is being provided. All business units are applying a universal prioritization model against all organization portfolios and are aligned to best strategic value.

Pitfalls to Avoid

Focus on top project risks. The PMO should deal with the critical path items identified in each of the portfolios and work to reduce their potential effect. Improving trend lines in project status health are emerging. The PMO should give more attention to supporting troubled projects and improving delivery prediction visibility through the portfolios. 3Ms metrics profiles are created to uncover opportunity and threat holistically in the organization derived from aggregated status reporting.

Level V: Community Buy-in Established

A change in workforce attitude has emerged within the culture. Project teams have an air about them that is fostering positive events. Common characteristics include the following: Executive buy-in and project management community buy-in exist for combined scope of all projects for the planned fiscal year. Force-ranked project calibration of the workforce is understood and accepted. The governance board is operational and responsible for portfolio delivery results and order. Some projects are deactivated because they are no longer viable. Projects are staggered according to availability of strategic resource(s). The entire customer community is educated about the strategic resource and does its best not to waste it. Operations plans are published to the governance board from the PMO. Sponsors, teams, functional executives, and other stakeholders have accurate delivery information that they need regarding status, acceleration opportunities, and delivery threats. Risk management is a normal part of status reporting at the project level. Risk mitigation is supported by the governance board, sponsors, and functional management. Project management metrics are established that support organizational goals. Boundaries between functional disciplines are torn down. Project vendors, team members, and functional executives understand their impact on project financial objectives. Vendors/contractors have incentives to seek delivery acceleration on critical items. There is an increased number of PMP®. A PMIS is being used throughout the project life cycle. The community is beginning to feel safe in reporting "bad" news, as problems are seen as opportunities to make a difference.

How to Move to the Next Level

Within the project management community meetings, the supply-side business units leadership meetings, and the governance board meetings, the PMO begins reporting new delivery accomplishments that are fostering business cost avoidance and early delivery news. The PMO should be measuring in six-month increments its fiscal value to the business it serves and be able to plan PMO-based action derived from these results for the next six months.

Pitfalls to Avoid

The PMO should be aware that everyone will not be successful. The behavioral processes implemented to date will raise the cloak of cover for poor performers wherever they may be. The PMO can help project managers deal with this dysfunction through mentoring and through standardizing project status reporting and status meetings. As this level of maturity is achieved, poor performance will surface. The project managers must be ready to act in a constructive manner to keep their initiative on track.

Level VI: Project Teams Delivering on Schedule 95% or More

Level VI brings about improved vision in project delivery predictability. Common characteristics include the following: Projects are completing within scope 95% of the time. Some projects are completing early. Resource assignments are calibrated to the project portfolio through the resource portfolio. Resource needs are manageable without excessive peaks and valleys, across all disciplines. Business partners are actively engaged tactically through their delegates at the project level. All project managers and teams have information in time to take preventative action on project threats and to take advantage of acceleration opportunities. Project teams are seizing delivery opportunities and have become adaptive in their attitude toward acceleration of project work. Quality issues preventing on-time delivery are documented and being addressed. Project teams are collectively managing their project budget within 10% of budget plan. Subcontractors manage projects using the same system as the company. The planning process always balances scope, schedule, and resources without overloading the system.

How to Move to the Next Level

PMIS tools are well utilized. Workers can see at a glance where their time must be applied, now and later. Management has begun to align the business with confidence on project estimates based on recent delivery successes. Project communication is taking place more and more offline as people realize that the need for urgency is related to staying informed about project opportunities and threats. People are no longer waiting to discuss project information at status meetings and thereby delaying action. The PMO continues to implement 3Ms metrics profiles that identify holistic opportunities for project delivery to improve further.

Pitfalls to Avoid

The PMO should be recognizing delivery successes everywhere as more and more success occurs. There should be more focus on people delivering great work to continue the drive to send the correct message back to the workforce. The worst thing the PMO can do at this level is not campaign for project delivery demonstrated brilliance. Evidence should be present from the workforce in terms of job satisfaction as demonstrated by performance.

Level VII: Project Teams Calibrated with Portfolios, More Projects in Fiscal Year

In Level VII, the business begins to see quantifiable payback in terms of unexpected budget money left over from projects completed earlier than expected. Common characteristics include the following: Project teams are using their delivery knowledge of scope interdependencies between projects to meet or optimize scope requirements ahead of planned delivery schedule. Everyone understands their workload and how it relates to project priorities. Strategic resources are no longer causing project delays. A team-based performance process has been implemented. All resources look for acceleration opportunities and threats in project work assignments. Resource utilization rates are improving and in alignment with the portfolios. Bad multitasking is visibly reduced. Portfolios are integrated to allow changes in one project or resource area to be proactively addressed when they impact other projects, resources, assets, and strategic objectives. Metrics, procedures, and training are used to raise visibility of delivery acceleration opportunities and to decrease delivery threats. The governance board is taking a global view of all portfolio costs. The governance board is balancing the portfolios by investing more in marketing and in strategic assets. The supply-side business leaders are becoming more aligned within their skill set and less directive in project selection. Business-side leaders are taking more responsibility for project delivery speed and work within the governance board to communicate opportunity and threats. Vendors are integrated into the project planning process and use the same procedures and methodology. Project selection is a formal process performed at speed. This process is adhered to and respected by all functional leaders and has become a "way of life." The governance board demands and supports project management methodology from all functional areas.

How to Move to the Next Level

Quantifiable return on investment is found in project delivery, resource utilization improvements, the order of asset improvement, and strategic objectives balanced with all portfolios. Resource portability is in full swing. The cost to do business in new development has decreased proportionately to the planned work for the fiscal year.

Pitfalls to Avoid

The work environment should be as safe as it can be to report bad news. The PMO should continue to find ways to improve the culture and to prevent a return to the carnivorous work culture. Implementing 3Ms metrics profiles that focus on predicting bad news so that trending analysis can be performed can lessen the impact of bad news.

Level VIII: Organization Delivering

Level VIII is nirvana for the organization and the project teams. By this time, there is no question about the value of project management to the business and to each individual in the workforce. Common characteristics include the following: All strategic objectives of the organization are achieved in the fiscal year. Over 95% of projects are completing on, and 10% or better of projects are completing early. Resource utilization rates are stable, yet improving in productivity. The organization is delivering more projects without the need to add resources. Every stakeholder understands and supports the connections between organization goals, projects, resources, and assets and understands performance standards. Suggestions for acceleration and better project mix are offered without solicitation The combined portfolios are balanced so that even several disasters do not affect meeting organization goals. A process of ongoing improvement is in place, with statistical controls and identification of biggest leverage points for improved quality. The governance board actively reallocates excess project budget to other project work. Vendors/contractors cannot be differentiated from organization staff.

Project management metrics maturity is integrated with all other processes and is continually reviewed for improvement. Metrics maturity is enabling more than 10% return on investment compared to baselined fiscal year work plan budget for the delivery of strategic initiatives compared to actuals.

Pitfalls to Avoid

Most PMOs are funded to a 50 to 80% level of what they actually need to operate. PMOs need to research methods to achieve problem resolution in terms of timeliness that will continue to enhance their demonstrated value to the business. Identifying and establishing key vendor support agreements over two- to three-year periods is essential to the lifeblood of the PMO.

WHERE IS YOUR BUSINESS IN THE METRICS MATURITY MODEL?

In this chapter, we reviewed the metrics maturity model and what should normally occur. Consider the resources and assets available to the business, and use this information to craft the metrics maturity improvement plan. If you are just beginning, consider organizing an approach in six-month increments that can be measured every month. The key to metric success is not how well the business defines process but how safe people feel in using metrics. When implemented, the 3Ms metrics profile can drive human behavior in the direction you want.

SUMMARY

The metrics maturity model will support for-profit and nonprofit entities alike. This point remains clear for all businesses. We have provided a metrics maturity approach that will help the business leadership sleep at night. More importantly, following this model will help project managers find new friends and help projects find new value. The only question now is what the sense of urgency is for everyone. What are the performance standards for moving up the ladder in your organization's maturity model? What is satisfactory performance?

QUESTIONS

28-1. Discuss the metrics maturity model and its overall value to a business.
28-2. Explain which is more important, the measuring process on the project or the measuring process on the organization.
28-3. The metrics maturity model is comprised of eight levels of maturity and is measured across nine knowledge areas of the PMBOK® defined by the Project Management Institute. True or false?
28-4. Level I of the metrics maturity model is the stage where the organization is identifying what the current situation is as it begins to develop the metrics maturity value proposition. True or false?
28-5. Explain Level I of the metrics maturity model and how a business would improve to Level II.
28-6. Discuss how to assess a metric maturity level.
28-7. Explain the consequences of a Level VI metrics maturity that has less than medium knowledge area ratings.
28-8. Where would a business seek to grow its return in investment value if it is at Level VIII? Discuss three to five possible opportunities and their value to a business.
28-9. Explain how important it is for a business to understand what is satisfactory performance for the workforce culture in all work tasks performed and why excellent performance on all tasks is not necessary to the business and can result in delay. List and explain the top three to five beneficiaries in order of value to the business for this concept.

This book has free materials available for download from the
Web Added Value™ Resource Center at www.jrosspub.com.

29

ROAD MAP SCHEDULE FOR IMPLEMENTING A 3MS METRICS PROGRAM

So far, we have presented the 3Ms methodology with rigorous procedures to define value of the project by way of creating key value areas (KVAs); how to prove that value was created by defining results in terms of objectives with metrics, weightings, and standards; and how the cumulative project objectives as calculated by a performance scorecard will show the total value that was delivered at the project level. Going up one level in the corporate hierarchy of objectives shows the cumulative value of all projects at the level of corporate objectives, or we could go down one level from the project level to the individual performance objectives and the performance scorecard of each team member. Regardless of whether you go up or down in the corporate hierarchy, 3Ms allows you to define value in precise quantitative and qualitative metrics, so at *any* level at *any* time for *any* reason you can get a snapshot or, if you prefer, a dashboard picture of progress for any reason.

What we have not done, as will be rigorously and clearly presented in this chapter, is give you a road map or step-by-step procedure for introducing the 3Ms. Regardless of how valuable we believe the 3Ms approach is, if it is not introduced properly and supported adequately, its introduction will be for naught. And like so many other valuable change management and continuous improvement initiatives, it too will fall by the wayside as a failure. The problem is that the 3Ms and the many other project management performance efforts failed because of the inadequate manner of their introduction that was later blamed on their intrinsic nature.

This chapter will detail the steps. Skip any step at your own risk. Every compromise of the steps, by skipping, shortening, or rushing, will add to the chance for failure. Realize also that the 3Ms will focus on metrics, leadership, commitment, and teamwork as they have never been looked at so thoroughly and systemically. 3Ms is not a workshop or a training program. It is a way of looking at the way you measure what you get paid to deliver, and it does so in a way that leaves no ambiguity regarding where efforts are being successful and who is accountable.

In Table 29-1, the steps are described as concrete actions to be taken by your 3Ms facilitator/trainer and your executives, project managers, and team. Follow the sequence of steps with the same sequence of populations, with the mastery of what has been presented to you, and with the approximate amount of time and the same timing, and you will have success with this program.

There are many ways to initiate a metrics project management program. It could be done as a mandate from a dictatorial figure proclaiming that from now on metrics will be the way all performance is baselined, managed, improved, and rewarded; there could be a consensus-building approach to try to get everyone in the project management community to buy-in to metrics; there could be a strictly educational approach where everyone attends classes on the 3Ms methodology; or there could be speeches and other means of persuasion that would tell everyone why metrics is good for them.

Essentially, the choices are broadly within the areas of power, education, and persuasion. Successful change efforts are those that employ the appropriate balance of all three. The newer discipline of organizational change management (OCM) combines all three in a very disciplined and sequential manner. It is about lining up the ducks in a particular way. This chapter will describe the sequence of steps that are a near guarantee of success.

HOW EFFECTIVE IS YOUR ORGANIZATION'S PROJECT METRICS SYSTEM?

Except for the examples in this book, the hierarchical alignment of metrics to support project management is a rarity. The following questionnaire, when filled out candidly by the executive level of any company, will clearly indicate to what degree the metrics do not exist or do exist and are not fully exploited as a project management tool at any level of the organization.

When these metrics are absent or not used, this only leads to a more challenging project management environment where project metrics, KVAs, and performance objectives will have no higher level objectives for alignment.

When the results of this survey show a weak use of metrics at the executive level, you can be sure that there will be a lot of conflict at the project management level. Fortunately, there are enough brilliant, passionate, committed project managers around who are able to make pretty good guesses about what their KVAs and performance objectives are, in spite of the ambiguity or absence of corporate objectives for project management alignment.

Table 29-1. Road Map for Implementing 3Ms Metrics Program

ID	Task Name
1	General work breakdown structure for implementing metrics at the organization level
2	Initiating phase
3	1st month
4	Conduct 1st metrics assessment to determine strengths and weaknesses of the program
5	Building a compelling case for change
6	One-on one interviews
7	Survey 20% of the workforce
8	Baseline current project management performance levels
9	Produce findings and recommendations presentation to sponsor
10	Obtain approval to proceed with selected recommendations
11	Determine value proposition for organization
12	Develop project charter
13	Obtain formal approval for project charter
14	Initiating phase complete for 3Ms implementation
15	Planning phase
16	2nd month
17	Develop project management plan
18	Obtain sponsor approval for project management plan
19	**Conduct workshop for project managers on 3Ms method and give out baseline data**
20	**1st workshop**
21	Review baseline organization data in workshop
22	Review baseline project delivery portfolio with project managers
23	Assess reasonability with project managers as a group
24	**Perform example exercise with group in constructing project profiles**
25	Review KVA development process
26	Review performance standard development process
27	Review reporting process to PMO
28	Assess process reasonability
29	Determine initial draft team member profiles related to defined metrics
30	**Perform workshop follow-up**
31	**Project manager meets with each team member to review team member metric**
32	Assess reasonability with each team member
33	**2nd workshop (3rd week)**
34	Review project 3Ms profiles with the project managers as a group
35	Review project portfolio critical path based on new project 3Ms profiles
36	Assess reasonability
37	Review project KVAs
38	Assess reasonability for organization
39	Construct 3Ms profile for organization rolled up from all reporting projects
40	Planning phase complete for project metrics implementation
41	Monitoring and controlling phase

Table 29-1. Road Map for Implementing 3Ms Metrics Program (continued)

ID	Task Name
42	**Executing phase**
43	**3rd month**
44	**Engaging the leaders at every level**
45	Identify strategic/tactical accountability at the executive level for each corporate goal
46	Hypothesize the improvements they want and why they would add value
47	Take data, conclusions, and recommendations to executives to formulate a picture of today's reality
48	**Winning the commitment of critical stakeholders**
49	Create focus groups to gauge readiness for, reaction to, and support of 3Ms metrics program
50	Develop communications strategy to keep executives and all stakeholders informed of areas of 3Ms
51	Training in 3Ms methodology starting at the top with the executive team
52	Create executive KVAs
53	With the executive leadership team, identify all variables that will help or hinder the achievement of a metrics program
54	**Designing 3Ms to deliver what is important**
55	3Ms organization profile is complete
56	3Ms corporate goal profiles are constructed
57	3Ms corporate objective profiles are constructed and ready to be implemented
58	3Ms team profiles are defined and ready to be implemented
59	Project portfolio approved with respect to 3Ms profiles
60	All team member 3Ms profiles are ready to be implemented for active projects
61	All corporate goal owners are in consensus with corporate goal 3Ms profiles
62	Planning phase complete for project metrics implementation
63	All corporate goal owners trained in 3Ms method
64	All corporate objective sponsors are trained in 3Ms method
65	All project managers trained in fiscal year 3Ms process and given baseline data to configure their projects
66	Conduct 2nd metrics assessment to determine strengths and weaknesses of the program
67	**Driving the program**
68	All project managers trained in fiscal year 3Ms process and given baseline data to configure their projects
69	**4th month**
70	Conduct 3Ms training of all project teams in 3Ms skills
71	With the next level down to the project teams, cascade the 3Ms downward
72	Conduct training in 3Ms methodology as applied to the variables identified by Measure
73	Group the variables identified in Manage into like functions — administrative, financial, etc.
74	Conduct team building to resolve or facilitate resolution of any conflict to accelerate the Manage phase of 3Ms

Table 29-1. Road Map for Implementing 3Ms Metrics Program (continued)

ID	Task Name
75	Conduct 2nd metrics assessment to determine strengths and weaknesses of the program
76	**5th month**
77	Revisit corporate goals and objectives and realign with project objectives
78	Apply specific consulting to areas of leadership, OCM, conflict resolution, the 3Ms
79	Focus on corporate culture change to institutionalize 3Ms linguistics and skills
80	**6th month**
81	Making 3Ms "our own," training of 3Ms champions and facilitators
82	Conduct 3rd metrics assessment to determine strengths and weaknesses of the program
83	Executing phase complete
84	**Closing phase**
85	Each corporate objective/corporate goal/organization 3Ms profile is assessed for performance
86	Project manager updates project book and provides final performance data to sponsor
87	Closing phase is complete
88	End of road map plan (from a 3Ms perspective)

Project Metrics System Questionnaire

Excellent = 4   Very Good = 3   Satisfactory = 2   Unsatisfactory = 1

1. **Quality of measurement system**: The extent to which the metrics are strategically linked and reflect the long- and short-term objectives of the organization
   a. There is strong agreement among the senior management team on measurable criteria for determining the success of project objectives _____
   b. Our leadership team has a set of scorecard measures that are tracked to provide feedback on project implementation _____
   c. Our top-level scorecard measures accurately reflect our project direction and objectives _____
2. **Balance**: The extent to which the coverage of the project measurement areas is adequate
   a. The measures we track reflect a good balance between desired results and the organizational drivers of those results _____
   b. The measures we track reflect a good balance between short- and long-term objectives _____

c. In which of the following areas are performance measures updated and reviewed by the top executive team at least semi-annually?
   Customers _____
   Human resource management _____
   Productivity and service quality _____
   Growth and innovation _____
   Financial performance _____
3. **Deployment**: The extent to which an effective process is used to effectively cascade measures throughout the organization
   a. The organizational strategy is well communicated and understood at all levels _____
   b. Specific project targets have been set for each of the scorecard measures of performance _____
   c. Subunits feel ownership of the measures in each performance area _____
4. **Alignment and embededness:** The extent to which the project measures are aligned with the performance and reward system in the organization
   a. Scorecard items are linked to important rewards _____
   b. Department performance measures are closely linked to strategic business unit measures _____
   c. Individual performance measures for team members are directly linked to unit and/or organizational project performance measures _____
   d. Senior management holds itself accountable for the overall scorecard results _____
5. **Continuous learning**: The extent to which the project measures are continually evaluated and updated
   a. Performance measures are updated and reviewed at least semi-annually _____
   b. The organization continuously evaluates and improves its measures and the methods used to collect project performance data _____
   c. Objectives of achievement are currently used to drive organizational change _____

Scoring Guide

- **>54+ points** — Your project measurement system is performing at a strong level (maximum = 76)
- **>36+ points** — Your project measurement system is effective in some areas, but not in others (maximum = 54)
- **<35 points** — Your project measurement system is not effective (maximum = 36)

A more general summary of the steps above is congruent with the OCM discipline. As we have said earlier, 3Ms is a profound and for some even life-changing exposure to a way of thinking about work, value, and money earned for producing certain results. For some, it can even be applied to the most intimate of relationships. Even when money is not part of the exchange, value is created by psychological rewards as in a romantic relationship. But even so, the value, the way it is created in measurable terms, the metrics, the weightings of each result, and the standards of performance are all equally rigorous, although seldom defined in a disciplined 3Ms way.

The OCM discipline has five major phases into which one could put all of the steps detailed above. Although different OCM models have different phases (from five to seven or eight), it is the steps that are all the same, regardless of how any model groups them into phases.

For our model, the five phases and the major steps that occur within each are:

Phase 1 **Building a compelling case for change** — Driven by the business strategy and with a sound financial rationale
    a. Metrics assessment
    b. Preparation of report
    c. Building executive support

Phase 2 **Engaging the leaders at every level** — Ensuring visible sponsorship and demonstrating commitment at the highest level
    a. Focus groups
    b. Surveys
    c. Presentation for feedback

Phase 3 **Winning the commitment of critical stakeholders** — Stakeholders need to be identified and rigorously managed
    a. Tailoring presentations for each group
    b. Focus groups for each stakeholder community
    c. Managed communication that is visible, frequent, and honest

Phase 4 **Designing 3Ms to deliver what is important** — Understanding what the business wants to achieve
    a. Getting the expertise on board
    b. Creating the mechanisms for monitoring progress
    c. Frequent line of sight toward the corporate objectives

Phase 5 **Driving the program** — Designing and driving the program ruthlessly to deliver the required business outcomes
    a. Early message that this is a long-term commitment (three to five years)
    b. Renewing energy by touting the most successful outcomes
    c. Allocating sufficient resources to troublesome areas

SUMMARY

Like the many other organizational change methodologies (quality circles, organizational transformation, diversity, etc.), 3Ms can have an equally profound impact on how the business is run and the corporate culture. If 3Ms is not to be seen as a "flavor of the month," as has often been true of these other methodologies, the introduction and "selling" of the program must be methodical and strategic. This chapter described a meticulous step-by-step approach, so that your implementation of 3Ms will be successful. Though there will be times when you might want to skip a step, you will do so at your own peril. The projects can be grouped into project management phases aligned with the PMBOK® or grouped into phases aligned with the OCM approach. More critical than the grouping of steps into phases is that the steps be covered.

QUESTIONS

29-1. Corporate objectives represent the aggregation of what other kind of objectives?

29-2. The 3Ms approach is most likely to fail because of:
  a. Intrinsic weaknesses in the methodology
  b. Lack of visible corporate leadership
  c. It is too complicated
  d. Communication about the business case is weak

29-3. 3Ms allows for you to define value in precise qualitative and quantitative metrics. True or false?

29-4. Messages regarding 3Ms progress should be tailored to individual values of the project managers. True or false?

29-5. What is the first group to be trained in 3Ms techniques?

29-6. Of the three approaches to effecting large-scale organizational change, which is the most important:
  a. Education
  b. Persuasion
  c. Power
  d. All three in the appropriate proportion are critical

29-7. The final phase of the 3Ms implementation is when 3Ms thinking is part of the corporate culture. True or false?

29-8. The metrics assessment instrument has the following five categories of questions: quality of the measurement system, balance, deployment, alignment and embededness, and continuous learning. True or false?

29-9. Organizing the implementation steps into the correct phases is as important as the steps themselves. True or false?

29-10. Focus groups, surveys, and presentations to get stakeholder feedback are used in which of the following phases:
   a. Building a compelling case for change
   b. Engaging the leaders at every level
   c. Winning the commitment of critical stakeholders
   d. Designing the business to deliver what is important
   e. Driving the program

30

BUSINESS CASE FOR IMPLEMENTING A 3MS MEASUREMENT PROGRAM

The following information is a general proposal template for implementing the 3Ms methodology in your business. The assumption behind this proposal is that the sponsoring advocates have done their homework.

EXECUTIVE SUMMARY/COMMITMENT LETTER

This proposal addresses enterprise support needed to improve the return on investment in the projects activated to achieve the organization's goals. This is a $xx million opportunity for our organization. Getting the right projects completed far more quickly is key to meeting executive and stakeholder goals. This capability will be accomplished by deploying a 3Ms methodology through the Enterprise Program Management Office (EPMO) with the following key objectives:

1. **Produce an executive-sanctioned, prioritized, and time-based enterprise portfolio** — This portfolio would be governed and visibly supported by the executive team. It would be utilized by all project and resource managers to ensure that decisions are made and resources are allocated according to executive mandate. Data in this portfolio would emanate from all business units. All executives and managers would receive reports to guide decision making and actions from a common base of data.
2. **Implement 3Ms methodology for all employees to establish the standards for essential performance** — This process deployment would be governed by the EPMO across the organization in a uniform and consistent manner. All employees would be measured according to uniform perfor-

mance standards in alignment with business objectives governed through corporate governance.

3. **Build knowledge and skills to improve 3Ms performance** — The EPMO structure and executive support increase management's ability to meet executive goals through faster and more effective project execution. Managers will effectively utilize progress data within the portfolio and 3Ms process methods and EPMO tools to improve delivery performance and manage the constantly changing composition of project delivery expectations.
4. **Track, report, analyze, and improve project performance** — This step provides quick-starting measurement and process utilization to collect, track, and process improve and perform project management activities on key project investments while providing strategic and tactical progress data to all stakeholders.
5. **Replace deficient project management processes with standard and best practice tools, methods, and processes** — In order to drive best practices across the organization, and be able to share information meaningfully, the organization needs a common language and measurement methodology that can be applied holistically to the organization so that defects can be made visible for management action.
6. **Drive higher value from project management training and skills development** — This step improves project management delivery capability by measuring current skills of the project management community, analyzing the collected data, and creating effective project management training curricula that focus on improving key project management weaknesses.
7. **Implement workforce cognitive skills to acquire business value for the organization** — To obtain consistent, needed executive information on a timely basis, employees will need help with learning how to recognize potential value from measured applications provided through the 3Ms methodology. The EPMO help desk will help users with readily available documented procedures and support when required.

SECTION 1: BUSINESS CASE

Project Overview

Implement the 3Ms methodology to improve return on investment in the $xx million project portfolio by a minimum of xx%.

Background

The business is seeking to improve its capabilities to deliver projects that are strategic to the vitality of the business. The need for this improvement has been demonstrated by the following:

- Lack of capability across top strategic initiatives to effectively collaborate to avoid project delivery delays
- Frequent priority changes, with constant disruption across the organization
- Inability to complete sufficient projects to counter competitive and economic threats
- Constant schedule and cost overruns
- Low resource utilization rates associated with poor planning integration processes
- Project teams competing for same scarce resources without the realization of which project is truly vital to the business

Objectives

1. Deliver the capability to create a balanced employee performance scorecard that positions the executives best to meet the organization's goals
2. Put in place 3Ms methodology processes for managing projects and priorities in the projects and for data gathering, reporting, tracking, analyzing, and improvement
3. Improve delivery of project outputs in both speed and quality
4. Allow more projects to be completed with the same resources by improving organizational knowledge for capacity to do so
5. Provide the information needed to support excellent executive decision making in project delivery

Strategic Corporate Alignment

Internal perspective	Effective management of capital
Operational excellence	Improve organizational process productivity and leverage strategic technology capabilities
Learning and growth	Results-oriented leadership and decision making and communicate and share knowledge across the organization

Opportunity Type

Select the appropriate box to demonstrate the type of opportunity this project provides:

- ☒ Increased revenue
- ☒ Increased productivity
- ☒ Decreased cost
- ☒ Decreased risk
- ☐ Regulatory compliance
- ☐ Maintenance

SECTION 2: SCOPE

Project Scope

- Identify minimum data requirements for implementing 3Ms methodology
- Develop and document 3Ms methodology best practices, in an easily accessible web-based tool

- Determine minimum data requirements needed for the 3Ms methodology
- Gather, report, and analyze initial 3Ms methodology data
- Establish and facilitate first EPMO 3Ms meeting
- Deliver a library of easily accessible user guides for project managers, resource managers, team members, sponsors, and executives for 3Ms methodology
- Develop and implement processes to enable all project managers to deliver on holistic performance standards prescribed by 3Ms methodology
- Add/hire staff to take on roles that provide effective 3Ms methodology enterprise support
- Implement necessary training/education/development of the 3Ms methodology processes

Impact Analysis

See Table 30-1 for a description of the impact the 3Ms methodology will have on each stakeholder.

Critical Success Factors

- Executive and EPMO/Project Management Office (PMO) support across the organization
- 3Ms methodology project management training and skills development at every level of the organization
- Quality marketing of the 3Ms method, its tools, and support
- Effective 3Ms tool training
- Executive ownership of the 3Ms methodology process and standard

SECTION 3: APPROACH

Proposed Solution

A project team, consisting of five senior project managers, will assemble initial data and select and implement all initial 3Ms methodology tools and data structures. This will allow for the project team to focus in on the hard and soft tools needed to further develop project management delivery rigor and discipline throughout the organization.

Alternatives Considered

- Continue to manage projects as we do now (lack of common measure and procedures). This alternative was eliminated because the opportunity represents over $xx million to our organization's bottom line.
- Minimum infrastructure — Begin with one senior project manager, no formal process governance, and no tools. This alternative was eliminated because an optimistic estimate of the amount of work required is several person-years. Our organization cannot afford to wait that long for the results. Also,

Table 30-1. Impact of the 3Ms Methodology

Stakeholder	Impact
Executives including CEO, CIO, CFO	Executives will have a standard view of how their project capital and resources are measured against all strategic projects. This enables more informed decision making and what-if scenario planning. Executives will have improved information around the implications of timeline constraints and scope changes. All projects will be prioritized by the executives.
Project Management Office	Project Management Office will have access to 3Ms processes, a portfolio view of the collection of projects, and detailed analysis of how the project resources are performing.
Project managers	Improved project management competencies, standardized life cycle, planning and scheduling methodologies, help with resource issues, issue tracking, and collaboration will help reduce project overruns. Most project managers will need training to leverage the capabilities of 3Ms methods provided. Sponsor support will be significantly enhanced. Cross-functional executive support will be more visible.
Team members	Team members will be called on to help improve delivery. They will better understand the link between their work and the organization's goals through the 3Ms processes. Team members will not make decisions on task priorities. Cross-functional barriers between team members will be broken down to improve work flow and quality.
Resource managers	Project priorities will be clear. Conflicts between project and resource managers will be significantly reduced through the 3Ms methodology application.

three members of the executive committee were involved in the assessment of capital investment for tools. They concluded that such tools are 100% vital to improving competitive business advantage by linking project progress to the personal performance standard.

- Temporary infrastructure — Build a PMO and disband it once the initial objectives are accomplished. This alternative was eliminated because we believe that the PMO will prove that it will continue to provide outstanding return on investment from improvement in project execution resulting from the 3Ms application. In fact, this is one of the metrics that the executive team will use to continually evaluate overall 3Ms process performance.

Assumptions

1. Deficient project managers will need to attend 3Ms methodology concept course.

2. All project managers who are managing portfolio projects will buy-in to the 3Ms methodology project guidelines, including using a standard 3Ms methodology suite as the project management measurement tool.
3. All organization units will ultimately use the 3Ms methodology tool to report status of their top projects.
4. 3Ms method and other training will be provided for all employees at every level. Executives will be vocal and positive in support of this training.
5. 3Ms methodology tool functionality will drive all organizational processes.

Obstacles

- Finding qualified resources to support the 3Ms methodology project
- Defining the best way to incorporate 3Ms method into every functional unit's need without sacrificing the need for a common structure
- Buy-in of functional units to move their measurement approach to 3Ms methodology project management and utilization of the 3Ms tools made available

Stakeholder Expectations

See Table 30-2 for the expectations that each stakeholder group can enjoy.

Project Organization

An organization chart for the 3Ms project is provided in Appendix I (include chart for your organization). Core team members and time commitments are identified in the project resource plan in Appendix II (include list of team members and planned commitments).

Procurement Plan

Jane Smith and John Doe have been our primary negotiators from corporate purchasing. We have negotiated a purchase price for 3Ms software and have surrounding agreements for maintenance, training, and consulting. In addition, we have a master consulting agreement in place with [supplying company name] to provide implementation consulting, training development, and project manager mentoring. We continue to evaluate alternatives in acquiring implementation expertise from external providers as opportunities arise.

Communication Plan

Upon executive authorization, the team will:

- Develop a welcome packet for participants, including background, expectations, schedule, key contacts, overview of the 3Ms methodology processes, etc.
- Develop training materials and presentation for 3Ms training in the new tools, reporting, and delivery acceleration strategies

Table 30-2. Stakeholder Expectations

Stakeholder	Impact
Executives including CEO, CIO, CFO	Reports and views of project performance based on standard 3Ms measures will provide timely, accurate, and relevant information for improved cross-collaborative decision making and strategic objective realization.
Project Management Office	Improved ability to view project delivery performance, to further develop project managers' skill sets and the capability to leverage learning from past projects. Will also look for corporate support.
Project managers	More stable, more advanced measuring tools and processes to assist them in planning and actively managing their projects. They must be able to efficiently and effectively control their projects, while maintaining a collaborative environment. There will be much less resource contention.
Team members	An easier method of tracking their personal performance. There will be much less conflict between project work and operational duties. Opportunities to do more in value for the business will become observable for the team member.

- Conduct 3Ms training for pilot participants
- Provide weekly communications to pilot participants, including status, results, recommendations for improvement, and request for feedback
- Provide one-on-one 3Ms methodology mentoring to discuss experiences and concerns
- Provide 3Ms project status updates, portfolio analysis, and recommendations to executive management at critical junctures
- Hold regular meetings with participants to discuss experiences, concerns, and successes
- Provide a pilot summary report for all key audiences
- Create content for the EPMO website regarding the 3Ms methodology activities and project managers' testimonials as they use the 3Ms approach (including FAQs, issues, etc.)
- Adapt pilot 3Ms methodology welcome packet to meet the needs of each new group of users and distribute prior to communication
- Conduct 3Ms methodology awareness sessions during business unit rollouts
- Coordinate with business unit contacts to promote the 3Ms methodology within their business units
- Present 3Ms methodology results/findings and future outlook at a project management network meeting
- Provide a conclusive rollout summary to all key audiences at the end of the 3Ms methodology implementation

Change Control Plan

As potential changes to the project baselined scope, time, and budget are identified, they will be documented by the EPMO implementation manager, logged, distributed to the change control committee and core team, and reviewed weekly (unless urgent). For urgent change matters, an emergency teleconference or meeting will be convened. The change control committee consists of the EPMO director, CIO, and CEO.

The core team will first review changes and escalate questions and recommendations to the 3Ms methodology project executive sponsor and business unit contacts as appropriate. Once a change has been accepted or denied, the request resolution is documented and the appropriate project documents are also updated to reflect any changes. The EPMO implementation manager will be responsible for managing this process.

SECTION 4: RISK

Risk Identification Matrix

See Table 30-3 for a description of the key risks of this project and the approach that the 3Ms methodology implementation team is planning to take.

SECTION 5: COSTS AND BENEFITS
(SEE APPENDIX III FOR DETAILED COST-BENEFIT ANALYSIS)

Project Costs Breakdown

See Table 30-4 for the cost breakdown summary.

Project Resource Costs Summary for Executing/Controlling Phase

1. Project manager — Project executing/control phase 17 weeks, 100% (external) = $102,000
2. 3Ms strategist lead — Executing/controlling phase 17 weeks, 50% (internal) = $34,000
3. Project management integration project leads (2) — Executing/controlling phase 17 weeks, 50% each (internal) = $34,000 each
4. Training/education coordinator lead — Executing/controlling phase 17 weeks, 100% (external) = $74,800
5. PMO help desk lead — Executing/controlling phase 17 weeks, 50% (internal) = $34,000
6. 3Ms trainer/mentor — Executing/controlling phase 17 weeks, 100% (external) = $74,800
7. Facility, training, and equipment support — $100,000 (estimated)

Table 30-3. Risk Identification Matrix

Description of the Risk	Quantification of the Risk	Risk Response
May have difficulty acquiring the appropriate core team, business unit, and external consultant resources needed for the project Too much delay in acquiring or assigning resources could result in a delay in critical path activities	This is considered a high-impact risk	Work closely with resource manager to assess and respond to resource needs Identify staff needs as far in advance as possible to allow enough lead time for acquisition Keep sponsor updated on resource issues and escalate as needed
Project team needs to coordinate with multiple departments/business units, which could result in communication breakdowns and spreading core team support too thin during pilot and rollout There can also be the at risk that the 3Ms methods might not be in alignment with some existing functional unit processes	This is considered a high-probability and high-impact risk	Detailed marketing and communication plan for how to handle cross-functional unit communication Align core team members to focus some of their efforts on specific business units Investigate staffing a position to specifically work with business unit configurations and implementations
Lack of buy-in for the 3Ms methodology implementation project at the senior management level will reduce or eliminate the enterprise-level benefits being targeted to achieve from implementation Employees may also resist cultural changes that would result from tool implementation	This is considered a high-probability and high-impact risk	Leverage functional unit contacts to uncover concerns/issues and develop a plan to address those at the functional unit level Leverage executive owner and sponsor to uncover senior management concerns/issues and develop a buy-in presentation; do not proceed with implementation until majority executive team support has been secured Work with functional unit contacts to uncover cultural change issues and incorporate a plan to address those during the functional unit rollout

Project Benefits

See Table 30-5 for a project benefits summary. Benefits can be verified using the following measures.

Table 30-4. 3Ms Methodology Cost Summary

Cost Category	Costs			
	Year 1	Year 2	Year 3	Year 4
Project costs				
Internal resources	$136,000			
External resources	$251,000			
Equipment and software	$250,000			
Other project impacts (training)	$100,000			
Total project cash outlay	$737,000			
Ongoing costs				
Internal resources				
Equipment (maintenance)				
Total ongoing cash outlay				
Total costs	$737,000			

Table 30-5. 3Ms Methodology Benefits Summary

Benefit Category	Benefits			
	Year 1	Year 2	Year 3	Year 4
Tangibles				
Support the implementation of project management standards		$1,920,000	$1,920,000	$1,920,000
Identify project risks and (resource) constraints		$1,584,000	$1,584,000	$1,584,000
Development cost improvements for 60 projects		$7,500,000	$7,500,000	$7,500,000
Portfolio management		$12,000,000	$12,000,000	$12,000,000
Intangibles				
Total benefits		$23,004,000	$23,004,000	$23,004,000

Support the Implementation of Corporate Project Management Standards

According to the Gartner Group (August 1, 2000), projects that follow a standard life cycle are more often completed on time, on budget, and within scope.

Estimated savings:

    # of projects × # of people × average hourly rate × hours saved

Example:

20 projects × 10 people × $60/hour × 40 hours/week × 4 weeks = $1,920,000

This example assumes time to market will be reduced by four weeks for 20 projects. Of course, the additional revenue that can come from new products delivered to market more quickly can make these benefits pale by comparison.

Verification: Baseline scheduling and cost estimates along with scope definition will be tracked and reported on a monthly basis.

Identify Project Risks and (Resource) Constraints

EPMO tools (3Ms methodology) will require project managers to examine their projects for risks, dependencies, constraints, and impacts on the business. Using rigorous standards to move projects from the planning to execution phase will reduce organizational costs.

Estimated savings:

# of projects × # of people × hourly rate × hours

Example:

6 projects × 10 people × $60/hour × 40 hours/week × 11 weeks = $1,584,000

The Gartner Group estimates that proper risk identification will result in the cancellation of 20% of projects before the execution phase. In the example above, savings assumes six projects will be canceled before execution begins. The time savings are the average for the execution and subsequent phases.

The benefits are actually much greater than portrayed. These resources can be used to execute other projects, which bring far greater value than just the cost savings.

Verification: The EPMO will track the number of projects in the project portfolio that were canceled because of risk and impact on the organization.

Development Cost Improvement

By the end of 200X, the enterprise will go from tracking less than half of the portfolio projects to more than 75%. Payback will occur from having better information to make decisions on the deployment and use of resources and capital. In addition, the significant increase in visibility, cross-functional executive support, and tracking of these projects will enable delivery of the portfolio of projects.

Estimated savings:

Average aggregated budget of (60 active) projects
in portfolio annualized = $150,000,000

5% annual delivery improvement in time and budget
for projects in the portfolio = $7,500,000

Verification: The executive team will recognize delivery improvements as reported in the EPMO portfolio reports. These reports will illustrate comparable differences between baseline delivery forecasts and current progress at a summary level to enable management decision action.

Portfolio Prioritization

The portfolio along with the EPMO phase review will answer the question: "Where do high-priority projects stand?" According to the Gartner Group, "Project delivery rates directly impact customer satisfaction, IT's value to the business, the enterprise's competitive edge, market share and profitability. A project portfolio management capability includes a set of organization-specific metrics pertinent to project delivery."

Estimated savings:

>   Elimination of 10 projects, at an average cost of $1,200,000
>   or annualized for a total expected savings of $12,000,000

This assumes that the project portfolio along with the EPMO phase review process assists management in making the decision not to implement a portfolio project based on organizational priorities.

Verification: The EPMO will use the 3Ms methodology with the portfolio management process to review and identify the number of projects that actively follow the life cycle and use the project control tools in the everyday management of the projects.

SECTION 5: TIMELINE

Project delivery timeline summary:

1. Project planning phase completed by 6/3/200X
2. Project executing/controlling phase completed by 11/6/200X
3. Project closing phase commenced by 12/3/200X
4. Project completed by 12/31/200X

SUMMARY

The business case for implementing the 3Ms methodology should define the benefits, time, costs, and feature functionality. Once the costs have been identified, the summary cost of the implementation effort (that includes operation expenses for the remainder of the fiscal year) becomes the baseline number against which the 3Ms methodology will be evaluated for value added to the organization.

QUESTIONS

30-1. Explain how the 3Ms methodology might bring financial value to any organization.

30-2. The executive proposal makes assumptions about why and how the 3Ms methodology expected benefits would occur. How could you substantiate those assumptions in a real organization?

This book has free materials available for download from the Web Added Value™ Resource Center at www.jrosspub.com.

31

SUMMARY

GAINING COMPETITIVE ADVANTAGE

There are many ways to compete in the global marketplace. If your competitors are able to produce the same product at a cheaper cost and/or price, you are likely to lose the market share you have unless you become better at what you do in spite of your higher unit costs.

Clearly, the gains to be realized from implementing a 3Ms methodology in your business are more than just minimal. They are *huge*! Why aren't more businesses realizing this? The answer is very simple. Traditionally, businesses have solved their problems by purchasing tool solutions instead of improving the human capital to perform the task. This is the result of "transactional management," where every management decision is treated as if it can be resolved in its finite self and that's it. The problem with this approach is that the associated gain in value for reapplication to future work is greatly diminished and not valued. Our approach to project management excellence is based on the need to manage the organization holistically through uniform measures that are predictive and/or detective in nature. It is in this manner that we can improve our "transformational management" competencies that build value incrementally from previous work value earned and learned.

Organizations that practice transactional management won't be around long if they compete in a competitive industry. Consequently, business professionals will not be around either if they practice the same. We all must be consistently vigilant to add value for the employer in everything we do or we risk the worst possible result — loss of our jobs. What must we do next? We recommend the following initial steps:

- Keep looking for ways to improve project delivery speed
- Be vigilant of workplace behavior for opportunities and threats
- Quantify and qualify personal value every six months with the 3Ms method

- Seek to implement common tools and processes that support your measured improvement

EXAMINING THE WORKPLACE

What is the personality of the workplace that 3Ms will be serving? The organization must be able to distinguish what it is today and where it needs to be over time. This information is used in constructing the 3Ms deployment plan regarding value and speed. High-anxiety work cultures require careful execution early on to set the 3Ms methodology framework in place. The choice sometimes requires a slower initial implementation, to be sure of gaining the buy-in before mandating standards and methodologies.

HITTING THE TARGET

The 3Ms methodology implementation focus should be clearly aimed at the major development-oriented project teams that are vital to achieving organization goals. It is here that 3Ms can instill the cognitive skills the project teams need to recognize and meet project delivery acceleration opportunities and/or delivery threats.

The more the environment encourages people to utilize 3Ms, rather than the organization forcing or enforcing its use, the better and faster the change will take place. As one team begins to understand the value of these new measurement skills, tools, and information, other project teams will see and learn too. The natural competitiveness among project teams, team members, functional units, etc. will help to proliferate the new techniques that successful project teams have discovered. They will "own" this discovery. Team members on successful project teams will be perceived as good people to work with because they will have learned how to collaborate to beat the project estimate for delivery. This is one of the most critical benefits of the 3Ms methodology. When projects complete early, business grows because the cost of development was less than predicted. The remaining monies left over can be reallocated to other projects that need funds.

If your organization is to have any hope of sustaining itself, the organization must accomplish this feat of delivery acceleration. In collecting, aggregating, and measuring project delivery data, the 3Ms methodology can make this happen by evaluating project progress uniformly for everyone involved.

RETURN ON INVESTMENT FROM IMPLEMENTING 3MS METHODOLOGY

Implementing the 3Ms methodology with the simplest of approaches will bring value to the organization because of the visibility of progress the 3Ms methodology processes will bring about. Organizations should expect to see a minimum 10%

return against the fiscal year budget for planned development project work on the project investment (return on investment) using the 3Ms methods.

The key to achieving the organizational return on investment in the first year is identifying the difference between the current organization project culture and what should be. These gaps can immediately be reduced and eventually eliminated over time. As project delivery process improvements are achieved, delivery value will follow. But the organization must do an excellent job of communicating progress and issues through organizational processes back to the workforce and to the senior executives. This must be a closed-loop communication cycle that communicates to all levels of the workforce to achieve the return on investment.

FINDING THE VALUE PROPOSITION OF PROJECT MANAGEMENT

As the 3Ms methodology becomes recognized by executives as a vital tool to help them achieve their goals, their influence and positive outcomes can also significantly increase. Organizations must do more than perform projects correctly. They must choose the correct projects. While many organizations begin their life focused on project management methodology, with significant results, we believe that the role of 3Ms methodology holds even greater value.

FINDING OUTSIDE EXPERTS

Support is available commercially through many consulting firms and nonprofit project management businesses. The Project Management Institute (PMI) should become the centerpiece of outside information for any organization. PMI represents the largest association of people seeking project management value anywhere. This organization is already driving many project managers to become experts, as noted by the PMI certification of Project Management Professional (PMP®). Dr. Schnapper and Steve Rollins are as qualified experts as you will find in this space. Contact Dr. Schnapper at mel@schnapper.com and Steve Rollins at Steve@PMOUSA.com if you seek expert support to implement this process in either consulting and/or training.

CONCLUSIONS

We hope we have provided sufficient information in "road map" manner to help you be more successful in implementing the 3Ms methodology — a process for helping to grow the business.

The information provided in this book has been a labor of love, passion, and intrigue, with tremendous intensity of thought. We have demonstrated that implementing the 3Ms methodology is vital to sustaining any organization, yet it is not rocket science. The critical success factors of implementing the 3Ms approach involve dealing with people, changing workforce behavior dynamics, and raising progress visibility for improved cross-collaboration.

In 2001–2005, more than five million people lost their jobs. In 2004, many businesses failed or lost significant shareholder value, eventually leaving the shareholder holding the bag (definition for worthless paper). Ignoring the cases of executive fraud, what was it that everyone had in common that led to these job losses? In our opinion, their organizations could not execute the correct portfolio of projects quickly enough to meet opportunities and threats. They could neither detect nor predict the threat in a reasonable time to allow management to apply appropriate corrective action. Too many people in these organizations were working on the wrong projects or moving those projects to completion too slowly, or the business had gaping holes in its accountability alignment from the top to the bottom.

If you decide to implement the 3Ms methodology, you have many choices of where to focus the team's efforts. Our recommendation is to clearly define the 3Ms methodology value proposition as a starting point. Remember that your customers include the executives, the project managers, the resource managers, and the team members. Check your customer satisfaction frequently, and adjust accordingly. After all, if you can't define and measure the value of the 3Ms methodology, then of what value is it?

This book has free materials available for download from the Web Added Value™ Resource Center at www.jrosspub.com.

INDEX

A

Acceleration opportunities, 148–149
Acceptance criteria, 217–218, 362
Accepted deliverables, 224–225
Accountability, 19, 99, 124–126, 152
Accuracy, 5
Acquisitions, plan, 331, 332, 333–336
Activity attributes, 236–237, 241–242, 244–245, 248–249, 255
Activity-based costing, 133
Activity cost estimates, 261, 266–267
Activity cost supporting detail, 261–262
Activity estimating, 357–358
Activity list, 235–236, 238–240, 254–255
Administrative closure procedure, 205–206
Alignment, 18, 108, 147, 148, 400
　of metrics, 73–80
　　strategic corporate, 407
Approval, 64
Approve, 100
Asset portfolio, 368–369
Asset value, corporate, 181
Assumptions, 219
Auditing, project fraud, 351, 353–354
Audits, project, 372–373
Authority, 99–103

B

Balance, 399
Balanced scorecard, 24

Baseline
　cost, 263–264, 267
　data, 74
　model, 75
　performance, 106
　quality, 280, 285–286
　schedule, 246–247, 251
　scope, 223, 228–229
Behavioral alignment of metrics, 73–74
Behavioral skills, 67
Benefits, 412, 414–416
Bonuses, 66, 125
Boundaries, project, 216–217
Budget, 31, 32, 34, 66
Budgeting, cost, see Cost, budgeting
Business case for implementing 3Ms, 405–417
　approach, 408–412
　business case, 406–407
　costs and benefits, 412–416
　executive summary/commitment letter, 405–406
　risks, 412, 413
　scope, 407–408
Business plan, 73
Business strategy, 114
Business unit, value proposition of, 151

C

Calendar, project, 248–249
Carrying costs, 136

423

Change
 organizational, 115
 resistance to, 171
 strategy, 116
Change control, integrated, see Integrated change control
Change control plan, 412
Change requests, communications management, 312–313
Changes
 communications management, 308–309, 310
 cost management, 262–263, 265–266, 269
 human resource management, 299–300
 integration management, 191–192, 198–200
 procurement management, 335–336, 342–343, 344
 quality management, 281–282, 287–288
 risk management, 324–325
 scope management, 219–220, 224, 225–226, 229
 time management, 237–238, 240, 243–244, 249, 252–253
Charter, project, develop, 185, 187–188
Checklists, quality, 278–279
C-level executives, 4, 152
Close project, 186, 187, 205–208
Coaching, 112
Code of conduct, team member, 357
Cognitive skills, 105, 149
Cognitivity, 22
Collaboration, 128
Collins, Jim, 132
Commitment, 119, 126
Communication, 421, see also Project communications management
 organizational, 117–118, 120
Communication plan, 117–118, 410
Communications management, see also Project communications management
 metrics maturity model, 381–394
Communications management plan, 307
Communications planning, 305, 306, 307
Competitive advantage, 419–420
Conflict, 100
 resolution, 15–16, 17, 19–20, 64, 108, 126–127
Consensus building, 16
Constraints, 218–219, 415

Consult, 100
Consultants, 112, 421
Contract
 administration, 331, 332, 333, 343–346
 closure, 331, 332, 346–348
  procedure, 206–207
 documentation, procurement management, 343–344
 management plan, select sellers, 340–341
 select sellers, 340
 statement of work, 334, 337–338
Contractors, 387
Contractual agreements, risk management, 323
Contributing value areas (CVAs), 45–47
Contribution, 65
Corporate asset value, 181
Corporate culture, 20, 21, 63, 111
 metrics and, 105–109
 team-building workshop, 113–114
Corporate goals, 75–78
 force ranking, 74
Corporate governance, see also Management oversight
 qualitative standards, 40–43
 reporting, 365, 366, 370–371
 role of, 175–176
Corporate governance team, 175–176
Corporate levels, value of metrics methodology, 14–16
Corporate mission, 75, 76
Corporate objectives, 5, 30, 75, 76, 147, 151, 152
 hierarchy of, 63
 portfolio, 367
 return on investment, 150
 risk management of, 149
Corporate vision, 75, 76
Corrective actions
 communications management, 310–311, 313
 cost management, 269–270
 human resource management, 300
 integration management, 192–193, 195–196, 202
 procurement management, 344–345
 quality management, 282, 286–287
 risk management, 325
 scope management, 229–230
 time management, 253

Index **425**

Cost, 412, 414–416
    baseline, 263–264, 267
    budgeting, 259, 260, 263–266
    control, 259, 260, 266–271
    development, 415
    estimating, 259, 260, 261–263
    management, see also Project cost management
        metrics maturity model, 381–394
Cost accounting, 133–135
Cost management plan, 263, 265
Cost optimization metrics program, 146, 147
Creativity, performance factors, 67
Critical path scheduling, 31, 152, 355
Critical success factors, 64, 408
Culture, corporate, 20, 21, 63, 111
    metrics and, 105–109
    team-building workshop, 113–114
CVAs, see Contributing value areas

D

Decide, 100
Decision making, 99–103
Defect repair, 285, 288–289
    integration management, 194, 197–198, 203–204
Deliverables, 16, 33
    accepted, 224–225
    integration management, 190, 204–205
    project, 217
    validated, quality management, 289–290
Delivery
    aligning the organization to optimize, 73–74
    opportunity, 105
    threat, 105, 148–149
Departmental objectives, 14, 15
Dependencies, 140
Deployment, 400
Development cost, 415
Duration, activity, estimating, 233, 234, 235, 244–245

E

Embededness, 400
Empowerment, 20–21

Enterprise Program Management Office (EPMO), 405, 406, 408, 411, 412
Environment, secure, 129
EPMO, see Enterprise Program Management Office
Equipment, investment in, 134
Estimate-at-completion, 268
Estimate-to-complete, 268
Estimating, cost, see Cost, estimating
Evaluation criteria, procurement management, 336–337
Excellent, 5, 24, 36, 37, 40, 41, 42, 44, 63, 107, 108, 146, 163
    numerical equivalent, 31
Execution, project, direct and manage, 186, 187, 190–195
Executives, 4
    accountability, 152
    applications of 3Ms, 123–126
    expectations of, 411
    impact of 3Ms on, 409

F

Feedback, 120
Final product, 207
Fiscal year business plan, 73
Fiscal year strategic plan, 73, 178–179
Focus groups, 111, 114
Force ranking corporate objectives/goals, 74
Forecasted completion, cost management, 268–269
Forecasts
    communications management, 309–310
    integration management, 196–197
Fraud, see also Project fraud entries
    detection, 22, 181
    management, 152, see also Project fraud management
        return on investment, 150
    prevention, 22, 180–181
Fraud management plan, 351, 352–353
Fraud management plan policy
    PMO management and, 371–372
Frequency, 5
Fulfillment, aligning the organization to optimize, 73–74
Functional objectives, aligning, 14, 15, 16
Funding requirements, 264–265

G

Globalization, 171
Goals, 75–78
  objectives versus, 16, 83–84
Goldratt, Eli, 131, 139, 140
Governance, see also Corporate governance; Management oversight
  qualitative standards, 40–43

H

Health checks, 24–25
Hierarchical alignment of metrics, 73, 76–77
History, 128
Human performance and development, 118
Human resource management, 112, see also Project human resource management
Human resource planning, 293, 294, 295–296

I

Improve workforce, 179–180
Individual level, value of metrics methodology, 22
Individual objectives, 75, 76
Inflationary reward system, 108
Inform, 100
Information distribution, 305, 306, 307–309
Information flow, 171–172
Information systems, project management, 374
Innovative objectives, 47
Integrated change control, 186, 187, 199–205
Integrated people solution, 115–116
Integration, see Project integration management
Interdependencies, 16
Internal control management plan, 359
Internal control portfolio, 369–370
Internal controls, project fraud management, 351, 352, 355–362, 373
Interviews, 111, 114
Inventory, 143
  investment, 137
Inventory $ days, 137, 138–139
Investment, 18–19, 134, 135–137, 149–150
Issue management, 360–361

J

Job responsibilities, 120
Job value, 151
Joint objectives, 44–45

K

Key result areas, 93
Key value areas (KVAs), 18, 31, 63, 76, 77, 78, 163, 411
  alignment of, 147
  changes in weightings of, 43–44
  contributing value areas and, 45–47
  defining, 146–147
  establishing, 32–35
    rules for, 34–35
  examples of, 33–34
  key questions, 71
  longevity of, 64–65
  performance factors, 67–68
  performance objectives to support, 125–126
  skills-building exercise for setting, 82
  team building and, 128
  weightings to change behavior, 124–127
Knowledge library, 207

L

Leadership, 63
  applications of 3Ms, 123–126
  assessment, 120
  development, 117, 120
  performance factors, 67
  style, 63
Lead time, 143
Linguistics, 17, 90, 106–107
Longevity, 128–129
Long-term training objectives, 32, 69–70, 71

M

Magnify phase, 9–10, 30, 90, 106, 170
Make-or-buy decisions, 134, 334–335
Manage phase, 7–9, 30, 63, 90, 106, 169
Management, 4
Management by objectives (MBO), 4
Management oversight, 175–184
  achieve fiscal year strategic plan, 178–179
  corporate governance role, 175–176

corporate governance team, forming, 176–178
improve corporate asset value, 181
improve profitability, 182
improve project throughput, 180
improve workforce, 179–180
manage project fraud detection, 181
manage project fraud prevention, 180–181
manage project selection, 181–182
Manager, conflict resolution, 127
Managerial skills, 68–69
Materiality risk, 358
MBO, see Management by objectives
Measure phase, 4, 5–7, 13, 16, 30, 63, 90, 105–106, 147–148
Measurement system, quality of, 399
Mentoring, 387, 389
Metric profile, 157–168
Metrics, see also specific topics
  alignment of, 73–80
  corporate culture and, 105–109
  methodology, value of, 13–27
    health checks, 24–25
    at higher corporate levels, 14–16
    at individual level, 22
    at operational level, 16–22
    skill mastery, 23–24
    target population, 22–23
    training, 23
  program/project management and, 89–97
  qualitative, 39–43
  quality, 278
  questions about, 3
  skills-building exercises, 81–85
  Theory of Constraints, 131–144
Metrics maturity model, 381–394
  Level I, 382, 385, 386–387
  Level II, 382, 385, 386–388
  Level III, 382, 385, 387–389
  Level IV, 383, 385, 388–390
  Level V, 383, 385, 389–391
  Level VI, 383, 385, 386, 390–392
  Level VII, 384, 386, 391–393
  Level VIII, 384, 386, 392–393
Metrics program, organizational project based, value proposition of, 145–154
  benefit realization, 148–150
  case study, 152–153

determining and justifying the need for, 151–152
  managing, 150–151
  models, 146–148
Metrics system questionnaire, 399–400
Milestone list, 236–237
Mission, 75, 76
Monetary rewards, 65–66
Monitor and control project work, 186, 187, 195–198
Monitoring system, 15
Monthly plan of record, 370–391
MS Project®, 18, 64, 65
Multiproject environment, 141–143
Multitasking, 142

N

Negotiation, 101
Nelson, Robert, 66
Net profit, 135–137
Network diagrams, 238

O

Objectives, 18, see also specific types
  aligning, 14, 15
  commitment to, 126
  defined, 35
  goals versus, 15–16, 83–84
  hierarchy of, 75, 76
  joint, 44–45
  project, 215
  self-test on, 83–84
  typology of, 47, 60
OD, see Organization development
Odiorne, George, 4
Operating expense, 135–137
Operational level, value of metrics methodology, 16–22
Organizational assessment, 114, 116–117, 119
Organizational change management (OCM), 111, 114–121
  action plan, 118–121, 396, 401, 402
  3Ms components of, 116–118
Organizational change strategy, 116
Organizational communication, 117–118, 120
Organizational metrics, alignment of, 73

Organizational process assets
  communications management, 307–308,
    311, 313–314
  cost management, 270–271
  human resource management, 301–302
  integration management, 207–208
  procurement management, 345–346,
    347–348
  quality management, 282–283, 289
  risk management, 326–327
  scope management, 230–231
  time management, 253–254
Organizational project-based metrics program,
    value proposition of, 145–154
  benefit realization, 148–150
  case study, 152–153
  determining and justifying the need for,
    151–152
  managing, 150–151
  models, 146–148
Organization chart, 295–296
Organization development (OD), 108,
    111–114
Outside experts, 421
Oversight, see Management oversight

P

Parkinson's Law, 141, 142
People, 115
Performance, overall value of, 65–67
Performance assessment, team, 298–299
Performance factors, 31, 67–68, 93, 163
Performance measurements
  cost management, 267–268
  time management, 251–252
Performance objectives (POs), 18, 31, 33,
    41, 63, 76, 77, 78, 93, 163
  action plans for, 64–65
  alignment of, 147
  changes in weightings of, 43–44
  contributing value areas and, 45–47
  establishing, 35–39
    questions for, 35–37
  format for, 38–39
  key questions, 71
  longevity of, 64–65
  performance factors, 67–68
  reward system and, 17

  rules for, 37–38
  skills-building exercise for setting, 81, 82
  to support key value areas, 124–127
  team building and, 128
  training objectives, 69, 70
Performance reporting 305, 306, 309–312
Performance reports, communications
    management, 309
Performance scorecard, 31, 32, 65–67
Personal skills, 68
Plan contracting, 331, 332, 336–338
Plan purchases and acquisitions, 331, 332,
    333–336
PMBOK®, 381, see also specific
    knowledge areas
  PMO management and, 366, 375–376
  project cost management, 259–260
  project human resource management,
    293–294
  project integration management, 185–186
  project procurement management, 331–332
  project quality management, 275–276
  project risk management, 317–318
  project scope management, 211–212
  project time management, 233–234
PMI, see Project Management Institute
PMIS, 390, 391
PMO, see Project Management Office
PMP®, 390, 421
PO, see Performance objectives
Portfolio management, 365, 366–370
Portfolio prioritization, 416
Predecessor relationships, 147
Preventive actions
  human resource management, 300–301
  integration management, 193, 196, 202–203
  quality management, 287
  risk management, 325–326
Priorities, 16–17
Problem-solving objectives, 47
Process, 115
Process improvement plan, 279
Procurement documents, 336, 338–339
Procurement management, see Project
    procurement management
  metrics maturity model, 381–394
Procurement management plan, 333–334,
    342
Procurement plan, 410

Index

Product, 207
Product scope description, 215–216
Profit, net, 135–137
Profitability, 143, 182
Program Management Office, 30
Program objectives, 30
Program/project management, metrics and, 89–97
Project acceptance criteria, 217–218
Project assumptions, 219
Project audits, 372–373
Project-based metrics program, 146, 147, 148
   organizational, value proposition of, 145–154
      benefit realization, 148–150
      case study, 152–153
      determining and justifying the need for, 151–152
      managing, 150–151
      models, 146–148
Project-based throughput optimization metrics program, 146, 147, 148
Project boundaries, 216–217
Project calendar, 248–249
Project charter, develop, 185, 187–188
Project close, 186, 187, 205–208
Project communications management, 305–317
   communications planning, 305, 306, 307
   information distribution, 305, 306, 307–309
   manage stakeholders, 305, 306, 312–314
   performance reporting, 305, 306, 309–312
Project constraints, 218–219
Project cost management, 259–273
   cost budgeting, 259, 260, 263–266
   cost control, 259, 260, 266–271
   cost estimating, 259, 260, 261–263
Project deliverables, 217
Project delivery speed, 419
Project execution, direct and manage, 186, 187, 190–195
Project fraud detection, 181
Project fraud management, 351–363
   fraud management planning, 351, 352–353
   internal controls, 351, 352, 355–362
   PMO and, 365, 366, 371–373
   project fraud auditing, 351, 353–354
   return on investment, 150
   transparent reporting, 351, 354–355

Project fraud prevention, 180–181
Project funding requirements, 264–265
Project human resource management, 293–303
   acquire project team, 293, 294, 296–298
   develop project team, 293, 294, 298–299
   human resource planning, 293, 294, 295–296
   manage project team, 294, 299–302
Project integration, metrics maturity model, 381–394
Project integration management, 182–210
   close project, 186, 187, 205–208
   develop project charter, 185, 187–188
   develop project management plan, 186, 187, 189–190
   develop project scope statement, 185, 187, 188–189
   direct and manage project execution, 186, 187, 190–195
   integrated change control, 186, 187, 199–205
   monitor and control project work, 186, 187, 195–198
Project investments, 149
Project-level 3Ms template, 29, 31–32
Project management
   considerations for success in, 140
   metrics and, 89–97
   templates, 373–374
   Theory of Constraints metrics, 139–141
   value of, 169–174
   value audit form, 169, 170–173
   value proposition, 421
Project Management Body of Knowledge, see PMBOK®
Project management information systems, 374
Project Management Institute (PMI), 421
Project Management Office (PMO), 5, 408
   director of, 3Ms profile for, 41, 92–94
   expectations of, 411
   impact of 3Ms on, 409
   information loop and, 172
   knowledge library, 207
   managing an organizational metrics program, 150–151
   qualitative metrics for, 39–43
   support from, 171
   value proposition of, 370–371

Project Management Office (PMO)
  management, 365–377
  corporate governance reporting, 365, 366, 370–371
  PMBOK®, 366, 375–376
  portfolio management, 365, 366–370
  project fraud management, 365, 366, 371–373
  tools, 365, 366, 373–374
Project management plan
  communications management, 314
  cost management, 271
  develop, 186, 187, 189–190
  human resource management, 302
  integrated change control, 200–201
  internal controls, 358–359
  procurement management, 346
  quality management, 281–281, 283, 290–291
  risk management, 322–323, 327
  scope management, 231
  time management, 249–250, 255–256
Project manager
  expectations of, 411
  impact of 3Ms on, 409
  3Ms profile for, 92–94
Project metrics system questionnaire, 399–400
Project objectives, 30, 215
  skills-building exercise for setting, 82–83
  typology for creating, 47, 60
Project organization, 410
Project portfolio, 366–367
Project procurement management, 331–349
  contract administration, 331, 332, 333, 343–346
  contract closure, 331, 332, 333, 346–348
  plan contracting, 331, 332, 336–338
  plan purchases and acquisitions, 331, 332, 333–336
  request seller responses, 331, 332, 338–339
  select sellers, 331, 332, 333, 339–343
Project quality management, 275–291
  perform quality assurance, 275, 276, 281–284
  perform quality control, 275, 276, 284–291
  quality planning, 276, 276, 277–281
Project requirements, 216
Project risk management
  qualitative risk analysis, 317, 318, 320

quantitative risk analysis, 318, 321
risk identification, 317, 318, 319–320
risk management planning, 317, 318–319
risk monitoring and control, 318, 323–327
risk response planning, 318, 321–323
Project schedule, 245–246
  internal controls, 359–360
  network diagrams, 238
Project scope, 105
Project scope management, 211–232
  scope control, 212, 213, 226–231
  scope definition, 211, 212, 213, 214–220
  scope planning, 211, 212, 213–214
  scope verification, 212, 213, 224–226
  work breakdown structure, 211, 212, 213, 221–224, 227–228
Project scope statement, 214–215, 221
  develop, 185, 187, 188–189
  integrated change control, 201–202
Project selection, 181–182
Project staff assignments, 296–297
Project status reports, 356–357
Project teams, 152
  acquire, 293, 294, 296–298
  develop, 293, 294, 298–299
  manage, 294, 299–302
  status reports, 354, 355–356
Project throughput, 180
Project time management, 233–257
  activity definition, 233, 234, 235–238
  activity duration estimating, 233, 234, 235, 244–245
  activity resource estimating, 233, 234, 235, 240–244
  activity sequencing, 233, 234, 238–240
  schedule control, 233, 234, 235, 250–256
  schedule development, 233, 234, 235, 245–250
Project work, monitor and control, 186, 187, 195–198
Promotability, 70, 71, 163
Proposals, request seller responses, 339
Purchases, plan, 331, 332, 333–336

Q

Qualified sellers list, 338
Qualitative metrics, 39–43, 76

Index **431**

Qualitative risk analysis, 317, 318, 320
Quality, 6, 31, 32, 34, 66
  definitions of, 36
Quality assurance, 275, 276, 281–284
Quality baseline, 280, 285–286
Quality checklists, 278–279
Quality control, 275, 276, 284–291
Quality control measurement, 284–285
Quality management, see Project quality management
  metrics maturity model, 381–394
Quality management plan, 277
Quality metrics, 278
Quality planning, 275, 276, 277–281
Quantitative metrics, 76
Quantitative risk analysis, 318, 321
Quantity, 6
Questionnaires, 111

R

Raw materials inventory, 136
Recruiting, 112
Regular objectives, 60
Reporting
  corporate governance, 365, 366, 370–371
  performance, see Performance reporting
  transparent, 351, 354–355
Requested changes, see Changes
Request seller responses, 331, 332, 338–339
Resource activity, estimating, 233, 234, 235, 240–244
Resource availability, 297–298
  procurement management, 341–342
Resource-based metrics program, 146, 148
Resource breakdown structure, 242
Resource calendars, 242–243
Resource investments, 149–150
Resource management, 148
  metrics maturity model, 381–394
Resource managers
  expectations of, 411
  impact of 3Ms on, 409
Resource portfolio, 368
Resource requirements, time management, 240–241, 247
Resources, 64
  reliability of, 140

Responsibilities, 295
Return on investment, 135–137, 149–150, 420–421
Reward system, 17, 22, 65–66, 108, 112, 125
Risk analysis
  qualitative, 317, 318, 232
  quantitative, 318, 321
Risk avoidance, 66
Risk identification, 317, 318, 319–320
Risk identification matrix, 412, 413, 415
Risk management, 31, 32, 34, see also Project risk management
  of corporate objectives, 149
  internal controls, 361
  metrics maturity model, 381–394
Risk management plan, 318–319
Risk management planning, 317, 318–319
Risk monitoring and control, 318, 323–327
Risk register, 319–322, 323–324
Risk response planning, 318, 321–323
Road map schedule for implementing 3Ms, 395–403
Role authority, 100, 101
Role/authority/decision grid, 15, 99, 108
Role/authority/decision making, 99–103
Role clarity, 64, 99
Role-level authority, 99, 101
Roles, 295
Routing objectives, 60

S

Salary, 125, see also Reward system
Satisfactory, 5, 24, 29, 35, 36, 37, 40, 42, 44, 63, 107, 108, 146, 163
  hierarchy of, 30
  numerical equivalent, 31
Schedule, 31
  baseline, 246–247, 251
  critical path, 152, 355
  for implementing 3Ms, 395–403
  model data, 246, 251–252
  network diagrams, 238
  project, 245–246
    internal controls, 359–360
Scope, 105
  baseline, 223, 228–229
  control, 212, 213, 226–231
  definition, 211, 212, 213, 214–220

management, metrics maturity model, 381–394
planning, 211, 212, 213–214
product, 215–216
project, management, see Project scope management
verification, 212, 213, 224–226
Scope management plan, 213–214, 220, 223–224, 226–227
Scope of work (SOW), 16, 17, 18, 21
Scope statement, 214–215, 221, 387
project
    develop, 185, 187, 188–189
    integrated change control, 201–202
Select sellers, 331, 332, 333, 339–343
Sellers
    request responses, 331, 332, 338–339
    select, 331, 332, 333, 339–343
Service, 207
Short-term training objectives, 32, 69, 71
Skill mastery, 23–24
Skill sets, 120
Skills-building exercises, 81–85
SMART objectives, 35
SOW, see Scope of work
Sponsor, 5
Staff assignments, 296–297
Staffing management plan, 296, 298
Stakeholders
    expectations of, 411
    impact of 3Ms on, 409
    manage, 305, 306, 312–314
Standards, 66, 76, 77, 78, 17, see also specific standards
    numerical equivalents, 31
Statement of work, contract, 334, 337–338
Status reports, 354–357
"Storming" phase, 115
Strategic alignment, 148
Strategic corporate alignment, 407
Strategic initiatives, 151
Strategic objectives, aligning, 14
Strategic plan, 73, 175–176
Strategic planning, 106, 124–126
Strategy, 114, 140
Student Syndrome, 140–141, 142
Subordinate, conflict resolution, 127
Succession, 112

Successor relationships, 147
Supply chain, 133
    metrics for, 137–139
Surveys, 114
SWOT analysis, 106

T

Tactical alignment, 148
Target population, value of metrics methodology, 22–23
Task estimates, 140
Team
    accomplishment, 65
    assignments, 64
    objectives, 60
    performance assessment, 298–299
    project, see Project team
    status reports, 354–355
Team building, 15, 127–129
    organization development workshop, 111–114
Team member
    code of conduct, 357
    expectations of, 411
    impact of 3Ms on, 409
    objectives, 30
    status reports, 354
    time entry, 360
Teamwork, 18, 120
    performance factors, 67
Technical skills, 68
Technology, 114, 115
    implementation of, 117–121
Theory of Constraints (TOC) metrics, 131–144
    characteristics of good metrics, 132–135
    multiproject environment, 141–142
    project management, 139–141
    supply chain, 137–139
    system as a whole, 135–137
3Ms metric profile, 157–168
3Ms metrics, see also Metrics; specific topics
    linguistics, 106–107
    management oversight, 175–184
    maturity model, 381–394, see also Metrics maturity model
    profile, 157–168

project communications management, 305–317
project cost management, 259–273
project fraud management, 351–363
project human resource management, 293–303
project integration management, 185–210
Project Management Office management, 365–377
project procurement management, 331–349
project quality management, 275–291
project risk management, 317–329
project scope management, 211–232
project time management, 233–237
3Ms of Performance, see also Magnify phase, Manage phase; Measure phase; specific topics
   alignment of metrics, 73–80
   application of, 123–130
   business case for implementing, 405–417
   corporate culture and, 105–109
   initiatives that support, 111–122
      organizational change management, 114–121
      organization development, 111–114
   management oversight, 175–184
   metric profile, 157–168
   metrics, see 3Ms metrics
   metrics maturity model, 381–394
   profile, 92–94
      metric, 157–168
      template example, 48–59
   program/project management, 89–97
   project communications management, 305–317
   project cost management, 259–273
   project fraud management, 351–363
   project human resource management, 293–303
   project integration management, 185–210
   Project Management Office management, 365–377
   project procurement management, 331–349
   project quality management, 275–291
   project risk management, 317–329
   project scope management, 211–232

project time management, 233–237
   road map schedule for implementing, 395–403
   scorecard, 106
   template, 29, 106, see also specific sections
      example, 48–59
      project level, 31–32
      questions per section of, 71
      value, defining, see Value
   value of, 13–27
      at higher corporate levels, 14–16
      at individual level, 22
      at operational level, 16–22
Throughput, 135–137
   project, 180
Throughput $ days, 137–138, 139
Throughput optimization metrics program, 146, 147
Time entry, team member, 360
Timeliness, 31, 32, 34, 66
Time management, see also Project time management
   metrics maturity model, 381–394
TOC metrics, see Theory of Constraints metrics
Tools, PMO management, 365, 366, 373–374
Training, 19, 23
   PMBOK®, 375–376
   objectives, 32, 68–70, 71, 163
Transactional management, 419
Transformational management, 419
Transparency, 16
Transparent reporting, 351, 354–355

U

Unsatisfactory, 36, 37, 40, 42, 44, 147, 163
   numerical equivalent, 31

V

Validated deliverables, 289–290
Value, 16–17
   defining, 29–61
      contributing value areas, 45–47
      joint objectives, 44–45
      key value areas, see Key value areas

performance objectives, see
Performance objectives
qualitative metrics, 39–43
definition of, 29, 32
determining, 22
how to create and exceed, 63–72
action plans per performance
objective, 64–65
performance factors, 67–68
performance scorecard, 65–67
promotability, 70, 71
training objectives, 68–70
work, 149
Value audit form, 172–173
Value proposition
business unit, 151
job value, 151
organizational project-based metrics
program, 145–154
benefit realization, 148–150
case study, 152–153
determining and justifying the need
for, 151–152
managing, 150–151
metrics program models, 146–148

PMO, 370–371
project management, 169–171, 421
Vendors, 136, 387
Very Good, 5, 24, 36, 37, 40, 41, 42, 44,
63, 70, 107, 146, 163
numerical equivalent, 31
Visibility, 147
Vision, 76, 124

W

Waste, 136
Weightings, changing, 43–44
Work, project, monitor and control, 186,
187, 195–198
Work breakdown structure, 65, 211, 212,
213, 221–224, 227–228
Work breakdown structure dictionary, 222, 228
Workforce, improving, 179–180
Work performance information, integration
management, 194–195
Workplace behavior, 419
Workshop, corporate culture team building,
113–114
Work value, 149